Current Issues in Women's History

Current Issues in Women's History

Editors

Arina Angerman
Geerte Binnema
Annemieke Keunen
Vefie Poels
Jacqueline Zirkzee

Language editor

Judy de Ville

R

ROUTLEDGE
London and New York

First published 1989 by Routledge
11 New Fetter Lane, London EC4P 4EE

Simultaneously published in the USA and Canada by Routledge
a division of Routledge, Chapman and Hall, Inc.
29 West 35th Street, New York, NY 10001

Printed in Great Britain by
Richard Clay Ltd, Bungay, Suffolk

British Library Cataloguing in Publication Data

Current issues in women's history.
1. Women. Historiography
I. Angerman, Arina
305.4′072

ISBN 0-415-00361-X (hb)
0-415-00362-8 (pb)

Library of Congress Cataloging in Publication Data

Current issues in women's history/edited by Arina Angerman . . . [et al.].
Papers presented at the International Conference on Women's History held in Amsterdam from 24–27 March 1986.
Includes index.
1. Women—History—Congresses. 2. Women—Historiography—Congresses. 3. Feminism—History—Congresses. 4. Sexism—History—Congresses. I. Angerman, Arina. II. International Conference on Women's History (1986: Amsterdam, Netherlands)
HQ1121.C85 1989
305.4′0973—dc19 89-3582

Contents

Preface 1

Selma Leydesdorff
Politics, identification and the writing of women's history 9

Londa Schiebinger
Maria Winkelmann: the clash between guild traditions and professional science 21

Lucia Bergamasco
Female education and spiritual life: the case of ministers' daughters 39

Päivi Setälä
Brick stamps and women's economic opportunities in Imperial Rome 61

Marijke Gijswijt-Hofstra
Witchcraft in the Northern Netherlands 75

Lydia Sklevicky
Emancipated integration or integrated emancipation: the case of post-revolutionary Yugoslavia 93

Amy Swerdlow
Female culture, pacifism and feminism: Women Strike for Peace 109

Mineke Bosch
Gossipy letters in the context of international feminism 131

Margot Badran
The origins of feminism in Egypt 153

Jo Anne Preston
Female aspiration and male ideology:
school-teaching in nineteenth-century New England 171

Alison Oram
'Embittered, sexless or homosexual':
attacks on spinster teachers 1918-39 183

Anne Laurence
Women's psychological disorders in seventeenth-century
Britain 203

Annelies van Gijsen
Pygmalion, or the image of women in medieval literature 221

Anna Clark
Whores and gossips:
sexual reputation in London 1770-1825 231

Maria Grever
On the origins of Dutch women's historiography:
three portraits (1840-1970) 249

Helga Grubitzsch
A paradigm of androcentric historiography:
Michelet's *Les femmes de la Révolution* 271

Willy Jansen
Ethnocentrism in the study of Algerian women 289

Notes on contributors with selected bibliographies 311

Index 319

Preface

Current Issues in Women's History is a selection from the papers presented at the International Conference on Women's History held in Amsterdam from 24-27 March 1986. At this conference, over a hundred lectures and workshops were presented by women from about thirty different countries. That women's history is a dynamic and promising field of research became very clear during the four well-attended days. The lectures offered were richly diverse in their contents because the organisers had made no restrictions as to possible themes, methods or periods. The conference was marked by its many discussions about differences in approach, amplified by the fact that the 800 or so participants came from many different countries and disciplines. All this made the conference a lively and also a unique event. As far as we, the editors of this collection, know, a conference on women's history with representatives from so many different countries has not taken place before. For this reason, and because we wanted to make the papers presented accessible to a wider audience, we decided to publish a selection from the wide range of research papers.

In keeping with the intention of the conference, we did not start from a specific notion of women's history. Our main criterion was that a particular piece of research was innovating or challenging in the presentation of its question, its use of sources or its theoretical orientation. Another criterion was that the research contained sufficient clues to be interesting for non-specialists in the relevant field. In order to see if our choices were justified, we often turned to specialists for advice.

Women's history in its present state can definitely not be called a crystallised field of research. Its history has known continual clashes of a theoretical nature, often emanating from differences in political ideas which in their turn are brought about by differences in class, culture and ethnic background. We believe that the confrontations at the conference connected with these different backgrounds will make an essential contribution to the changing and narrowing down of the questions and methods employed. This goes in particular for the heated discussions at the conference about the white nature of women's history. These made once again apparent that the West shows the dogged tendency to universalise, consciously or subconsciously, its findings with respect to the non-Western research areas. This is why in this collection we had hoped to compensate for the underrepresentation of non-Western contributions at the conference. Unfortunately, we have not succeeded in doing so. We found Selma Leydesdorff prepared to write about the different items of discussion in the introductory article to the collection as a whole, which makes her the only author to have found a place in *Current Issues* not on the basis of a lecture.

The idea of compiling this collection not thematically, but by accentuating the possible similarities and/or differences in approach, was inspired by our view that the various developments within women's history should be placed side by side. In order to make this diversity and these similarities appear as clearly as possible, we asked each author to discuss explicitly the choice of her research subject, her research question, the place these two have in the relevant historiographic tradition, and finally the way in which she dealt with her source material. On the basis of the ways in which the authors incorporated these guidelines into their articles, we have formulated in the following paragraphs a number of current issues as we see them. The cross-connections that we found enable us to give a further illustration of recent developments within women's history.

One of the first research themes of women's history involved research into the actual presence or absence of women in power structures and organisations, and the degree to which women could make their influence felt inside or outside of these structures and organisations. The causes of the powerless positions that women, according to the results of such research, often appeared to have were especially found in the general, seemingly unchangeable power structures that men were felt to personify. Research into social structures and institutions on the one hand and the possibilities of women to function within such structures on the other hand is still carried out today. However, the idea that there is an immediate connection between being female and an *a priori* limitation of opportunities has been abandoned. The new nature of this research often appears from the fact that more questions are formulated which are time- and situation-related, and that those opportunities are investigated that actually were open to women. New source material has led to surprising changes in existing opinions. Londa Schiebinger, in her article about an eighteenth-century astronomer, shows for instance that it is no longer merely important to rescue great women scientists from obscurity. What matters is to reconstruct precisely how social trends such as professionalisation and modernisation encouraged or discouraged women to fight for a position in the academic world.

Lucia Bergamasco examines what effects changes had in the theological opinions of seventeenth-century Puritan preachers on the place intended for women within this religious community in New England. On the basis of letters and religious writings of two preachers' daughters, Bergamasco shows that the changed views meant that preachers' daughters received a thorough intellectual education and in addition were brought up with strong moral beliefs regarding their tasks in society. In their upbringing, we trace diffuse patterns of expectation with respect to being female, which formed the basis of emotional conflicts at a later age.

Päivi Setälä, like Bergamasco, adjusts the image of uninfluential women, but her location is Ancient Rome. In addition to discussing the existing legal rights for women in general, Setälä shows by means of a brickstone analysis that a group of land-owning women did succeed in exercising economic and political influence.

Marijke Gijswijt-Hofstra is another author who takes a critical look at the prevailing image of women. Her paper - about the popular theme of witchcraft - shows that the question why women were overrepresented at large witch-trials cannot be explained only by characterising the relevant period as misogynist, but that a careful analysis of the religious and social context forms a necessary step towards a further explanation of this phenomenon.

Not only have the individual opportunities and obstacles for women - discussed in the previous paragraphs - always appealed to people's imagination, but there has also always been an interest in their collective performance. Initially, research concentrated on the struggle of feminist movements as such, and the degree to which the women involved had succeeded in bringing their demands to fruition. In the first instance women researchers looked for recognition of their own feminist ideals and in that light judged the feminist nature of women's movements from the past. They described a feminist fight in terms of a united movement against an unequivocal oppression. Soon it became apparent that such a description was not valid. They realised that the fight of a feminist movement cannot be judged by contemporary, universally validated, feminist standards but that it would have to be examined in the context of its own time and place. From the paper of Lydia Sklevicky, for instance, it becomes clear that the fact that the women's organisation in Yugoslavia was incorporated into the structure of the state machinery was highly decisive for the possibilities of this organisation. On the one hand, this incorporation gave the organisation a clear basis, on the other, it made its functioning exceedingly dependent on state politics. The official existence of this women's organisation within the party could be used rhetorically by the government to show that oppression of women no longer existed in its socialist society. This led to an area of tension between the rhetoric of party officials and the space that was actually given to the women's organisation.

To what extent feminist motivations can be the products of their time becomes clear from the paper by Amy Swerdlow. The Women Strike for Peace movement, active in the early 1960s in the USA, made motherhood the stake of its political fight against the arms race. This argument enabled the movement not only to involve very many women in its fight but also to achieve the necessary political effect. Swerdlow indicates how much the effect of the appeal to motherhood was connected with the socio-political circumstances of that period.

If the articles of Sklevicky and Swerdlow show two women's movements concerned with the realisations of their respective interests, to Mineke Bosch the key question is quite a different one, namely the extent to which the participants in a movement manifest themselves individually. By means of the many letters which a number of women within the International Women's Suffrage Alliance wrote to one another, Bosch creates a lively picture of the way in which their personal and business interests were interwoven.

From Margot Badran's article it becomes clear that the Western assessment of the origin of women's movements does not in any way apply to Egypt. In the West, their origin is attributed to the increasing separation of private and public spheres, whereas in Egypt it appears that feminism arises when the strict isolation of women begins to lessen. Badran also undercuts the notion that Egyptian feminism is a movement initiated by the West. She supports her claim by previously unused source material and interviews.

The idea that there is no clear-cut distinction between the powerful and the powerless, and that such oppositions are not always immediately evident, has made women historians look for different sources and new means of analysis. Since language contributes to constitute social opinions and ideas about power relations within the mental framework of people, analysis of meaning and of changes in meaning can give insight into the ways in which a certain culture does or does not restrict women. By comparing different texts about a certain subject we can reconstruct global images which in their turn demonstrate feelings about being female or the feminine. That the ideas of contemporaries may vary about this is apparent from Jo Anne Preston's paper. She compares the motivations that women themselves formulated for wanting to become schoolteachers to the motivations educationalists ascribed to them. In New England in the period 1835-80, there were pleas to employ more women as teachers, because their female qualities would make them suitable. The women themselves, however, showed little motherly inspiration in their letters; instead they gave reasons such as the wish for economic independence and an interest in science and literature.

A century later, in the 1930s, British educationalists expressed entirely different opinions when they discussed the suitability of the spinster as a schoolteacher. Alison Oram shows that educationalists in the Depression used the argument that spinsters were 'embittered, thwarted women with overtones of sexual frustration' and for that reason were highly unsuitable as teachers. In their attempts to exclude spinsters from teaching, experts could avail themselves of opinions formulated by the rising sexology.

Anne Laurence analyses how psychological disorders are couched in concepts in professional writings and ego-documents of 'patients'. With her analysis, Laurence tries to gain insight into the traditions within which these concepts are handled. The tradition in which an author finds her/himself is decisive for the meaning which she/he assigns to a certain disorder. For instance, a lawyer, obliged for the sake of his profession to ascertain the personal responsibility of the patient with a psychological disorder, would attribute a different meaning to the disorder than the patient herself, who would seek to understand the how and why of her disorder. Seventeenth-century women saw their psychological disorders in a religious context, for which they used terms such as 'demonic temptation' and 'divine inspiration'. For the twentieth-century woman historian this context does not make the task of charting the experiences of these women easy.

The article of Annelies van Gijsen gives a revision of the literary-critical significance that is attributed to courtly literature. After a careful analysis of the stories of Pygmalion and Narcissus, Van Gijsen concludes that the courtly genre merely reveals the self-confirmation of male heroes instead of their reverence of women.

In her paper, Anna Clark analyses aspects of the spoken language of working-class women as they can be traced in reports of defamation cases around 1800. By analysing the meaning of terms of abuse, Clark finds that their use is a gauge for the social stratification in a working-class neighbourhood in London. Because of the sharpening of the divisions between the lower and the lower-middle classes, the norms of the middle classes began to play a crucial part in determining the social stratum to which a person belonged. Since, according to these norms, to be the object of verbal abuse was harmful to a woman's reputation, women were more inclined to take the matter to court if they had achieved higher positions on the social ladder.

Three of the articles in this collection are historiographical and/or methodological in nature. Maria Grever pleads the recognition of a women-historical tradition. Many women in the past wrote history; they often unjustly passed into oblivion. Women wrote history, for instance in the form of historical novels, on the one hand because they had no access to the contemporary institutions of scholarship and on the other because the novel form offered better opportunities for formulating aspects of the lives of women. Thus the writings of women historians *avant la lettre* are interesting not only because they contain information about the women described, but also because they throw light on the possibilities for women to manifest themselves as writers.

Helga Grubitzsch's article deals with the other side of Grevers' story. In the dominant male historical tradition, research is almost always presented as being sex-neutral. At a closer inspection it turns out to concern merely the male perspective. Grubitzsch finds that this androcentrism can even be found in historical works that are explicitly about women. Because every woman historian has to deal with sources and historiography written by men, Grubitzsch gives a careful analysis of *Les femmes de la Révolution* by J. Michelet to display in how many different ways androcentrism can manifest itself.

It is still a fact that the Western academic tradition tends to describe non-Western societies by means of Western categories. Feminist researchers show a similar tendency to universalise their discoveries, as has already been pointed out in the discussion of Badran's paper. In her article, Willy Jansen wonders to what extent Western scholars are justified in investigating the history of non-Western women; an issue which came up repeatedly at the conference. She is amply aware of the biases of Western historians or anthropologists. As a result of a discussion of Western historical and anthropological research of Algerian women she argues that, provided certain aspects of ethnocentrism are recognised and explicitly incorporated, Western scholars can avoid biases in their research.

We think that these articles may offer sufficient ground for further consideration of research methods and points of view within women's history and that these proceedings of the conference may lead to a follow-up. Finally we would like to express our gratitude to everyone who has contributed to the realisation of this publication. First of all, the women who devoted themselves for two years to the organisation of the conference. The *Landelijk Overleg Vrouwengeschiedenis* (The Dutch National Network of Feminist Historians) formed, from its membership of students and researchers of women's history, the organising committee of this presentation and exchange of current research in women's history. Secondly, we should like to mention Ciska Pattipilohy for her role in judging non-Western contributions; and Carla Laan and Karen Peters, who unfortunately had to abandon their editorial work prematurely. Thirdly, all the authors who had to meet our many requirements and who have done so in a very pleasant manner, and those who assisted us with all our English correspondence: Bram Dijkshoorn, Gerard Steen, and Els Klijnsma, who also did part of the language editing. Furthermore, all those who freely gave their time to advise us concerning the contents of this collection: Nelleke Bakker, Margret Brügmann, Lilian de Bruijn, Fia Dieteren, Saskia Grotenhuis, Pauline Hagemeijer, Anton van Hooff, Els Kloek, Susana Menendez, Arthur Mitzman, Marijke Mossink, Brita Rang, Marion de Ras, Dineke Stam, Marja van Tilburg, Petra de Vries, Mirjam Westen and Jolande Withuis. We are also very grateful to the institutions whose financial contributions to this collection have been indispensable: the Prins Bernhard Fonds, the University of Amsterdam and the Women's Advisory Committee at the University of Amsterdam.

The editors
May 1988

Translated by Lonette Wiemans

Selma Leydesdorff

Politics, identification and the writing of women's history

In spite of the great differences in the ways in which women's history is made and studied, there nevertheless appears to be a great deal of common ground. Time and again there is that moment of recognition, that feeling that all women are involved in the same things. Great women leaders from the past make us feel proud; we admire their fight for equal rights and we feel that we recognise something in their struggle with the contradictions in their lives. Do we not all feel ambivalent about the conflict between what is expected of us as women and what we really want in society? Feelings of identity, however, depend on whom it is that we study, for we are also quite capable of feeling appalled by women in whom we do not recognise anything of ourselves, women with whom we cannot possibly identify and whom we do not really understand at all. Apart from the identification with great women another kind of identification is possible. Many of us feel great involvement with unknown women, women who have disappeared nameless in history. No matter how quantitative our approach to them may be, there are moments at which all those anonymous women emerge from obscurity. This may be when we study an old manuscript, when we hold an old garment or when we read a statement from a contemporary author. Almost all women historians involved in studying women from the past are familiar with these moments of identification, disapproval or pride. Their research can be seen as a passionate exploration and a desire to increase knowledge.

If one element can be said to have characterised the International Conference on Women's History, it was this exchange of enthusiasms. Most women researchers identify with the object of their research. This leads to a situation in which canons of scholarship dissuade researchers from any such identification. Women researchers are therefore often, somewhat belittlingly, said to be 'emotionally involved'. Yet it is this very identification with women forerunners that marks the common ground by means of which the ties with the vast field of the women's movement keep coming up for discussion. Again and again the exchange of views proves possible, even where specialist subjects are concerned. Systematically, women historians attempt to discuss the traditions which generated differences, and they all realise that there is no point in imprisoning themselves in the subdisciplines of history.

The first part of this introduction will deal chiefly with the differences in the ways in which women's history is written. Where do these differences come from and how do they relate to national traditions? Next I shall look at how these differences are related to the degree of integration of women's history into the academic world, and what consequences this integration has had for the way patterns of identification are dealt with within the practice of women's history.[1]

I believe that it is necessary to take a closer look at the issue of conscious and unconscious patterns of identification within the practice of women's history, primarily because the search for identification has, from the onset, been one of the foundations of feminist historiography. In the course of time, however, attitudes towards such a strong involvement have changed; new questions as well as new fields of interest have come up for discussion within women's history. All this has made identification difficult, if not impossible.

I am aware with everything that I am writing at the beginning of this collection that an overall vision is impossible, even though this was so much the underlying aim at the conference. Of course, my views have been defined by Western practice, and of course I am a product of the way in which women's history has slowly gained a place at the universities in the Netherlands. It was exactly the consequences of what was described as Western academicism that were criticised at the conference by women from non-Western countries where women's history has not (yet) acquired this status.

Differences

In spite of the fact that feminist historians have exchanged their ideas internationally practically from the start, the differences in the research papers presented at this conference appeared to be nationally determined. Historiography remains linked to national, historical traditions. In some countries, historiography is interwoven with legitimisation by the authorities, in other countries, more with social movements. Women's history in Germany, for instance, shows obvious traces of a national historiography trying to come to terms with the atrocities of the past. In Germany, much research is carried out into the ways in which Nazism oppressed women. It is interesting to compare this German tradition of women's history about Nazism to the literature from the United States on the same subject. In the United States, the focus of research appears to have shifted from the question how oppression works - the (justified) repetition of the charge against fascism - to the issue of how the great mass of women faced fascism. This latter question is then asked from an explicitly feminist perspective.

In Great Britain, women's history has, from the start, been closely linked to labour history and is therefore strongly oriented towards the position of women within the labour process - the relation between paid and domestic work and the problems surrounding the organisation of women. In Italy, women's history has developed parallel to the women's movement as very much a cultural tradition. This will be apparent from the fascinating periodical *Memoria.* And in France, with its philosophical tradition, women's history has been influenced by modes of thought that other feminist historians can only grasp with great difficulty. Here too, the national character of historiography is present: in the bicentennial year of 1989 women are involved on a large scale in the historiography of the French Revolution.

To us, Dutch historians, the variety of all these different approaches at the conference seemed at first kaleidoscopic. Soon, however, it became apparent that the differences were not only on a national level, but that every form of feminist historiography implies a political stand, leading to different scholarly views. This became especially apparent in the lectures given by non-Western women. They made clear to what extent historiography can be

'Eurocentric' and 'Western-oriented'.

Two examples: to a Western European woman it is almost inconceivable that anyone would choose to wear a veil voluntarily. She would probably refer to veiling as the umpteenth proof of how badly women are treated in Islamic countries. Upon closer consideration such unequivocal conclusions appear to be largely based on a lack of knowledge about Islamic countries. Anyone who attended the lectures about these countries will have learned that wearing the veil has political and religious significance, and that if you describe this custom within a historical perspective, it implies that women are expressing an opinion about political developments. After all, wearing the veil is for many girls an act of protest against westernisation, which has brought many bad things as well as good ones. It is also an act which veils women again, and this often goes hand in hand with the resumption of traditional women's roles. No historiography should refrain from assessing these changes. Again and again we take up positions in a debate that raises more questions than it answers.

The historiography of women in Latin America has a strong political character as well. The Latin American women at the conference argued that Western women use terms like *machismo* and *marianismo* too easily, while to Latin American women these terms do not refer to reality. In Latin America there is a multitude of relations between men and women; these cannot all be gathered under the heading of *machismo.* The historiography in Latin America is characterised by a strong solidarity with resistance groups against dictatorial regimes which oppress not only women but men also. The Latin American women argued that you cannot accuse men of machismo while at the same time fighting alongside them. In the heated discussions that followed, some referred to Frantz Fanon, who has shown that this 'equality in the fight' proved to be an illusion in the Algerian liberation movement. Of course the effects of the decolonisation of Algeria cannot be applied unthinkingly to Latin America, firstly because the latter has a longer liberal tradition, secondly because the power relations between men and women in Latin America are quite different. Only on a superficial level do we see the woman as ally of the man as a parallel feature in both these liberation struggles. The division of the gender roles, however, remains intact, which becomes painfully clear when the joint fight is over.

This, at first glance, political use of historiography was seemingly at odds with much of the research presented at the conference, so that it appeared as if the 'academic' women's history had turned permanently away from politics. Sometimes the scale tipped and women engaged in a polemic against all this 'political stuff'. It was scholarship that we were concerned with, and politics is a separate issue. Unfortunately, in the present state of affairs this point of view means that some women scholars distance themselves verbally from the women's movement by conforming to existing scholarly practices.

Women's history as an academic subject

Women's history has acquired academic status in a number of countries: with here a single accepted woman scholar, and there an isolated chair, sometimes even complete departments at universities such as those in the United States and in some parts of France. Integration into universities is important: the fight against existing forms of historiography has, after all, from the beginning been one of the aims of feminist historians. This has had implications for the extent of their political involvement.

At the conference, there appeared to be a division between historiography in those countries where women's history has gained a place at universities or has become an accepted scholarly subject, and those countries where this is not the case. No woman employed at a university will deny that there is a tension between political involvement in a movement and the kind of academic work which is expected of a woman scholar. Especially from scholarship one expects more than just political involvement. This certainly applies to those women who do not work within departments of women's studies or do not hold a position in women's studies.

Gaining academic acceptance has often resulted in abandoning the initially interdisciplinary character of women's history. This interdisciplinary approach existed at a number of levels: first of all at the level of exchange between the different branches of historical scholarship, secondly at the level of exchange with other scholarly subjects, and thirdly at that brought about by the theoretical questions put forward by feminism. This interdisciplinary emphasis was based on the need for insight into the social mechanisms that have contributed to the current position of women. In order to achieve this insight, women historians drew comparisons between cultures. They looked at the differences between their own culture and other civilisations, but they also examined the historical relativity of their own society. In doing so, they crossed the borders of their own subdiscipline and often the limits of history itself. In the Netherlands, for instance, anthropology has always been considered important in answering the questions brought forward by feminist historiography. That women's history has become an object of scholarly research has led to a decreased ability, on the part of the researchers, to identify with the subject of their studies - they have been forced to distance themselves from their work.

Changes in identification

A great deal of feminist historiography originated from a need for a past with which the feminist movement, but also women individually, could identify. Identification, and not only with the past, has from the start been a high priority with feminists. By telling each other their stories and by identifying with one another, women have learned to realise that their problems are not individual ones, and thus they have found a common ground on the basis of which they could start their political fight. This fight was given a historical basis by referring to a long line of predecessors, all of whom were supposed to have grappled with the same, and therefore with our, problems. Were the Amazons not after all fabulous predecessors? And were witches not women who had courageously opted out of the laws of society? There was also identification with the role of the victim. Women were victims of the system, of male supremacy and male violence. At the conference, this identification with the victim featured in the discussion on racism and historiography. The accusation made by some women that many of the papers presented ignored the role of the whites as oppressors in the non-Western world, led to confessions of guilt and discussions about the way in which research could be conducted into this painful aspect of European and American historiography. There was quite a fight to occupy the role of victim: some women suddenly declared themselves oppressed because they came from farmers' or labourers' families. It seems to me that this is not the right way to deal with this problem. Even admitting that women's history is ethnocentric does not take us any further.

In our initial aim of finding women in history with whom we could identify, we tried to find evidence of their resistance. On the other hand, however, there was the oppression of a much larger group of women: those who stayed at home to do the washing. We felt a certain compassion for these women who had so entirely accepted their lot. But in the course of the years we began to see that this oppression was not as unequivocal as we had believed at first. For instance, it turns out that the common washplace by the river or in a town was a place of women's culture, where a special kind of power was developed. The fact that the area was out of bounds for men enabled the women to make good use of this place. So there was more to these non-militants than first met the eye. This erroneous judgment on 'non-resisting' women paralleled the way in which the women's movement judged the 'passive' majority that had not joined it. The women's movement explained this so-called passivity by introducing the concept of *false consciousness.* In actual fact women were born free, in legal terms they were born as either citizens, free-born individuals or as 'human beings', depending on their country of birth. It was simply that men obstructed the realisation of this freedom; that women were even content with their lot could only be explained by false consciousness. It had to be explained to these women that they were not serving their own real interests. The reasoning behind this idea, which was initially adopted by quite a number of women historians, is that, in principle, every person fights for his or her freedom. Anyone who does not fight this battle has a blind spot. However, the women's movement has become aware of the fact that things are not that straightforward. Women historians especially have repeatedly pointed out within the women's movement that all the millions of women from the past cannot possibly be lumped together and 'accused' of suffering from false consciousness.

Apparently, we need other concepts in studying the experience of the everyday life of women from the past. The dichotomy between oppression and resistance, from which the notion of false consciousness has been derived, is an oversimplified model of explanation. Did this not stem from the fact that for the women's movement, initially, it was important to prove with examples from the past that women have actually always wanted to be free, just as they do today? This view was too much determined by our desire to identify with women in history. There is, however, no point in simply rejecting these identifications. We too have been greatly inspired by them. At the same time we should realise and acknowledge that there are many women historians today who wish to concern themselves also with women with whom they cannot immediately identify.

The ultimate aim is to create historical narratives in which the experiences of the oppressor stand side by side with those of the oppressed. Neither of these experiences is the less true, but time and again it becomes apparent that the experience of the oppressed improves the existing historical picture better than the experience of the oppressor. This change is expressed in historiography by means of what may be described as a feminist variant of the history of mentalities. This has complicated the identification with the past, and in this respect such a historiography is less successful in meeting the direct needs of political feminism.

Studying what is not immediately obvious

Studying mentalities has shown us how strong the bars are of what the French historian M. Vovelle has called 'the dungeons of long duration'. These bars are not only strong because they prevent people from breaking out, but also because many people did not perceive the dungeons as such. The study of mentalities has pushed the resistance-oppression dichotomy to the background and with it the notion of false consciousness. New questions were raised about the unconscious and about language; these were new keys in the study of mentalities. However, it also meant creating distance in order to see more clearly. Identifying with people who led completely different lives is no longer a matter of course. By considering the past with more distance we have learned to see how superficial the immediately apparent is.

Let me give an example from my book about Jewish, proletarian Amsterdam, for which I interviewed many of the survivors from the concentration camps. At first sight the position of women in Jewish culture seems bad: women are excluded from worship, they have many domestic tasks, and decisions in public life are made by men. Upon investigation, I came across an incredibly strong professional honour on the part of these women, similar to that of Jewish women in Eastern Europe: they had learned a trade, had been in employment, and they talked about this with pride. Every mother wanted her daughter to learn a trade first and then get married. Jewish women, unlike most Dutch gentiles, did not regard the profession of servant-girl as a real trade. A woman had to be able to earn her own living and a servant-girl was too dependent. It was not considered a disgrace if a woman kept on working after her marriage, and this was also in opposition to the dominant ideology. In a culture which was so oppressive to women there was apparently a general pattern of economic independence for them. How then did oppression work within this culture? And why do many studies of the position of Jewish women overlook this economic independence?

Along with the shift in the area of attention of women's history, the study of women apart from their social context or from their opposition to men simultaneously ceased. Once again women are increasingly presented in research not only by means of what can be discovered explicitly about them, but in history rewritten on the basis of more indirect information, by giving women once again a place in their social context and incorporating their changing opposition to men. In doing so, historians make creative use of new methods of historiography and reflect on matters such as symbolic order, ideology and language.

With regard to the changing social context and the relativity of our own positions we could learn a great deal from women in the Third World. By showing us their different viewpoints they have made us realise how temporary, how relative and how transitory our own cultural and economic order is. They have continually inspired me, at any rate, with new outlooks on how to view women. One example is the necessary use that these women make of oral traditions, which are often still lively. The way in which these traditions have been integrated into the historical picture made me realise the necessity of analysing these stories which have often been handed down from generation to generation. Oral sources are of great importance to women's history, for we lack written ones of many aspects of the lives of women from the past.

The written source often gives a distorted picture. A well-known example of this is the report of a factory inspector who described the women workers in the factory he visited as being 'almost naked'. This does not mean that they were almost naked, but that they did not wear the layers of underclothes that his middle-class wife wore. Such distortions often exist in the painted record of historical 'reality' as well: in the Netherlands, factory girls were portrayed by the painter Jan Toorop, who pictured the hideous existence of the candlemakers in Amsterdam around 1900. For anyone with the slightest education in history the most striking fact is that in this factory, which did not yet have a conveyer-belt, the workers were seated in straight lines. What this reveals is merely Toorop's fascination with lines, for every other observer perceived the factory floor as chaotic, which, for that matter, also seems a distortion to me. The factory girls were called 'wax lights', according to tradition because they took on the colour of the candles. However, another tradition has it that the name only referred to the profession of candlemaker. The first version is dominant, and has always been used by the labour movement to protest against the bad working conditions in the factories. The girls would almost certainly have been pale, but it seems unlikely that they took on the colour of the candles, if only because it could be very hot in the factory. It is much more likely that at such high temperatures they perspired and became quite red in the face. We come across similar distortions in the statistics, which, certainly in the Netherlands, do not mention women's labour. Further investigation into the phenomenon of home industries makes one realise that industrialisation in the Netherlands was on such a scale that home industries must have existed. Only they were not registered anywhere, which is why women's labour hardly exists, as far as the statistics are concerned.

The above-mentioned examples give us an inkling of aspects of history which are often forgotten or ignored, and feminist historians have specialised in searching out the story behind the sources. They are no longer just concerned with naming what is clearly visible; they are also concerned with a story which is not described in so many words. Through accounts, for instance about what is expected of men, we learn a great deal about expectations with respect to women. In many writings claims are made about the antagonism between male and female. What we have to do is find out what forms this has taken. That is why 'male' and 'female' should not be taken as fixed data, but as the result of ideological and political changes. The question now arises as to why so many oppositions at a first glance have nothing to do with the one between male and female, but which in fact do refer to it.

Historiography of what is absent, what is forgotten

I would like to make a plea for a historiography of that which is not immediately visible and, one step further: a historiography of that which has been forgotten. This should be seen as an effort to rewrite history by re-introducing into the historical picture those elements which conjure up unpleasant feelings and are therefore in danger of being forgotten or omitted. Such a historiography, based on what has been forgotten, needs to be further worked out. It could profit from what we have found out, for instance, from oral history about forgotten historical events. After all, the knowledge gained in oral history about the course of ideological processes and their assimilation on the individual level, can be extrapolated to earlier periods. Earlier on I referred to an example from my own research. The economic independence of Jewish women no longer existed in their consciousness. I discovered it only by questioning the repeated statement made by these women that in later years they did not go out to work, and really did do just the housework. Why did they keep emphasising this, and what norm did it confirm? It cropped up at the same time as interviewees proudly announced that they had practised a 'trade' for years, and the statement appeared often. Why this repeated confirmation? Feminist historiography can form part of the quest for such conscious and unconscious repressions in the memory of an individual and of a culture. How these conscious or unconscious repressions in the lives and experiences of women could have come about, is a matter which calls for quite detailed research. How can we explain that the asymmetry between men and women has been retained in images in which this is not immediately recognisable, such symbolic oppositions as intellect and emotion, science and superstition, strong and weak, culture and nature, work and home? It may well be that in dealing with so many historical pictures we do not know whether we have to do with shifts in the lives and experiences of women themselves, or with a shift in the notion of 'femininity'. An example again from my own research: in many Jewish communities in Europe, it was quite normal that women were responsible for the economic functioning of the family, so that men could devote themselves to 'higher matters'. Being female thus implied economic independence; being male, on the other hand, was not defined as such.

A historiography which traces what has been forgotten about women and what they themselves have repressed will have to reconsider the basis of its theories. We shall have to consider carefully what the concepts 'being female' and 'femininity' mean in context. In addition, the differences on the level of symbolic presentation can provide much information. We can no longer be concerned only with filling the gaps that other historians have left open. Neither can we be solely concerned with our need for immediate identification. We must first of all ask ourselves why so much about women has been forgotten, repressed or omitted. This will also re-kindle the discussion of the relationship between science and politics.

Note

1. Every article one writes finds its inspiration in the works of others. Sometimes one re-interprets problems that have been discussed elsewhere. I would particularly like to mention an article by the anthropologist M.Z. Rosaldo which has been an inspiration to women's history in the Netherlands: 'The use and abuse of anthropology: reflections on feminism and cross-cultural understanding', *Signs: journal of women in culture and society,* vol. 5, no.3 (1980), pp. 389-417. See also: J.W. Scott, 'Survey article: women in history II. The modern period', *Past and present,* no.102 (1983), pp. 141-57; G. Pommata, 'La storia delle donne: una questione di confine' in N. Tranfaglia (ed.), *Gli strumenti della ricerca* 2 (Firenze, 1983), pp. 1434-69. A final inspiration is to be found in the work of L. Passerini, *Torino operaio e facismo. Una storia orale* (Bari, Laterza, 1984).

Translated by Lonette Wiemans

Londa Schiebinger

Maria Winkelmann: the clash between guild traditions and professional science

In 1984, only 5 per cent of all physicists and astronomers in the United States were women.[1] What is even more shocking is that women earned only one-quarter of what men in those fields earned. According to statistics from the United States Department of Labor, this represented the widest pay gap for any profession in the United States.[2] This situation is much the same around the world.

Why are there so few women scientists? Historians have been slow to research the problem of women in science. Since Christine de Pisan's first look at this subject in 1405, works on women scientists have been primarily lexicons of 'women worthies' - women who despite all obstacles made significant contributions to science.[3] In recent years, a new field of inquiry - gender and science - has begun to explore deeper cultural barriers which block women's access to science. Those working in this rich and varied field are still interested in uncovering the history of women scientists from the obscurity of the past. More than that, they employ gender as a category of historical analysis, and look at women scientists in relation to changing trends in the political and economic function of science and its institutional forms.[4] The focus has turned from a simple celebration of great women scientists to a more careful study of what social trends encourage or discourage women to participate in science.

To uncover the origins of current tensions between women and science, I return to an important juncture in the history of science - the seventeenth and eighteenth centuries, when new academies were founded to foster the new experimental sciences. It would be a mistake to think that there were no qualified women scientists when these academies first opened their doors. An example of this is the case of Maria Winkelmann[5] at the Royal Academy of Sciences in Berlin.[6] Already a seasoned astronomer when her husband, Academy astronomer Gottfried Kirch, died in 1710, Winkelmann asked to be appointed in her husband's place. Despite the fact that the President of the Academy, Gottfried Leibniz, was among her backers, her request was denied. The story of Maria Winkelmann's rejection by the Academy illustrates patterns in women's participation in early modern science. On the one hand, craft traditions fostered women's participation in astronomy; through apprenticeships, they gained access to the secrets and tools of the trade. Winkelmann was not an exceptional woman; between 1650 and 1720, more than 14 per cent of German astronomers were women.[7] These craft traditions, however, were counterbalanced by other trends, both old and new. For centuries, women had been excluded from universities. In many ways, the new trend of professionalisation served to reaffirm this traditional exclusion of women from intellectual culture. There were those at the Berlin Academy who judged it improper for a woman to practise the art of astronomy, and advised Winkelmann to return to her 'distaff' and 'spindle'.[8]

Craft traditions in astronomy

In order to understand Maria Winkelmann's story, we must first understand how it was possible for women to participate in astronomy in the seventeenth century. If universities were closed to women, how could they receive a training in astronomy? Edgar Zilsel was among the first historians to emphasise the importance of craft skills for the development of modern science in the West.[9] Zilsel located the origin of modern science in the fusion of three traditions: the tradition of letters, exemplified by the literary humanists; the tradition of logic and mathematics, exemplified by the Aristotelian scholastics; and the tradition of practical experiment and practical application, exemplified by the empirical artist-engineers.[10] The new value attached to the traditional skills of the artisan allowed for broader participation in the sciences. Of the various institutional homes of astronomy, only the artisanal workshop welcomed women. Women were not newcomers to the workshop: it was in craft traditions that the fifteenth-century writer Christine de Pisan had located women's greatest innovations in the arts and sciences - the spinning of wool, silk and linen, and 'creating the general means of civilized existence'.[11] In the workshop, women's contributions (like men's) depended less on book learning and more on practical innovations in illustrating, calculating or observing.

The position of women in the crafts was stronger than has generally been appreciated. In fifteenth-century Nürnberg and Cologne, for example, craftswomen were active in nearly all areas of production: of the 38 guilds that Margret Wensky has described in her study of working women in Cologne (a city where women's economic position was especially strong), women were full members of between 20 and 24.[12] Women's membership in these guilds conferred on them limited civic rights - they could buy and sell, and be represented in a court of law. They could not, however, hold city office. Of course, astronomers were never officially organised in guilds, yet the craft traditions which moulded all aspects of working life in early modern Europe were also very much alive in astronomical practices. This was especially true in Germany, where stirrings of industrialisation came late.[13]

Maria Margaretha Winkelmann, daughter of a Lutheran minister, was born at Panitzsch (near Leipzig) in 1670. Her education followed a pattern often found in the trades, a common one for both young men and young women. Educated privately by her father (and after his death, by her uncle), the young Winkelmann made great progress in the arts and letters; she took a special interest in astronomy from an early age.[14] She received advanced training in astronomy from the self-taught Christopher Arnold, who lived in the neighbouring town of Sommerfeld. Winkelmann served as an unofficial apprentice at Arnold's house, learning the art of astronomy through practical experience in observation and calculation. Although young women trained as apprentices, they could not become journeymen. Journeymen might travel from master to master; young women, by contrast, took what training was available in their homes. At least within the sciences, there is no example of a woman apprentice travelling from one master to another. For a woman, the single most important factor for her future in science was her father. Winkelmann trained with Arnold outside her home, but her case was extraordinary because she was an orphan.

Astronomy in late seventeenth-century Germany was not, however, organised entirely along guild lines, and women's exclusion from universities created additional inequalities between women's and men's education. Had Maria Winkelmann been male, she would probably have continued her studies at the nearby universities of Leipzig or Jena. Leading male astronomers, such as Johannes Hevelius, Georg Eimmart and Gottfried Kirch, held university degrees, though not in astronomy. Hevelius, for example, was a beer-brewer by profession and had been educated in jurisprudence.[15] This was not uncommon; mathematics and astronomy in this period were not autonomous disciplines. Most astronomers studied one of the ancient professions: law, theology or medicine.[16] Although women's exclusion from universities set limits to their participation in astronomy, it did not exclude them entirely.[17] Debates about the nature of the universe were rife in university halls, and yet the practice of astronomy - the actual work of observing the heavens - took place largely outside the universities.

After her apprenticeship, a scientifically-minded woman often married a scientist in order to continue practising her trade.[18] It was at the astronomer Christopher Arnold's house, where Maria Winkelmann served her unofficial apprenticeship, that she met Gottfried Kirch, Germany's leading astronomer. Although Winkelmann's uncle wanted her to marry a young Lutheran minister, he eventually consented to her marriage to Kirch.[19] By marrying Kirch, 30 years her senior, Winkelmann secured her place in astronomy. Knowing she would have little opportunity to practise astronomy independently, Winkelmann moved, in typical guild fashion, from her position as assistant to Arnold to become an assistant to Kirch. Kirch also benefited from this marriage. In Winkelmann, he found a second wife who could look after his domestic affairs, and also a much-needed astronomical assistant who could help with calculations, observations and the making of calendars.[20]

In 1700, Kirch and Winkelmann took up residence in Berlin, the expanding cultural centre of Brandenburg. In the late seventeenth century, the route to Berlin was very different for men and for women. His university education at Jena, and his apprenticeship to the well-known astronomer Hevelius, afforded Kirch the opportunity to move from the household of a tailor in the small town of Guben to the position of astronomer at the Royal Academy of Sciences. Winkelmann's mobility, on the other hand, came not through education, but through marriage. Although each came via a different route, both served at the Berlin Academy: Gottfried as Academy astronomer, Maria as an unofficial but recognised assistant to her husband.[21]

Although guild traditions gave women access to the practice of science, it is important not to see this in romantic terms. Women's position in astronomy was similar to their position in the guilds: valued, but subordinate. Only a few women, such as Maria Cunitz or Maria Winkelmann, directed and published their own astronomical work.[22] More often a woman worked in various supportive positions, editing her husband's writings or performing astronomical calculations.

Comets and calendars: Winkelmann's scientific achievement

In 1710, Winkelmann petitioned the Academy of Sciences for a position as calendar-maker. Was she merely a wifely assistant, engaged in the tedious computation characteristic of what Margaret Rossiter has defined as 'women's work'?[23] Or was she a qualified astronomer, capable of setting and carrying out her own research?

Although Maria Winkelmann is little known today, she was celebrated in her time.[24] Her scientific accomplishments during her first decade at the Berlin Academy were many and varied. It was her habit to observe the heavens every evening from nine o'clock onwards.[25] During the course of an evening's observation in 1702, Winkelmann discovered a previously unknown comet - a discovery which should have secured her position in the astronomical community. Her husband's position at the Academy, for example, was partly due to his discovery of a comet in 1680. Today there is no question about Winkelmann's leading role in the discovery; in the 1930s, F.H. Weiss published Winkelmann's original report of the sighting of the comet, which was in his private possession.[26] In his notes made on that night, Kirch also recorded that his wife found the comet while he slept:

> 'Early in the morning (about 2:00 A.M.) the sky was clear and starry. Some nights before, I had observed a variable star, and my wife (as I slept) wanted to find and see it for herself. In so doing, she found a comet in the sky. At which time she woke me, and I found that it was indeed a comet... I was surprised that I had not seen it the night before.'[27]

Since this sighting was the first 'scientific' achievement of the young Academy, a report of the comet was immediately sent to the King. However, the report bore Kirch's name, not Winkelmann's.[28] Published accounts of the comet also bore Kirch's name, which unfortunately led many historians to attribute the discovery of the comet to Kirch alone.[29]

Why did Winkelmann let this happen? She was certainly not hesitant about publishing; she was to publish three tracts under her own name between 1709 and 1711.[30] Her inability to claim recognition for her discovery was partly due to the fact that she had had no training in Latin, the shared scientific language in Germany at the time. This made it difficult for her to publish her discovery in the *Acta Eruditorum*, which was then Germany's only scientific journal. More important to the problem of assigning credit, however, was the fact that Maria and Gottfried worked closely together. The tasks of husband and wife did not divide along modern lines - he was not fully professional, working in an observatory outside the home; she was not fully a housewife, confined to hearth and home. Nor were they independent professionals, each holding a chair of astronomy. Rather, they worked very much as a team and on common problems.

During her years at the Berlin Academy, Winkelmann came to know Leibniz, who expressed a high regard for her scientific abilities. In 1709, Leibniz presented her to the Prussian court, where Winkelmann explained her sighting of sunspots. In a letter of introduction, Leibniz wrote:

> 'There is [in Berlin] a most learned woman who could pass as a rarity. Her achievement is not in literature or rhetoric, but in the most profound doctrines of Astronomy... I do not believe that this woman easily finds her equal in the science in which she excels... She observes with the best observers, she knows how to handle marvellously the quadrant and the telescope [*grandes lunettes d'approche*].'[31]

Leibniz added that if only she had been sent to the Cape of Good Hope instead of astronomer Peter Kolb, the Academy would have received more reliable observations.[32]

At the Academy, Winkelmann made important contributions in calendar-making. Unlike many major European courts, the Prussian court did not yet have its own calendar. In 1700, the Reichstag at Regensburg ruled that an improved calendar, similar to the Gregorian calendar, was to be used throughout German territory. The production of an astronomically accurate calendar became a major project for the Academy of Sciences, which had been founded in the same year. In addition to fixing the days and months, each calendar predicted the position of the sun, moon and planets (calculated using the Rudolphine tables), the phases of the moon, eclipses of the sun or moon to the hour, and the rising and setting of the sun within a quarter of an hour for each day. The calendar was also of monetary interest to the Academy. In 1700, the King granted the Academy a monopoly on the sale of calendars, and throughout the eighteenth century, the Academy derived a large part of its revenues from these sales.[33] This income made the position of astronomer particularly important.[34] The sale of calendars depended on their more popular aspects. Calendars, referred to by Leibniz as 'the library of the common man', had been issued at least since the fourteenth century and they owed much of their popular appeal to astrology.[35] Until 1768 there was little distinction between calendars and farmers' almanacs; each predicted the best times for haircutting, blood-letting, the conceiving of children, the planting of seeds and the felling of timber.

The attempt to become Academy astronomer

Gottfried Kirch died in 1710. It fell to the executive council of the Academy - which consisted of Leibniz as President, the Secretary J. Jablonski, his brother, the court pastor, and the librarian Cuneau - to appoint a new astronomer. It was vital to make this appointment quickly, as the Academy depended on the annual revenues from the calendar. The situation was bleak.[36] Apart from one in-house candidate, Jablonski could think of no one who qualified for the position. Even though there were few candidates, Maria Winkelmann's name did not enter their deliberations.[37]

This is even more surprising when one considers that her qualifications were not all that different from her husband's. They both had long years of experience preparing calendars. They had both discovered comets: Kirch in 1680, Winkelmann in 1702. They both prepared *ephemerides*, and recorded numerous other observations. What Winkelmann did not have, and which nearly every member of the Academy had, was a university degree.

Since Winkelmann's name did not come up in discussions about the appointment of astronomer, she submitted it herself, along with her credentials. In a letter to the Secretary, Jablonski, she asked that she and her son be appointed assistant astronomers in charge of preparing the Academy calendar.[38] Her argument for her candidacy was twofold. Firstly, she argued that she was well qualified, since she had been instructed in astronomical calculation and observation by her husband. Secondly, and more importantly, she had been engaged in astronomical work since her marriage, and thus had been working for the Academy since her husband's appointment ten years earlier. Indeed, she reported that 'for some time, while my dear departed husband was weak and ill, I prepared the calendar from his calculations and published it under his name'. She also reminded Jablonski that he had had occasion to remark on how she 'lent a helping hand to her husband's astronomical work' - work for which she was paid a wage. For Winkelmann, a position at the Berlin Academy was not only an honour, it was a means of supporting herself and her four children. Her husband, she wrote, had left little money.

Jablonski was aware that the Academy's handling of Winkelmann's case would set important precedents for the role of women in Germany's leading scientific body. In September 1710, the Secretary warned Leibniz:

> 'You should be aware that this approaching decision could serve as a precedent. We are tentatively of the opinion that this case must be judged not only on its present merits, but also as it could be judged for all time. For what we concede to her could serve as an example in the future.'[39]

Winkelmann's repeated requests for an official appointment at the Observatory were not welcomed by the Academy. Jablonski wrote to Leibniz on the matter:

> 'That she be employed in an official capacity to work on the calendar or to continue with observations simply will not do. Already during her husband's lifetime the society was burdened with ridicule because its calendar was prepared by a woman. If she were now to be kept on in such a capacity, mouths would gape even wider.'[40]

Leibniz was one of the few at the Academy who supported Winkelmann. During the council meeting of 18 March 1711 (one of the last meetings over which he presided before leaving Berlin), Leibniz argued that the Academy, considered as either a religious or an academic body, should provide widows with housing and salary for six months as was customary. At Leibniz's request, the Academy granted Winkelmann the right to remain in Academy housing for a little longer; the proposal that she be paid a salary, however, was defeated. Instead, the council paid her 40 thalers for her husband's observation notebooks. Later that year, the Academy showed some goodwill towards Winkelmann by presenting her with a medal.[41]

The Academy never spelled out its reasons for refusing to appoint her to a position in the Observatory. Winkelmann, however, traced her misfortunes to her sex. In a poignant passage, she recounted her husband's assurance that God would show his grace through influential patrons. This, she wrote, does not hold true for the female sex. Her disappointment was deep: 'Now I go through a severe desert, and because...water is scarce,...the taste is bitter.'[42] Despite the fact that Winkelmann had been involved in preparing the calendar for ten years and knew the work well, the position of Academy astronomer was awarded to Johann Heinrich Hoffmann. Hoffmann was an undistinguished astronomer who today has vanished into obscurity. During his tenure at the Academy, he was twice censured for poor work.[43]

Did Winkelmann have a legitimate claim to the post of assistant astronomer? How did she imagine that her requests to continue the calendar project would be taken seriously? It was as the wife of an artisan-astronomer that Winkelmann enjoyed a modest measure of respect at the Academy. When she petitioned the Academy council to allow her to remain as assistant calendar-maker, she invoked age-old guild principles.[44] In most cases, guild regulations gave a widow the right to run the family business after the death of her husband. Widows' rights followed three general patterns. In some guilds, widows were allowed to work as independent masters as long as they lived; in others, widows were allowed to continue the family business, but only with the help of journeymen or apprentices, while in yet others, they 'filled in' for one or two years to provide continuity until their eldest sons came of age.[45] Within the lower echelons of the Academy, widows were allowed to continue in their husbands' position. A woman whom we know only by the name of 'Pont', widow of the keeper of Academy mulberry trees, was allowed to complete the last four years of her husband's six-year contract.[46] This is what Winkelmann also wished to do. After the death of her husband, she tried to carry on the 'family' business of calendar-making as an independent master. Yet, as we have seen, the Academy refused her request. Winkelmann found that traditions which had once secured women a (limited) role in science were not to apply in the new institutions.

Although the Academy retained vestiges of an older order, it also contained the seeds of a new one. The founding of the Academy in 1700 represented the first step towards the professionalisation of astronomy in Germany. Earlier observatories - those of Hevelius in Danzig and Eimmart in Nürnberg - had been private. The Academy's Observatory, however, was not private, but a public ornament of the Prussian State. The astronomers were no longer owners and directors of their own observatories, but employees of the Academy, selected by a patron on the basis of personal merit, rather than on the basis of family tradition. This shift in character of scientific institutions from private to public had dramatic implications for the role of women in science. As astronomy moved more and more out of the private observatories and into the public world, women lost their threshold in modern science.

Although Winkelmann could not continue her work at the Berlin Academy, she did continue her astronomical work. On leaving the Academy, Winkelmann moved with her family to Baron von Krosigk's private observatory, where she and Gottfried Kirch had worked while the Academy Observatory was under construction. At Von Krosigk's observatory, Winkelmann reached the height of her career. With her husband dead and her son away at university, she enjoyed the rank of 'master' astronomer. She continued her daily observations and had two students to assist her, since she was now a master.[47] The published reports of their joint observations bear her name. In 1716, the Winkelmann-Kirch family received an invitation from Peter the Great of Russia to practise astronomy in Moscow.[48] The family decided instead to return to Berlin when Winkelmann's son Christfried (along with J.W. Wagner) was appointed Observer at the Academy. Thus Winkelmann returned once more to the task of observation and calendar-making, this time as assistant to her son.[49]

But still all was not well. The opinion that women should not do astronomy, at least not in a public capacity, still prevailed.[50] In 1717, Winkelmann was reprimanded by the Academy Council for talking too much to visitors at the Observatory. The Council recommended her to 'retire to the background and leave the talking to Wagner and her son'. A month later, the Academy again reported that 'Frau Kirch meddles too much with Society matters and is too visible at the Observatory when strangers visit.' Again the Council warned Winkelmann 'to let herself be seen at the Observatory as little as possible, especially on public occasions'.[51] As family friend and Academy Vice-President A. des Vignoles recorded, there were those who found it wrong for a woman to practise astronomy. Maria Winkelmann was forced to make a choice. She could either continue to badger the Academy for a position of her own or, for the sake of her son's reputation, she could retire to the background as the Academy requested. Des Vignoles wrote that she chose the latter option. Academy records show, however, that the choice was not hers to make. On 21 October 1717, the Academy resolved to remove Winkelmann - who apparently had paid little heed to their warnings - from the Academy premises. She was obliged to leave her house and the Observatory. Despite this, the Academy did not want her to abandon her duties as a mother; Academy officials expressed their hope that she 'could find a house nearby so that Herr Kirch [her son] could continue to eat at her table'.[52]

Winkelmann quit the Academy's Observatory in 1717 and continued her observations at home 'behind closed doors', as was thought appropriate, a move which Des Vignoles judged detrimental to the progress she might have made in astronomy. With few scientific instruments at her disposal, she was forced to abandon astronomical science. Maria Winkelmann died of fever in 1720. It was the opinion of a close observer that 'she merited a fate better than the one she received'.[53]

The consequences for women's participation in science

As the case of Maria Winkelmann illustrates, the poor representation of women in the Berlin Academy of Sciences cannot be traced simply to an absence of women qualified in science. Rather, the exclusion of women resulted from policies consciously implemented at an early period in the Academy's history.

The Academy did not, however, make its decisions in a vacuum. Larger developments, both scientific and social, set limits within which the Academy manoeuvred. The professionalisation of the sciences (a gradual process which took place over a period of two centuries) weakened craft traditions within the sciences, which in turn weakened women's position in those sciences. With the gradual professionalisation of astronomy, astronomers ceased working in family attics-cum-observatories as they had done in the days of the Kirch family. As late as 1704, Gottfried Kirch recorded in his diary: 'July 4, [the sky was] light early. But I was unable to use the floor [to make observations through windows in the ceiling] since the washing from two households was hanging there. It was a pity, because I missed the conjunction of Jupiter and Venus.'[54] Kirch's complaint reveals a striking juxtaposition of science and private life that began to disappear in the course of the eighteenth century. With the increasing polarisation of public and private spheres in the eighteenth and nineteenth centuries, the family moved into the private sphere of hearth and home, while science migrated to the public sphere of university and finally industry.

With the privatisation of the family, husbands and wives ceased to be partners in the family business, and women were increasingly confined to the domestic role of housewife and mother. A wife such as Maria Winkelmann-Kirch could no longer become assistant astronomer to a scientific academy through marriage. With the changes in the social structure of science, women's participation in science also changed. On the one hand, women attempted to follow the course of public instruction and certification through the universities, like their male counterparts. These attempts, however, remained unsuccessful until nearly two centuries later, at the beginning of the 1900s.[55] A second option open to women was to continue to participate within the (now private) family sphere as increasingly 'invisible assistants' to scientific husbands or brothers.

Although there were three honorary women members of the

Berlin Academy in the eighteenth century, the election of a woman purely on scientific merit did not take place until 1949, when the physicist Lise Meitner was elected - but only as a corresponding member. The first woman awarded full membership was the historian Liselotte Welskopf in 1964. Since the founding of the Academy in 1700, only 14 of its 2,900 members have been women. Of those 14 only four have enjoyed full membership. As of 1983, no woman has ever been appointed to a leadership role as Academy president, vice-president, general secretary or head of any of the various scientific sections.

Notes

1. *Women and minorities in science and engineering*, National Science Foundation, January 1986, p. 61. I would like to thank Christa Kirsten and the staff of the Zentrales Akademie Archiv der Akademie der Wissenschaften der DDR; Gerda Utermöhlen and the staff of the Leibniz Archive, Niedersächsische Landesbibliothek, Hannover; and the staff of the Observatoire de Paris for their kind assistance with material for this essay. My thanks also to the Deutscher Akademischer Austauschdienst, the Rockefeller Foundation and the National Endowment for the Humanities for providing support for this research and for my larger project on women in the origins of modern science. A number of friends and critics read and commented on earlier drafts of this manuscript: Robert Proctor, Richard Kremer, Margaret Rossiter, Roger Hahn, Merry Wiesner and Lyndal Roper.

2. Men working in the fields of physics and astronomy earn on average $674 per week. Women in these fields earn only $166 per week. Bureau of Labor Statistics 1983, published in Carole Bodger, 'Salary survey: who does what and for how much?', *Working Woman*, January 1985, p. 72.

3. Christine de Pisan, *The book of the City of Ladies* (1405), trans. Jeffrey Richards (Persea Books, New York, 1982), pp. 70-98. The phrase is Natalie Davis'.

4. See Londa Schiebinger, 'The history and philosophy of women in science: a review essay', *Signs*, vol. 12, no. 2 (1987), pp. 305-32. See also Joan Scott, 'Gender: a useful category of historical analysis', *American Historical Review*, vol. 91, no. 5 (1986), pp. 1053-75.

5. When writing the history of women, we immediately encounter problems, even in small matters such as what name to use for our main character. To employ the married name unconsciously reveals a nine-

teenth- and twentieth-century bias. I have elected to use Maria Winkelmann's maiden name throughout, since this is the name she used for her publications. The use of the maiden name is also consistent with the practice of the day. The astronomer Maria Cunitz, for example, published under her maiden name; midwives listed in eighteenth-century Prussian address lexicons also used their maiden names (their married names were given in parentheses). It should be pointed out, however, that Winkelmann also referred to herself as 'Kirchin' (the feminine form of Kirch, her husband's name) in her correspondence with Leibniz and Academy officials, trading (I assume) on her husband's name in her quest for employment. Academy officials referred to her as 'Kirchin' or 'widow Kirch'.

6. The Berlin Academy first bore a Latin name: the Societas regia scientiarum. It was also commonly known as the Brandenburgische or Berlin Societät der Wissenschaften. In the 1740s, it took a French name: Académie Royale des Sciences et Belles-Lettres. In the 1780s, it became the Königlich Preussische Akademie der Wissenschaften, which it remained until its reorganisation after the Second World War, when it took its present name, the Akademie der Wissenschaften der Deutschen Demokratischen Republik. For simplicity I have referred to the Societät der Wissenschaften as the Berlin Academy or the Academy of Sciences.

7. Between 1650 and 1710, a surprisingly large number of women (Maria Cunitz (1610-64), Elisabetha Hevelius (1647-93), Maria Clara Eimmart (1676-1707), Maria Winkelmann (1670-1720) and her daughters Christina (1696-1782) and Margaretha (active in the 1740s)) participated in German astronomy.

8. Alphonse des Vignoles, 'Eloge de Madame Kirch à l'occasion de laquelle on parle de quelques autres femmes & d'un paison astronomes', *Bibliothèque germanique*, vol. 3 (1721), pp. 115-83, esp. 181.

9. See Edgar Zilsel, 'The sociological roots of modern science', *American Journal of Sociology*, 47 (1942), pp. 544-62, esp. 545-6; Arthur Clegg, 'Craftsmen and the origin of science', *Science and Society*, 43 (1979), pp. 186-201; Paolo Rossi, *Philosophy, technology, and the arts of the Early Modern Era*, trans. Salvator Attansasio (Harper & Row, New York, 1970); Rupert Hall, 'The scholar and the craftsman in the scientific revolution' in Marshall Clagett (ed.), *Critical problems in the history of science* (University of Wisconsin Press, Madison, 1959), pp. 3-23.

10. Zilsel, 'The sociological roots of modern science', pp. 544-62, esp. 545-6.

11. De Pisan, *The book of the City of Ladies*, pp. 70-80.

12. Margret Wensky, *Die Stellung der Frau in der stadtkölnischen Wirtschaft im Spätmittelalter* (Böhlau, Cologne, 1981), pp. 318-19.

13. Jean Quataert has warned against conflating important distinctions between guilds and households. Jean H. Quataert, 'The shaping of

women's work in manufacturing: guilds, households, and the state in Central Europe, 1648-1870', *The American Historical Review*, vol. 90, no. 5 (1985), pp. 1122-48. In the case of astronomy or entomology, however, the greater danger has been to ignore almost entirely both of these forms of production. Here I use the term craft to refer to household production, and guild to refer to regulated crafts.

14. Although many scientific papers of the Kirch family survived, few of their personal papers did. On the whereabouts of the Kirch papers, see D. Wattenberg, 'Zur Geschichte der Astronomie in Berlin im 16. bis 18. Jahrhundert II', *Die Sterne*, vol. 49, no. 2 (1972), pp. 104-16. Most of what we know of Winkelmann's life comes from an eulogy written upon her death by family friend and Academy Vice-President Alphonse des Vignoles, 'Eloge de Madame Kirch', pp. 115-83. See also G. Hellmann (ed.), *Das älteste Berliner Wetter-Buch 1700-1701* (Berlin, 1893) and P. Aufgebauer, 'Die Astronomenfamilie Kirch', *Die Sterne*, vol. 47, no. 6 (1971), pp. 241-7.

15. See Johann Westphal, *Leben, Studien und Schriften des Astronomen Johann Hevelius* (Universitäts-Buchhandlung, Königsberg, 1820).

16. Copernicus, for example, studied law and medicine. Robert Westman, 'The astronomer's role in the sixteenth century', *History of Science*, 18 (1980), pp. 105-47, esp. 117.

17. A university education was not absolutely essential for the practice of astronomy; see E. Zinner, *Die Geschichte der Sternkunde von den ersten Anfängen bis zu Gegenwart* (Springer, Berlin, 1931), p. 590.

18. See Londa Schiebinger, *The mind has no sex: women in the origins of modern science*, forthcoming.

19. Des Vignoles, 'Eloge de Madame Kirch', p. 173.

20. 'Lebens Umstände und Schicksale des ehemahles berühmten Gottfried Kirchs', *Dresdenische Gelehrte Anzeigen*, 49 (1761), pp. 769-77, esp. 775.

21. See Erik Amburger, *Die Mitglieder der deutschen Akademie der Wissenschaft zu Berlin 1700-1950* (Akademie Verlag, Berlin, 1950), p. 173.

22. The Silesian astronomer Maria Cunitz (1610-64) was known for her astronomical tables, used for calculating the position of the planets. Maria Cunitz, *Urania Propitia* (Oels, 1650).

23. Margaret Rossiter, 'Women's work in science, 1880-1910', *Isis*, vol. 71, no. 258 (1980), pp. 381-98. See also her *Women scientists in America: struggles and strategies to 1940* (Johns Hopkins University Press, Baltimore, 1982), pp. 51-72.

24. Winkelmann was at least mentioned in early histories of astronomy. These sources include biographical information, but no analysis of women's position in early modern science. During her lifetime, she was cited in the German editions of Christian Wolff's 'Mathematisches Lexicon' (1716) in J.E. Hofmann (ed.), *Gesammelte Werke* (Georg Olms, Hildesheim, 1965), part I, vol. 11, p. 972. Wolff reported that 'of special

glory to the German nation is Kirch's widow, who is well studied in astronomical observation and calculation'. (This tribute was dropped, however, in the 1741 Latin edition of Wolff's work.) In his *Historia astronomiae*, Friedrich Weidler picked up the review of her publications from the *Acta Eruditorum* (Wittenberg, 1741, p. 556), as did Joseph Jérôme Le Français de Lalande (*Bibliographie astronomique: avec l'histoire de l'astronomie* (Paris, 1803), p. 359). Jérôme de Lalande included Winkelmann in the short history of women astronomers that introduced his popular astronomy textbook for women, *Astronomie des dames* (Paris, 1786, 'Préface Historique'). J.E. Bode, astronomer of the Berlin Academy and Winkelmann's great-nephew, referred to Winkelmann in his 'Chronologisches Verzeichniss der berühmtesten Astronomen, seit dem dreizehnten Jahrhundert, ihrer Verdienste, Schriften und Entdeckungen', *Astronomisches Jahrbuch für das Jahr 1816* (Berlin, 1813), p. 113. In the nineteenth and twentieth centuries, Winkelmann appeared most often in popular histories of astronomy or in articles about women astronomers. In his semi-popular *Geschichte der Astronomie*, Rudolf Wolf gave much attention to women's achievements, beginning with those of Hypatia (R. Oldenbourg, Munich, 1877, p. 458). See also E. Lagrange, 'Les femmes-astronomes', *Ciel et Terre*, 5 (1885), pp. 513-27, esp. 515-16; Alphonse Rebière reprinted Lagrange's account in his *Les femmes dans la science*, 2nd edn (Paris, 1897), pp. 153-4; H.J. Mozans also repeated this account in his *Woman in science* (1913; repr. MIT Press, Cambridge, Mass., 1974), pp. 173-4. For more recent accounts see R.V. Rizzo, 'Early daughters of Urania', *Sky and Telescope*, vol. 14, no. 1 (1954), pp. 7-9; Diedrich Wattenberg, 'Frauen in der Astronomie', *Vorträge und Schriften*, 4 (1963), pp. 1-8. Lettie Multhauf included highlights from Winkelmann's life in Charles Gillispie (ed.), *Dictionary of scientific biography* (16 vols., Scribners, New York, 1973), vol. 7, pp. 373-4.

25. Letter from Winkelmann to Leibniz, Leibniz Archive, Niedersächsische Landesbibliothek, Hannover, Kirch, no. 472, page 11.

26. F.H. Weiss, 'Quellenbeiträge zur Geschichte der Preussischen Akademie der Wissenschaften', pp. 223-4. A copy of Winkelmann's report is to be found in the Paris Observatory, Kirch papers, MS A.B. 3.7, nr. 83, 41, B.

27. Kirch papers, Paris Observatory, MS A.B. 3.5, nr. 81 B, p. 33.

28. Adolf Harnack, 'Berichte des Secretars der brandenburgischen Societät der Wissenschaften J.Th. Jablonski an der Präsidenten G.W. Leibniz (1700-1715) nebst einigen Antworten von Leibniz', *Philos.-histor. Abhandlungen der königlichen Akademie der Wissenschaften zu Berlin*, vol. 3 (1897), nr. 22.

29. See Wattenberg, 'Zur Geschichte der Astronomie in Berlin', p. 107.

30. See Maria Winkelmann, 'Vorstellung des Himmels bey der Zusammenkunfft dreyer Grossmächtigsten Könige' (Potsdam, 1709); and Maria

Winkelmann, *Vorbereitung, zur grossen Opposition, oder merckwürdige Himmels-Gestalt im 1712* (Cölln an der Spree, 1711).

31. 'Letter from Leibniz to Sophie, Januar 1709' in Onno Klopp (ed.), *Die Werke von Leibniz* (11 vols., Klindworth, Hannover, 1864-88), vol. 9, pp. 295-6.

32. Leibniz refers here to the attempt to obtain an exact measurement of the lunar parallax. The attempt failed because Von Krosigk's apprentice astronomer was irresponsible and only occasionally made observations. Hans Ludendorff, 'Zur Frühgeschichte der Astronomie in Berlin', *Vorträge und Schriften der Preussischen Akademie der Wissenschaften*, vol. 9 (1942), pp. 3-23, esp. 15.

33. Aufgebauer, 'Die Astronomenfamilie Kirch', p. 244.

34. Ibid., p. 246.

35. Adolf von Harnack, *Geschichte der Königlich Preussischen Akademie der Wissenschaften zu Berlin*, 2nd edn (3 vols., Georg Olms, Hildesheim, 1970), vol. 1, p. 124; Wolf, *Geschichte der Astronomie*, pp. 94-105.

36. Harnack, 'Berichte des Secretars', nr. 112.

37. Ludendorff judged Winkelmann to be among the leading astronomers of her day; see Ludendorff, 'Zur Frühgeschichte der Astronomie in Berlin', p. 12.

38. Letter from Maria Margaretha Kirchin to the Societät der Wissenschaften zu Berlin, 2 August 1710. Original in Kirch papers, Archives of the Akademie der Wissenschaften der DDR, I-III, 1, pp. 46-8. A copy also exists at the Leibniz Archiv, Niedersächsische Landesbibliothek, Hannover; Jablonski 440, Blatt 154-65.

39. Harnack, 'Berichte des Secretars', nr. 115. Unfortunately, Leibniz's response to Jablonski has not been preserved.

40. Harnack, 'Berichte des Secretars', nr. 116.

41. 'Protokollum Concilii, Societatis Scientiarium', 15 December 1710, Archives of the Akademie der Wissenschaften der DDR, I, IV, 6, 1. Teil, p. 54; 18 March 1711, pp. 65-6; and 9 September 1711, p. 93. Unfortunately, we do not know why Winkelmann received a medal.

42. Letter from Winkelmann to the Council of the Berlin Academy, 3 March 1711. Archives of the Akademie der Wissenschaften der DDR, Kirch papers, I, III, 1, p. 50.

43. Harnack, 'Berichte des Secretars', nrs. 143, 144.

44. Winkelmann did not explicitly invoke guild principles; her requests, however, followed well-established patterns in the organised crafts and free arts. See Merry Wiesner, 'Women's defence of their public role' in Mary Beth Rose (ed.), *Women in the Middle Ages and the Renaissance: literary and historical perspectives* (Syracuse University Press, Syracuse, 1986), pp. 1-28.

45. See Wensky, *Die Stellung der Frau*, pp. 58-9; Ketsch, *Frauen im Mittelalter*, vol. 1, pp. 29, 204 and 210.

46. 'Protokollum Concilii, Societatis Scientiarum', 23 September 1716, Archives of the Akademie der Wissenschaften der DDR, I, IV, 6, 2. Teil, pp. 230-2.

47. Christfried Kirch, *Teutsche Ephemeris* (Nürnberg, 1715), p. 82.

48. Des Vignoles, 'Eloge de Madame Kirch', p. 180.

49. 'Protokollum Concilii, Societatis Scientiarum', 8 October 1716 and 6 April 1718, Archives of the Akademie der Wissenschaften der DDR, I, IV, 6, 2. Teil, p. 236.

50. Des Vignoles, 'Eloge de Madame Kirch', p. 181.

51. 'Protokollum Concilii, Societatis Scientiarum', 18 August 1717, Archives of the Akademie der Wissenschaften der DDR, I, IV, 6, 2. Teil, pp. 269, 272-3.

52. Des Vignoles, 'Eloge de Madame Kirch', p. 181.

53. Ibid., pp. 181-2.

54. Quoted in Zinner, *Die Geschichte der Sternkunde*, p. 583, and Wattenberg, 'Zur Geschichte der Astronomie in Berlin', p. 166.

55. Women were not formally admitted to German universities until the early twentieth century. Laetitia Böhm, 'Von dem Anfängen des akademischen Frauenstudiums in Deutschland', *Historisches Jahrbuch*, 77 (1958), pp. 2298-327.

Lucia Bergamasco

Female education and spiritual life: the case of ministers' daughters

At the time that I considered writing a paper for the International Conference on Women's History, I was deeply immersed in my research on the friendship between Sarah Prince and Esther Burr, two New England young ladies from prominent clerical families who lived around the middle of the eighteenth century. In fact, I had just finished a chapter on Sarah Prince's spiritual journal and her tormented dealings with a marriage proposal. Some basic questions were still puzzling me, namely: why did she tenaciously refuse to marry, and why did she yield only after her father's death?[1]

I then decided to set aside Sarah Prince's relationship with her beloved friend Esther Burr, and instead compare Sarah's experience to those of Jane Colman, another young lady from a distinguished Bostonian clerical family, who lived a generation earlier and who appeared to be similar in many ways to Sarah Prince, both in upbringing and character. The paper for the Conference was originally intended to be a basic presentation of some points for discussion, such as the accomplished education which these two women received from their fathers, their intense relationship with them, and their preferred commitment to a life of piety and intellectual pursuits.[2] Writing an article from that brief paper is more problematic, since my research on women's cultural environment in early eighteenth-century New England is still continuing. Also, given the different nature of the sources, my questions can only be tentative, posed as a sort of preliminary hypothesis.

With regard to Jane Colman (1708-35), we have the *Memoirs of the life and death of the pious and ingenious Mrs. Jane Turell* written by her husband, the Reverend Ebenezer Turell, after her death in childbed at the age of 26, which include some extracts of Jane's writings (mainly but not only pious), and letters to her father and to other members of her family. She was the daughter of Benjamin Colman (1673-1747), a prominent Bostonian pastor, learned and genteel, who had spent some years in England, taking part in literary circles himself, having an inclination for poetry and for elegant and gently sentimental religious expressions.[3] Benjamin Colman, a moderate and mildly Pietistic cleric who officiated from 1699 up till his death, was pastor of the Brattle Street Church, the first church in Boston to adopt a liberal policy towards admission to the Sacraments as well as women's participation in church affairs.

From Sarah Prince (1728-71), we have the manuscript of part of her spiritual journal, as well as references to her in Esther Burr's letter-journal (addressed to Sarah Prince and written between 1754 and 1757) and some *Devout Meditations*, published after her death along with her funeral eulogy in the *Boston Evening Post.* Her father, Thomas Prince (1687-1758), pastor of the prestigious Old South Church in Boston, was an affable and genteel erudite, who had also lived in England and travelled extensively in Europe. He was devoted to serious historical research - in 1736 he published the first volume of a *Chronological History of New England* - and was the possessor of a very extensive library. An advocate of Evangelical Pietism, although not a vehement character, Thomas Prince became a passionate protagonist of the great religious revival between 1740 and 1742, known as the Great Awakening.[4]

Jane Colman and Sarah Prince grew up in a religious and cultural elite where Evangelical Pietism played a crucial role. Pietism had indeed been gaining popularity in New England churches from the end of the seventeenth century up to the middle of the eighteenth. Along with its sentimental religiosity, Pietism seems to have produced a concomitant special consideration for women. The number of printed sermons, funeral eulogies and elegies dedicated to women increased consistently during this period. Certainly while New England society was becoming increasingly secular women were filling up the congregations, leaving men behind in their religious zeal. However, the sentimentalisation of religion was also a characteristic of the period, and seems to have gone hand in hand with a general extolling of feminine virtues.[5] Eminent ministers of the time (including of course Benjamin Colman and Thomas Prince) paid tributes to women's Christian excellence as well as to their talents, not only in managing household affairs (woman's earthly territory), but also in their handling of human relationships. In a way, women's intellectual activities could be grouped under a spiritual heading. Indeed women were urged from the pulpit to read the Scriptures and devotional books extensively and furthermore were encouraged to write spiritual journals, reflections and commentaries on the Scriptures, letters of counsel and of consolation, and so on. These activities were to be carried out at home and the resulting literature could circulate among the parishioners under close pastoral supervision. This occurred in spite of the fact that in orthodox churches women were excluded from verbal expression in public worship - although they could fully express themselves in their own prayer groups - and from theological elaboration, the latter being reserved for pastors only.[6]

It was in this atmosphere of pastoral attention to feminine virtue that Jane Colman, and later Sarah Prince, were given an extensive education by their fathers. What is surprising is the degree of serious scholarship, even erudition, which was attained, for we have good reason to believe that ministers' daughters enjoyed a better education than most of their contemporaries.[7] In a way, ministers' daughters formed an intellectual elite among pious women of their time. Jane Colman and Sarah Prince were the elite's elite, championing female intellectual achievement as well as religious devotion.

The question of why Benjamin Colman and Thomas Prince took such care to ensure that their daughters were learned remains unanswered and deserves further study. I can only suggest the following hypothesis. Perhaps the two pastors, themselves well-read in the Classics, were pursuing the Renaissance ideal of the learned gentlewoman. If so, they were responding to the literature which championed the cause of female intellect and learning. After all, Cotton Mather, the leading Pietist and erudite of Boston, revered and befriended by Thomas Prince and certainly much respected (if not loved) by Benjamin Colman, was a staunch admirer of the 'learned maid' Anna Maria van Schuurman. These pastors believed in spiritual equality between men and women, which afforded them sufficient grounds for believing in their intellectual equality and therefore in the possibility of their pursuing intellectual goals. However, we should not forget that ministers' daughters formed an exceptional group. Only a few like our heroines were actually learned, in a way the exception that proves the rule which was justified by its exemplarity; a prototype, as it were, to be presented to the public for emulation if not for imitation.[8] Be that as it may, both Benjamin Colman and Thomas Prince invested a great deal of energy and received a great deal of satisfaction in educating their respective daughters both intellectually and spiritually.

Jane Colman

Jane Colman was born in Boston in 1708, the first surviving child of Benjamin Colman; one had died in early infancy. Since her birth she had been of a sickly constitution. In a way Jane Colman had been a miraculous child, for as her father relates in her funeral sermon, she had been near to death three times before she had attained the age of 18 months. Her recovery from the third illness was an inexplicable fact which caused the pastor who was praying with the dying child to foresee an unusual future for her.[9] As is often the case with sickly children, Jane was extremely sensitive and responsive to parental attention. Her lack of physical strength was compensated by an exceptional liveliness of mind. Benjamin Colman's detailed description of Jane's character and upbringing is worth quoting:

> 'In the midst of this bodily weakness her soul made uncommon Improvements for an Infant State; and it may be much the more for the weak State of the Body; for she had no Strength to run about and play like other Children, which was then our Grief. We made it therefore our daily Pleasure, and our Diversion, to learn her Letters, and Prayers to God her Maker, Redeemer and Sanctifier, and to fill her little Mind with Stories of all the Holy Men on Sacred Record.'[10]

At this early age, Benjamin Colman was careful to show his daughter where true excellence lay, and to encourage her mind in religious thought:

> 'to strike her Admiration and Affection with true Excellency and Perfection; for which End I took care to speak to her of every thing in a just and proper Manner, if possible to convey regular ideas into her, as of the Greatness and Goodness of God, so of all that relates to his worship and Service'.[11]

By the time Jane was able to walk she had absorbed 'a little treasure of sacred knowledge'. In this remarkable description of pedagogical success, it is noteworthy that the Holy Scriptures were administered with such skill to an infant, and that this religious instruction paved the way for a broader humanistic education. Jane's husband, the Reverend Ebenezer Turell, who greatly admired her, stresses in his *Memoirs* of Jane the importance of Benjamin Colman's gentleness and affection in educating his daughter. As he says, Jane's knowledge was instilled in her by her father in the 'easiest and kindest Manner', for he loved to infuse knowledge

> 'in her little Mind as fast as it grew capable of receiving it. He first talk'd into her all he cou'd in the most free and endearing Manner, and then supply'd her with the best Books of every kind, suited to her years and Inclinations, without making them a Task or a Burthen.'[12]

Since she was very intelligent and inclined to study, Jane Colman provided a fertile ground for her father's pedagogical skills. The modern reader may, however, find his methods strikingly seductive. As the *Memoirs* continue, it becomes evident that Benjamin Colman expressly sought to bind his daughter's mind and heart to him:

> 'His next care was to teach her to read his Hand, and then by writing to her, in a Manner becoming him and proper for her, he insinuated himself more and more into her Affections, and increas'd the Reverence of Him, and the Desire of his Esteem. The way to merit and obtain that, he let see was by a prudent,

> humble, virtuous and religious conduct, upon the principles and Motions of Christianity, the Fear of God, and the desire to please her Heavenly Father.'[13]

As the quotation points out, Jane Colman was burdened with the remarkable task of 'pleasing' two fathers from the very start, the mundane and the celestial. As regards her earthly father, Jane pleased him exceedingly, for we learn that 'before her second Year was completed [she] could speak distinctly, knew her Letters, and could relate many Stories out of the Scriptures to the satisfaction and pleasure of the most judicious'. On one occasion the Governor of New England and some other gentlemen placed her on a table and grouped around her, entertaining themselves with her stories.[14] She was, in fact, an infant prodigy. The story of Jane Colman's education continues in this exceptional and prodigious vein:

> 'Before she was four years old so strong and tenacious was her Memory, she could say the greater Part of the Assembly Cathechism, many of the Psalms, some hundred lines of the best Poetry, read distinctly, and make pertinent Remarks on many things she read.'[15]

Jane's 'tender and gracious' mother's interventions are barely mentioned; we are told only that she prayed for her daughter and gave her 'wisest counsels'. At this early age Jane was already able to pray both by set forms and, more importantly, *ex corde*, which means under direct inspiration of the Spirit. It is also significant that although she could read at age four, and learn stories, psalms and poetry by heart, Jane only learnt to write at a later age. Her biographer relates: 'at nine or ten (if not before) she was able to write', for he finds a letter dated 1718 of 'her honored father to her' in response to a letter from Jane. In 1721, the year of the great smallpox epidemic in Boston, Jane began to keep a diary, at the early age of 14. She wrote many pieces of prose as well as an essay describing her own life. The biographer does not mention whether it was a spiritual or a mundane autobiography. She wrote poetry extensively between her fourteenth and eighteenth year, her father helping her with constructive criticism and corrections as well as praise.[16] It is of interest to know that Jane was well acquainted with what her husband calls 'Divinity, History, Physick, Controversy, as well as Poetry', and that she absorbed all these intellectual riches from the lips of her father when he read aloud to her during the long winter evenings.[17] It is not unlikely that she pursued the study of these subjects independently when alone, since she enjoyed free access to her father's extensive library. In any case Ebenezer Turell is positive in affirming that 'before she was 18 she had read and digested all the English Poetry and Polite pieces in prose, printed and Manuscript in her Fathers well furnished library'.

Jane Colman's thirst for knowledge was so great, that she would borrow books from friends and spend whole nights reading. She seems to have been sympathetic to the idea of elevating the honour of her sex, as her husband affirms, by her intellectual accomplishments and her devout and pious life.[18] In this Jane seems indeed to have been responsive to literature which vindicated female intellect, and to clerical praise and encouragement of feminine spiritual accomplishments. Her social station no doubt helped her to cherish so 'laudable' an 'ambition', as her husband calls it.

She married in August 1726. In her new life she decided to diminish her intellectual activities somewhat, which suggests that Jane had maintained a steady flow of poetry or essays in prose before her marriage. Her husband, indeed, relates:

> 'Then she made her custom to make some essay in Prose or Verse, once in a month or two; but to read from Day to Day as much as her duties of Mistress of a household would allow her. But she made the writing of Poetry a Recreation and not a Business.'[19]

Despite his admiration for Jane's gifts, Ebenezer Turell thus intended to make very clear that a married woman had only two serious activities in life: the care of her family and the care of her soul. Indeed, after her marriage Jane grew more and more preoccupied with her spiritual state, as if responding to a vocation of this type while still clinging to her literary habits. Now her piety, which had always been strong, became burdened with guilt and with regret for having wasted so much precious time on 'useless books' instead of working seriously at her salvation.[20]

Jane Colman continued to apply to her father for religious advice and consolation, as if her husband, who was also a pastor, could not help her. Once Benjamin Colman gently redirected her to her husband's counsel and library:

> 'You mourn the time spent in reading useless Books, you do well, I am glad you see the Emptiness and Folly of them. Mr Turell has a Library for you to be repairing to, let him put proper and profitable Books into your Hands.'[21]

Benjamin Colman was reminding her that now that she was married she would do better to rely on her husband rather than on her father. As for the 'useless books', I wonder whether both Jane Colman and her father meant the novels or 'romantic' adventures and narratives which were circulating in Great Britain and the Colonies of that time. It is hard to believe that Benjamin Colman would have used the words 'emptiness and folly' to describe philosophical or scientific works, or works of poetry and literature. In fact, apart from novels and adventurous narratives, those 'useless books' may include the 'polite pieces' mentioned above by Ebenezer Turell, as well as all the 'mundane' (not classic) works of literature that passed through the hands of 'polite' ladies of the time, whether they were truly cultured or not. The Reverend Turell certainly possessed the Classics in his library, as well as philosophical works, since they were the routine background of all college graduates. Perhaps, however, Benjamin Colman meant works of religious consolation for Jane to 'repair to', and the role of her husband was to be that of spiritual counsellor and comforter now, since her intellectual formation had already been her father's responsibility.

Jane depended on her father to an extraordinary extent. Allowances may be made for the celebrative bias of the *Memoirs* (which fall into the category of hagiography), a bias that in itself is worth taking into account, since it forcefully emphasises the relationship between Benjamin Colman and his daughter. Yet, even allowing for the implicit exaggerations of hagiography, we cannot help wondering whether Jane's dependence was not a result of the 'tender' and 'insinuating' ways, to use the biographer's expression, which Benjamin Colman had used in her upbringing. It may be worth noting that on one occasion Jane Colman wrote a letter of apology to her father, for having been too forward in her expression of love and admiration of him. Benjamin Colman answered with paternal tenderness, gently rebuking her for her 'error' and significantly associating the role of a father with that of a spouse:

> 'You ask me to forgive the Flow of your Affections, which run with so swift a Current of filial Duty as may carry You beyond yourself sometimes, and make you wanting in that Respect which you aim at expressing. It is true, my Dear, that a young fond and musical genius is easily carry'd away thus; and never more than when it runs into the Praises of what it loves; and I would have you therefore careful against this Error, even when you say your thoughts of Reverence and Esteem to your Father, or to a Spouse, if ever you should live to have one. It is easy to be lavish and run into foolish Flatteries. I think you have done well to correct yourself for some of your Excursions of this kind toward me.'[22]

This quotation, which takes place with other pedagogical interventions of Benjamin Colman, is to my mind rather revealing with regard to Jane Colman's affective demands and to her father gently keeping her in her place.

Be that as it may, Jane Colman developed what her father called a 'Hysteric Distemper' which caused her considerable trouble, namely 'Swiming of Head and Inquietude of Mind', and 'A Timorous Temper'.[23] It is not unlikely that while in her teens, Jane's father made her understand that she could not cling to him all her life, and that marriage was her destiny. The above quotation seems to corroborate this hypothesis. She did indeed marry, but her dependence on her father remained, and was apparently gladly accepted by her husband either out of respect for the eminence of Benjamin Colman's culture and his social position, or perhaps simply because he himself may have felt comfortable as a son. It may be noted that sons-in-law and daughters-in-law were generally referred to as son and daughter.

Jane Colman's scrupulous adherence to her spiritual duties was praised by her father, but he criticised her spiritual distress and her doubts in preparing for communion. Indeed she would spend whole nights in prayer and great self-abasement, deeming herself unworthy and sinful. Benjamin Colman opined that a good Christian ought to rely more on the mercy and grace of Christ than continually to repine at his own sinful nature:

> 'She early gave herself to God, but her timorous Disposition restrained her from proceeding early to the Lord's Table; nor was it without much Conflict of Soul and great Distress through Fear of coming unworthily, that she at last came into full Communion. She afterwards exceeded, to her and her Consort's great Discomfort in her Preparation for Communion Days; which was her infirmity, and I do not praise her for it. Good Christians should take more the Comforts of Religion in their way to Heaven.'[24]

Although one should not apply this to all such cases as a general rule, one cannot help considering a psychological explanation for Jane Colman's tormented spirituality. This explanation is merely an hypothesis: did she aspire to an unattainable union with God because of the impossibility of 'uniting' spiritually, intellectually or emotionally with her beloved father for the rest of her life? In order to corroborate this interpretation of the *Memoirs* of Jane Colman, we should analyse her own writings, both spiritual and mundane, but as the search for them - if they still exist - has not yet begun, we can only make our hypothetical deductions.

Sarah Prince

The life of Sarah Prince (1728-71) follows a pattern similar in some respects to that of Jane Colman. Unfortunately we do not possess her biography, nor did she write an autobiography as far as we know. As I mentioned at the beginning of this paper, we only have access to part of a spiritual journal, many references to Sarah Prince in her friend Esther Burr's letter-journal, some printed spiritual meditations and a funeral eulogy. On the whole, the character of Sarah Prince still remains rather mysterious. She was born in Boston in 1728, the fourth child of Thomas Prince and Deborah Denny. Of her upbringing we have no detailed description; we only know that she was carefully and lovingly educated by her father, who apparently delighted in it, for 'he made a pleasing employment...to cultivate her infant mind, and guide her in the exercise and improvement of those talents with which she was so liberally endowed'. This quotation, from the *Boston Evening Post* soon after her death in 1771, goes on to describe the results of such an education: 'And the early advances she made in useful knowledge, together with the benevolent disposition which graced her whole deportment, more than answered the fondest expectations of her kind parent.'[25]

This eulogy seems to emphasise the special care taken by Thomas Prince to educate Sarah. He greatly enjoyed educating all his children, however (his only son Thomas attended Harvard with brilliancy); 'it was no small part of his labour and happiness, to impress on his children a suitable sense of religion; and properly to form their sentiments, manners and taste'.[26] If on the one hand the quotation seems to allude to a religious and moral education, it also shows how religion and morality went hand in hand with manners and taste, which was a typical combination of the time.

Surprisingly enough, no mention whatsoever is made of Sarah Prince's mother in the sources. Neither Thomas Prince, Sarah nor her admirers ever refer to her. On the other hand in Sarah's spiritual journal we find an expression of gratitude for her unusual upbringing which specifies her father's role as well as that of a sister:

> 'I praise the bountyfull Lord for the Distinguishing helps he affords me (beyond almost any of my age and sex) of Divine Knowledge and Christian Piety. For to have such a Father such Ministers such a Sister such Books as he favoured me with how can I be Eno' thankful.'[27]

We should not be misled by this quotation, for being learned in Divinity, if not in Christian Piety, required a complete humanistic education. As for the sister, this was the pious Mercy Prince, who had been dead for some years at the time of the entry in Sarah Prince's journal. Indeed, at this date all Sarah Prince's siblings were deceased: her sister Deborah in 1744, her brother Thomas in 1748 and her sister Mercy in 1752, aged 21, 26 and 27 years respectively. They had all died of consumption, all had been celibate, all had been exemplary as Christians and dedicated Evangelicals. Sarah was the youngest and the only survivor in her family, believing herself to be as close to death as her brother and sisters had been, since her own constitution was not strong. Her special relationship with her father may have commenced or intensified after the deaths of her siblings.

From Esther Burr's letter-journal we know that Sarah led an exceptionally pious life and that she was very active intellectually. With regard to her spiritual life, an examination of Sarah's spiritual journal and meditations confirms her friend's opinion as well as that of any hagiographer; her daily routine consisted of prayer and meditation, setting apart certain days for special self-abasement, prayer and fasting, preparing herself carefully for Communion, reading the Scriptures and devotional books and regularly attending at a female prayer group. A more interesting aspect of Esther Burr's journal is the glimpse we get of Sarah Prince's intellectual activity and tastes. Having been thoroughly educated, Sarah probably had a knowledge of Latin, which may have enabled her to read the Classics in her father's library. Presumably she was also well read in the works of moral philosophy which were taught at Harvard and had circulated widely in the colonies since the beginning of the eighteenth century.

Esther Burr also informs us that Sarah 'produced' some prose pieces, whose nature is unknown but likely to be religious or moral, and that, of course, she wrote poetry. Of the English poets, Sarah appears to have shown a preference for Edward Young, whose melancholy poems she sometimes paraphrased or quoted. As for her opinion of Isaac Watts' religious works, they formed the everyday literary diet of devout people and of Pietists in particular. Sarah Prince's cultural appreciation was wide and pluralistic, as had been the case with Jane Colman; indeed, both women had acquired this appreciation through the educational pattern of male intellectuals. Thus Esther Burr's letters provide information about Sarah Prince's critical reading of Samuel Richardson's novels *Clarissa* and *Pamela*, as well as of other contemporary English authors.[28] Besides her devotional activities, Sarah probably occupied her time with the reading of and writing about mundane subjects, subjects as were not directly of a religious nature, for it seems that the sharp distinction between the religious and the mundane was not perceived by devout intellectuals of the time, especially with regard to works of philosophy, morality and poetry.

Sarah Prince, like her sisters before her, attended the meetings of a women's prayer group throughout her life. However from

Esther Burr's journal it appears that Sarah was surrounded by a circle of women friends who had all adopted classical pen-names.[29] This fact indicates the existence of some sort of regular female get-togethers other than the prayer group, or possibly a kind of feminine 'circle' or 'society' meeting for cultural purposes. Since the Colman and Prince families were well acquainted, as were all the leading clerical families of Boston, we have good reason to suppose that Jane Colman's brilliant intellectual attainments did in fact set a precedent for feminine learning and piety to which Sarah Prince and other gentlewomen could aspire.

In addition, it is quite a significant aspect of the changes taking place in colonial society that Sarah Prince added love for humankind and patriotism to her life of religious devotion and learning. This was a legacy from her brother and father, who had both been praised for their patriotic feelings. Indeed, we have information from two sources that Sarah was active in the patriotic cause and was in contact with the British radical historian Catharine Macaulay during the 1760s. In 1759 Sarah married the merchant Moses Gill, future Lieutenant-Governor of Massachusetts, who with his brother John belonged to a patriotic circle. Furthermore, John Gill and Benjamin Edes were the owners of the *Boston Gazette*, the radical paper of Boston.[30] This information about Sarah Prince's intellectual and patriotic activities forms an illuminating background against which we can read her otherwise exclusively religious writings.

In some ways Sarah Prince's spirituality appears similar to that of Jane Colman. Throughout her spiritual journal she expresses a sense of guilt and desperately struggles to attain total submission to God's will. She also displays unremitting efforts to achieve a mystical union with Him. Yet this attitude, not uncommonly found in Puritan spiritual journals of the time, takes on a different meaning when one considers that during the very period that Sarah's spiritual struggle was at its peak, she was also considering an offer of marriage which she found herself unable to accept. From Esther Burr's journal we learn that Sarah had three suitors during the years 1754-7, and had also had a brief relationship with a young pastor, a short-lived affair about which we have no details.

As for the marriage offer, it is again from Esther Burr's journal that we know of its existence, for in her spiritual journal Sarah is very careful to avoid any direct mention of it. Sarah Prince limits herself solely to cryptic allusions, which, together with the information given in Esther Burr's journal, reveal that the man was a rich widower with two children, and of good character and sober tastes, since he showed his willingness to marry so pious and learned a lady as Sarah Prince. However, in one of her letters to Esther Burr (as the latter reports), Sarah alluded to the fact that she found it impossible to hold her suitor in high enough esteem, although by other accounts he seems to be well-endowed with good qualities.[31]

For about three years, Sarah made agonised entries in her spiritual journal without actually being able to come to a decision. All through this long period she stubbornly waited for 'divine direction' in this affair. A most mysterious expectation, indeed, for it is hard to understand from Sarah's spiritual language what her wishes were; also she hardly appears to have been urged to accept by her friends and acquaintances. She seems to have taken the good social position of her suitor into consideration, once referred to by her as 'a golden bait',[32] but apparently she did not find him very attractive, which made her feel guilty of 'carnal' (in this sense materialistic) temptation. She desperately tried to cling to God, declaring Him to be her supreme and only love, and to wait for His will to be manifest, since she repeatedly claimed not to know her own heart,

> 'Lord Pity and help for thou art my chosen Portion - I renew my choice and beg that I never may retract it but let me be tyed to thee by a thousand-fold stronger Obligation - What is ther here in this barren land to solace me? I cant take pleasure in Creatures - I cant take pleasure in myself; tis thee abstractly thee, O thou Alltogether Lovely One, that is worthy my Homage, Love, Choice, pursuit and Obedience, and Let me have thee and I will gladly forego all for thee! I can't take up with Less!'[33]

At times she felt herself to be a 'weaned child waiting to know the Mind of God'. Whenever Sarah was about to give a definite answer to her suitor, her heart and mind were in a turmoil, fearing to succumb to the pressure of her friends or the temptation of a comfortable life, instead of yielding to God's will. She was in fact riding an exhausting psychological seesaw, for when she herself felt ready to accept, God would inspire her to revoke this decision. Then when God was seemingly making His will manifest that she should accept the offer, it was Sarah who could not help feeling a deep revulsion against it.[34]

The part played by Sarah's love of God in her attitude towards this marriage offer is very complex indeed. She was trying to 'delegate' God to make the choice in her place, just as she was trying to put God in the place of human gratification (a very Evangelical wish), but she was unable to do either. In spite of much prayer and meditation, she could not help feeling depressed and anguished, caught as she was between 'carnal' temptation, the pressure of her environment and the will of God. If her feelings towards the man were so uncertain, then marriage was merely a social duty to be performed without much hope for love in the future. Therefore she apparently preferred to remain single, pious and with her books for company. Paradoxically, in some respects Sarah Prince was adhering to the Puritan tradition regarding marriage, which - along with the duty of marriage - dwelt on the possibility of love coming after marriage; she had unsuccessfully tried for three years to envisage this possibility. On the other hand, Sarah was perhaps responding to the new sentimental climate that increasingly required a couple to be in love before marriage. Evangelicism, the 'religion of the heart' with which Sarah's being was so deeply impregnated, may have increased her sentimental expectations toward marriage as well.

Yet we cannot help thinking that Sarah Prince's relationships with men were at best complex. What can we deduce from the following declaration: 'I never felt that intense desire after creatures which I feel for the blessed God.'[35] Who were these creatures that Sarah was unable to desire? She certainly loved her friend Esther Burr passionately, as well as Esther's husband Aaron Burr (whose death in September 1757 marked the cessation of any allusion to the marriage affair in Sarah's journal), not to mention her sisters and brother. It is not unlikely that she was referring to men, since she wrote this entry at the beginning of January 1757, when she devoted much time to meditation and prayer in order to be inspired by God regarding her matrimonial decision. Eventually Sarah Prince married Moses Gill in March 1759. We do not know whether he was ever one of the suitors mentioned earlier. By that time her friend Esther Burr had been dead for a year, but, more significantly, in October 1758 her beloved father Thomas Prince had died. In the years which followed her marriage, she never wrote in her spiritual journal with the same intensity and anguish that she felt during the time she was uncertain about marrying. It was as if her commitment to devotion, which with her studies had been her most profound satisfaction, had fatally weakened.

This interpretation is credible if we take the daily writing of a spiritual journal to be unquestionable proof of devotion. In fact, I wonder what had happened in Sarah Prince's mind that stopped her from writing regularly in her spiritual journal after her marriage. A lack of time, once she became mistress of a household, does not seem a sufficient explanation. However, the care of her family, and the intense social relations which were typical of that period, may have turned Sarah from her almost obsessive dedication to piety. Indeed, I suspect a change in the structure of her relationship with people in general and with men in particular, since Sarah Prince was now obliged to associate daily with a husband; we do not know whether she loved, esteemed or respected him. If we are to believe her journal, her exclusive relationship with God seems indeed to have weakened after her marriage, and that not without guilt, although the entries in which she laments her coldness of heart do not convey the torment and anguish of the years 1755-8.

However, if we are to take Sarah Prince's *Spiritual Meditations* seriously, her piety did remain with her always. As her editor relates, she selected her writings for publication, which may suggest that she did not wish to publish any other article from her hand, whether literary or patriotic, unless under a pseudonym. Thus the *Meditations* appear as a spiritual legacy that Sarah Prince intended to leave for public reading. Like her spiritual journal, they reveal her mystical inclination, reaffirming in a calm, serene tone the absolute supremacy of the love of God, the contemplation of His perfection, the pleasure of total submission to His will, the sacrifice of all human emotional attachment to His love. If Sarah Prince never actually voiced her regret for the time she had spent with her books, in the *Meditations* she repeatedly emphasised her opinion that a state of true holiness did not need books and study, which after all were nothing in comparison with the contemplation of the Divinity: 'The world affords nothing but toil, vanity and tumult; Friendship is but a partial, and Ease a temporary pleasure; riches give no satisfaction to my mind; books and study, my favourite employments, will not please always'; and again, in a prayer for the time of Communion:

> 'I bid a glad adieu to every thing else as my *good*, and take *my God for my all*, to love him, and to live upon him. I will not love husband, parent, friends, houses, lands, riches, pleasures, nor any thing in compare with *my God, my All*!'[36]

Conclusion

The spiritual struggle of Sarah Prince and her personal life are analysed in my dissertation, which I hope will shortly be published in book form. In this article, I tried to give a précis of the above in order to compare Sarah Prince's experiences with those of Jane Colman. In spite of the different nature of the sources I consulted, it appears that the relationship they enjoyed with their fathers played a central role in the lives of these pious and learned gentlewomen, and that they made a desperate effort to achieve a spiritual and emotional equilibrium. Having been 'launched' or 'seduced' into a life of great intellectual achievement and spiritual excellence, they were obliged in the end to bring themselves down to the restricted territory of domestic obligations. In fact, being pious and learned did not exempt them from the duties of marrying and running their households; duties which were especially extolled by the Puritans. In spite of their outstanding upbringing and intellectual activities, the two women found themselves obliged to comply with the traditional role and function that society, and their fathers, had imposed upon them.

It is small wonder that they resisted: by the way of illness - the hysterical distemper - in the case of Jane Colman, or the endless uncertainty and spiritual passions of Sarah Prince. Jane Colman apparently yielded to social and parental expectations early on by marrying young, although she tried to keep that privileged and exquisite relationship with her father. Her tormented dealings with God may be considered as the negative side or even the failure of her efforts to merge her life of piety and study and her life as a married woman into a harmonious whole. No wonder that her father blamed her for it.

Sarah Prince resisted longer, since she did not marry until she was 31. During the 1755-8 crisis she had to endure the criticism and pressure of her friends and acquaintances concerning her ambivalence and hesitancy towards her suitor. Unfortunately her father's opinion in this matter remains unknown. During this time of confusion and distress, she tried to substitute the Christian duty of loving God for the Puritan duty of marrying. In many instances it appears clearly that Sarah Prince preferred her life as a single woman, completely fulfilled by her devotion and her intellectual activities ('books and study my favourite employment'), to the satisfaction of running an upper-class household. Only when she had lost her father and his love, which she calls 'one of Natures tenderest ties' and her most unique union, did she give up and accept what seemed to be the will of God: the duty of marriage.

Notes

1. For the friendship between Esther Edwards Burr and Sarah Prince, see my article: Lucia Bergamasco, 'Amitié, amour et spiritualité en Nouvelle Angleterre au XVIIIe siècle: l'expérience d'Esther Burr et de Sarah Prince', *Annales ESC*, vol. 41, no. 12 (1986). Their family life, as well as their spiritual and intellectual experiences, forms the first part of my thesis entitled 'Condition féminine et vie spirituelle en Nouvelle Angleterre au XVIIIe siècle', PhD thesis, Ecole des Hautes Etudes en Sciences Sociales, Paris, 1987.

2. These points did indeed provoke a lively discussion, for it became apparent that in other instances - for example Anna Maria van Schuurman - the relationship between learned women and their fathers had been crucial in forming the choice of a life of learning and celibacy. A few months after the ICWH an interesting article appeared in which the paternal educational role of some women writers is defined as seductive: Beth Kowaleski-Wallace, 'Milton's daughters: the education of eighteenth century women writers', *Feminist Studies*, vol. 12, no. 2 (1986), pp. 275-94.

3. Ebenezer Turell, *Memoirs of the life and death of the pious and ingenious Mrs Jane Turell, who died at Medford, March 26 1735, Aetat. 27. Collected chiefly from her Manuscripts by her consort the Rev. Ebenezer Turell... to which are added two sermons preach'd at Medford... by her father Benjamin Colman D.D.* (London, 1741 (1st edition Boston, 1735)); for Benjamin Colman see Ebenezer Turell, *The life and character of the Rev. Benjamin Colman* (Boston, 1749); Clifford K. Shipton, *Sibley's Harvard graduates* (Boston, 1933), vol IV; *The Dictionary of American Biography;* Perry Miller, *The New England mind,*

from Colony to Province (Cambridge, Mass., 1953).

4. Sarah Prince Gill, manuscript Journal, Boston Public Library; Thomas Prince, *Dying exercices of Mrs Deborah Prince and devout meditations of Mrs Sarah Gill, daughters of the late Rev. Thomas Prince* (printed Edinburgh, reprinted Newbury Port, Boston, 1789). The journal of Esther Edwards Burr is available in microfilm at the Beinecke Rare Books and Manuscripts Library, Yale University. Here I refer to the recent edition of it by Carol F. Karlsen, Laurie Crumpaker (eds), *The journal of Esther Edwards Burr 1754-1757* (Yale University Press, New Haven, Conn., 1984). For Thomas Prince, see *Dictionary of American Biography;* Samuel Drake, *Some memoirs of the life and writings of the Rev. Thomas Prince, with a pedigree of his family* (Boston, 1851). Shipton, *Sibley's Harvard graduates* (Boston 1931), vol. V. By 'Evangelical Pietism' historians mean the more sentimental religiosity, both in verbal expression and in attitude, that spread throughout New England from the end of the seventeenth century onwards, in agreement with as well as in opposition to milder forms of Calvinism. In fact, Pietism remained faithful to the tenets of Calvinist orthodoxy, such as predestination and total surrender of the will to the movement of the Spirit; it did not change its doctrine until the beginning of the nineteenth century. Cf. F. Ernest Stoeffler, *The rise of Evangelical Pietism* (Brill, Leiden, 1971); Edwin S. Gaustad, *The Great Awakening in New England* (Gloucester, Mass., 1965); Norman Fiering, *Jonathan Edwards' moral thought and its British context* (Chapel Hill, N.C., 1981); David D. Hall, *The faithful shepherd: a history of the New England ministry in the seventeenth century* (University of North Carolina Press, Chapel Hill, N.C., 1972); Charles Hambrick-Stowe, *The practice of piety: Puritan devotional disciplines in 17th century New England* (Chapel Hill, N.C., 1982); Robert Middlekauff, *The Mathers: three generations of Puritan intellectuals 1596-1728* (Oxford University Press, London, New York, 1971).

5. Cedric Cowing, 'Sex and preaching in the Great Awakening', *American Quarterly*, 20 (1968), pp. 624-44; Mary Maples Dunn, 'Saints and sisters: Congregational and Quaker women in the Early Colonial Period', *American Quarterly*, Winter 1978, pp. 582-601; Emory Elliott, *Power and the pulpit in Puritan New England* (Princeton University Press, Princeton, N.J., 1975); also 'The development of the Puritan funeral sermon and elegy 1660-1750', *Early American Literature*, 15 (1980), pp. 150-64; Margaret Masson, 'The typology of the female as a model for the regenerated: Puritan preaching 1690-1730', *Signs*, Winter 1976, pp. 304-15; Gerald F. Moran, 'Religious renewal, Puritan tribalism and the family in 17th century Connecticut', *William and Mary Quarterly*, 2 (April 1979), pp. 237-54; also 'Sisters in Christ: women and the church in 17th century New England' in Janet Wilson James (ed.), *Sisters in Christ: women in American religion* (University of Pennsylvania Press, Philadelphia, 1980), pp. 47-65; Richard

Schiels, 'The feminization of American congregations 1730-1830', *American Quarterly*, 1 (Spring 1981), pp. 46-62; Laurel Thatcher Ulrich, 'Vertuous women found: New England ministerial literature 1668-1735', *American Quarterly*, 28, 1 (1976), pp. 21-40.

6. See Cotton Mather, *Ornaments for the daughters of Zion* (Cambridge, Mass., 1692), pp. 23-45; Tabitha Rediviva (Boston, 1713), pp. 29-30; Benjamin Colman, *The duty and honor of aged women* (Boston, 1713). On spiritual writing as a devotional duty see Charles Hambrick-Stowe, *The practice of piety*.

7. Illiteracy was widespread amongst women in the American colonies and declined only at the end of the eighteenth century: cf. Kenneth A. Lockridge, *Literacy in colonial New England: an enquiry into the social context of literacy in the early modern West* (Norton, New York, 1974); Linda Kerber, *Women of the Republic: intellect and ideology in revolutionary America* (University of North Carolina Press, Chapel Hill, N.C., 1980); Mary B. Norton, *Liberty's daughters: the revolutionary experience of American women 1750-1800* (Boston, 1980). These books have extensive chapters on women's education, although no particular details about the daughters of pastors. These last were in fact exposed to greater social pressure as far as education was concerned, since they were constantly watched by the entire community. If we take the example of Timothy Edwards (father of the great theologian Jonathan Edwards, who was himself the father of Esther Edwards Burr), we know that in 1711 he left detailed instructions to his wife Esther Stoddard (herself the educated daughter of an eminent minister) for the education of his daughters and his son Jonathan, which included Latin as well as reading and writing exercises: cf. Ola Elizabeth Winslow, *Jonathan Edwards 1703-1758: a biography* (New York, 1940), p. 44. As for domestic skills, women were instructed by their mothers as well as by other women, relatives or friends, at whose homes they would spend part of their adolescence.

8. Indeed, the purpose of Ebenezer Turell's *Memoirs* was to set an example to upper-class New England girls in general and to daughters of pastors in particular. Introducing the two funeral sermons by Benjamin Colman, Turell explained that he intended to 'provoke Emulation' and to encourage parents to develop their children's souls and 'inspire our Daughters in particular with Desires to improve in Knowledge and Goodness under the instructions of their wise and gracious parents', *Memoirs of the life of Mrs. Jane Turell*, p. cvi. In the postscript he addressed himself openly to pastors: 'Ministers especially have great Advantages herefor, and are under special Obligations to be Examples to their Flocks, in this Rule of their own House', ibid. p. 80. Cotton Mather, not surprisingly, had also educated his daughter Katharine, who, when she died of consumption at the age of 27, was eulogised as 'an accomplished Gentlewoman and an early erudite in the Hebrew and Sacred Geography': Cotton Mather, *Vic-*

torina: a sermon preach'd on the decease and at the desire of Mrs Katharine Mather (Boston, 1717).

9. Ebenezer Turell, *Memoirs of the life of Mrs Jane Turell*, pp. 164-6.

10. Ibid., p. 166.

11. Ibid., p. 166.

12. Ibid., p. 80.

13. Ibid., p. 80.

14. Ibid., p. 5.

15. Ibid., p. 9.

16. Ibid., pp. 6-9.

17. Ibid., p. 26.

18. Ibid., pp. 25, 33.

19. Ibid., p. 26.

20. Ibid., p. 37.

21. Ibid., p. 41.

22. Ibid., p. 16.

23. Ibid., p. 170.

24. Ibid., p. 168.

25. Thomas Prince, *Devout meditations of Mrs Sarah Gill*, p. 54.

26. *Six sermons by the late Thomas Prince A.M., published from his manuscripts by John Erskine D.D.* (Edinburgh, 1785), pp. iv-v.

27. Sarah Prince, Journal, 6 March 1757.

28. Karlsen, Crumpaker (eds), *Journal of Esther Edwards Burr*, pp. 22-3, 39, 98, 102, 105, 107-8. For Thomas Prince's library see *The Prince Library: a catalogue of the collection of books and manuscripts* (Boston, 1870).

29. Karlsen, Crumpaker (eds), *Journal of Esther Edwards Burr*, p. 184.

30. For the Gill family, see *The Dictionary of American Biography*, under John Gill, and Thomas Bellows Wyman, *The genealogies and estates of Charlestown, Massachusetts, 1629-1818* (Boston, 1878), pp. 408-11. Little information could be gathered for Moses Gill; in fact the couple Sarah Prince-Moses Gill deserves further research, if anything, for the patriotic activities in which both must have been engaged. For Sarah Prince's relations with Catharine Macaulay and for the John Adams testimony on it, see Monica Letzring, 'Sarah Prince Gill and the John Adams-Catharine Macaulay correspondence', *Proceedings of the Massachusetts Historical Society*, vol. 88 (1976), pp. 107-11.

31. Karlsen, Crumpaker (eds), *Journal of Esther Edwards Burr*, pp. 193-6, 231-3.

32. Sarah Prince, Journal, 25 Feb. 1757.

33. Ibid., 5 March 1757.

34. Ibid., 12 March 1757, 6-10 May 1757.

35. Ibid., 19 Jan. 1757. On some occasions during their correspondence, Sarah Prince made derogatory remarks to Esther Burr about the married state. For instance, on 23 August 1755, Esther Burr was obliged to

defend married people in general: 'These poor fettered folks you seem to pity so much I look upon as the happest [sic] part of the world, and if I was to wish you any ill for your severity on us, it should be that you might never be married, but such a friend as I am cant wish you a very great Ill nor any Ill. We are not obliged to you for your seeming Pity, for in the first place we dont want it, and in the second place you dont pity us, but Envy us for our happy lot. Say dont you? The Old saying is, you may know who is shot by their fluttering. Now nothing is more common than for persons to run out against the married state, and say they never intend to be married, etc., when they are just upon the point of determining to except of the first offer. Hant you observed this?' Karlsen, Crumpaker (eds), *Journal of Esther Edwards Burr*, p. 145.

36. Thomas Prince, *Devout meditations of Mrs Sarah Gill*, pp. 36-7.

Päivi Setälä

Brick stamps and women's economic opportunities in Imperial Rome

Women's history studies concerning Antiquity

Women's history studies concerning Greece and Rome are varied and active at present. In accordance with present trends in women's history, this field has also shifted the focus of interest from the study of misery to themes of strength and status. It is no longer permissible to write about women in the 'obligatory' last chapter on hairstyles and dress. Greek women's history studies have drawn attention to conflicts and tensions between public and private spheres of life, as well as the value set upon the *oikos*, the domestic sphere.[1] The economic opportunities of women in ancient Greece have also been investigated, and were observed to have been surprisingly broad in scope.[2] A book has been published on the Hellenistic woman in general, with concrete examples of women who were in charge of their property, as well as concluding contracts and having a definite influence in both private and public matters.[3]

The Roman woman was always known to have been active in public and private spheres. This was already acknowledged by Roman male authors. Inscriptions (writings on hard materials such as gravestones and brick stamps) have added to the information provided by contemporary literature, and they clearly demonstrate the economic activities of women.

In her manual of women's awareness, *Le deuxième sexe*, Simone de Beauvoir states that Roman women were free in vain. She writes as follows:

> 'A woman can inherit, she has the same right as the father to require her children to obey her, she may draw up a will, with her dowry she can free herself from the yoke of marriage; she can obtain a divorce herself and remarry as she wishes. But her liberation remains a negative one because she is not offered any practical opportunities to use her powers. Her economic independence exists only on paper because it does not entail any political influence.'[4]

Despite this, I would claim that the liberal rights of inheritance and marriage guaranteed women the opportunity to play a part and have influence in their communities. One does not have to be a Marxist to realise that prosperity brings about influence. An interesting question is to what purpose or in whose favour women used their prosperity. Be that as it may, the separateness of both spouses' property is a fact, and one which guaranteed a certain independence for women.

Roman law and the status of women

It is no novelty to stress the great discrepancies between the Roman code of legal norms and the true situation. These discrepancies are especially prominent in the case of women's status and opportunities. This aspect has been pointed out in several reliable studies in the past few years.

There are indications of the economic independence of women as early as Republican times. At that stage, some women had acquired a considerable amount of property. The *Lex Voconia* of 169 B.C. can be interpreted as proof of this. It permitted making a will in favour of one's daughter, which was probably legalised specifically because of its being a common practice. It also contained stipulations to prevent more affluent persons from making women their heirs, and to prevent women from inheriting more than male heirs. Very soon, however, the stipulations and statutes were disregarded and the law was abandoned.[5] The traditional concept of a striking difference between the status of women in Republican times and those in Imperial times does not in fact have any basis. Although Roman law retained certain limitations on the possibilities open to women for a long period, it also provided numerous loopholes. In fact, women controlled large-scale properties from the end of Republican times onwards.

The dowry (*dos*) was originally meant as economic aid to the husband for the financial burden of marriage. In accordance with its other function, it was designed to secure the woman's income if the marriage ended. Marriage was not a legal relationship, and society was uninterested in the economic relations of the spouses or their morals. Therefore divorce was also a private matter. Similarly, both spouses remained in control of their respective property, and each was responsible only for his or her own debts. Thus, in a free marriage (*sine manu*), which prevailed nearly universally around the birth of Christ, the property of each spouse remained separate. Roman law also retained the guardianship of women (*tutela mulierum*), although this was a mere formality in Imperial times. Women took care of their property themselves, and the respective guardian was not responsible for it.[6] In this connection reference has often been made to Cicero's wife Terentia, whose business dealings are well known, but whose guardian's name remains undiscovered.

In Imperial times women were able to inherit and bequeath property, control their dowries, free their slaves, buy and sell land and make free and generous donations. Tacitus also stressed the power of women in his account of Calvia Crispinilla, who married two consuls, but neither of the marriages produced children. Tacitus mentions that because of her wealth and the lack of heirs she was a very influential Roman.[7]

It is self-evident that in all communities wealth and prosperity bring about personal influence, which is not limited to private life but also extends to the public domain. This was especially the case in the Graeco-Roman world, where private donors were central in providing social respect, and it could be seen particularly in the Eastern provinces. It has also been noted that the influence of women was more evident on a local level and in the smaller towns.[8]

Research on the Roman family has been very impressive in many respects. It has stressed the importance of daughters and the status of women as 'structurally central family members'. The following results have been obtained: women maintained close contact with their own families, sons and daughters were equal in upper-class Roman families, also in the opinion of the father, and the mother's family was valued and respected as well.[9] The history of the Roman woman is seen to progress from membership of the father's family to membership of the family formed by her husband and children. The nuclear family unit became the centre of basic social obligations. This course of development is well suited to Christianity, which made the family the foundation of social order.

Brick stamp data

Roman brick stamps provide information on landownership and the production of bricks in the city of Rome and environs during the first three centuries A.D. or thereabouts. The production of bricks was important to the growing capital, whose population has been estimated at a million. On the basis of transport conditions in this period, the region of production of Roman brick stamps can be limited to the near vicinity of the city and the area of the Tiber, i.e. north of Rome.

Brick stamps have been of interest to researchers because they make the dating of buildings possible, and they also mention the names of members of the uppermost classes of society. In comparison with other inscriptions (e.g. funerary inscriptions), brick stamps can be dated with relative precision. One of the reasons for this is because they mention persons known from several other sources, and many of the stamps also have consular datings. Many problems relating to brick stamps and the production of bricks have been solved by a Finnish team of researchers.[10]

The historian has access to almost all the brick stamp material known in Antiquity, which is exceptional in classical studies. Therefore we have knowledge of all landowners and producers of bricks. The stamps indicate that of the persons mentioned, *dominus* is used to refer to the owner of the land (*praedia*) or the clay bed (*figlinae*), which means that the dominus was the landowner. A second person, the *officinator,* is defined either as a foreman in the service of the landowner or as a manufacturer of bricks, a private entrepreneur independent of the actual landowner. The domini were obviously from a higher social group than the officinatores. In my dissertation I have studied the dominus group, and on the basis of the brick stamps we know they were landowners in the near vicinity of Rome, but we do not know for certain their relationship to the brick production industry. A total of 150 landowners are known, of which one-third were women. The land areas were adjacent to Rome, and for this reason they were of value both politically and socially.[11]

Women as landowners

Of the female landowners (*domina*), over 70 per cent were of the senatorial class, while the corresponding proportion of men was 10 per cent less. From the middle of the second century A.D. women owners of brick land equalled the men in number. Because the immediate vicinity of Rome was important, the influence of these women was of great consequence. One should not underestimate the importance of landed property in Roman society.

The significant proportion of women landowners finds its explanation in the equal inheritance among sons and daughters under Roman law and the liberal marriage laws. The brick lands were frequently inherited by children from their parents, and most often they were bequeathed by fathers to daughters. Spouses are mentioned in the stamps as landowners, both separately and jointly, and the same also applies to siblings. I identified two-thirds of the brick landowners as relatives of some other landowner, which may be seen as an indication of the fact that the Romans tried to keep landed property within their families, at least in the vicinity of Rome. Romans always entertained sentimental feelings towards the owning of land. On the basis of the brick stamps, I wish to stress that in the highest circles of society, parents in increasing numbers transferred their property to their children. Preference for cognate relatives instead of agnate relatives gave female landowners an advantage because they also inherited their husbands' property. The brick stamps indicate that spouses owned brick lands as much jointly as separately.[12]

The central importance of children as heirs supports the idea of the central importance of the family in Roman society. Similarly, the inheriting of daughters from their mothers suggests that economic responsibilities among mothers and children were more extensive than was implied in legal texts. This is also indicated by the case of Cicero's family, where Terentia was expected to participate in the maintenance of the children. A Roman married couple did not constitute an economic unit. The possible confiscation of Cicero's property did not apply to Terentia, nor did Cicero have any say in the management of his wife's property.[13]

The large amount of property owned by women can be partly explained by the fact that in some cases women were the only children of their parents. This applied to two Domitia Lucillas; the elder Domitia Lucilla was the granddaughter of Cn. Domitius Afer, a man of considerable wealth. Domitia inherited from her grandfather, her father and her uncle, who adopted her. She also inherited property from her maternal grandfather, on the condition that her husband would not have any right to the inheritance. Domitia Lucilla married three consuls, but these marriages produced only one daughter, who bore her mother's name. The husbands are not mentioned in the brick stamps, where the only heir is the daughter. The daughter, Domitia Lucilla the younger, married M. Annius Verus, whose father had been a consul three times and was an owner of brick areas. Domitia the younger had a son and a daughter. The son grew up to be the Emperor Marcus Aurelius, and the daughter is mentioned in brick stamps along with her spouse. Domitia the younger lived as a widow for about 20 years. Through these two women large areas of land were acquired by the Emperor.[14]

The central importance of women can also be explained by the fact that these women lived longer than their husbands and therefore inherited their brick areas as well. The bequeathing of property by husbands to their wives also indicates the significance of the nuclear family unit. We can also find possible support for the theory that in some families the brick lands were given to the daughter rather than to the son. Cases of daughters inheriting brick lands from their fathers include at least Asinia Quadratilla, Cusinia Gratilla, Domitia Lucilla the elder, Anna Cornificia, Anna Fundania Faustina and Iulia Procula. In my dissertation I suggested that inheritance of brick lands by daughters would only have applied to the cases of Neratia Quartilla and Pedania Quintilla. Both were from political *gentes* of great power whose male representatives belonged to the Emperor's inner circle. It is, of course, possible that sons inherited land which was unsuitable for the production of bricks.[15]

It has been aptly said that we see Roman society as an iceberg, and similarly we have the most information about the very highest strata of society. It has been estimated that of the senatorial males of the first three centuries A.D. 50 per cent are known, while the corresponding figure for women is 15-20 per cent. The prosopographic list of the senatorial class includes a total of 868 women, of whom 78 per cent married senators.[16] The majority of the women brick landowners came from this class.

The brick stamps also prove that women of the senatorial and equestrian classes were important in a society based on familial ties. In these circles, marriages were contracted between families and were both political and economic transactions. Rome was governed by these networks of families, and the relatives of wives and mothers were important for forming contacts and for bringing prosperity to the family.[17]

Economic activity of women

The starting-point of my dissertation was that at least all domini were known to be landowners. On the basis of brick stamps, we do not know anything about the relation of the domini to the production of bricks. Research done in the 1980s into the economic history of Antiquity, however, has stressed the participation of the Roman upper class in production and commerce. It was previously maintained that a member of the upper class could only be a landowner. The primary nature of landownership should not be questioned as such. On the other hand, interest should be focused on the discrepancies between Roman social norms and praxis. Recent archaeological excavations and new studies of inscriptions indicate that the upper class also was involved in commerce and production.[18] The economic practices of individuals were therefore more complex than agriculture and related means of livelihood alone. The Roman upper class was more business-minded than was hitherto assumed.

These results point to a reassessment of the female domini, of whom some at least may have had an interest in the actual production of bricks alongside their ownership of the land.[19] The brick industry offered a means of prosperity, and it may have been one of the reasons for acquiring land. Good clay beds were no doubt much sought after. An example of a Roman woman who was active in economic affairs is Flavia Seia Isaurica, who owned six clay-bed areas which produced bricks. Her brick stamps mention 16 officinatores, who were probably foremen in her employ. It may also be assumed that in the case of stamps with only one name, the women landowners had more to do with the actual production of bricks. In this connection ten women are known, e.g. Neratia Quartilla.[20]

One could suggest that when agriculture found itself in a state of crisis in early Imperial times, active owners of brick-clay areas - women included - saw the significance of the brick industry with regard to amassing wealth. In this sense they were ahead of their time, and succeeded in investing their property in a highly lucrative manner.

As well as the domini, brick stamps also mention officinatores. Unlike the domini, they were not from the upper classes of society. The officinatores have been defined either as independent producers of bricks or foremen in the employ of others. The available sources concerning this period do not provide any straightforward answer to this problem. Both interpretations are of interest with respect to the position and status of women.[21] Women officinatores have been interpreted as being independent tenants or entrepreneurs as such, because it was assumed that being employed to direct the actual work would also have entailed participation in the production of the bricks. This, in turn, was seen as being unsuitable for women, although we know of women who participated in other forms of physical labour. As independent entrepreneurs, the women officinatores would have been active in economic affairs. Two of the women officinatores are mentioned in connection with land areas of two different domini, which supports the idea of independent entrepreneurship. Half of the known women officinatores were employed in brick-clay areas owned by the Emperor. The officinatores were not bound by the traditions of the community as the senators were with regard to the unsuitability of economic activity.

Some brick stamps also mention *conductores* and *negotiatores*. Of the five conductores, one was a woman who was either a tenant or a contractor of the brick-producing areas owned by the Emperor Commodus. Two negotiatores are known, also from the *Figlinae Publilianae*, which was owned by a woman, Aemilia Severa. Their names were Iunia Antonia and Iunia Sabina. The negotiatores have been interpreted as being business people in an intermediary position between the producers of bricks and the builders. The

Figlinae Publilianae testifies to a female-dominated organisation.[22]

A recent study has stated that the independence and influence of Roman women, or feminism as it has also been called, flourished for a period of about one hundred years only, around the birth of Christ. During this period women competed on an equal basis with men for wealth.[23] However, the brick stamps show that the economic activity of women continued for three hundred years in Imperial times. At the end of the second century A.D., there were equal numbers of male and female landowners. It can therefore be concluded that research has not yet been able to interpret the message contained in the inscriptions, and especially the brick-stamp data.

Economic opportunities of women

Corresponding activity in economic affairs is found on the part of the women of Pompeii. Pompeii's most famous woman, Eumachia, was a respected priestess and the protectress of the wool-fullers' guild (*patrona* of the *collegium fullonum*). The economic interests of Eumachia's family were linked to the brick and amphora industries, as well as to foreign trade. Eumachia's house by the forum has been called a club for business people, where shippers and those engaged in foreign trade gathered. We also know of Faustilla from Pompeii, who as a pawnbroker controlled the flow of capital in her city. Likewise, women in business are encountered in the spice and textile trades. In Pompeii property was put up for sale at public auctions, where women bought and sold without the intervention of their guardians.[24] Women were active in public affairs as well. The life-style of the women of Pompeii will no doubt have had its pendants elsewhere.

Women's history has called attention to women's opportunities for influence in activities related to religion. It is believed that they provided women with psychological and social space for mobility. From the economic point of view, notice has been taken of those women who donated considerable sums to religious communities. There is evidence of this all over the Roman Empire.[25]

I have already stressed that Roman women were active in the management of their own wealth and property. The letters of petition sent to the Emperor, to which the latter sent replies or rescripts, are proof of this. Women applied to the Emperor for justice in matters of inheritance, marriage and property. About one-fifth of the known rescripts are replies to women's petitions. The petitions indicate the self-sufficiency of women, which was honoured by the Emperor in his replies. From these sources many active businesswomen are known. Examples of a single year's rescripts tell, amongst other things, of the produce of landed property given as a dowry; a present given by a wife to her husband which included slaves and other goods; landed property in connection with dowries and testaments; a landed estate which produced oil and wine for the market, over which the *mater familias* had administrative power, and about a certain Marcia who initiated court proceedings against her debtor. Of the ladies who received the rescripts, a considerable number worked in the provinces.[26] Therefore women's activities were carried out not only in the centre but also in the periphery. The petitioners also applied to the Emperor in small property matters, which shows that the self-sufficiency of women was not only an upper-class privilege. Among the petitioners there were many liberated women, which is interesting in that recent studies have drawn attention to the economic activities of freed persons.[27] These women may have been the representatives of their masters, but the number of economically independent persons was significant. With regard to women, this is supported by the examples from Pompeii, as well as the imperial rescripts and inscriptions. Grave inscriptions tell of capable women who, upon the death of their husbands, took over their business affairs and continued them successfully. The expression 'from her own funds' is also mentioned in the inscriptions.[28]

Despite the data provided by the brick stamps, the case of Cicero's wife and the wealth and prosperity of the women of Pompeii, economic and social histories of Antiquity still appear with no mention of women, which attests to the strength and durability of male-dominated traditions.

Influence of Roman women

The economic emancipation of Roman women was based on liberal marriage and inheritance laws. Although the law preserved some aspects detrimental to the position and status of women, their own prosperity and wealth were recognised facts. One problem of women's history, whether the available sources of the past refer mainly to exceptional women of the upper classes, is especially important in relation to the otherwise limited source material of Antiquity. It is certain that the 'visibility' of the Roman woman was a result of her wealth and prosperity, which no doubt distorts our image of the proportion of the wealthy in the overall scene. However, data from inscriptions and papyri, amongst other sources, also relate to the economic activities and interests of so-called ordinary women.

Landownership by women in the vicinity of Rome, as indicated by the brick stamps, gives cause to stress the central importance and influence of women in the capital. The brick stamps show that it was desirable to keep property within the family, which was readily understood as the nuclear family unit consisting only of the father, mother and children. Blood ties were consequently a main rule in Roman inheritance practices. Information from brick stamps supports the view that the Roman woman of Imperial times identified with, and therefore belonged to, both her father's family and via marriage to her own family. Studies of families have stressed the increased importance of children and the ensuing consolidation of the status and position of the mother.

As an historian, one may ask how women achieved influence in their communities with their property. In Antiquity, respect and status depended on donations to one's community, which women are known to have made. This was also the route to public life. The influence of women can be seen as well in the literary expression 'leading women and men', used by Tacitus and Suetonius amongst others.

The Roman woman of Imperial times used her property as she pleased. She could make wills and testaments to her sons, daughters, husband and the children of her siblings. Women were institutionalised heiresses, not only as daughters but also as wives and mothers. The Roman will was a family matter, and the most important member of the family was the child - be it a son or a daughter.[29]

There have not yet been any studies on the economic effects of Roman inheritance and marriage laws. I would claim, however, that in this respect too, women played an important role. Simone de Beauvoir wrote that Roman women were free in vain. In my opinion her private wealth made the Roman woman an influential and visible member of her community.

Notes

1. Sally Humphreys, *The family, women and death: comparative studies* (Routledge & Kegan Paul, London, 1983).
2. David M. Schaps, *Economic rights of women in ancient Greece* (Edinburgh University Press, Edinburgh, 1979).
3. Sarah B. Pomeroy, *Women in Hellenistic Egypt: from Alexander to Cleopatra* (Schocken Books, New York, 1984).
4. Simone de Beauvoir, *Le deuxième sexe*, vol. 1 (2 vols., Editions Gallimard, Paris, 1949), pp. 151, 153.
5. Beryl Rawson, 'The Roman family' in Beryl Rawson (ed.), *The family in ancient Rome: new perspectives* (Croom Helm, London & Sydney, 1986), pp. 1-57; J.A. Crook, 'Women in Roman succession' in Rawson (ed.), *The family in ancient Rome*, pp. 65-7.
6. Crook, 'Women in Roman succession', pp. 58-82.
7. Ramsay MacMullen, 'Women's power in the Principate', *Klio*, 68 (1986), pp. 434-43; Tacitus, *Hist.*, 1.73.
8. Ramsay MacMullen, 'Woman in public in the Roman Empire', *Historia*, 29 (1980), pp. 208-18; Riet van Bremen, 'Women and wealth' in Averil Cameron and Amelie Kuhrt (eds), *Images of women in Antiquity* (Croom Helm, London & Canberra, 1983), pp. 223-42.
9. Judith P. Hallett, *Fathers and daughters in Roman society: women and the elite family* (Princeton University Press, Princeton, New Jersey, 1984), pp. 299-346.
10. Margareta Steinby, *La cronologia delle figlinae doliari urbane dalla fine dell'età repubblicana fino all'inizio del III sec.* Estratto dal Volume 84, 1974, dal Bullettino della Comm. Arch. Communale di Roma (Roma, 1974); Tapio Helen, *Organization of Roman brick production in the first and second centuries A.D.: an interpretation of Roman brick stamps.* Annales Academiae Scientiarum Fennicae. Dissertationes Humanarum Litterarum 5 (Helsinki, 1975); Päivi Setälä, *Private domini in Roman brick stamps of the Empire: a historical and prosopographical study of landowners in the district of Rome.* Annales Academiae Scientiarum Fennicae. Dissertationes Humanarum Litterarum 10 (Helsinki, 1977).
11. Setälä, *Private domini*, pp. 13-19.
12. Ibid., pp. 230-41.
13. Suzanne Dixon, 'Family finances: Terentia and Tullia' in Rawson (ed.), *The family in ancient Rome*, pp. 93-120.
14. Setälä, *Private domini*, pp. 107-9.

15. Ibid., p. 239.

16. M.-Th. Raepsaet-Charlier, *Prosopographie des femmes de l'ordre senatorial romain aux deux premiers siècles de notre ère.* Diss. à paraître dans les Mémoires de l'Académie royale de Belgique. Classe des Lettres (Bruxelles, 1967-77).

17. Setälä, *Private domini*, pp. 242-4.

18. John H. D'Arms, *Commerce and social standing in ancient Rome* (Harvard University Press, Cambridge, Mass., and London, 1981).

19. Margareta Steinby, 'I senatori e l'industria laterizia urbana' in *Epigrafia e ordine senatorio I-II* (Tituli 4-59, Atti del Colloquio Internazionale Roma 1981 (Rome, 1982)), pp. 227- 37.

20. Setälä, *Private domini*, pp. 119-21.

21. Helen, *Organization of Roman brick production*, pp. 112-13.

22. Setälä, *Private domini*, pp. 50-2.

23. Vito Antonio Sirago, *Femminismo a Roma nel primo Impero* (Rubbettino, Rome, 1983), pp. 187-98.

24. Elisabeth Lyding Will, 'Women in Pompeii', *Archaeology*, vol. 32, no. 5 (1979), pp. 36-7.

25. MacMullen, 'Woman in public in the Roman Empire', pp. 208-18.

26. L. Huchthausen, 'Herkunft und ökonomische Stellung weibliches Adressaten von Reskripten des Codex Iustinianus (2. und 3. Jh.u.Z.)', *Klio*, 56 (1974), pp. 199-228.

27. P.W. Garnsley, 'Independent freedmen and the economy of Roman Italy under the Principate', *Klio*, 63 (1981), pp. 359-71.

28. Sarah B. Pomeroy, *Goddesses, whores, wives and slaves: women in classical Antiquity* (Schocken Books, New York, 1975), pp. 190-204.

29. Crook, 'Women in Roman succession', p. 79.

Marijke Gijswijt-Hofstra

Witchcraft in the Northern Netherlands

The first Dutch historian to write a comprehensive book on the history of European as well as Dutch witch-trials was Jacobus Scheltema.[1] His book was published in 1828, and was given the significant and rather self-complacent subtitle: *A contribution to the glory of our fatherland.* With this subtitle he referred to the executions for witchcraft in the Netherlands, which commenced later, were less frequent, and ceased 60 to 100 years earlier than elsewhere. Except for the first one, Scheltema's conclusions still hold, although later research has shown his list of Dutch witch-trials to be in need of supplementation and correction.[2]

Scheltema's statements concerned the territory of the former Northern Netherlands, later known as the Republic of the United Provinces. At that time, parts of the present-day Netherlands were not included, such as most of North Brabant and Limburg. While partly maintaining Scheltema's geographical delimitation for the sake of argument, there is much to be said for enlarging the scope of the subject and its time span. The interpretation of witch-trials has much to gain if one considers them as part of witchcraft on a broader socio-cultural scale. Since witchcraft has proved to be an ongoing concern during the centuries after the executions for witchcraft had ceased, the time boundaries have to be shifted towards a less distant past as well. One may even assume that Dutch witchcraft, like witchcraft elsewhere, does not yet belong to the past.

Obviously, much depends on the way witchcraft is defined. Anthropologists and historians have proposed several diverging distinctions between witchcraft and sorcery. In European witchcraft literature, it has become rather fashionable to reserve the term *sorcery* for ritual acts to attain harmful or beneficial ends. Witchcraft mostly implies harmful sorcery or *maleficium*, and always one or more specifically demonological elements summed up in manuals for witch-hunters, like the *Malleus maleficarum*, the *Hammer of witches*, published in 1487. According to these demonological doctrines, witches - mostly females - derived their magical powers from a pact with the Devil, thereby renouncing God. This pact was sealed by sexual intercourse. Witches were also supposed to attend nocturnal meetings, known as sabbaths. However attractive such a distinction between sorcery and witchcraft may seem, it often proves rather difficult to fit 'witchcraft' phenomena neatly into one of these categories. Besides, this distinction does not adequately reflect former usage. It therefore seems sensible to use either of these terms in an encompassing sense - preferably in accordance with former usage. Different types of witchcraft or sorcery can then be indicated by means of adjectives, or by original and more specialised terms. The term *witchcraft* will be used here in a general way, as an umbrella-term, to refer to ideas and acts of men and women, with as central element the human control of the succession of events with the aid of magical forces.

When speaking of witchcraft in the Dutch context, it should be understood that the former encompassing Dutch term was *toverij*. This concept covered various types of magical beliefs and activities like maleficent witchcraft, whether or not - but mostly not - combined with demonological elements such as the Devil's pact and the sabbath. Illness and death of men and animals, failure of dairy or beer production and of the harvest, setbacks in affairs of love, or bad luck when fishing, and even shipwrecks could be attributed to witchcraft. *Toverij* also referred to counter-magic or white magic as practised by cunning men and women, fortune-tellers and exorcists, or by private persons applying magical arts themselves. Our knowledge of the development of the past uses and meanings of *toverij* and various related terms is still incomplete. This is also the case regarding shifts in the lines of what was conceived to be normal or tolerable in the sphere of witchcraft. It has become clear, however, that lay magistrates as well as church authorities took action against several forms of witchcraft until well into the seventeenth century, and even later. The judicial and ecclesiastical punishments of non-harmful witchcraft, slander and scolding, or even mistreatment in connection with suspicions of maleficent witchcraft, were to continue long after trials for maleficent witchcraft had stopped or noticeably declined after the second decade of the seventeenth century.

This brings me to the important theme of the infrequency and the early ending of the Dutch executions for witchcraft. According to the present state of research, an outline of Dutch trials for maleficent witchcraft may be expressed as follows.[3] Though not belonging to the Republic, the region of Limburg will be dealt with briefly first. From this politically and juridically much divided region, many witch-trials, including several which resulted in death sentences, have been traced, mainly occurring between the 1520s and the 1680s. These trials increased in number after 1590 until they reached a peak in the second decade of the seventeenth century. The Roermond 'panic' of 1613 was the most extensive one, with at least 39 women and one man burned at the stake. Nothing like this ever happened in the northern provinces.

Here, the largest series of prosecutions happened in the Groninger Ommelanden, with 20 executions for maleficent witchcraft, mainly women, in 1547. A smaller peak followed in this same region with the execution of 5 women in 1562. In Westerwolde, now part of the province of Groningen, 7 women were sentenced to death in 1587, and 9 women and 3 men in 1589. As far as we know, no other part of the Northern Netherlands shared a similarly high frequency of peaks or such a large number of death sentences. Two other large series of trials occurred in 1595. One of them took place in Peelland, a region in North Brabant, which then belonged to the Southern Netherlands and is therefore beyond our Dutch scope. These Peelland trials resulted in the death of 19 women. In the same year, a total of 6 women and 2 men were executed for witchcraft in Amersfoort and in Utrecht. Smaller concentrations occurred in Utrecht, with the burning of 4 women in 1533, in Amsterdam with the execution of another 4 women in 1555, and in Schiedam, where 5 women were condemned to the stake in 1585. Most other trials for maleficent witchcraft were isolated, or sometimes came in small concentrations of two or three, for instance when several members of one family were accused of this crime.

Apart from in Limburg, records of most executions for witchcraft have so far been found in the province of Groningen and in Westerwolde. Out of a total of about 60 known trials, 54 executions occurred in these regions. According to our present information, the number of executions, though not always the number of trials, has been much lower in other provinces. From Gelre, Utrecht, Holland and North Brabant, approximately 20 executions are known in each case. Very few trials for maleficent witchcraft have so far been found in the remaining provinces of Friesland, Drenthe, Overijssel and Zeeland. The Court of Friesland has never been known to pass a death sentence for maleficent witchcraft. However, witchcraft research in Friesland still has a long way to go. Continuing research in Drenthe has not yet led to the discovery of any death sentences either. In Overijssel the case is similar; records of only one execution have been found. The somewhat incomplete archives of Zeeland have so far revealed 3 deaths at the stake: one of a recidivist woman fortune-teller in 1541, and the other two of women who confessed to maleficent witchcraft and a pact with the Devil in 1565. Not counting Limburg, and according to the present state of research, the total number of executions is less than 150.

The first execution for maleficent witchcraft was recorded in 1472 in Gelre. In the wake of burnings in adjoining German territories, more burnings followed in Gelre during the first decades of the sixteenth century, under the reign of Duke Karel of Egmond. The executions then spread towards the north and the west. In Utrecht the first execution took place in 1520, while in Amsterdam this happened some 20 years later and on the advice of Utrecht. Most burnings in Groningen and Westerwolde followed after trials in neighbouring East Friesland. These more severe actions against maleficent witchcraft, which are also to be observed in the Southern Netherlands from the 1490s onwards, were an expression of the changing attitudes of the church and secular authorities towards witchcraft as a crime. They were also connected with the gradual introduction of Roman law and *ex officio* criminal proceedings.

There were several waves of witch-trials: those in Utrecht in the 1520s and 30s, in Groningen in the 1540s, smaller ones in the 1550s in Gelre, and 1560s in Groningen and Holland. In the mid 1580s a new wave of trials began. This was manifest in Westerwolde, Gelre, Utrecht, Holland and North Brabant, and also in the

Limburg regions. Except for the latter, the end of this wave meant the end of the burnings as well. According to our present knowledge, the last burning in Holland took place in 1591 (Schoonhoven) or 1592 (Goedereede), or possibly even in 1608 (Gorinchem). In North Brabant the last one was in 1595 (Peelland), in Utrecht in 1596 (Rhenen) and in Westerwolde in 1597. The last execution in Gelre is registered in 1603 (Nijmegen); in 's-Heerenberg, which did not recognise the jurisdiction of Gelre, a woman was burned in 1605. In Limburg the burnings continued until the 1630s. Suspicions and accusations of witchcraft concerned first of all a *maleficium*, or bewitchment. One way to interpret misfortune was to ascribe it to witchcraft. Protracted or sudden illness of men and animals, as well as recurrent failures of dairy production, were found to be associated with witchcraft. Wise men or women could help to diagnose a bewitchment and discover the culprit. The accused were mostly women, not necessarily old or unmarried; they were seldom midwives, but they always lived near to the bewitched. Victims of bewitchment were men, women and also many children. Preceding conflicts or tensions between both parties could only be traced in some of the witchcraft cases. They concerned matters of envy, power or property, interests or feuds between families. However, preceding conflicts were by no means a necessary condition for accusations of witchcraft: a reputation for practising maleficent witchcraft, or merely living in each other's neighbourhood, could also lead suspicions in a certain direction. Certainly the uttering of witchcraft accusations had the effect of disturbing relations between people, if they were not already problematic.

Theories of learned men concerning witchcraft seem to have remained relatively unknown to the people directly concerned with bewitchments. The traditional learned view of witchcraft - both maleficent witchcraft and counter-magic - as expressed by Augustine and Thomas à Kempis, was still accepted by most theologians and jurists of the Netherlands in the fifteenth and sixteenth centuries. According to this view, witchcraft practices are vain; they cannot be the cause of any ill effects. Magic is a system of signs, which is based on an agreement or an explicit or implicit pact with demons. Effects of witchcraft can be attributed solely to the activities of demons, which in turn can only take place with the consent of God. Copulation with demons forms no part of this idea, nor are women in particular associated with witchcraft.

A largely deviant theory was developed by the Dominicans Institoris and J. Sprenger in their *Malleus maleficarum* (1487). According to them, the pact with the Devil is sealed by copulation, and mainly women are tempted to practise witchcraft, which is the worst form of heresy. Also contrary to the traditional view, the authors of the *Malleus* stress the real effects of *maleficia.* Witches can fly through the air with the assistance of demons; however, on the subject of nocturnal gatherings of witches, sabbaths, they are not quite clear. Their vision of witchcraft and the pact with the Devil had hardly any following in the theological literature of the Netherlands. In the Southern Netherlands, this situation was changed when the Jesuit Martinus Delrio published his *Disquisitionum magicarum* in 1599; this was written very much in the spirit of the *Malleus.* The magistrates of the Northern Netherlands were seldom inclined to consider witchcraft in terms of the *Malleus,* though they did come to accept the traditional notion of the Devil's pact during the sixteenth century.

Without going into differences in judicial organisation and procedural law between the provinces, the legal proceedings in cases of maleficent witchcraft can be summarised as follows. Though a charge could be brought by anybody who suspected someone of maleficent witchcraft, *ex officio* proceedings were more commonly instituted. In the first case, the accuser had to prove his charge, and if he failed to do so he ran the risk of being punished for witchcraft himself or being obliged to give satisfaction to the accused. If the magistrates learned of any reputations or suspicions of witchcraft, they could decide to make inquiries and to question the suspected person. Therefore much depended on the attitude of the magistrates concerned. It was beyond dispute that maleficent witchcraft, based on a pact with the Devil, was classed as a capital offence. However, the inclination to institute proceedings varied, even within the same jurisdiction. Once a prosecution had begun, the attitude of the magistrates was again of the utmost importance. Their questions and threats, with or without the use of torture, could result in a confession of *maleficium* and a pact with the Devil - which required the death sentence - and also in the naming of accomplices, who could then in their turn be summoned. The latter was the case during the trials in Groningen, Utrecht, Holland, Peelland and Limburg. Nocturnal dancing and witches' organisations were reported on only a few occasions; demons were seldom mentioned as participants. The relationship between demons and witches was a personal one; copulation certainly did not belong to the continually recurring aspects of the Devil's pact. More often this pact was sealed by a solemn pledge on the part of the witch and by a gift from the Devil. Both men and women confessed to involvement in these same procedures, though the latter were much more frequently concerned.

Apart from trials for maleficent witchcraft, there were fairly regular instances of slander suits connected with maleficent witchcraft, and trials for non-harmful witchcraft as well. This last category included cases of fortune-telling, magical healing or white magic, and they often resulted in banishment and sometimes in acquittal. In these trials male suspects no longer formed a minority. Proceedings for slander rarely resulted in the death sentence for one of the parties, though some examples of both are known. Usually the outcome was that accusations of witchcraft had to be withdrawn.

What happened after the trials for maleficent witchcraft had ceased or declined to a considerable extent? It should be borne in mind that systematic research of the period after the last burnings is still rather scarce, but presumably less so than elsewhere in Europe. We may assume that trials for maleficent witchcraft became exceptional - not counting Limburg - after the second decade of the seventeenth century. However, accusations of maleficent witchcraft continued to result in slander suits until the beginning of the nineteenth century, as is apparent from research in Drenthe. Some later examples are known of trials for mistreatment of women who were forced to reverse their alleged bewitchment. The last known case of this type took place at the beginning of the twentieth century. For the rest, judicial concern with witchcraft was limited to the repression of the more professional forms of counter-magical activities. Up till the beginning of the twentieth century, exorcists or fortune-tellers and similar magical healers are found to have been banished or otherwise punished more or less regularly.

But the repression and intervention in cases of witchcraft were by no means exclusively worldly affairs. Unfortunately, very little is known about the role of the Dutch Roman Catholic church before the Reformation. We know much more about the Protestant churches. Since the reforms in the 1570s and 80s, their attitude towards witchcraft was made known at synods, classical and church council sessions, and in the catechism. From the very beginning the Calvinist clergy were confronted with the task of teaching the true faith, and exhorting church members to adopt a Christian way of life. The Heidelberg catechism (1563) was to become the official confession book, and the catechism preachings on Sunday afternoons soon became compulsory. The national synod of Dordrecht (1618-19) decided to make this regionally developed practice the official national policy. The catechism preachings soon resulted in a stream of publications of so-called catechism explanations. According to continuing research, about 120 such explanations were published between 1588 and 1730.

The catechism explanations were supposed to be read by all church members before attending the Sunday afternoon sermon. Each Sunday of the year had its own theme. Three of them especially were relevant to the subject of witchcraft: Sunday 10 was the doctrine of providence and of the almighty God; Sunday 34 dealt with the first commandment and with themes like idolatry, witchcraft, fortune-telling and the invoking of saints; Sunday 52 was the prayer: deliver us from Evil. These explanations consider God to be almighty and the Devil to be subject to His will; this is quite in accordance with traditional theological views. Misfortune can be interpreted either as an ordeal of the faithful or as a punishment of the wicked for unchristian behaviour. The Devil is regarded as a seducer and a liar, having much knowledge and power, but being subject to the laws of nature. He can cause illness in a natural way and he can help fortune-tellers. Witchcraft is forbidden; it is considered to be a pact between man and the Devil. This pact is of a dual nature. There is an indirect pact, which does not necessarily originate directly from the Devil, although ultimately it does. This indirect pact concerns so-called white magic: healing of the sick, tracing of lost or stolen goods, and exorcising. The second form is the direct pact, which is intended to harm men, livestock and crops. The direct pact is punishable by law, whereas the indirect pact, white magic, is considered to be punishable by the church. All catechism explanations emphasise the use of white magic, almost to the point of obsession. The subject of white magic merges into that of superstition, which refers to the erroneous ascription of a certain potency to objects, words, gestures or signs. Examples of so-called papist superstitions occur many times. Towards the end of the seventeenth century, definitions of witchcraft tend to become somewhat mitigated: what was formerly supposed to be witchcraft was frequently interpreted by clergymen as deceit or conjuration.

Dutch historians like R. Fruin and J. Huizinga, and in their wake H.R. Trevor-Roper, have attributed the early ending of the Dutch witch burnings to the subordinate position of the supposedly pro-witch-hunt Calvinist clergy.[4] However, there is much evidence to the contrary. The catechism explanations emphasise white magic and papist superstitions rather than maleficent witchcraft. The Utrecht theologian G. Voetius, though known to be a protagonist of the punishment of maleficent witchcraft, warned against hasty or careless acceptance of doubtful proofs of witchcraft. In his opinion it was better to acquit the guilty than to condemn any innocent person.[5] This cautious attitude obviously reflects a long-standing tradition of prudence when applying legal procedures. By the way, not only has the Calvinist clergy's preoccupation with maleficent witchcraft been exaggerated, but Balthasar Bekker's contribution to the ending of witch-trials has also been overrated. Bekker's book *The enchanted world* (1691), which deals with the negligible role of the Devil in human affairs and which was much criticised by his colleagues at the time, was published when trials for maleficent witchcraft already belonged to the past in many parts of Europe.[6]

Another indication of the clergy's attitude and behaviour towards witchcraft is provided by the minutes of church council meetings. Up till the end of the seventeenth century, and sometimes even later, the repression of counter-magical activities formed part of the wider programme of disciplining church members according to the Christian doctrine and way of life. The protectionary measures taken by church members themselves against maleficent witchcraft as well as their making use of the services of professional magical healers and fortune-tellers, were forbidden and punished. Offenders were punished by censuring them in front of the church council or during divine service, preventing them from attending the Lord's Supper for one or more times, or withholding an attestation from them when they wanted to move house. Papist superstitions were to be banished and quarrelling church members reconciled, since peaceful relations were considered to belong to a Christian way of life. The church council minute-books of an expanding city like Amsterdam show no marked differences in this respect to those of rural villages in Zeeland or in Overijssel. It is also becoming clear that there was a strict division of labour between the church and the magistrates. The church organisations did not personally punish professional healers and fortune-tellers, but only urged the magistrate to do so, should the case arise. The Dutch church councils performed nothing like the police function ascribed by C. Larner to the Scottish kirk sessions.[7]

A rather interesting example of joint handling of a case of slander connected with witchcraft is worth mentioning. It concerns an accusation of witchcraft against two sisters with regard to the death of two women. These events took place in or near the village of Hoek in Zeeland, in 1674.[8] The church council tried to reassure a group of worried church members, whose spokesman was the local surgeon. Could it be that this surgeon's remedies had failed, and that he had therefore resorted to witchcraft accusations? We will never be able to find out. Be that as it may, the suspected sisters, as well as their suspected mother and aunt, applied to the nearby court of Terneuzen for an act of purgation. None of the Hoek church members appeared in court to accuse them, and so the four women were given their act of purgation early in 1675. Although the members of the church council had never suspected the women of witchcraft, it proved to be rather difficult to get the dissenting church members to accept the verdict. The surgeon in particular refused to be reconciled even with the church council, let alone with the four acquitted women. It took four years, as well as the death of the minister, before the quarrelsome surgeon repented and life returned to normal.

Though much remains to be discovered and discussed regarding Dutch witchcraft, a few words should be devoted to a tentative examination of Dutch witchcraft material. As the European witchcraft debate has been focused on witch-trials, this subject will be further discussed. There are two main interrelated problems connected with the witch-trials in Europe: their geographical and chronological distribution, and, more particularly, the spreading of mass trials. The concentration of witch-trials in the sixteenth and seventeenth centuries, and the practically exclusive occurrence of mass witch-trials during the same period, require slightly different explanations. The formal structure of these explanations, however, can be identically expressed in terms of structural vulnerability, mobilisation and counter-mobilisation. The term *structural vulnerability* refers to preconditions or necessary conditions. Without their presence, no witch-trials could occur. But given their presence, some kind of mobilisation or trigger was necessary to start off witch-trials. Generally speaking, structural vulnerability to witch-trials contains two components: the component of witchcraft beliefs and practices, and the component of acts against witchcraft and suitable judicial procedures. Structural vulnerability to isolated witch-trials came into existence when acts against witchcraft were joined to traditional witchcraft beliefs and practices, whether or not combined with demonological elements, as found in the *Malleus*. If, in addition, these demonological versions of witchcraft had been gaining the upper hand, and the use of judicial inquisitorial procedures was accepted without or with less than the usual restrictions, then there existed a state of structural vulnerability to mass witch-trials as well. Of course, the existence of both kinds of structural vulnerability, as well as their absence, needs to be explained too. However, one should guard against all-embracing explanations in terms of a general crisis, fear or misogyny. Given a situation of structural vulnerability to isolated or mass witch-trials as well, some kind of mobilisation could bring about these trials. The initiative could rest with those who considered themselves to be direct victims of witchcraft, with their family, with the professional magical healers whose advice they had sought, with the magistrate, with professional witch-hunters, or with a combination of several of these categories. Counter-mobilisation and measures to increase a state of lessened structural vulnerability could function as a brake on the effects of mobilisation.

If we apply this explanatory scheme to the Dutch variant, it may be concluded that the Northern Netherlands, later the Republic, was structurally vulnerable to isolated trials of maleficent witchcraft from the fourteenth century until well into the seventeenth century, whereas the structural vulnerability to trials of non-harmful witchcraft continued to exist for three more centuries. Structural vulnerability to larger witch-trials seems to have been practically non-existent: on the whole, neither magistrates nor clergy appear to have been impressed or obsessed by demonological doctrines like the one constructed in the *Hammer of witches*. This cannot be explained as part of a general sceptical attitude, since many of them did not deny the possibility of maleficent witchcraft. Whatever explanation may be put forward in the future, it is clear that the idea of an heretical sect of mainly female witches, threatening human society and therefore having to be exterminated, found no fertile soil in the Northern Netherlands. Here, like elsewhere, most isolated accusations of maleficent witchcraft concerned women. On the other hand, the judicial aspect of structural vulnerability to larger witch-trials was present to a rather critical extent. *Ex officio* legal procedures, including torture in order to obtain confessions, were gaining ground over accusatorial procedures during the course of the sixteenth century. However, these procedures were mostly applied in a somewhat conscientious manner by magistrates who did not feel personally threatened by a formidable and diabolical sect of witches. Cautiousness in handling matters of evidence was typical of most Dutch magistrates. The simultaneous continuation of slander suits, instituted according to the accusatorial procedure, might be seen as another brake on judicial structural vulnerability to mass trials.

Still, as we have seen, a few larger witch-trials occurred, like those in the provinces of Groningen, Utrecht and North Brabant. The Groningen trials followed in the wake of witch-trials in nearby East Friesland: they might well have been inspired by them, especially since in both cases ideas about witches' organisations and nocturnal gatherings have been found. The rather de-centralised judicial organisation in those particular areas of Groningen left much scope for individual judicial functionaries to proceed one way or the other in cases of witchcraft. Therefore, these large trials can be said to have resulted from a temporary situation of structural vulnerability, in which some local judges were willing to find definite solutions to the witchcraft problem, once they were confronted with accusations by an injured party. Peelland, in North Brabant, also had a de-centralised judicial organisation, and demonological elements like the pact, copulation and the sabbath were expressed in abundance during the questionings at the 1595 trials. It is not clear how the magistrates became impressed by this demonological doctrine. The larger Utrecht trials in 1595 are even more problematic. Here, a central court was concerned, but very little is known about the ideas of its members.

The Dutch variant is not exceptional in its relatively low intensity of witch-trials; it shares this characteristic to a certain extent with England. The exceptionally high figure of about 80 executions in the English county of Essex (1560-1645) gives an indication of this.[9] The population of Essex at that time was 100,000 inhabitants, compared to about one million in 1500 and one and a half million in 1600 in the Northern Netherlands, where less than 150 executions took place, not counting those in Limburg. In England, a relative lack of demonological witchcraft ideas was combined with accusatorial legal procedures, torture not being permitted. It was only during the period of disruption of local government and justice caused by the Civil War that the witch-hunters M. Hopkins and J. Stearne were able to turn Essex in 1645 into a state of structural vulnerability to mass witch-trials. Continental demonological ideas were then introduced, together with legal procedures like pricking, the water-ordeal and various forms of near-torture. In Flanders and the Walloon provinces, a total of at least 250 burnings took place before 1684. Denmark, Norway and Sweden had more executions: in Denmark, about the same number of executions (approximately 1,000) took place as in Scotland, whose population was almost double that of the former. Germany, Switzerland, France and Luxemburg produced much higher figures *per capita*. In Italy and Spain, where the Inquisition was in charge of judicial inquiries into witchcraft, the number of executions remained lower and ceased altogether *circa* 1620. The Spanish and Italian inquisitions are known not to have been impressed by demonological witchcraft ideas, and to have employed a high standard regarding the acceptability of proofs of witchcraft.[10]

The Dutch variant becomes more exceptional if the early ending of trials for maleficent witchcraft is taken into account. This was not due to changes in structural vulnerability. Maleficent witchcraft remained punishable by law, and continued to play a part in the lives of many people. The early cessation of witch-trials and executions - which made a significant contribution to the score of low intensity - is partly due to the absence of central exhortations to prosecute witchcraft, and to the absence of a rigid reformational or counter-reformational climate. Where these elements were present, as in parts of Limburg, or in France and Scotland, [11] there was more likelihood of continuing prosecutions. The political developments during the first decades of the Dutch

Revolt, and the resulting perpetuation of local and regional autonomy, as well as the religious pluriformity of the day paved the way for the early ending of the Dutch burnings. The fact that they stopped was mainly due to the limited receptiveness of learned circles and magistrates to demonological witchcraft theories, in combination with the growing reluctance of magistrates to accept confessions and other data as proofs of witchcraft. It is not yet apparent to what extent this critical attitude can be considered as an aspect or result of the early development of the medical and natural sciences in the Republic.[12] It is extremely doubtful, however, that we could gain by suggesting that witch-trials were no longer 'necessary' in the Republic because of the relatively high standard of living and education, the preponderance of cities over countryside, and the advantages of an open urban culture.[13] Apart from the dubious explanatory effect of functionalist reasoning that witch-trials were 'necessary', performed indispensable functions, and stopped when there was no more 'need' of them, we are confronted with the problem of how to demonstrate possible connections between the above-mentioned developments and the progress of the witch-trials. For pointing out correlations is merely the first step toward interpretations.

There still remains the question of the overrepresentation of women in the trials for maleficent witchcraft. Apparently we are confronted with a paradox: approximately 90 to 95 per cent of the Dutch trials for maleficent witchcraft concerned women, which is an even higher percentage than in most other parts of Europe. On the other hand, trials and burnings in the Netherlands were fewer than in any other country, and they ended earlier. Some historians have been inclined to interpret witch-hunting or witch-trials as woman-hunting. The reason why women were prosecuted should, according to them, automatically include the reason why there were prosecutions for witchcraft. Other historians have rightly objected to this view, however, because it neglects the prosecution of about 20 per cent of males in the European witch-trials. Larner preferred to describe witchcraft as sex-related rather than sex-specific, which means that there was no direct relationship between witch-hunting and woman-hunting.[14]

This still leaves us with the problem of the overrepresentation of women in witch-trials. This question can only be answered in a general way by referring to the stereotype of witchcraft, which, according to N. Cohn and C. Larner, was directly related to women: witches were considered to be women. This centuries-old popular witchcraft stereotype was to be incorporated into the learned and demonological stereotype from the end of the fifteenth century onwards.[15] However, one should bear in mind that there have been less uniformly women-centred witchcraft stereotypes, either popular or learned. The case of Finland illustrates the need for differentiation rather well.[16] Here we find a combination of a popular male witch, or rather magician stereotype, and a comparatively late introduction of demonological witchcraft doctrines in parts of the country. Women were only prosecuted on a large scale after the introduction of ideas on witchcraft as expressed in the *Malleus maleficarum*, but even then the number was never greater than about 60 per cent. For the rest, mostly professional male magicians and their clients were prosecuted.

The Dutch case also poses some problems as to the presence of a women-centred popular witchcraft stereotype. On the one hand, we are confronted with the overrepresentation of women in the trials for maleficent witchcraft. Was this overrepresentation due to the existence of a popular female witch stereotype, or could it be that the pattern of the witch-trials does not reflect the whole pattern of witchcraft accusations? If we assume that women had fewer chances of defence than men - which still has to be proved - and were therefore more likely to be involved in trials of maleficent witchcraft, then the existence of a popular female witch stereotype cannot be taken for granted. It should also be borne in mind that a greater involvement of women in matters of illness and death - the misfortunes most frequently ascribed to witchcraft - might have resulted in a larger number of accusations being made against them. On the other hand, seventeenth-century witchcraft accusations in the Dutch provinces of Overijssel and Drenthe show no distinct sex division: both men and women were called witches by members of both sexes - though men more by men and women more by women - thereby referring to their supposed bewitchments, their powers to bewitch, or merely to their being disagreeable.

It is obvious that more specific answers to the problem of female overrepresentation are only to be expected if more specific questions are posed. One should examine the existence of witchcraft stereotypes: whether women and men were associated with different types of witchcraft, both at a popular and a learned level. Which view was held by the magistrates who performed the interrogations? Were they convinced that witchcraft was based on the Devil's pact, and if so, on which definition of a pact (either the traditional theological view of a pact as an agreement related to a system of signs, or the demonological doctrine described in the *Malleus* of a formal pact sealed by copulation)? One should also look into the possibly divergent chances of defence between men and women. It is even more important to consider the position of women compared to that of men in various social groupings and contexts, especially regarding their concern with health and healing - whether magical or not - and the care of their family and animals. Would it not be plausible to suggest that, given a belief in the possibility of bewitchments, those who were most concerned with these matters ran more risk of being suspected of witchcraft if anything went wrong? This could also help to explain the inverse relationship between the percentage of female witches and the number of trials for maleficent witchcraft in the Northern Netherlands. The Dutch variant, with its few trials and burnings, its early cessation of the same, and a very high percentage of women accused of maleficent witchcraft, is not a paradox after all.

This brings me to my final remarks: Dutch witchcraft research is well on its way to broadening the conventional horizon of witch-trials. This research not only draws attention to the problem of the absence or low intensity of witch-trials, but also explicitly considers trials for maleficent witchcraft as part of the total judicial witchcraft policy. The local witchcraft scene is stressed as a *conditio sine qua non,* and the attitude and behaviour of church authorities towards witchcraft, as well as their relationship with the magistrates in these matters, are viewed as relevant dimensions for the interpretation of witch-trials. However, witchcraft research is no longer restricted to the problems of witch-trials. The function of witchcraft in local communities and the witchcraft theories of various social groupings, including their mutual influence, occupy an important place in Dutch witchcraft research. This approach to witchcraft, both during and after the period of the trials, proves to be very fruitful: witchcraft sheds light on the ways in which people thought, behaved and lived together. That may well be its essential charm.

Notes

1. Jacobus Scheltema, *Geschiedenis der heksenprocessen: eene bijdrage tot den roem des vaderlands* (Vincent Loosjes, Haarlem, 1828).

2. In 1982 the Dutch interdisciplinary study group 'Witchcraft and sorcery in the Netherlands' was set up. More than half of its 30 participants have contributed articles to a new survey on Dutch witchcraft and witch-trials: Marijke Gijswijt-Hofstra, Willem Frijhoff (eds), *Nederland betoverd: toverij en hekserij van de veertiende tot in de twintigste eeuw* (De Bataafsche Leeuw, Amsterdam, 1987). An earlier publication by the study group is: Willem de Blécourt, Marijke Gijswijt-Hofstra (eds), *Kwade mensen: toverij in Nederland,* special number of Volkskundig Bulletin, 12, 1 (1986). An annotated bibliography of witchcraft and sorcery in the Netherlands will be published *c.* December 1987. Several doctoral dissertations on Dutch witchcraft are being prepared as well. An English version of *Nederland betoverd* is planned for 1988.

3. See the list of Dutch witch-trials in Gijswijt-Hofstra, Frijhoff (eds), *Nederland betoverd,* the various contributions to this book, and also De Blécourt, Gijswijt-Hofstra (eds), *Kwade mensen.*

4. R. Fruin, 'Het geloof in wonderen' in *Robert Fruin's verspreide geschriften,* X (Martinus Nijhoff, 's-Gravenhage, 1905), pp. 1-38; J. Huizinga, 'Nederland's beschaving in de zeventiende eeuw' in *Verzamelde werken,* II (M.D. Tjeenk Willink en Zn, Haarlem, 1948), pp. 412-507; J. Huizinga, 'Erasmus' in *Verzamelde werken,* VI (M.D. Tjeenk Willink en Zn, Haarlem, 1950), pp. 179-274; H.R. Trevor-Roper, *The European witch-craze of the 16th and 17th centuries* (Penguin Books, Harmondsworth, 1969), pp. 98-9.

5. G. Voetius, *Selectarum disputationum theologicarum,* III (Utrecht, 1659), p. 612.

6. Balthasar Bekker, *De betoverde weereld* (Amsterdam, 1691-3).

7. Christina Larner, *Enemies of God: the witch-hunt in Scotland* (Chatto & Windus, London, 1981).

8. Marijke Gijswijt-Hofstra, 'Toverij in Zeeland, een status quaestionis' in De Blécourt, Gijswijt-Hofstra (eds), *Kwade mensen,* pp. 107-51.

9. Alan Macfarlane, *Witchcraft in Tudor and Stuart England* (Routledge & Kegan Paul, London, 1970), pp. 61-3.

10. See for Flanders and the Walloon provinces: F. Vanhemelryck, *Heksenprocessen in de Nederlanden* (Davidsfonds, Leuven, 1982); F. Vanhemelryck, 'Bijdrage tot de studie van de heksenwaan in de zuidelijke Nederlanden van de XVde tot de XVIIde eeuw', *Volkskunde,* 82 (1981), pp. 31-41. For Denmark, Norway and Sweden: Jens Christian V. Johansen, 'Als die Fischer den Teufel ins Netz bekamen... Eine Analyse der Zeugenaussagen aus Städten und Landbezirken in den jütischen Zaubereiprozessen

des 17. Jahrhunderts' in Christian Degn, Hartmut Lehmann, Dagmar Unverhau (eds), *Hexenprozesse: deutsche und skandinavische Beiträge* (Karl Wachholtz Verlag, Neumünster, 1983), pp. 159-66; Gustav Henningsen, 'Hexenverfolgung und Hexenprozesse in Dänemark' in Degn, Lehmann, Unverhau (eds), *Hexenprozesse*, pp. 143-9; Brian P. Levack, *The witch-hunt in early modern Europe* (Longman, London and New York), 1987, p. 188.

For Germany, Switzerland, France and Luxemburg respectively: G. Schormann, *Hexenprozesse in Deutschland* (Vandenhoeck & Ruprecht, Göttingen, 1981); E. William Monter, *Witchcraft in France and Switzerland: the borderlands during the Reformation* (Cornell University Press, Ithaca and London, 1976); Robert Muchembled, 'Sorcières du Cambrésis: l'acculturation du monde rural aux XVIe et XVIIe siècles' in Marie-Sylvie Dupont-Bouchat, Willem Frijhoff, Robert Muchembled (eds), *Prophètes et sorciers dans les Pays-Bas XVIe-XVIIIe siècle* (Hachette, Paris, 1978), pp. 155-261; Marie-Sylvie Dupont-Bouchat, 'La répression de la sorcellerie dans le duché de Luxembourg aux XVIe et XVIIe siècles' in Dupont-Bouchat, Frijhoff, Muchembled (eds), *Prophètes et sorciers*, pp. 41-154.

For Italy and Spain: Gustav Henningsen, *The witches' advocate: Basque witchcraft and the Spanish Inquisition (1609-1614)* (University of Nevada Press, Reno, 1980); Levack, *The witch-hunt*, pp. 201-6.

11. Muchembled, 'Sorcières du Cambrésis' and Larner, *Enemies of God*.

12. Willem Frijhoff, 'Kerk en heks: troebel water', *Archief voor de geschiedenis van de katholieke kerk in Nederland*, 25 (1983), pp. 100-16; 115.

13. I. Schöffer, 'Heksengeloof en heksenvervolging: een historiografisch overzicht', *Tijdschrift voor geschiedenis*, 86 (1973), pp. 215-35, 234.

14. Larner, *Enemies of God*, p. 92.

15. Norman Cohn, *Europe's inner demons: an enquiry inspired by the great witch-hunt* (London, Chatto Heinemann, 1975); Larner, *Enemies of God*, pp. 92-4.

16. Timo Kervinen, 'Observations on witch trials in the 16th and 17th century (Finland)', paper for symposium: *Witchcraft, sorcery and crime in early modern Europe*, Stockholm 30 August - 2 September 1984.

Lydia Sklevicky

Emancipated integration or integrated emancipation: the case of post-revolutionary Yugoslavia

The idea that the issue of women's emancipation was once and for all taken care of by the safe hands of the revolutionary government and administration, after its consolidation of power in 1945, is a commonplace in any mainstream reflection on the position of women in post-revolutionary Yugoslavia. The repudiation of the women's movement's complex history in the inter-war period, which has been pushed into oblivion and become inaccessible to new generations, only encouraged the idea that the socialist development era was the starting point for the liberation of Yugoslav women.[1] It was only the development of feminist perspectives during the mid-1970s[2] that has prompted its questioning. The considerable lack of women's historical consciousness was a natural consequence of the absence of historiographic tradition to draw upon when researching past activities of women in general, let alone when dealing with their struggle for emancipation.[3] Anyone who wants to study the organised activities of women in the post-revolutionary social context, whether to explore these activities from the point of view of their emancipatory goals and potentials, or merely to analyse the profound changes in the role of women in various dimensions of social life, is in danger of missing the point by ignoring its history.

The Anti-Fascist Women's Front (AWF), the official and sole existing organisation of women in Yugoslavia after the revolution, was instituted in 1942, but it was in operation right from the beginning of the armed resistance (1941). It was established on the initiative of the Communist Party (CP), but its membership included the broadest possible selection of women. In this manner it could claim the exclusive heritage of the complex and controversial development of the pre-war women's movements. Even though the claims of the vocal and articulate autonomous pre-war bourgeois feminist movement did not diverge essentially from those of the so-called proletarian (i.e. communist-inspired) one, the main difference - apart from the autonomous character of the former, and the espousal of the model of a classical affiliated organisation by the latter - was that its critique of the system aimed at improving it and not overthrowing it. This explains the label 'conservative' attached to the bourgeois feminist movements, as well as the irreconcilable animosity of the CP's ideology and its activists towards any mention of the term feminism. The autonomous women's movement, aware of its inability to cope with the imminent threat of war, dissolved quietly during 1940. The women of the proletarian women's movement, accustomed to a life of danger, harassment and secret operations,[4] were well prepared for the events to come. They formed the core force of the AWF, mobilising women from all social strata (but mostly peasants) for the resistance and revolution.

During the first years of the Second World War, the AWF enjoyed a considerable degree of autonomy in relation to the National Liberation Movement (NLM) and the People's Government (PG), established on the territory liberated by the partisan forces. It had a rather steep hierarchical structure of its own; there was a sense of identification with the organisation by its members; the emancipatory goals as a relevant type of motivation were stressed, etc. The AWF underwent its first reorganisation in 1944, when this autonomy, relative in regard to war-time circumstances, was replaced by its immersion into the monolithic structure of the NLM (it became subordinated to the People's Government bodies).[5]

After the war, in the period of the consolidation of revolutionary changes, the AWF was seen as an important vehicle for organising women. The new state was building a strong and centralised structure of government, emulating the USSR model while at the same time retaining the rhetoric of the movement, i.e. relying upon the Popular Front (PF) tradition - a coalition made up of various different political and interest groupings. In a centralised type of government, the function of this rhetoric was to transmit influence and gain the widest popular support by means of organisations. The AWF happened to be the largest of such organisations, appealing to more than half the population.

The problem I want to discuss in this article is to what extent the way in which the AWF was conceived, and in which it functioned after the liberation, was instrumental in carrying out the emancipation of women as a long-term social process and one of the top priorities in the ideology of the socialist revolution. What organisational and institutional resources or options were available to women themselves to articulate the meaning and formulate the strategies of the liberation from their specific, gender-related oppression? By reconstructing the constant shifts in the organisational model of the AWF (1945-53) as they were formulated in response to its organisational environment, mainly the revolutionary government and the CP as the leading social force behind it, I wanted to establish the degree of autonomy the AWF disposed of when formulating the strategies, tactics and execution of the emancipatory process. Did the AWF's organisational schemes provide it with sufficient resources and power for such a task in a war-ravaged, underdeveloped country with a deeply rooted patriarchal culture - political culture being a part of it - with 70 per cent of the population still living in rural areas, and a heavily stressed trend towards the industrialisation of the country?

The sources I based my research upon consist of the archival material of the Croatia AWF's proceedings (conferences, consultations, activities, directives, etc.),[6] which present almost 'virgin' material since it has not as yet been catalogued or worked on. Since I wanted to reconstruct the organisation's structure as objectively as possible, omitting the passions, desires and wishful thinking of the women who participated in it, I refrained from collecting supporting evidence from possible oral history sources. In this phase of my research I did not interview any of the AWF functionaries and members. It is a sober starting-point for my continuing monographic research with regard to my previous experiences in writing about the AWF during the Second World War. Most of the women participants, usually the ones who were the high-ranking members of the organisation and still held considerable positions of power afterwards, are eager to present their own experiences, visions and memories as the only true version. Further stages of my research will, of course, have to try to take into account these different visions, based on oral history from the participants - women from different levels within the AWF's hierarchy - allowing them to voice their own very personal idiosyncrasies.

Having started my research with no analytical work to draw upon, I read all the documents available, classifying them according to their relevance and potential to: (a) reconstruct certain aspects of the problem, e.g. the modification of the organisational model and its correlation to the priorities as expressed in this article, or the changes in the interpersonal dynamics of the AWF activists, the attitudes towards the 'socialist' family, etc.; (b) explain the course of events (i.e. why a certain option was preferable to others).

I feel justified in generalising my findings by using material from Croatia's AWF archives because the organisation's policy was formulated by the AWF's Federal Central Council in Belgrade, whose guidelines were followed or implemented by all the republican AWF organisations. Consequently, the archival collection of the AWF of Croatia contains all these guidelines, the exchanges on the federal-republican level, and the minutes of all the meetings held in Belgrade by the Yugoslav AWF.

In my reading of the archival documents, I also tried to be sensitive to the changes of discourse used - the discourse theory, in effect, proposes that the way we speak and write reflects the structure of power in society. The archival documents I have consulted provide information for the researcher on two levels: the first one is the discourse of the political and organisational directives, pamphlets, public manifestos and women's press,[7] sent from high-ranking councils to low-ranking ones, and using a type of *agit-prop* language. Amongst other things, it anticipates the possible future existence of a community of equals as a real entity. The revolutionary optimism, the faith in victory and expression of powerful emotions, such as revolutionary zeal and fervent belief in the immediate achievement of a just society, are directed towards mobilisation of members for action. The obligatory smiling women, agricultural or factory workers, who spared no effort to overturn the production norms, or the message of a little girl in folk costume to the readers of *Woman in Struggle* (October 1945) in childish handwriting: 'Mummy, vote for Tito and the Republic for a better and brighter children's future', illustrate some of the imagery used to support it.

The second one is a critical and informative discourse which can be found in the reports sent by low-ranking councils to the high-ranking ones, as well as in the discussions of the women delegates at different AWF conferences or briefings. It is characterised by critical judgements, sobriety, realistic assessment of concrete situations, and self-critique, as well as an accurate perception and articulation of specific manifestations of discriminatory practices against women. As examples I could quote the analyses and often semi-classified information on teenage prostitution, ghastly conditions in maternity wards, destitute and homeless orphans, the laying-off of pregnant women workers, etc.

These two types of discourse are almost constantly interwoven. The former is the projection of desires, ideals and ideology which can still be found in the written reminiscences of former participants, and is directed from the AWF's inner circle to the broader membership and the general public. The latter is an expression of a lucid, even feminist (in the sense of women-centred) perception. However, its public articulation is confined solely to the higher-ranking members, who are firmly embedded in the power structure of the establishment.

In the immediate post-war period (1945-6), the government set a number of tasks which 'all women' had to carry out by mediation of the AWF. These were the following:

- the support of the People's Government, including the struggle against the black market, illegal price-increases, etc.;
- the fight against illiteracy, organising all kinds of vocational training, mainly for more skilled tasks in industrial work and for the improvement of agricultural production, as well as courses in domestic science, etc., in order to integrate women into the workforce;
- organising help for working mothers (crèches, kindergartens, etc.);
- improving health care for women, such as building maternity wards;
- assisting the Unions in the organisation of women workers.

However, in the words of one of Croatia's AWF leaders: 'The AWF has no specific tasks of its own, but as a part of the Popular Front it should co-operate closely with the People's Government.'[8] This shows reluctance to assess the relevance, if not the primacy, of the women-centred tasks listed. It is evident that the ambiguous attitude by the government towards the status of the AWF ('broader' social goals versus women-centred ones) resulted in an obvious contradiction, echoed in the following statement by Anka Berus, the only female government member in Croatia, who was Minister of Finance and honorary official of the organisation: 'The AWF's organisations have no separate guide-lines, but nevertheless they ought to have an organisational structure which is solid enough to ensure the participation of each single woman in the people's efforts and the people's endeavour.'[9]

The new socialist woman the AWF was supposed to educate was a composite of a humble and self-sacrificing worker, a mother and a political subject participating in meetings and voluntary work until the small hours of the morning, clearing away the debris, building new houses, etc.; tender but without showing sentimentality, demonstrating her femininity by deed (caring for wounded soldiers, orphans, her own children), but not by a frivolous appearance (I have been told of occasions when young women were expelled from the CP merely because they were wearing lipstick).[10]

I labelled the organisational structure of the AWF, which had been conceived to meet the tasks formulated by the PG, the organising and educational model. It is 'educational' in the sense that, during the period of the consolidation of revolutionary changes in society, the explicit stress was on teaching women of all social strata to accept these changes.

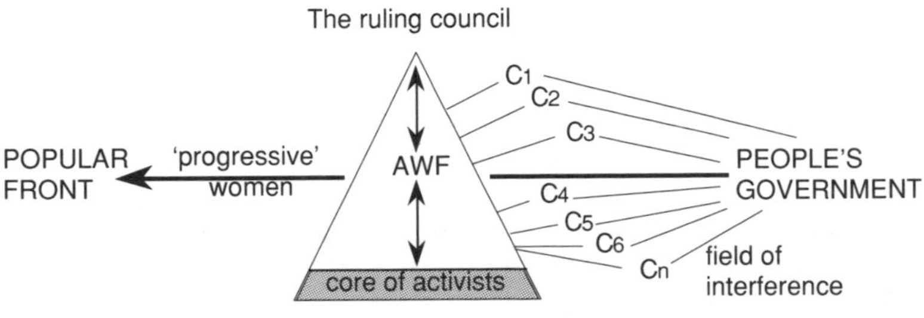

Figure 1: The organising and educational model of the AWF (1945-8)

As can be seen, the organisational structure of the AWF was hierarchical: each of its levels was represented by its own council, the lower ones (village, city) having a broader base consisting of ordinary members, whereas the higher ones (county, region) were composed of delegates, all of them united by the republic's council and consequently by the federal council. While most council members at lower hierarchical levels were volunteers, each council had a paid professional to do the paperwork and to receive and administer directives from the higher-ranking ones. The republican and federal councils had a varying number of such professionals, usually heading the existing committees, whose number also varied according to the top priorities of the moment.

The fact that it is possible to make a diagram of the organisation's structure as a rather steep pyramid with a broad base and an identifiable top, indicates, in terms of the sociology of organisations, a certain degree of intra-organisational autonomy, thus guaranteeing a possibility of articulating other goals besides the ones entrusted to it by the PG. The existence of such a possibility is also indicated by the fact that there were two lines of communication: a vertical one and a horizontal one. The former operated in two directions, from the lower levels to the higher ones and vice versa, and the latter permeated the whole structure through the *agit-prop* committee and its instruments - the AWF's official organ *Woman in Struggle*, pamphlets, a women's radio programme and a women's bookshop in Zagreb's main square.

The ambivalent character of the organisation's status is clearly exemplified by the fact that 'progressive' women were immediately told to join the People's Front, since they were regarded as already educated in political terms, while the 'not-so-progressive' women - those insufficiently socialised (indifferent, frightened, or even hostile) for revolutionary purposes - remained within the organisation and joined various committees (C): for social welfare and health, education, economy, *agit-prop*, etc., whose tasks were formulated by the People's Government.

This model functioned fairly efficiently during the early post-war period, and the women devoted much time and energy to a great variety of social work and the reconstruction of the country. Nevertheless, in spite of the obvious enthusiasm and collective sacrifice of its members, it was often emphasised by the AWF leadership that 'all these activities are not sufficiently exploited to raise political consciousness',[11] i.e. the degree of identification with the revolutionary policies was considered insufficient.

The forces of social regulation (the PF, PG and CP), which were expected to back the AWF's educational function, were often criticised by AWF activists and functionaries. The CP was reproached for putting the 'worst people available' at the disposal of the AWF and for regarding the AWF as a mere supplier of physical labour and different public services. However, the fact that female CP members or leaders were criticised for disparaging any work concerning the 'woman question' and the AWF is particularly suggestive. It reflects a deeply-rooted attitude characteristic of the rather low position the 'woman question' has held within the hierarchy of social priority goals in Yugoslavia up till now.[12] The PG and the PF were upbraided for not taking into account the specific role and tasks of the AWF, for ignoring its problems during their meetings, and for not having more women in leading positions in their ranks. An often repeated grievance concerned the discrepancy in private and public behaviour:

> 'Many comrades, leaders of the PF, army officers and leaders of the PG don't encourage or even allow their wives to participate in the activities of the PF or AWF. This is a frequent occurrence, thus making the functioning of the AWF among the people extremely difficult.'[13]

Soon a gradual slackening of AWF activity was noted: in Croatia alone, the organisation ceased to exist in 1,500 villages (as opposed to the war period), so that in 1947 Cana Babović, President of the Yugoslav AWF, expressed her dissatisfaction:

> 'It has been noted in all republics that work done by women is in most cases sporadic and carried out through some short-lived campaigns... The AWF has not succeeded in mobilising women *en masse* to participate in the current political, social and economic life of this country. Another point is that we do not have anything special, anything specific, any problem that we as women should strive to solve.'[14]

In 1948 the conditions in the AWF were judged as 'disorderly' by the CP and PG, which, in connection with the political trauma brought about by Yugoslavia's break with Stalin, resulted in an attempt to re-define the organisation. For the first time the stress was overtly on the ideological indoctrination of women. As Vida Tomšič,[15] the new federal AWF President put it, the task of the AWF was to educate women 'in the spirit of socialism' - the Yugoslav as opposed to the Soviet brand - 'not the dreary bureaucratic socialism which actually sets limits to every aspect of life'.[16] She explained that the re-defined AWF should not be perceived as the kind of firm organisation where the vertical link is the primary one (meaning that she criticised the degree of autonomy that the AWF had disposed of). Instead, the AWF was 'our Party's organisational form for work among women' and consequently 'every Party directive is its directive as well, and the political work of the Popular Front is present in the AWF, and as far as that is concerned there are no specific directives'.[17]

With regard to this definition, we will now deal with the following model of the AWF, which I have called the model of transmission of directives and mobilisation.

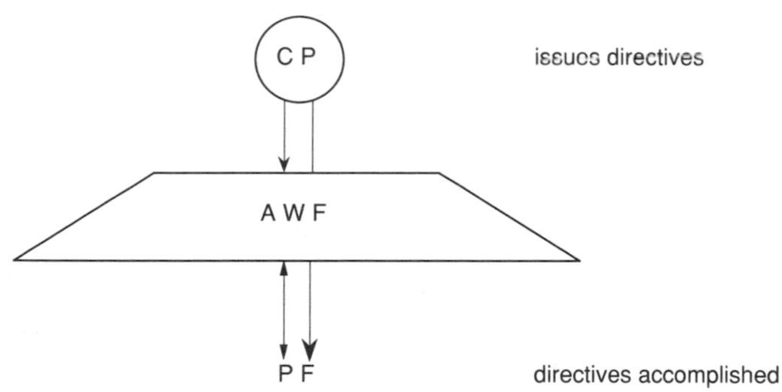

Figure 2: Model of transmission of directives and mobilisation (1948-9)

One of the directives thus transmitted was the anti-Soviet propaganda, which became one of the AWF's most important ideological issues in this period, and as such was applicable to the image of the *new* 'new woman':

> 'We can see in the Russian newspapers how badly dressed all the women are there, which is presented as being necessary for socialism. But this denies everything we are looking for - beauty,

joy and diversity. It is necessary to teach women how to dress attractively, how to run their households, and how to do it quickly.'[18]

Vida Tomšič's words present an image of 'enlightened femininity' (good looks *and* efficient homemaking), combined with the proclaimed new roles of worker and political activist, which was probably typical of one aspect of Yugoslav socialist development.

Notwithstanding constant achievements of the AWF, especially as a lobby and an agent of formulating and carrying out the social policy tasks aimed at improving the standard of living of women and children (health care, education, development of social services, etc.) in the postwar period,[19] a letter sent to the AWF in 1950 by the Central Committee of the Yugoslav CP expressed doubts about the organisation's potential and identity, and a certain dissatisfaction with its performance. Once again it proposed, or rather imposed, a reorganisation of the AWF. The first suggested step was the complete de-professionalisation of the organisational apparatus. The rationale was that the existence of professional functionaries was seen to be an obstacle to the functioning of a mass organisation.Therefore, all the AWF's professional staff were dismissed: some were re-directed to the PF councils dealing principally with issues such as social welfare and health, and some of them to lower government positions. The measure of de-professionalisation might indeed be viewed as a serious attempt to moderate the increasingly bureaucratic system of the AWF, as if its rigidity was personified by its professional functionaries. All the AWF work became voluntary, and it ceased to be even nominally an autonomous organisation. Through its organisational status, it became an elective committee of the PF, i.e. its members were elected 'among the people' within the territory of the respective basic units of the PF.

The immediate result of this kind of reorganisation was that 'among the people' it was interpreted as the abolition of the AWF. Due to this misunderstanding, most of the AWF work concerning women-centred issues ceased, and as far as PF policies were concerned, women were not asked to contribute. As the only possible response to this development, Vida Tomšič attempted to salvage what she could. To make the AWF operational at all, she claimed that an even stronger vertical line was needed[20] for the specifically women-centred tasks, thus contradicting her former plea for the primacy of the horizontal link. The result was a transformation of the AWF's organisational structure in two successive phases, both of which illustrate blatantly the overall confusion and the desire to achieve the impossible - on the one hand to retain the hierarchy (horizontal link), which would ensure the organisation's functioning, and on the other hand to abolish it by immersing it into the PF as a response to the general party-line. The final product had a somewhat oxymoronic appearance:

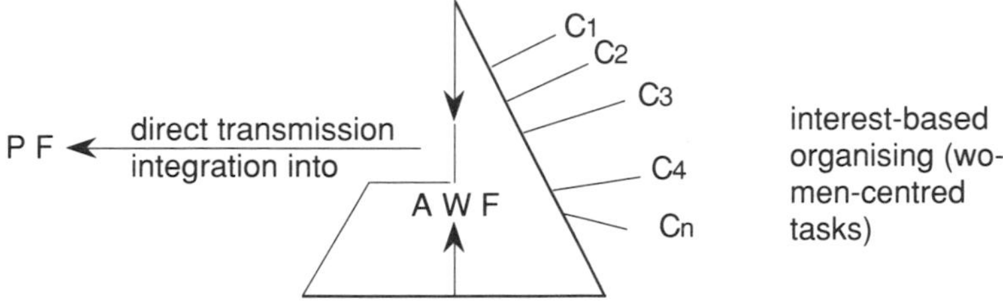

Figure 3: The dualistic model of the transitional phase (1950-3): first phase (schizophrenic structure)

As can be seen, various committees attempted to deal with women-related tasks as before, while at the same time they were supposed to give unconditional support to the policies of the PF.

This obvious contradiction was resolved to some extent after the Third Congress of the Yugoslav AWF (October 1950), when it was decided that the organisation as a whole was to be integrated into the PF as a committee of its respective council. This meant that women were to become members of the PF without any mediation of their organisation, that what was left of the AWF had no vertical line whatsoever, and that there were no possibilities left for gathering or organising women on a grass-roots level. At that point, the AWF dissolved in a number of small and mutually unrelated units, called 'actives', and integrated into the PF on respective hierarchical levels.

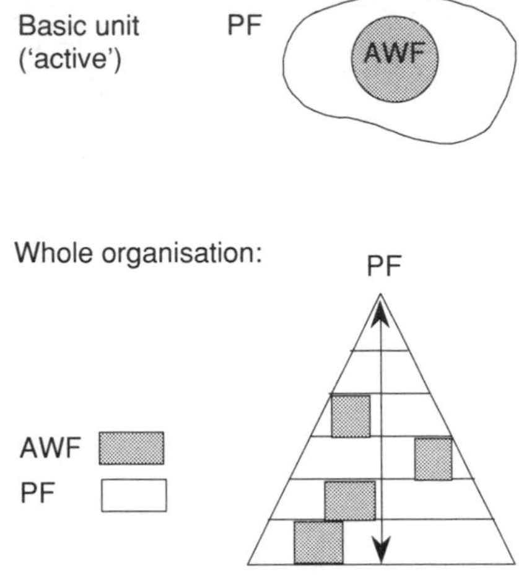

Figure 4: The dualistic model of the transitional phase (1950-3): second phase

The focal point of the AWF's 'independent work', its 'actives', as stated in the Resolution of the Third Congress, was the protection of mother and infant, providing help for working mothers,[21] and collaboration with the PG and other mass organisations for the purpose of mobilising women to participate fully in economic and political life. The main conclusion of the Resolution was that the mass organisation had to be transformed into 'the instrument of the people for its own education as well as a place for people's political and cultural edification, where the greatest opportunities will be available for the development of initiatives and for the criticism of negative tendencies'.[22]

The changes in the image of the 'socialist woman' were never made explicitly. Implicitly they could be seen in the increased attention given to the traditionally 'feminine' issues in the AWF's organ *Woman in Struggle*, from the beginning of the 1950s onwards: family, housekeeping, fashion, popular medicine, entertainment, cultural life, etc. The 'serious' subjects, i.e. general political themes, gradually faded away. The image of the ascetic combatant-cum-worker-cum-political activist was gradually and silently being abandoned. However, the abolition of the minimum of organisational prerogatives incapacitated any collective action by women themselves. The final result was the changing of the mass organisation, however rigid and inefficient it may have been in certain areas, into an amorphous organisation - a contradiction in terms.

What it was like to be in a situation in which many different categories of women faced serious problems, and in which women as a social group experienced explicit disadvantages in their professional and political life,[23] is a purely rhetorical question. The critical and informative discourse of the AWF shows an acute awareness of pressing problems such as: the tendency to lay off pregnant women and single mothers; the harassment of children born out of wedlock; the desperate conditions of 'children's homes' (orphanages); the dissatisfaction of women in the labour force (jobs which were too strenuous, complete equalisation of work norms for men and women doing manual work, and other conditions which forced women to leave their employment); battered wives; the exploitation of women within marriage; adolescent prostitution, etc. In the last analysis, it meant the denial of any possibility of either an autonomous articulation of interests, or a grass-roots activism and a publicly articulated female solidarity.

The conclusion I propound here is that the total integration of the emancipatory process into the 'ideological apparatus of the state'[24] meant that emancipation became something 'practised' on women, as inarticulate objects of the social-political process, instead of making them its legitimate subject.

The approach I used, which is an interpretation of the nature of the emancipatory process in post-war Yugoslavia, has some inherent limitations. Firstly, I am aware that this process is multi-dimensional, and that its scope is limited by its own two basic co-ordinates:

1. the political emancipation of women: securing equal rights and acquiring a political power-base by means of the women's organisation as a place of interest articulation;
2. women's cultural emancipation: fighting the limits set by ascribed gender roles, and radically questioning the patriarchal culture as a whole.

My efforts to decipher the confusing (and confused) discourse of the AWF's self-comprehension, by condensing it into the proposed organisational models, provides a basis for an understanding of the erroneous methods of the first aspect of the emancipatory process. I tried to meet that requirement by being sensitive to the shifts of discourse from the populist one in the immediate post-revolutionary period, to a more opaque and redundant one as the political system became more articulated during the early 1950s.

Cultural emancipation, with its inherent subtleties and complexities, might possibly require a different approach. However, it is quite obvious that for a considerable number of women, especially the ones with no previous experience in taking a public stand, the young ones and the peasants, freed from the burden of paternal authority, taking part in the activities of the AWF was certainly an emancipatory experience. But the so-called progressive women (those who were politically conscious and in favour of the revolution) were constantly showing signs of divided loyalties by supporting organisational schemes dictated by 'broader' and 'more relevant' political needs, at the evident expense of the AWF and women in general. This can be explained by the actual situation in a poor country devastated by a cruel and bloody war whose victors worked hard to make a utopian dream of a socialist society come true.

But the dissenting voices of the AWF's rank and file members at its Fourth Congress (1953), which were raised in bitter disappointment at its complete extinction (even its name perished), give us a hint that through the agency of the AWF, Yugoslavian women's cultural emancipation has been furthered. Before committing ourselves to a final judgement about this period of women's history in Yugoslavia, we should be aware that time is still running its course.

Notes

1. L. Sklevicky, 'Konji, zene, ratovi, itd.: problem utemeljenja historije žena u Jugoslaviji' in L. Sklevicky (ed.), *Kultiviranje dijaloga: Zena i društvo* (Biblioteka Revije za sociologiju, Zagreb, 1987).

2. Slavenka Drakulić-Ilić, '"Six mortal sins" of Yugoslav feminism' in R. Morgan (ed.), *Sisterhood is global* (Anchor Press/Doubleday, New York, 1984), pp. 736-8.

3. For example, in spite of the lip-service rendered to the prominence of the role the AWF (Anti-Fascist Women's Front) played in the NLM (National Liberation Movement), a monograph on the organisation's war-time development (1942-5) was not available for almost 40 years

afterwards. Also, the existence of the so-called bourgeois women's movements which were active before the Second World War has been virtually ignored.

4. The Yugoslav CP was illegal during most of its pre-war existence.

5. L. Sklevicky, 'Organizirana djelatnost zena Hrvatske za vrijeme narodnooslobodilaćke borbe 1941-1945', *Povijesni prilozi*, Zagreb, 3 (1984), pp. 83-127.

6. This collection is kept in the Archives of the Institute for the History of the Workers' Movement of Croatia in Zagreb (AIHRPH), under the code KZDAZH.

7. The AWF edited a number of local and regional newsletters during the NLM period, and its central organ, the magazine *Zena u borbi* (Woman in Struggle) has continued to be published ever since (in 1958 the title was changed and it became simply *Zena*, and from 1967 onward it has been edited in the form of a scholarly bi-monthly magazine).

8. Milka Vranešević, 'On the forms of the Anti-Fascist Women's Front and of its organisation', speech, 1946, AIHRPH, KZDAZH Collection, 1/1945.

9. Anka Berus, 'On the tasks of the women of Croatia', AIHRPH, KZDAZH, 1/1946.

10. A clear-cut utopian projection of the 'new woman' was virtually never articulated in any period of the AWF's existence. The schematic formula: worker-cum-political subject-cum-mother is implicitly conceived in most of the writings.

11. Berus, 'On the tasks of the women of Croatia'.

12. Vjeran Katunarić, *Zenski eros i civilizacija smrti* (Zagreb, 1984), p. 239. Discussing the 'typical socially accepted attitudes to the "woman question"' of the present day, sociologist Vjeran Katunarić explains the attitude of 'pseudo-universalism' as 'a desire for momentary equality for all people to avoid any active resistance to those in power'.

13. 'On deficiencies and errors of the AWF and on incorrect attitudes of some Popular Front organisations and of the Government towards the AWF', AIHRPH, KZDAZH, 18/1948.

14. Cana Babović, 'The closing speech at the plenum of GO AFZ Hrvatske', AIHRPH, KZDAZH, 6/1947.

15. Vida Tomšič (1913 -), one of the first women to become an elected member of the Central Committee of the CP in 1940. At the 5th National Conference in 1940 she was in charge of formulating the party-line concerned with the woman question. In 1945 she became a member of the Slovene Government as Minister for Social Policy. In 1948 she was elected President of the Federal AWF. She was also awarded the 'People's Hero' order.

16. Vida Tomšič, AIHRPH, KZDAZH, 15/1948.

17. Vida Tomšič, AIHRPH, KZDAZH, 33/1949. I should remind the

reader at this point that one of the main objections to the Resolution of the Information Bureau, which triggered off Yugoslavia's break with Stalin, was that the YCP diluted its influence by immersing in mass organisations (like the PF, youth organisations, the AWF, etc.), thus betraying the socialist revolution. The stress on the primacy of the CP's directives and the repeated claim that all these organisations were only its transmittors are two consequences of such a development. This also explains the overlapping of the AWF's and PF's aims.

18. Vida Tomšič, AIHRPH, KZDAZH, 15/1948.

19. As an example I quote the results of the AWF's preoccupation with child care (the information has been compiled from different AWF reports and refers to the situation in the People's Republic of Croatia). The organisation initiated (i.e. lobbied for them at different ministries, etc.) the establishment of: 79 pre-natal care centres, 40 childcare centres, 4 children's hospitals, 8 children's wards in hospitals, 22 maternity wards, 59 crèches, 93 kindergartens and 24 restaurants for children.

20. Vida Tomšič's discussion at the meeting: I.O. AFZ Hrvatske, 26.5.1950, AIHRPH, KZDAZH, 47/1950.

21. Due to incomplete data, the ratio of working mothers to nonworking mothers is not available.

22. 'The Resolution of the Third Congress of the AWF of Yugoslavia', AIHRPH, KZDAZH, 48/1950.

23. The decline of the number of women in economic and political life was also noted in President Tito's speech at the Sixth Congress of the YCP: 'I quote figures which clearly show the incorrect attitude towards women: in 1939 there were 197,736 women in employment; in 1947 the number increased to 199,236, in 1948 to 376,836 and in 1949 to 465,166; however, in 1950 the number of employed women fell to 434,222, in 1951 to 375,166, and in 1952 it must have also fallen by some thousands, although as yet we do not have the precise data... A similar trend can be seen with regard to the number of women in the government.' Josip Broz Tito, *Govori i članci* (Naprijed, Zagreb, 1959) vol. VII, pp. 299-301.

24. L. Althusser, as quoted by Nicos Poulantzas, *Država, vlast, socijalizam* (Globus, Zagreb, 1981), pp. 25-31.

Amy Swerdlow

Female culture, pacifism and feminism: Women Strike for Peace

This essay is situated within the historical, theoretical and tactical debates among United States feminists regarding the uses of female culture in radical movements for social change. These debates are part of an on-going discussion regarding the relationship of sex difference to sex equality. For feminist peace activists the pressing question today is whether peace groups that make their appeal to women on the basis of female difference, particularly woman's identification with nurture and moral guardianship, do not in the end undermine woman's political power and even the cause of peace. Critics of the politics of moral motherhood allege that gender-based women's peace groups project the kind of essentialist view of women that re-enforces the notion of biology as destiny and legitimises a sex-role system that, in assigning responsibility for nurture and survival to women alone, lays the basis for male violence in the family and the state.[1] Simone de Beauvoir, who was a leading proponent of the equality over difference viewpoint, put it this way shortly before her death:

> '...women should desire peace as human beings, not as women. And if they are being encouraged to be pacifists in the name of motherhood, that's just a ruse by men who are trying to lead women back to the womb. Women should absolutely let go of that baggage.'[2]

This apparent dichotomy between traditional female culture and feminism has been challenged by a number of historians of women, who point out that in the nineteenth century and the early decades of the twentieth century, middle-class white women in the United States used the ideology of 'domestic true womanhood' to build political movements that expanded women's role beyond the domestic sphere, and that this dialectic was an essential aspect of the most important women's reform movements in the United States, from moral reform and temperance to abolition and peace.[3] Those who have traced the history of the Women's Christian Temperance Union, for instance, have shown how the largest mass organisation of women in the history of the United States influenced thousands of women to support labour reform, suffrage and peace, under the conservative slogan 'For Home, God and Country'.[4]

My work on Women Strike for Peace (WSP), a separatist, maternalist, grass-roots women's peace movement of the 1960s, follows in this tradition. It is part of a growing body of historical and theoretical work on the relationship of maternalism and female culture to power, both personal and political.[5] By analysing WSP's feminine rhetoric and tactics in relation to its global political assumptions and its gender consciousness in the context of United States politics in the 1950s and early 60s, I hope to provide further historical evidence that difference and equality are not opposite categories, and that to pose one against the other is both a-historical and undialectical. The story of WSP provides fresh evidence that women's reform movements are not static. In the 1960s, the women who invoked traditional culture to legitimise their radical dissent found that the decision to engage in radical politics, and the process of political struggle, placed them in direct contradiction to the sexual division of labour they had formerly accepted without question. In addition, their rejection of male political culture forced the women of WSP to develop a non-hierarchical, participatory, creative and playful political format that foreshadowed feminist peace politics in the 1970s and 80s, particularly the Women's Pentagon Action of 1981.

This paper argues that in 1961 maternalism was the only possible political vehicle for a broad-based women's peace movement, given the regressive political climate of the previous decade. In addition, the WSPers themselves were totally lacking in feminist consciousness, although many were well-educated women who had been active in a variety of movements for social justice. They had been victims of the historical amnesia that beset the first wave of feminism in the United States as all mention of the women's rights struggle was eliminated from public discourse, even in left-wing circles, and written out of the historical record. Today, however, after two decades of feminist consciousness-raising, women's peace protest based purely on the notion of female difference is regressive and simplistic. The women's peace movement must go beyond maternalism to extend so-called female values into every level of society, and into the consciousness of both sexes, if it is to rescue the planet from the men who would destroy it.

Women Strike for Peace burst upon the American political scene on 1 November 1961, when an estimated 50,000 women in over sixty cities walked out of their kitchens and off their jobs in a one-day, nation-wide peace strike.[6] As a radioactive cloud from a Russian nuclear test hung over the American landscape, and the United States was threatening to hold its own series of atmospheric explosions, these women staged the largest female peace action of the twentieth century. According to the *Los Angeles Mirror*, it seemed as if 'A wave of feminine determination swept the country through marches and protests.'[7] The women strikers did more than march, however. They put advertisements in local papers, sent delegations to local officials - from governors to school-board members - held community rallies and wrote thousands of letters to President Kennedy and Soviet Premier Nikita Khruschev, demanding that they 'End the arms race, not the human race.' The slogans of the strike addressed issues of particular concern to women. 'Pure milk not poison' and 'Let the children grow' were the most widely used. A placard which hung from the neck of a little girl sitting in a push-chair expressed the maternalist consciousness of the peace strikers. It read, 'I want to grow up to be a mommy some day.'

Following a decade noted for its regressive politics of nostalgia and marked by the Cold War abroad, McCarthyist political repression at home, and the celebration of female domesticity and sexual passivity in the family, the sudden appearance of thousands of militant women strikers puzzled the media and public officials.[8] It even amazed the strikers themselves. The women seemed to have emerged from nowhere, as they belonged to no unified or identifiable organisations, and their leaders were totally unknown as public figures.[9] They were actually responding to a call from a handful of women in Washington, D.C., who had become alarmed by the acceleration of nuclear testing and the growing number of Cold War confrontations between the United States and the Soviet Union, which they feared would develop into a push-button nuclear holocaust.

The founders of Women Strike for Peace, as the movement which emerged from the strike came to be called, had met as members of the male-led Committee for a Sane Nuclear Policy (SANE) in Washington, D.C. However, they had become alienated from SANE because of its hierarchical structure, its emphasis on political lobbying instead of direct action and its acquiescence to Cold War pressure, manifested in SANE's exclusionary policy toward communists and former communists. The organisers of WSP were brought together by Dagmar Wilson, a successful children's book illustrator, who identified herself for the purposes of the strike simply as a housewife and mother. She and the other initiators sensed that the time had come for women - ordinary housewives and mothers - to take direct action because men, on the right and the left, could no longer be counted upon for leadership or protection.[10] After much deliberation, this small group decided to issue a call to women across the nation to suspend for one day the regular routine of home, family, jobs and to stage a dramatic appeal to all governments on behalf of all the world's children to reverse the nuclear arms race.

The call to strike, drafted in Washington, circulated swiftly throughout the country, from woman to woman, via traditional female networks such as word of mouth in playgrounds, supermarkets, and doctors' surgeries; via telephone and Christmas card lists, church and temple contacts, and by letter to the members of local chapters of national women's groups such as the League of Women Voters. Eventually the call was spread through existing peace groups, such as SANE and the Women's International League for Peace and Freedom (WILPF), neither of which offered official support. The only piece of political or social philosophy expressed in the call to strike identified the Washington organisers more with the culture of domesticity than with radical politics. 'Nations disagree as families disagree', the women proclaimed. 'Women believe that nations can solve differences as families do without killing each other.'[11] This theme of social housekeeping, used by women reformers since the nineteenth century, would be invoked frequently by WSP in the years to come, although the leaders of the movement had no historical memory of either the words or deeds of their pacifist predecessors.

Most of the women who joined the strike in November 1961, and those who participated in the national movement that grew out of it, were in their mid-thirties to late forties. They came from liberal to left-wing political backgrounds, having been associated with liberal democratic, Quaker, pacifist, socialist, anarchist or communist causes in the years before the Second World War.[12] The majority were university- and college-educated women who had been employed outside the home before, during, and immediately after the war. Unlike Jane Addams, Emily Balch and Alice Hamilton, who led the Women's Peace Party and the United States delegation to the international women's peace conference at The Hague in 1915, the leading activists of WSP were not professional women.[13] Most had succumbed to social pressure in the late 1940s and throughout the 50s to retire from the work-force and become resident housewives and mothers. They had returned to the home because they had been convinced by Dr Spock's best-selling baby and child care manual and by the other Freudian child development experts, that full-time care of a child by its biological mother was the only way to ensure well-adjusted, productive, successful children who would build the post-war world of justice and peace to which they were committed.[14] The women of WSP had grown to adulthood in an optimistic, if difficult, era marked by depression and war. They shared the liberal and radical conviction of the 1940s that society could be re-ordered in the interests of social justice and peace, through the direct efforts of ordinary people of good will like themselves. As socially concerned women, the WSPers viewed motherhood as more than a responsibility to the private family. They saw it as a service to the community, and to social progress.

Dorothy Dinnerstein has described the psychological process of depoliticisation and privatisation that pushed these women out of radical politics in the 1950s. According to Dinnerstein, people like the WSPers spent the decade of the 1950s in moral shock caused by the twin traumas of Stalinism and McCarthyism. They lost their optimism and their capacity for social connectedness. In this condition, Dinnerstein suggests, they withdrew 'more or less totally, more or less gradually, more or less blindly into intensely personalistic, inward turning, thing and place oriented life'.[15] What the women of WSP withdrew into, with society's blessing, was the manageable sphere of home, children and local community. When their children no longer required full-time care, many of the WSPers were propelled by their earlier social, political and humanitarian concerns to become active in Parent-Teacher Associations (PTA), the League of Women Voters, the Democratic Party and church or temple reform groups. Some were already involved in peace groups such as SANE and the WILPF, others had returned to school or did part-time work in 1961, but very few of those who served as key women in WSP were employed full-time outside the home.[16]

It took the escalation of the nuclear arms race and the example of the civil rights sit-ins in the South to give the WSPers the sense of urgency and opportunity that are the necessary ingredients for political activism. When the WSPers took to the streets in 1961, they were a disorganised band of middle-class housewives with liberal, radical and pacifist backgrounds, pleading for the world's children in the domestic, maternal language they had learned from their mothers and had been using themselves on a daily basis for over a decade.

At a time when Cold War dissenters in the United States were dismissed by the press, the public and political leaders as either 'commies' or 'kooks', and when a popular slogan of the right was 'Better dead than red', the maternal language of WSP brought a positive response from the media. The image projected by WSP of respectable middle-class, middle-aged women and liberal politicians picketing the White House to save the human race helped to legitimise the movement's radical critique of United States foreign policy. By stressing motherhood instead of political ideology, by behaving like the kindly lady-next-door, and by never seeming to threaten the sexual division of labour and power, WSP was able to gain support from the President of the United States, who had been elected on a Cold War platform, but who was also interested in building a constituency for the test ban.[17]

When questioned about the sexual rebellion that could be inferred from WSP's Lysistrata-like action, Dagmar Wilson, who became the movements's spokesperson, reassured the public that WSP posed no threat to the sex-role *status quo.* 'Our organisation has no resemblance to the Lysistrata theme or even to the suffragettes', Wilson told a reporter from the *Baltimore Sun*: 'We are not striking against our husbands. It is my guess that we will make the soup that they will ladle out to the children on Wednesday [1 November 1961].'[18] Wilson was not dissembling. She herself chose to work at home as a children's book illustrator to ensure a well-run household and be available to her children. She certainly intended to make the soup her husband would dispense. In the years to come WSPers often complained to each other that household duties were being neglected during particularly active periods, but they blamed only themselves or the nuclear crisis for the neglect. Little or no help was expected from husbands in the home. WSP justified, and also trivialised, its militant peace strike as an appropriate and socially constructive female response to male misbehaviour. 'You know how men are', Wilson explained.

> 'They talk in abstractions and prestige and the technicalities of the bomb, almost as if this were all a game of chess. Well, it isn't. There are times, it seems to me, when the only thing to do is let out a loud scream. Just women raising a hue and cry against nuclear weapons for all of them to cut it out.'[19]

The press reports of the November first peace strike delighted the participants because they felt that they had been heard. The media comments would be considered unacceptably condescending today, but the women strikers in 1961 were happy to have their slogans mentioned, and their presence noted, after years of invisibility at home. Typical was the *Newsweek* story.

> 'They were perfectly ordinary looking women with their share of good looks; they looked like the women you would see driving ranch wagons, or shopping at the village market, or attending PTA meetings. It was these women by the thousands who staged a demonstration in a score of cities across the nation this week, protesting atomic testing. A strike for peace they called it and - carrying buggies or strollers - they marched on city halls and Federal buildings to show their concern about nuclear fallout.'[20]

The 'key women' of WSP understood that the projection of a traditional and respectable middle-class image was essential for attracting a positive, or at least a benign, response from the media, and that only through sympathetic media coverage could the movement reach the ears of the women it wished to recruit, and the hearts and minds of the men in power. But this image was not artificially contrived. The WSP participants were, indeed, ladylike, middle-class white mothers: beneficiaries of the rising affluence of their class. The 'key women' of WSP, those who created the rhetoric, tactics and image, had sufficient free time and discretionary funds to devote to political volunteerism, endless telephoning across the country, and travelling to meetings and demonstrations far from home. These women enjoyed the luxury of contemplating the issues of survival in the nuclear age and acting on their convictions, because they were free of the struggle for daily survival faced by poor women, black and white. WSP was certainly not a working-class movement concerned with class struggle. In reviewing WSP press releases, pamphlets and publications, as well as internal documents, I have come across no mention of, or debates over, issues such as domestic poverty of labour reform, but there is evidence of a good deal of discussion about racial justice and co-operation with the civil rights movement. I believe this is due not only to WSP's fear of sounding too radical, but also to the fact that Cold War anti-Communism had eliminated the issue of class conflict from public discourse, while the black movement for civil rights had made the issues of racial justice a topic for debate in the White House, the halls of Congress and in homes all over the United States. It is not surprising, then, that members frequently discussed whether or not WSP should join the two issues of peace and civil rights. At WSP meetings the question was frequently asked, 'Why are there no black women here?', but there was little self-criticism concerning the absence of poor white women. It was not until the Vietnam war that WSP joined the issue of militarism abroad with that of poverty at home. However, by then the WSPers had been re-radicalised, along with large sections of the general public.[21]

Responding to public fear of deviance, sexual or political, WSP boasted that its members 'are no odd-ball types, but pillars of the community'.[22] *La Wisp*, the Los Angeles newsletter, reported:

> 'Our public image is good... We made a distinctly good impression on all those who saw us walking, and received several fine

compliments. For instance: One of the reporters who interviewed us went out of his way to tell us back at the Press Club the guys had decided that we were the prettiest picket line they had ever seen. A Lieutenant of the Police...commented favorably on our appearance - and our decorum, too...'[23]

Being well-dressed and ladylike, which meant wearing hats and white gloves, speaking politely and deferring to male authority was not a pose for WSPers, but a manner they had been taught early in life, and had practised for most of their adult years. Even in their youth as socially concerned and politically aware women, they had deferred to men. In 1961 they had become extremely critical of male political culture and male political power, but they were still trying to please individual men.

The women of WSP chose to focus on the powerlessness of mothers in the face of male nuclear brinkmanship, because that was the most obvious form of oppression and contradiction in their lives. Many of the WSP activists were moved by political and religious convictions that far transcended maternal thought, but it was their maternal role and practice that they felt was most under attack in 1961.[24] What was particularly threatening and offensive to the WSP women was the contradiction between the way mothers were praised and extolled, and their perception that motherhood would be rendered obsolete by the nuclear menace to their own children and future generations.

The women who struck for peace on 1 November 1961 could not be pushed back into their kitchens again, even though they often apologised for being in the public arena and promised to return home as soon as the nuclear crisis was over.[25] By the end of 1962, they had transformed their one-day action into a national movement, with local groups in sixty communities and offices in ten cities. With no paid staff and no designated leadership, thousands of women in different parts of the country, most of them previously unknown to each other, managed to establish a loose communications network capable of swift and effective direct action on a national and international scale. This participatory framework tapped a vast reservoir of moral outrage, energy and political talent: female capacities that had been submerged or under-utilised during the 1950s. From its inception, WSP viewed itself as a participatory movement of women who were consciously opposed to tight organisation and leadership. As each group was autonomous, the women often duplicated efforts and crossed wires, but they preferred overwork to what one of the founders called 'formalist hierarchical impediments'.[26] WSP was apologetic about its much-debated and innovative format, which was referred to as 'our un-organisation'. The women defended it as energising, but showed little understanding of its theoretical contribution to feminist political culture. It is interesting to note that the young men of Students for a Democratic Society (SDS), while also rebelling against hierarchy in society and on the left, were more aware of their place in the radical political tradition, and of their power to name. They called their loose structure 'participatory democracy', and predicted that it foreshadowed the new social order. The WSPers, as middle-aged women, were too diffident and too fearful of being presumptuous to theorise, or even to reveal that their political tactics came from considered thought. Everything WSP did seemed spontaneous, pragmatic, practical and improvisational; and for the most part it was. What the women did not understand was that they were building theories in the feminist mode, in struggle, combining observation, experience and emotion.

Continuing to insist upon the right of mothers to oppose national policies dangerous to children, WSP won public sympathy for itself in a dramatic confrontation with the House Committee on Un-American Activities of the United States Congress (HUAC), which staged a full-scale investigation of the movement in December 1962. The alleged purpose of the HUAC investigation was 'to determine the extent of Communist Party infiltration into the peace movement, in a manner and to a degree affecting the national security'.[27] The WSP women, sensing that the investigation was an attempt to intimidate any woman who might become politically active, declared that they would not be stopped by HUAC, 'because...more and more it's obvious that it has to be "the women" who speak for mankind'.[28] The tactics and rhetoric WSP employed to meet the fearsome challenge from the dreaded HUAC were cool, feminine, non-ideological and pragmatic - totally different from those of radical groups called before the committee in the 1940s and 50s. In their testimony at the hearings, the WSPers were so effective and witty in evoking traditional assumptions regarding mothers' rights versus male insensitivity and rigidity that they succeeded in holding the committee up to public ridicule and damaging its standing with the press, the public and Congress. Eric Bentley, in a history of the committee which he called *Thirty Years of Treason*, gave WSP credit for striking the crucial blow in 'the fall of HUAC's Bastille'. Other historians have concurred.[29]

The feminine guerrilla theatre created by WSP at the HUAC inquisitions was so different from the tragic tone that marked earlier investigations, such as that of Alger Hiss or the 'Hollywood Ten', that many reporters perceived the political inquisition as a playful battle of the sexes in which the 'ladies' won the day. The report in the *Vancouver Sun* (British Columbia) was typical of many others:

> 'The dreaded House Un-American Activities Committee met its Waterloo this week. It tangled with 500 irate women. They laughed at it. Kleig lights glared, television cameras whirred, and 50 reporters scribbled notes while babies cried and cooed during the fantastic inquisition.'[30]

The *Detroit Free Press* commented:

> 'The House Committee can get away with attacking college students in California, government flunkies who are forced to shrive their souls to save their jobs, and assorted misguided dogooders. But when it decides to smear an estimated half-million angry women, it's in deep trouble.'

The *Detroit Free Press* wished HUAC 'nothing but the worst'.[31] The hearings were a perfect foil for the humour of Russell Baker, syndicated columnist of the *New York Times*, who declared:

> 'If the House UnAmerican Activities Committee knew its Greek as well as it knows its Lenin, it would have left the women peace strikers alone. Instead, with typical male arrogance, it has subpoenaed 15 of the ladies, spent several days trying to show them that woman's place is not on the peace march route, and has come out of it covered with foolishness.'[32]

The battle of the sexes between WSP and HUAC demonstrates that reliance on female culture can give women the freedom, creativity, humour, common sense, and courageous outrageousness that rigid and ideological male-led organisations often lack.[33]

After this victory, WSP continued to conduct an intensive, consistent and broad-based political campaign for a nuclear test ban treaty and for multilateral disarmament. The movement used standard pressure-group tactics such as lobbying and petitioning, coupled with direct action and face-to-face meetings with women like themselves across national and ideological boundaries. In April 1962, 51 WSP activists, ordinary housewives, travelled to Geneva to focus public attention on the 17-nation disarmament conference and to demand that it produce a test ban treaty. In Geneva the WSPers met with women from several European countries, including a representative from the Soviet Union. Together they staged a non-violent silent march to the Palais des Nations, despite the fact that such manifestations were prohibited by Swiss law. At the Palais, they managed to interrupt the proceedings of the conference and to force Arthur Dean and Valerian Zorin, the United States and Soviet chief negotiators, to receive and acknowledge a petition from 50,000 American women demanding an immediate end to atmospheric tests. The promise by Zorin and Dean to keep the negotiations going and to take seriously their responsibility to the children made international headlines.

In organising national and international direct actions, WSPers often used the informal housewifely techniques they had learned in their daily routine of managing households, running church luncheons and organising bake sales, League of Women Voters forums and school car pools. The WSP telephone network that could reach key women across the country in a matter of hours was an immediate and democratic vehicle for the women which was familiar and effective. WSP also employed common female images unashamedly, turning them into political symbols. At one White House demonstration the New York women carried a tea towel hundreds of feet long, on which thousands of women had inscribed their signatures in opposition to the nuclear arms race. This enormous tea towel was attached to the White House fence. Some women were embarrassed by the use of such a degrading image, but for most of the WSPers it was a symbol of both the powerlessness and the potential power of the housewife. It also attracted TV cameras, which was always a consideration for WSP.

At another demonstration the women affixed pictures of their own children to their spring hats, using them as political symbols. Maternal language was employed consistently in WSP rhetoric and metaphor. An example is a statement in the Los Angeles newsletter; 'WSP is two years old', *La Wisp* declared:

> 'We all know what two year olds are like - lovable, busy, noisy, but not easy to get along with. WSP is a typical two year old. We've gotten some of what we wanted, but we want more. A partial test ban treaty is not enough.'[34]

Despite their domestic language and imagery, the WSP leadership displayed a high level of political acumen in the campaign for the test ban: a sense of the strategic moment for pressure and a talent for research, self-education and public relations not expected of non-professional women of their time. I.F. Stone, the highly respected and independent radical journalist, stated in 1970 that he knew of no anti-war or radical organisation of any kind in the United States which had been 'as flexible and intelligent in its tactics, and as free from stereotypes and sectarianism in its strategy'. In 1970 Stone was apparently as insensitive to the issue of sex-role stereotyping as were the WSPers.[35] They reprinted Stone's comment with pride in the national publication *Memo*.

Carrying through a campaign of self-education on the hazards of nuclear fallout was a transforming experience for many WSPers. Women who had previously deferred to experts and who had quaked when they had to speak before an audience recognised that they had become experts themselves, and public speakers in demand. They delivered addresses at churches, temples and Parent-Teacher Association meetings, and testified at congressional hearings. They wrote articles for local papers and movement periodicals, whilst educating their senators and representatives on the contamination of milk by the radioactive isotopes strontium-90 and iodine-131. Because of WSP's non-hierarchical format, every woman was considered a leader and a spokesperson. The Washington organisers described as 'uncanny' the way all the WSP women sounded alike when they spoke in public or to the media without a mutually agreed-upon script. The reason for this unanimity of approach was an agreement that every woman speak only as a mother, and in no other capacity. When she did speak publicly, a

WSPer was urged to discuss only the broadest issues of survival in the nuclear age. If she spoke in any other capacity, as a scientist, educator or lawyer, she was asked to make it clear that she spoke as a professional and not as a WSPer, as the two designations were obviously viewed as contradictory.

In the early 1960s there was a great deal of unity in WSP regarding the issues of nuclear testing, disarmament, *détente* with the Soviets, and general support for the United Nations. Disagreements did arise within the movement about whether or not to engage in civil disobedience, support unilateral disarmament, or oppose United States policies in Cuba and Vietnam. This was due to a belief on the part of the organisers that WSP possessed the potential to become one of the largest mass movements of women in the history of the United States, but only if it took the broadest possible stand on the broadest issues. The WSP debate over civil disobedience and opposition to the Vietnam war, which threatened movement unity, was eventually resolved by history. As the Vietnam war escalated and American troops were sent to South-East Asia, the WSPers, as pacifists, were forced to take a stand. And as they grew angrier and more frustrated by their inability to end the war, civil disobedience became a tactic the women employed frequently and with growing courage, particularly in relation to conscientious objection.

The politics of motherhood did not serve WSP well during the years of struggle for United States withdrawal from Vietnam. As the youth movement grew in strength and prominence, WSP lost its initiative and its visibility. This puzzled the women, but they rarely complained, as they seemed content to return to positions of support rather than leadership. They were particularly interested in aiding the young men who resisted military call-up and the war, some of whom were their own sons. Advice and financial support for conscientious objectors, statements of complicity with those who refused to fight, prison visitations, and observation and monitoring in the courts where conscientious objectors were being tried, were all part of the day-to-day political tasks of WSP women. These actions, most of the women felt, were ideally suitable for moral, militant, socially concerned mothers. Despite the fact that WSP played only a secondary role in the peace movement from the mid-sixties until the end of the war, it is important to note that the women never acted as a ladies' auxiliary, nor did they take orders from any other political group. The movement made its own decisions on policy and tactics, supported only those national anti-war actions and organisations of which it approved and participated in coalitions as an important, if secondary constituency. WSP developed its own campaigns and rhetoric to bring thousands of mothers into peace protest under the slogan, 'Not our sons, not their sons', but it was the sons and not the mothers who were the principle actors.

Did WSP's successful campaign for the test ban treaty of 1963, including its rhetorical victory over HUAC, reinforce sex-role stereotypes and thus weaken women politically? I believe that the answer is a qualified 'no'. WSP brought women forward into the political struggle in a period of political and sex repression. The WSP movement made public speakers, political strategists, pamphlet writers and local, national and international leaders out of formerly unknown housewives and mothers. In speaking, writing, talking, and walking for peace, in standing up to HUAC and in travelling to Geneva to demand responsibility and progress at the 17-nation disarmament conference in 1962, and by joining with women from Europe and the Soviet Union, WSP demonstrated that women could be creative and militant political thinkers and actors, while still referring to themselves only as mothers and housewives. WSP was also able to move its constituency from concern over practical maternal issues, such as the contamination of milk by nuclear fallout, to specific gender demands. When the WSP activists in Washington, D.C., and New York City decided to focus public attention on the 17-nation disarmament conference in Geneva in 1962, it became clear to them that neither the United States nor the Soviet Union included women on their negotiating teams, so WSP demanded that women be included in all negotiating decision-making bodies relating to foreign policy, war and peace. When the women became tired of begging members of Congress to cut off funds for the war, the movement helped to elect its own legislative chairperson, Bella Abzug, to the House of Representatives.[36]

The Birmingham Feminist History Group has suggested that the feminism of the 1950s seemed to be more concerned with integrating and foregrounding femininity than in transforming it in a fundamental way.[37] It is clear that WSP followed this pattern. The movement was not concerned with the abolition of traditional gender roles, but rather with using gender ideology to advance the political influence of ordinary women. In so doing, however, they were placing both the roles and the ideology in question. WSP helped to change the image of the good mother from passive to militant and from private to public. In proclaiming that the men in power could no longer be counted on for protection, WSP challenged one of the most important myths of the militarists: that wars are waged by men to protect women and children. By stressing global issues and international co-operation among women rather than private family issues, WSP exposed the key element of the feminine mystique, which was the domestication and privatisation of the middle-class white woman.[38] By making recognised contributions to the achievement of an atmospheric test ban treaty, WSP also raised women's sense of political efficacy and self-esteem. WSP's greatest achievement was the way in which its maternalist struggle against the bomb made clear to its members and to the public that the familial and the personal are political, and that the private and public sphere are one.

Notes

1. Ellen DuBois, *et al.*, 'Politics and culture in women's history: a symposium', *Feminist Studies*, 6 (Spring 1980), pp. 26-64; Kathy Kahn, 'Gender ideology and the organizers', *Resist* (December 1980), pp. 1-2, 6; Ellen Willis, *Village Voice*, 23 June 1980; Judy Houseman, 'Mothering, the unconscious and feminism', *Radical America*, 16 (November-December 1982); Jean Bethke Elshtain, 'Women, war and feminism', *The Nation*, 14 June 1980, p. 1; Dorothy Dinnerstein, *The mermaid and the Minotaur: sexual arrangements and the human malaise* (Harper, Colophon Books, New York, 1976), pp. 207-28; Micaela di Leonardo, 'Morals, mothers, militarism: antimilitarism and feminist theory (a review essay)', *Feminist Studies*, 11 (Autumn 1985), pp. 599-618.

2. Alice Schwartzer, 'Simone de Beauvoir talks about Sartre', *MS* (August 1983), p. 37.

3. Barbara L. Epstein, *The politics of domesticity* (Wesleyan University Press, Middletown, Connecticut, 1981); Blanche Glassman Hersh, *The slavery of sex* (University of Illinois Press, Urbana, Illinois, 1978); Keith E. Melder, *Beginnings of sisterhood* (Schocken Books, New York, 1977); Mari-Jo Buhle, 'Politics and culture in women's history: a symposium', *Feminist Studies*, 6 (Spring 1980), pp. 55-64.

4. See: Ruth Bordin, *Women and temperance: the quest for powerful liberty,*

1873-1900 (Temple University Press, Philadelphia, 1981).

5. Temma Kaplan, 'Female consciousness and collective action: the case of Barcelona, 1910-1918', *Signs*, 7 (Spring 1982), pp. 545-66; Sara Ruddick, 'Preservative love and military destruction: some reflections on mothering and peace' in Joyce Trebilcot (ed.), *Mothering: essays in feminist theory* (Rowan & Allanheld, Totowa, N.J., 1984); Carol Gilligan, *In a different voice* (Harvard University Press, Cambridge, Mass., 1982); Barbara Steinson, 'The mother half of humanity: American women in the peace and preparedness movements in World War I' in Carol Berkin and Clara Lovett (eds), *Women, war, and revolution* (Holmes and Meier Publishers, Inc., New York, 1980).

My own research on WSP is based on investigation of a full run of the national publications, several local newsletters, the files of the (national) Washington office and the New York office, both of which contained movement correspondence, plus hundreds of pamphlets, newspaper clippings, local newsletters and scrapbooks. I have examined the Los Angeles papers, which are now in the Swarthmore College Peace Collection, and all articles on the movement published in popular magazines and movement journals. Dagmar Wilson, founder of WSP, has opened her own papers to me. In addition, I have had access to 53 volumes of FBI records based on its surveillance of WSP.

6. The U.S. wire service Associated Press reported on November 2nd: 'The radioactive cloud from Russia's mighty nuclear explosion was following the expected path but was picking up speed as it headed toward Alaska', *Sacramento Union*, 2 November 1961. In San Francisco, the California State Health Department reported that 'slightly radioactive rain' was falling, Newsweek, 13 November 1961, p. 22. See also: *Los Angeles Times*, 2 November 1961; *Los Angeles Mirror*, 1 November 1961. The figure of 50,000 women was an estimate based, according to Washington founders, on reports from women in sixty cities across the country. In order to verify this figure I tallied the highest numbers reported either by strike groups or local papers and could arrive at a total no greater than 12,000. Nevertheless, this was the largest national peace demonstration of the twentieth century, and the media constantly referred to that number.

7. *Los Angeles Mirror*, 1 November 1961.

8. The most persuasive analysis of the connection between the Cold War abroad and the celebration of female domesticity is that both are a nostalgic response to the threat of the bomb and rapid changes in world politics, economics and demographics. Containment of Communism abroad was paralleled by containment of the woman at home to maintain the romanticised and mythologised America of strong men, strong government and world power. Elaine Tyler May, in a brilliant article, 'Explosive issues: sex, women and the bomb in postwar America', forthcoming in Larry May (ed.), *Promise and peril: rethinking postwar American culture*

(University of Chicago Press), points out that taming fears of the atomic bombs and taming women were so connected that a civil defence pamphlet published by the U.S. government actually personified dangerous radioactive rays as 'sexy female bombshells'. Appropriately, during the post-war years the slang term for a sexy woman outside the home was a 'bombshell'.

9. The decline in women's peace activism and national leadership in the second half of the twentieth century can be seen by comparing the group that organised the Women's Strike for Peace in November 1961 with the Women's Peace Parade Committee of 1914, which formed hastily at the outbreak of the First World War. Fanny Garrison Villard, a nationally famous philanthropist, suffragist and pacifist and the well-known descendant of a distinguished reform family, was chosen as peace leader. Other well-known suffragists on the committee included Harriet Stanton Blatch, daughter of Elizabeth Cady Stanton, and Carrie Chapman Catt. Leading figures in the field of social work, like Lillian Wald, Lavinia Dock and Mary K. Simkovitch were also part of the parade committee, along with labour leaders Mary Drier, Leonora O'Reilly and Rose Schniederman. A few other notable women involved officially in the organisation were Mary Beard, Charlotte Perkins Gilman and Henrietta Rodman.

10. This information is based on interviews with WSP founders Dagmar Wilson, Eleanor Garst and Folly Fodor, and with Washington, D.C. activist Barbara Bick. They were conducted on 6 November 1976. Those interviewed indicated that the women who founded WSP were also frustrated by the bureaucratic and hierarchical structure of the United States section of Women's International League for Peace and Freedom (WILPF). They found that the WILPF leadership inhibited spontaneous and local direct action. A letter from Evelyn Alloy of Philadelphia, written in March 1962 to members of the WILPF Executive Committee, indicates the sort of constraint upon local direct action that led WILPF members to become active in WSP. Alloy, who became a key woman in WSP, asked: 'What degree of autonomy does a State branch have? I would hope that the State Board does not become so timid that it wants all PAC projects to be submitting flyers, etc. to Mrs. Olmstead and Mrs. Hutchinson [Executive Director and President] for approval.' 'Evelyn Alloy to Executive Committee', WILPF, 27 March 1962, WILPF Papers, Swarthmore College Peace Collection, Swarthmore, Pennsylvania. An internal Evaluations Committee of the 1962 WILPF annual meeting alleged that while the young women were 'champing at the bit' on peace action and wanting an exchange of ideas on pamphlets, leaflets and publicity techniques, they were being treated to over-long speeches by VIPs instead. 'Suggestions of Evaluations Committee of WILPF', Annual Meeting, May 1962, WILPF Papers, Swarthmore College Peace Collection.

11. 'Dear..., The other night I sat with a few friends', Draft of call to

strike, Washington, D.C., 22 September 1961, mimeographed, WSP Document Collection, Swarthmore College Peace Collection.

12. The term *Democrat* refers to members of the Democratic Party in the United States. Liberal democrats in the 1950s were supporters of Adlai Stevenson.

13. For an account of the Woman's Peace Party and the Hague Conference, see Marie Louise Degen, *The History of the Woman's Peace Party* (Garland Publishing, New York, 1972).

14. See Dr Benjamin Spock, *The common sense book of child care* (Duel Sloan and Pearce, New York, 1945); Lawrence K. and Mary Frank, *How to be a woman* (Bobbs Merrill Company, Inc., New York, 1954); Ashley Montagu, 'The natural superiority of women', *Saturday Review*, 27 September 1958, pp. 13-14.

15. Dinnerstein, *The mermaid and the Minotaur*, pp. 259-62.

16. Sixty-five per cent of the women had either a Bachelor's or a higher degree, at a time when only 6% of the female population over age 25 had a Bachelor's or more. Seventy-one per cent of the WSP women were suburban or city dwellers, with the highest concentration in the East Central states, the West Coast and the Midwest, and with low participation in the Mountain states and the South. The WSPers were concentrated in the 25 to 44 age bracket. Only 5% of the group were 'never marrieds'. Of the married women, 43% had from one to four children under six and 49% from one to four or more children over 18. Sixty-one per cent of the women involved in WSP were not, at the time of the questionnaire, employed outside the home. Nearly 70% of the husbands of the WSPers who responded to the survey were professionals. Only 4% of the WSPers were members of professional organisations.

Thirty-eight per cent of the women who responded claimed not to belong to other organisations, or at least did not record the names of any other organisations in response to questions concerning community activities. Forty per cent were active in a combination of civic, race relations, civil liberties, peace and electoral political activities. Boulding concluded that many of the WSPers were non-joiners. As for their goals in joining the WSP, the Boulding survey revealed that 55% gave abolition of war or multilateral disarmament as their primary goals, and 22% gave non-violent solution of all conflicts, political and social. This indicated that the majority were not committed pacifists. The remainder chose as their goals a variety of proposals for world government or limited international controls, such as a test ban treaty. With regard to their reasons for taking part in WSP activities 28% of the women said they had joined the movement due to concern over fallout, testing and civil defence. Another 4% mentioned the Berlin Wall Crisis; but 41% listed no specific event, just an increasing sense of urgency concerning the total world situation and a need to make a declaration of personal responsibility. Elise Boulding, *Who are these women?* (Institute for Conflict Resolution, Ann Arbor, 1962).

17. Commenting on a WSP march at the White House on 15 January 1962, President John F. Kennedy told the nation in his regularly scheduled news conference that he thought the WSP women were extremely earnest: 'I saw the ladies myself. I recognized why they were here. There were a great number of them... I understand what they were attempting to say, therefore, I consider their message received', *New York Times*, 16 January 1962. In November 1963, eight of the largest mass circulation women's magazines published an interview with the President regarding women's role in the campaign for nuclear disarmament. Kennedy stated: 'I have said that control of arms is a mission that we undertake particularly for our children and our grandchildren, and they have no lobby in Washington. No one is better qualified to represent their interests than the mothers and grandmothers of America.' When asked if groups like Women Strike for Peace embarrassed him, he replied, 'Some groups may be more controversial than others but I think they are probably very good too... There is great pressure against peaceful efforts... These women's groups, working for peace and disarmament are very valuable because they help balance off that pressure', *Woman's Day*, November 1963, pp. 37-9, 141-2.

18. *Baltimore Sun*, 29 October 1961.

19. *Washington Star*, 26 October 1961.

20. *Newsweek*, 13 December 1961, p. 21.

21. For a more detailed narrative history and organisational study of the formative years of the WSP (1961-3) and its campaign for a nuclear test ban treaty, see Amy Swerdlow, 'The politics of motherhood: the case of Women Strike for Peace and the test ban treaty', unpublished PhD thesis, Rutgers University, 1984.

22. Eleanor Garst, 'Women middle class masses', *Fellowship*, 28 (November 1962), pp. 10-12.

23. *La Wisp*, November 1962, p. 9. WSP Document Collection, SCPC.

24. See the preamble to the platform of the Woman's Peace Party, which stated: 'As women we are particularly charged with the future of childhood and with the care of the helpless and the unfortunate...As women we are called upon to start each generation onward toward a better humanity. Therefore, as human beings, and the mother half of humanity, we demand that our right to be consulted in the settlement of questions concerning not only the life of individuals but of nations be recognized and respected.' 'Addresses given at the organization meeting of the Woman's Peace Party', Washington, D.C., 10 January 1915, Woman's Peace Party, Chicago, 1915, p. 11.

25. Betty Friedan commented in *The feminine mystique:* 'It is perhaps a step in the right direction when a woman protests nuclear testing under the banner, "Woman Strike for Peace". But, why does the professional illustrator who heads the movement say she is just a "housewife", and her

followers insist that once testing stops they will stay happily at home with their children?' Betty Friedan, *The feminine mystique* (Dell Publishing Co., Inc., New York, 1976), p. 361.

26. *Liberation*, December 1966, p. 33.

27. U.S. Congress, House Committee on Un-American Activities, 'Communist activities in the peace movement (Women Strike for Peace and certain other groups), hearings before the Committee on Un-American Activities on H.R. 9944'. 87th Congress, 2nd Session, 1962, p. 2057.

28. 'Letter from Women Strike for Peace, Washington, D.C., to "Dear WISPs"', mimeographed, WSP Document Collection, SCPC.

29. Eric Bentley, *Thirty years of treason* (Viking Press, New York, 1971) p. 95; Charles DeBenedetti, *The peace reform in American history* (Indiana University Press, Bloomington, Ind., 1980), pp. 167-78, states: 'WSP activists challenged for the first time the House Un-American Committee's practice of identifying citizen peace seeking with Communist subversion... The open disdain of the WSP for HUAC did not end the Congress' preference for treating private peace actions as subversive. But it did help break the petrified anti-Communism of Cold War American politics and gave heart to those reformers who conceived peace as more than military preparedness.'

30. *Vancouver Sun*, 14 December 1962.

31. *Detroit Free Press*, 13 December 1962.

32. Russell Baker, 'Ladies turn peace quiz into Greek comedy', *Detroit Free Press*, 16 December 1962.

33. For a full description of the WSP-HUAC confrontation, see Amy Swerdlow, 'Ladies Day at the Capital: Women Strike for Peace confronts HUAC', *Feminist Studies*, 8 (Autumn 1982), pp. 493-520.

34. *La Wisp*, 8 November 1963, p. 1.

35. 'I.F. Stone to National Office, Women Strike for Peace, Washington, D.C.', reprinted in *Memo*, special commemorative issue (April 1970), WSP Document Collection, SCPC.

36. Maxine Molyneux, in an article which attemps to clarify the difference between women's issues and feminist issues, proposes that the transformation of women's general concern over issues such as health and welfare into specific gender demands is an essential dynamic of feminist politics. Maxine Molyneux, 'Mobilization without emancipation? Women's interests, the state, and revolution in Nicaragua', *Feminist Studies*, 11 (Summer 1985), p. 232.

37. Birmingham History Group (Britain), 'Feminism as femininity in the 1950s?', *Feminist Review*, 3 (1979), pp. 48-65.

38. Betty Friedan identified a cultural ideal she named 'the feminine mystique'. It established the suburban housewife as the American ideal. 'She was healthy, beautiful, educated, concerned only about her husband, her children, her home.' Betty Friedan, *The feminine mystique*.

Mineke Bosch

Gossipy letters in the context of international feminism

> 'If you are idling your time away in the mountains, I am sure you will be glad to get gossipy letters, and so you must expect to read mine whenever they come.'[1]

This is a quote from one of the letters in the book *Lieve Dr. Jacobs* (Dear Dr Jacobs), which Annemarie Kloosterman and I compiled on the occasion of the fiftieth anniversary of the International Archives for the Women's Movement (IAV) in Amsterdam in 1985.[2] Our starting point was to make a meaningful selection of letters, primarily from the Aletta Jacobs Collection.[3] After reading several hundreds of letters, mostly from suffragists and feminists in the IAV-archives, as well as several collections in the USA, we decided to tell the story of the International Woman Suffrage Alliance through the letters of five women. Or to tell the story of five women: Anna Howard Shaw, Carrie Chapman Catt, Aletta Jacobs, Rosika Schwimmer and Rosa Manus, all in the Alliance, through their letters. The 'or' is an inclusive 'or'; we tried to do both at the same time. Before going into this story, however, I want to make a few preliminary remarks concerning the relation between gossipy letters and the writing of history.

It is a common belief among historians that history is improved when biography, or the history of a particular person, is related to general historical aspects. There is even a tendency to value the history of an (in a sense invisible) individual life, only in so far as it sheds any light on the social, economic or political climate in which the subject of a biography lived or the (in a sense impersonal) institutions to which she or he belonged, mostly in the public sphere. Underlying these assumptions is a widely accepted notion of 'history as a science' that unites even women's historians, who otherwise question each other's opinions on women's history in many ways. It is a notion in which history is expected to produce general knowledge in a language full of theoretical concepts and abstractions. History that does not obey these unwritten rules is easily dismissed as so-called *petite histoire.*

The exclusion of *petite histoire* from academic historical discourse finds a parallel in the exclusion of gossip from (semi-) public discourse. Thus Phyllis Rose, in the introduction of her book *Parallel lives,* equates her inquiry into the marriages of a few carefully selected Victorians with gossip. She still needs to defend this kind of research, but she does it with the enlightened argument that 'gossip may be the beginning of moral inquiry, the low end of the Platonic ladder which leads to self-understanding'.[4] Patricia Meyer Spacks has since published her delightful book on *Gossip.*[5]

Gossip, always seen as a female genre, is often too easily dismissed as irrelevant. Spacks, however, was not deterred by what she suspected to be a prejudice: on the contrary, she decided to analyse the social discourse always associated with gossip, and discovered a whole range of different kinds of gossip. By way of a definition she conceived of a continuum. At one extreme, gossip manifests itself as distilled malice. This gossip plays with truths and half-truths and serves certain purposes for the gossipers. At the other end of the continuum lies 'serious gossip', which exists only as a function of intimacy, and achieves no other end than disinterested self-expression and self-understanding. In between are all the modifications of these extremes.

Since she was most interested in the serious gossip that takes place within the intimacy of the dyad conversation, Spacks made it into a model for the interpretation of the novel and borderland prose, like published letters and biographies. Thus she was able to explain how the endless personal details revealed in published correspondence:

> 'dignify small truths rather than trivialize large ones... Lady Mary [Wortley Montagu]'s letters, taken seriously in full detail, can help the reader value the small remark - in life as well as on

the page. They do not, like tragedy, for instance, emphasize the grandeur of the human spirit; they insist rather, on the compelling persistance of personality.'[6]

Our wish to edit the 'gossipy letters' of Anna Howard Shaw and others was in no small measure inspired by genuine curiosity about those human aspects of life which tend to be the subject of gossip. Who were these women who organised such an extensive women's support network? What did they laugh, worry and talk about? Did they quarrel, or did they make love underneath the soft blanket of universal sisterhood? These questions were not new in all respects. Apart from the above-mentioned curiosity, they were also inspired by developments within the historiography of feminism. The debate on 'Politics and culture in women's history' has assessed the importance of taking women's experience and women's sense of solidarity into account when writing the history of feminist movements.[7] This had also indicated the study of love letters and other unpublished material that could reveal informal bonds between women which contributed to establish their formal organisations.

However, we wanted our questions to go beyond the debate on 'Politics and culture'. Although this debate was primarily intended as a discussion of feminist politics in women's history, it is nevertheless interesting to note that more than once an appeal was made on behalf of metahistorical arguments, most often defending research that was seen as typical for the women's culture approach, such as Nancy Cott's *The bonds of womanhood* and Carroll Smith-Rosenberg's essay 'The female world of love and ritual', as well as Blanche Wiesen Cook's article on 'Female support networks and political activism', to name only a few.[8] MariJo Buhle, for instance, stated in her contribution to the debate in *Feminist Studies* that a 'new wave of sympathetic research' had allowed the story of the Women's Christian Temperance Union (WCTU) to come inside the parameters of feminist history. According to her, Cott's study had been especially instrumental in this development: 'It is clear that the heuristic scholarship of Cott and others already allows us to look past the abstractions of previous historians.'[9] Buhle claims here that by carefully interpreting the sources, the women historians had been able to overcome feminist abstractions like the enduring subjection of women, and one of its corollaries, that women become historical subjects only when they start to become politically active in the public sphere.

Although Buhle calls Cott's scholarship 'heuristic', the expression 'sympathetic research' reminds me rather of the *Verstehen*, the 'understanding' that is central in the hermeneutical conception of history. It is interesting here to consider an article by Bonnie Smith, in which she argues that it was not Mary Beard's thesis that women were a force in history which was her most important contribution to the history of women, but her radical hermeneutics as expressed in her books *America through women's eyes* and *Laughing their way*.[10] Rather than constructing another linear (though feminist) version of history, Beard let women speak for themselves, thus showing the multiple perspectives at work in history itself.[11] In the debate on 'Politics and culture', a parallel was drawn more than once with Beard's polemics with feminist historians in the 1930s and 40s. Beard's conviction that women had been active participants in history, rather than passive victims in this parallel, is equated with the conception that women's culture should be central in women's history. As Bonnie Smith showed, however, this parallel lacks a full understanding of Mary Beard's effort. Beard did not want to substitute one feminist truth for another, she wanted to deconstruct the idea of historical truth itself in order to overcome all abstractions, whether feminist or not.

There were, therefore, different reasons for our wishing to edit a selection of gossipy letters. In the first place we wanted to write a history of the suffrage movement as the story of a few women in particular: active feminists who debated together, who intrigued, loved and hated each other; women who were human, sometimes maybe 'all too human', who were corseted or definitely not, who used morphine sometimes, or favoured the colour blue. In making their letters central, however, we were also aiming at a second goal, namely to overcome all kinds of 'feminist abstractions' apparent in the history of feminism.

Our principal target was the idea of *universal sisterhood* that seems to dominate every interpretation of the international women's organisations at the turn of the century. Adopted from Elizabeth Cady Stanton's address to the women who had gathered to found the International Council of Women in 1888, the concept of universal sisterhood became a *Leitmotiv* in all descriptions of the history of international feminism which invariably culminate in the

1915 women's peace conference in The Hague.[12] Although most historiography pays lip-service to critics of the universal character of this limited white, western-oriented, (upper) middle-class sisterhood, it does not do so effectively when the term universal sisterhood is maintained as a central interpretative theme, even to the point of disregarding the clear-cut divisions within the world of organised feminism itself. Such interpretations reinforce contemporary ideology of feminist solidarity, but they do not reveal its problematics.

The gossipy letters we edited confirm many of Patricia Meyer Spacks' observations. Certainly the gossip in the letters had many different aspects. Moreover, it drew our attention to 'small truths', hitherto unnoticed when researching public sources. For instance, the fact that among professed equality-feminists, being Jewish played a more important role than the suffragist ideology could acknowledge; or that the suffragism of the National American Woman Suffrage Alliance differed radically from the suffrage cultures of their sister organisations in Europe; or, finally, that the 1915 women's peace conference in The Hague could be seen as an act of feminist dissidence just as well as an outburst of female solidarity. If the many details and particulars in the suffragists' letters do not contribute so much to ideals of feminist solidarity and universal sisterhood, they do emphasise the importance of personality, nationality, class, ethnicity, etc., also in the history of feminism.

In this paper I have concentrated on the letters from Anna Howard Shaw and Carrie Chapman Catt to Aletta Jacobs on the one hand, and the letters from Aletta to the Hungarian feminist Rosika Schwimmer on the other hand. Aletta Jacobs had met Anna Howard Shaw and Susan B. Anthony in 1899 at the third conference of the International Council of Women in London. Her acquaintance with Carrie Chapman Catt dated from the first conference of the International Woman Suffrage Alliance in Berlin in 1904. After this conference, both Catt and Shaw stayed a few days with Aletta Jacobs in Amsterdam. This acquaintance was continued during the trip Aletta and her husband Gerritsen made through the United States later in the same year. From then on, Aletta had a regular correspondence with both women. The letters of Rosika Schwimmer were probably all destroyed by Aletta Jacobs, who guarded her heritage jealously. Differences of opinion in 1915 were probably the cause of a final break.[13] Fortunately the Schwimmer-Lloyd Collection gives proof of an intensive exchange of letters dating back to 1902, when Aletta Jacobs visited Hungary for the first time. This same collection includes letters from Dutch women like Martina Kramers, of whom hardly any records have been kept in the Netherlands.[14]

The letters from Anna Howard Shaw and Carrie Chapman Catt to Aletta Jacobs

At first glance the letters from Anna Shaw to Aletta Jacobs seem to be very different from the letters of Carrie Chapman Catt, both in tone and in content. Shaw's letters are all perfused with warmth and intimacy. On many pages she contemplates the feelings of friendship she has for Aletta Jacobs. In her very last letter to Aletta, written on Thanksgiving Day in 1918, she writes:

> 'Oh dear Doctor, there are so few real friendships in the world that those which do exist should be prized above all things, so today in recounting some of my blessings, they are so many that I cannot recount them all, in the foreground are my dear friends and out of the larger group a few, for whom I am especially grateful; among them is my dear Doctor, so on this thanksgiving day I am thankful for you.'[15]

From the beginning of their correspondence Aletta Jacobs is drawn into the intimate circle of friends around Shaw, the President of the National American Woman Suffrage Association. Letters from Aletta to Anna are shared with Lucy E. Anthony, Shaw's life-companion, and Rachel Foster Avery, who lived for many years with Anna and Lucy; or postscripts are added and messages passed. In the light of this, it is no coincidence that in the Aletta Jacobs Collection, Lucy's letters can be found among Anna Shaw's correspondence with Aletta.

The shared love and memory of Susan B. Anthony plays a vital role within this circle of friends. Thus Lucy writes to Aletta from Oregon, where she assists Shaw in a suffrage campaign just after Susan B. Anthony has died:

> 'Since arriving a lovely letter from you has been forwarded and Aunt Mary, Miss Shaw and I thank you very much for it. I think that all of those who loved and were loved by dear Aunt Susan will always feel nearer together.'[16]

A year later, when Aletta Jacobs writes to Shaw for photographs of pioneers to be exhibited during the coming international conference in Amsterdam, Shaw replies that one of the photographs she is sending need not be returned. It is a picture of Susan Anthony that 'hangs up now over our desks and seems like the living presence of Aunt Susan to us'. She continues: 'Mrs Avery and Lucy and I are going to have a copy made for you, your own dear self.' Shaw repeats emphatically that the photograph is a present from the three women to Aletta:

> 'So this is not a gift to the Association or by the Association at all, but just a personal remembrance from us three who love you so very dearly and who are so interested in your good service and share in our admiration for our Dear Aunt.'[17]

The distinction Anna Shaw makes here between 'us three' and 'the Association' is interesting, although rhetorical. Rather than confirming this distinction, it testifies to the existence of a community in which personal lives and feminist politics were completely interwoven. In this respect Shaw's life seems to have been no different from the lives of the women in the more visible women's communities, such as the women's colleges, or the settlement houses which arose in the United States during the second half of the nineteenth century.[18] Suffrage work may not have taken place within such visible and clearly defined boundaries, but for women like Anna Shaw it was also true that they worked not only from nine to five but day and night for the Cause.

Indeed, as recent studies have argued, the ideology of sisterhood that nurtured the building of so many female institutions was also the moving spirit behind the suffrage movement from the 1890s onwards.[19] Anna Howard Shaw could figure as a model example for this argument. In her suffragism, a theoretically vague but passionate identification with women was paramount over any other feminist principle or practice. Central in all her activities was a deeply felt sense of sisterhood turned into reality. Dedicated suffrage colleagues had to become cherished friends, and respected women were to be converted into devoted friends of the Cause. All had to become members of the one and only suffrage family around Anna Shaw, sometimes literally. Susan B. Anthony, for instance, was lovingly referred to as 'Aunt Susan' by many feminists. However, it seems that Anna Shaw could not content herself with so symbolic an aunt. By making her household with Lucy E. Anthony, the niece of Susan, in a way Susan became her real aunt.

Suffrage politics were therefore politics of friendship to a large extent, and personal letters obviously played a significant role in such politics. This is the reason why Shaw's letters do not always seem to be entirely above suspicion as to whether the suggested intimacy is truly disinterested and sincere. Do they truly express the 'serious gossip' that exists as a function of intimacy? In a situation in which the boundaries between public and private life are blurred to such an extent, gossip definitely has a public, political dimension. Some of this gossip can be functional, in that it articulates the views women share but cannot voice in public. The light-hearted gossip among feminists, which mocks at 'men in general', can be seen as such. Shaw's letters frequently bear witness to her opinion of the opposite sex, often humorous but during the First World War increasingly bitter: 'Men, I am convinced, never grow up and of all animal creation are the least capable of reason' was certainly not her most negative comment at that time. I see parallels in the privately exchanged views on subjects such as militancy or the younger generation within the suffrage movement. Such gossip implicitly reaffirms the ideology of sisterhood and strengthens feelings of solidarity, of sharing inside information that is not shared with outsiders. It thus serves a political end.

However, in Shaw's correspondence a less edifying type of gossip frequently surfaces which also serves a political end, albeit a very personal one. It is the kind of gossip that is very close to 'distilled malice' on Spacks' continuum. Thus for seven years, from December 1908 until December 1915, when Catt becomes President of the National American Woman Suffrage Association, no letter from Shaw to her overseas friend seems complete without a sneer at Mary Garrett Hay, the friend and life-companion of Carrie Chapman Catt:

> 'Miss Hay seems to be in the forefront of everything. She is living with Mrs Catt and seems to take the responsibility of almost all the household in her own hands. I do not think there is any hope of breaking that affair off'

sighs Anna in a letter dated 14 December 1908. In Anna's confessions to Aletta, sometimes one cannot dismiss the impression that the confessions are not only for Aletta's ears, but also for Catt's. An example of this is the long lament that Shaw sends to Aletta Jacobs when the latter is travelling around the world with Catt. Nobody had longed more than Anna Howard Shaw to take the trip Aletta is making with Catt at that very moment: 'I felt that we could do it successfully and without friction just as we did our campaigning here for years before an outside influence prompted by jealousy felt it would weaken our influence if our friendship were broken.' After Catt's husband died, Shaw had tried to persuade Catt that she needed a change for her physical and mental well-being, without Miss Hay of course:

> 'If Miss Hay had gone with her it would have been impossible for either of them to have forgotten it. However, my interest was misunderstood and misinterpreted. Had Mrs. Catt known how with all my soul I had longed to do that very thing since the W.C.T.U. had sent its Temperance missionaries out, she would not have misunderstood. I tried to tell her several times, but somehow I never could open my heart to Mrs. Catt. Not that she was ever unkind or unsympathetic, but because I felt she distrusted me, because she had distrust preached constantly to her.'[20]

Even passages like this contain important information about the movement's politics. They reveal a considerable amount of the ineffective power-play between Catt and Shaw that had so much influence on the North-American suffrage association.

With regard to such undisguised sympathies and antipathies, Catt's letters to Aletta Jacobs seem to be very different. Certainly the heights and depths of Shaw's prose are missing from the pages of Catt's correspondence. Always under control, it seems as if neither severe criticism nor the loftiest of praise were within Catt's power to bestow; and *Schwärmen* would be the last thing for her to do. Her letters to Aletta Jacobs reveal a good businesslike companionship, which even becomes rather playful and light-hearted after their joint world trip:

> 'My dear Aletta: This American monkey has been swung by her *tail* so vigorously ever since she stepped on this Continent, that she is dizzyheaded; her body is tired, and her *tail* sore! I am sure the Dutch monkey is having the same experience.'[21]

Jacobs describes the background to this esoteric language in her autobiography. In front of an office in Manila a monkey, obviously for the amusement of the office-clerks, was tied to a tree. Aletta had drawn Catt's attention to the sad plight of the animal, whereupon Catt had remarked dryly: 'That monkey is just as we, aren't we just as fast tied on the suffrage tree? When will we be freed?'[22]

Although Catt draws Aletta into her intimate circle by using private jokes in a manner similar to Shaw, at the same time her letters seem to be more distanced and more sincere. Such observations could easily lead to a confirmation of earlier conclusions by historians, which all stress the differences between the two succeeding suffrage leaders. In present historiography, Catt is invariably presented as the 'professional organiser' and Shaw as the 'amateur reformer'.[23] And indeed, when one compares the letters, there are many examples of Catt taking a much more unbiased stand in a much more sober language than Shaw. Further proof could be that Mary Garrett Hay was definitely not included in any friendship with Catt, as is shown by the presence of only one small note from her hand amongst Catt's correspondence in the Aletta Jacobs Collection. Obviously private life and politics were kept more at a distance.

Yet, closely examining Catt's letters to Aletta Jacobs, I do not think the differences are really so great that they can be called principal differences, rather than gradual ones. I think that Catt and Shaw had more in common than not in feminist ideology and practice. Catt also wrote letters which consisted of nothing else but first-rate gossip of all kinds. These suggest to me that the differences between Catt and Shaw are of a far less radical nature than is generally assumed. Take the following example: when feelings ran high among the officers of the Association, and Anna Howard

Shaw was confronted by strong resistance from her Board members in the Washington conference in 1910, Aletta Jacobs is alarmed by what she hears: the wonderful working relationship and friendship between Anna Shaw and Rachel Foster Avery has come to an abrupt and definite end. True, Catt's letter to Aletta is far from emotional, but it reveals her way of handling such situations:

> 'I am sorry she [Anna] told you about the difficulty in Washington, for such matters are quite unintelligible to the people of another country. It is a hard story to tell and will be a harder one for you to understand as it involves so many personal relations. Stripping the story of all personalities, I will tell you my version.'[24]

There follows an extensive explanation of the problems in the Association, in which at least one thing becomes very clear: although Anna Howard Shaw has the most wonderful talents, she is the sole cause of the Association's trouble. It may be right to blame Shaw, as many scholars do, for not having any organisational talents, but to hold her personally responsible for the Association's misfortunes is not fair. Other women, like Catt, let things happen the way they happened.

Reading Catt's letters showed me then that Catt and Shaw stood on common ground. Perhaps the two women differed in style and character, but the feminist framework within which they operated was the same. Superficially it may seem that Catt was the professional organiser, capable of drawing lines between personal and political arguments and motives. However I think she was only more clever. The following example shows that Catt did not hesitate to use gossip and persuasion rather than formal procedures to solve internal differences of opinion either. In 1913 the Dutch suffragist Martina Kramers, editor of *Jus Suffragii*, the journal of the Alliance, was put under this personal kind of pressure by Catt. Contrary to what the annals reported up till now it appears that Martina did not give up her post as editor of *Jus Suffragii* of her own free will.[25] In the spring of 1913, a plan was conceived to establish the International Press Office in London, and to publish *Jus Suffragii* from the new office. However, when Kramers did not show any readiness to resign as editor and publisher, Catt tried a different tack. For years, Kramers had had an extra-marital relationship with a certain 'Bobbie', and Catt now took advantage of this. In a letter she pressed Kramers to step down quietly because, she said, in American circles rumours were rampant about Kramers' free love. The reproach was not levelled specifically at Kramers' 'illicit' relationship. As Catt wrote: 'In my judgement such matters are largely personal and must be governed by one's own conscience, but they cease to be personal or individual when one carries them into public work.'[26] In her answer, Kramers pointed out that in this particular case, Catt used gossip and rumours in order to get rid of her. After all, when rumours had circulated about the homosexuality of two women in the Alliance, Anita Augspurg and Käthe Schirmacher, or about Aletta Jacobs, who was suspected to be an abortionist, Catt had refused to lend her ear to the scandalmongers. Kramers wrote:

> 'You think that blasting my position is little compared to the "moral" gain you strive for in expelling me. If so, you must act as your conscience dictates just as I do. But you shall do it openly and have all the credit for it which the Americans who regard me with "horror and repugnance" will give those who vindicate their morals.'[27]

Of course, this example was not only taken because of its savoury subject matter. Indeed, it is interesting to see that the suffrage movement had to deal with controversial topics such as homosexuality and abortion, but the letters tell us a lot more than that. They are not only revealing as to Catt's 'sisterly exhortations', but also Kramers' letter speaks volumes. It is a frank and unambiguous defence, not covering up any of her opinions or activities. In it she explicitly asks Catt not to influence the organisation's policies by means of personal machinations:

> 'Don't you be enticed into using your authority to take sides in such questions. Let the ballot pronounce; that is what it is secret for. Is not the essential part of the task of a President to make people understand exactly what they are voting for or against and so do away with all confusion or issues. I hope soon to see that as President you refuse to discuss personal life of candidates, and that as friend you will some time give me an

opportunity to present to you the man I love.'[28]

If my first point was that differences between the letters from Catt and Shaw to Aletta Jacobs are balanced by the many similarities that the two share, my second point is that the real difference is between the North-American and the European suffrage correspondence under discussion. The letters from Aletta Jacobs and Martina Kramers to Rosika Schwimmer convey a completely different atmosphere existing within this correspondence.

The letters from Aletta Jacobs to Rosika Schwimmer

Perhaps this difference could be best expressed by a quote from one of Aletta's letters to Rosika Schwimmer, written just before the propaganda trip to Austria and Hungary which Aletta made in 1906 with Carrie Chapman Catt:

> 'Can you tell me what the women doctors want to know about Neo-Malthusianism. They don't want a lecture, do they? If so, it must happen in private, without press or propaganda. It isn't so much that I am afraid of publicity, but it will harm the cause of woman suffrage. People are so stupid, they confuse everything. And everything that has to do with sex may not be mentioned, it may only be done. Also I don't know what Catt thinks about this. It is strange, but I have never talked to her about it.'[29]

The quotation shows that Aletta was very much aware of the subject of Neo-Malthusianism, and also that she was involved in it, even as President of the Dutch Women's Suffrage Association. Although her long-term experience as a feminist forbade her to tell the whole story, even as late as 1924 when writing her autobiography, her letters to Rosika Schwimmer reveal that Aletta Jacobs never detached herself from Neo-Malthusianism. The meeting with the women doctors in Hungary was by no means an exception.

However, the most important point here is that Aletta's letters to Rosika Schwimmer show that the two women shared a broad feminist perspective. In these letters, more than one delicate matter is openly discussed which apparently cannot be discussed with

Catt or Shaw. In one of her letters to Rosika, Aletta Jacobs writes that the subject referred to can better be talked about than written down. This is not a sign of political caution, unlike similar observations made by Shaw. What she means here is that the discussion of Schwimmer's predilection for morphine, in connection with the repression of her suppressed sexual desires, requires a subtler treatment than Jacobs was capable of expressing in German. Everything is discussed: prostitution, white slavery, child protection, and there are even hints about homosexuality.

In addition, a broad range of activities taking place in their spare time becomes apparent from the correspondence. The first thing Jacobs wanted to do in Hungary in 1902 was to visit the women's reformatory in Maria Nostra. In 1909 she went to a medical conference in Sarajevo (Yugoslavia), where the prostitution question was on the agenda. She took advantage of the opportunity to visit the town's red-light district, and to inquire into the results of regulation and government control.

Moreover, Aletta and Rosika discussed feminist theory. Aletta, who translated Charlotte Perkins Gilman's book *Women and economics*,[30] inspired Rosika to do the same; Rosika in her turn sent Aletta many of her articles for criticism. A courageous act, for Aletta could be severe: 'I have read your short story with interest, but I don't understand it really. Did you ever meet a whore that already practised such a long time and still cherished such ideals?'[31] For her book on marriage ideals and ideal marriages (*Ehe-Idealen und Ideal-Ehen*) Rosika took the Jacobs-Gerritsen marriage as one example of an ideal marriage, although finally it was left out, probably as a result of Aletta's protests.[32]

Of course, one could very well argue that the relationship between Aletta Jacobs and Rosika Schwimmer was exceptional, and thereby account for its openness. Their friendship was indeed something out of the ordinary. Aletta was the one who introduced Rosika into the greater world of international feminism. Perhaps their easy comradeship can also be explained by their common Jewish background. The many references to Jewry in Aletta's letters to Rosika are certainly very unusual for the Dutch suffragist. Yet I think that the main body of their correspondence, in which so wide a range of issues is discussed, is not exceptional for European suffragists.

As we have seen, Martina Kramers' answer to Catt in 1913 was remarkable for its frankness. Her letters to Rosika Schwimmer have this same quality. Rosika became personally acquainted with Martina's lover: witness a few letters from 'Bobbie' in the Schwimmer-Lloyd Collection. One of them has been amended by Martina: 'There, proof that not *all* socialists here in Holland are our enemies. You don't need to show this to Aletta, it's no use with her.'[33] Indeed, not everything is discussed equally frankly, even among European feminists, but it is obvious that Martina and Rosika talked about the connection between socialism and suffrage in a way that is quite impossible to imagine among the leading North-American suffragists in the Alliance. The letters written by Aletta and Martina to Rosika are unquestionably gossipy letters, but it is a manifestation of gossip in which feminist theory is explored and feminist principles and opinions are checked and reflected upon. It is the kind of gossip that Patricia Meyer Spacks claims exists as a function of intimacy, a means of self-expression and a form of solidarity.

Suffragism in the United States and in Europe

The difference in tone and content between the European and the American-European correspondence can be related to the distinct suffrage cultures in Europe and in North America. Since it is impossible to elaborate on this here, I will restrict myself mainly to citing Catt (through Mary Gray Peck) on this issue. After her first propaganda tour of Austria, Hungary and Bohemia (Czechoslovakia) in 1906, Peck wrote that Catt had now acquired first-hand knowledge of the situation in Europe and how it affected women, and she thought that it differed radically from the situation in the United States:

> 'Women were in the majority in Europe. For ages Europe had been a battle-ground of contended races and ideologies. It was profoundly disharmonious and militarized. Masculine dominance was the continental tradition as it never was in the democratic New World. Standing armies took European men away from normal social life for a considerable portion of their existence. There were not enough men to go around in marriage, prostitution was regarded as necessary by governments, irregu-

> lar liaisons were condoned if not encouraged. Out of these conditions grew a sex cynicism on the part of many European feminists which shocked American suffragists, while the Europeans were diverted by what seemed to them incredible naïveté on the part of Americans.'[34]

One can only wonder what exactly was on Catt's mind to make her draw such a conclusion. Was masculine dominance responsible for the exclusion of German and Austrian women from political meetings and the legal prohibition of forming political associations? And the 'sex cynicism' supposedly abounding in Europe, did that refer to the militant policies of British suffragettes or the pacifism of Aletta Jacobs and Rosika Schwimmer that did not stop at 'motherly persuasion', or did it refer to the German suffragists who openly supported the homosexual emancipation movement in Germany? Catt hints at the existence of principal differences between North-American and European women, but she is unable to express these differences.

I think Catt's vagueness is revealing. The President of the Alliance never inquired deeper into feminist questions than was necessary to develop compelling ideology and design effective strategy. Her suffragism, like the suffragism of Anna Howard Shaw, was inspired by an idea of sisterhood which dominated the North-American suffrage movement from 1890 onwards. It was a pragmatic and a-political concept of sisterhood, phrased in idealistic sentimental terms. Its aim was to create the greatest possible assembly of women. It was a myth forced upon reality. Its most precious watchwords were political neutrality and unity. It was precisely in this manner that European suffragism differed most radically from North-American suffragism.

Even though the North-American model began to be imitated in Europe, European suffragism always represented more than the joint struggle to obtain the vote. European suffragists never reached the stage in which strategy prevailed over principal feminist politics, and the vote was seen as an end in itself. Suffragism in Europe as such bore more resemblance to the women's rights feminism that Elizabeth Cady Stanton favoured than the suffragism that Susan B. Anthony left as her imprint on the North-American suffrage movement. Indeed, Elizabeth Cady Stanton had spoken of universal sisterhood, but she never wanted the differences between women to be denied or concealed. As a result, the suffrage movement was divided over feminist political issues in several European countries, which often resulted in more than one suffrage organisation.

Gossipy letters and the idea of universal sisterhood

'Within our Alliance we must develop so lofty a spirit of internationalism, a spirit so clarified from all personalities and ambitions that its purity and its grandeur will furnish new inspirations to all workers in our Cause.'[35] In every Presidential address, Carrie Chapman Catt elaborates on this theme. Public statements such as this led women's historians to conceive of the international women's movement as an expression of universal sisterhood. The personal correspondence between members of the Alliance sheds a different light on the movement. Catt's constant exhortations may be seen as the North-American attempt to silence European influx with its capacity for division, rather than as proof of the unity and supra-national character of the Alliance.

Indeed, this European influx was much more important than the official Alliance history has recorded. In *Journey towards freedom*, a history of 50 years of the Alliance which was written by one of its pioneers, Adele Schreiber, it is maintained that Catt founded the Alliance in 1902.[36] Other sources, however, more accurately ascribe the initiative to two German radical-suffragists, Anita Augspurg and Lida Gustava Heymann. The precise reason for the initiative may even be seen as symbolic of the European contribution to the Alliance. Furious that a suffrage meeting at the 1899 Conference of the International Council of Women in London was forced to admit anti-suffragists, the two women decided to found an international body which was separate from the Council.[37] I use the word 'symbolic' because it demonstrates the European capacity for making feminist history full of complexities. One might even wonder if Catt would have taken the initiative in 1902, had such faction not occurred. It is highly likely that Catt tried to take over the initiative strategically, thereby taking advantage of dissension and, at the same time, limiting the damage. The impact of European suffragism on the Alliance is finally proven by the 1915 women's peace conference in The Hague. Certainly this conference cannot be seen as the result of universal sisterhood. A minority in the Alliance, undaunted by a majority vote against such a conference in wartime, organised it *à titre personnel* under the leadership of Aletta Jacobs. Officially the Alliance remained aloof, and, which is even more significant, neither Catt nor Shaw went over to The Hague in 1915.

In a letter to Aletta, Shaw exhausts herself in an enumeration of excuses.[38] Catt, as befits the President, shows her concern in an extensive letter, written one month after the peace conference. Apparently she is shocked by its immense success and by the tremendous impression the conference made upon public opinion. In many resolutions she recognises Alliance policy and proposals, and even reflects upon the possibility that the minority who took the initiative might 'prefer a different international organization, which shall be linked together with peace propaganda rather than a non-partisan and neutral suffrage organization'.[39] Catt was right to worry about the future. The conference in The Hague could only have been organised by neglecting the majority vote in the Alliance concerning this subject. It definitely caused a breach in that it led to the foundation of the Women's International League for Peace and Freedom, which of course required attention and energy that would otherwise have gone to the Alliance.

The gossipy letters to and from Aletta Jacobs give proof of the existence of an extensive international sisterhood. However, to conceive of this sisterhood as a universal sisterhood, a sisterhood that painlessly transcended differences of personality, nationality, class, ethnicity and ideology, is to ignore the information that these letters also provide: that the sisterhood was dearly bought, frequently by neglecting the differences between these women, or drowning them in the ocean in between.

Notes

1. Anna Howard Shaw (AHS) to Aletta Jacobs (AJ), 14 December 1908, in Aletta Jacobs Collection, IAV (AJ-IAV).

2. Mineke Bosch, Annemarie Kloosterman, *Lieve Dr. Jacobs: brieven uit de Wereldbond voor Vrouwenkiesrecht, 1902-1942* (Feministische Uitgeverij Sara, Amsterdam, 1985).

3. The IAV was founded in 1935 by Rosa Manus, Johanna W.A. Naber and W.H. Posthumus-Van der Goot. The first collection to be housed

there was the Aletta Jacobs Collection, which consists primarily of international correspondence. The many letters from women like Alexandra Grippenberg, Susan B. Anthony, Olive Schreiner, Charlotte Perkins Gilman and Emily Hobhouse reflect the versatility of Aletta Jacobs' feminism. The letters in the last decade of the nineteenth century often deal with material requested by Aletta Jacobs for her and her husband Gerritsen's library, which was sold to the Crerar Library in Chicago as the Gerritsen Collection in 1904. The letters written between 1900 and 1920 deal with suffragism and peace activities. The letters dating from the twenties testify to a renewed emphasis on birth-control. An article published in the USA in 1920 sparked off a large stream of letters asking for more information. Long before the IAV was closed in June 1940 - after two months of Nazi occupation - and its contents shipped to an unknown destination, the Aletta Jacobs Collection had been hidden and thus survived oblivion as one of a very few collections.

4. Phyllis Rose, *Parallel lives: five Victorian marriages* (Vintage Books, New York, 1984), p. 9.

5. Patricia Meyer Spacks, *Gossip* (University of Chicago Press, Chicago and London, 1986).

6. Spacks, *Gossip*, p. 77.

7. 'Politics and culture in women's history: a symposium; Ellen Dubois, MariJo Buhle, Temma Kaplan, Gerda Lerner, and Carroll Smith-Rosenberg', introduction by Judith R. Walkowitz, *Feminist Studies*, vol. 6, no. 1 (1980), pp. 26-64.

8. Nancy F. Cott, *The bonds of womanhood: 'woman's sphere' in New England, 1780-1835* (Yale University Press, New Haven and London, 1977); Carroll Smith-Rosenberg, 'The female world of love and ritual', *Signs*, vol. 1, no. 1 (1975), pp. 1-29; Blanche Wiesen Cook, 'Female support networks and political activism: Lilian Walld, Crystal Eastman, Emma Goldman' in Nancy F. Cott, Elizabeth H. Pleck (eds), *A heritage of her own: toward a new social history of American women* (Simon and Schuster, New York, 1979), pp. 412-44.

9. 'Politics and culture', p. 38. Barbara Sicherman, in the unpublished 'Survey of recent United States scholarship on the history of women' (Bucharest, 1980), uses similar arguments in assessing the importance of 'recent studies, that by concentrating on women's "separate sphere" have greatly added to our knowledge of women as historical agents... This research has yielded some of the best empirical studies of distinctly female behavior and attitudes.' The terms 'heuristic' and 'empirical' are used rather light-heartedly, which reflects the unsophisticated way in which philosophy of history is incorporated into (women's) history. The idea of history as an empirical science is very dubious.

10. Mary Beard, *America through women's eyes* (Macmillan, New York, 1933); Martha Bensley Bruere, Mary Ritter Beard (eds), *Laughing their way:*

women's humor in America (Macmillan, New York, 1934).

11. Bonnie G. Smith, 'Seeing Mary Beard', *Feminist Studies*, vol. 10, no. 3 (1984), pp. 399-416. I elaborated these questions in two articles: Mineke Bosch, 'Women's culture in women's history: historical notion or feminist vision?' in Maaike Meijer, Jetty Schaap (eds), *Historiography of women's cultural traditions* (Foris Publications, Dordrecht, Holland and Providence, USA, 1987), pp. 35-52, and Mineke Bosch, 'Egodocumenten: bronnen van kennis en plezier', *Tijdschrift voor Vrouwenstudies*, vol. 8, no. 2 (1987), pp. 203-20.

12. For instance: Edith F. Hurwitz, 'The international sisterhood' in Renate Bridenthal, Claudia Koonz (eds), *Becoming visible: women in European history* (Houghton Mifflin Company, Boston, 1977), pp. 326-46, and Rebecca L. Sherrick, 'Toward universal sisterhood' in Elizabeth Sarah (ed.), *Reassessments of 'first wave' feminism* (Pergamon Press, Oxford and New York, 1983), pp. 655-61. Indeed, Rebecca Sherrick questions the idea of universal sisterhood: 'leaders from Anthony and Stanton to Addams, Catt, Jacobs and Heymann spoke and wrote often on the themes of solidarity and sisterhood. It is not apparent though whether their rhetoric reflected, masked, shaped or distorted reality' (p. 661). However, she should address the historians rather than the feminists regarding their use of notions like 'universal sisterhood'.

13. It is difficult to assess 'what really happened'. Certainly there were differences of opinion about policy matters concerning the handling of the press in 1915. Rosika favoured the mobilisation of mass sentiments, while Aletta Jacobs believed in a more 'diplomatic role' for women. However, both women were 'strong characters', to put it mildly. Rosika Schwimmer was controversial in her own time, which seems to repeat itself in present-day research. Barbara Kraft, in *The peaceship: Henry Ford's pacifist adventure in the First World War* (Macmillan, New York and London, 1978) passes a downright negative judgement: 'Many examined her methods and misread her motives. Certain of her wisdom and judgement, the Hungarian feminist practised a pious hypocrisy, shading the truth in her favor, sometimes slightly, sometimes grossly, to persuade others to her ends. She wanted power not for personal aggrandizement but to ensure that her ideas, which no one was as capable of enacting as herself, were realized. Once obtained she used power to gratify her ambition and to force acknowledgement of her supreme position. Because she gave unselfishly of herself to what she took to be a common purpose, she considered her behavior - including her flair for high living when she was in the money, her own or someone else's - above criticism and commensurate with the dignity and importance of the work' (p. 205). Anne Wiltsher, in her book *Most dangerous women: feminist peace campaigners of the Great War* (Pandora, London, Boston and Henley, 1985) also recognises the ambivalence of Rosika's legacy, but her judgement differs radically from Kraft's:

'No one was neutral about Rosika Schwimmer. A human dynamo with a forceful personality and tireless energy, she was somebody you either loved or hated - frequently people did both at different times. Known as the "comedienne" of the European women's movement who provoked "shouts of laughter" from female audiences for her pungent attacks on the male sex, she was much in demand as a speaker and could make men laugh their way into agreeing with women's suffrage by her clever use of satire, driven home by dramatic hand gestures' (p. 10). Rosika is clearly the heroine of this book about the 1915 peace efforts.

14. The Schwimmer-Lloyd Collection in the manuscript division of the New York Public Library (SL-NYPL) is a large collection consisting of 945 linear feet, or 1,777 boxes. It contains the personal papers of Rosika and Franciska Schwimmer, Lola Maverick Lloyd, and both families' papers. There are special files on the Ford Peace Expedition, the Ford Neutral Conference, the International Committee for Immediate Mediation, the World Center for Women's Archives and the Campaign for World Government. On the history of European feminism, it contains invaluable material in the form of letters from German, Hungarian and Austrian women, many of whose papers were lost in the Second World War.

15. AHS to AJ, Thanksgiving Day 1918, in AJ-IAV.

16. Lucy E. Anthony (LEA) to AJ, 3 April [1906], in AJ-IAV.

17. AHS to AJ, 26 March 1907, in AJ-IAV.

18. Estelle Freedman, 'Separatism as strategy: female institution building and American feminism, 1870-1930', *Feminist Studies,* vol. 5, no. 3 (1979), pp. 512-29.

19. Ellen Carol Dubois (ed.), *Elizabeth Cady Stanton - Susan B. Anthony: correspondence, writings, speeches* (Shocken Books, New York, 1981); Aileen S. Kraditor, *The ideas of the Woman Suffrage Movement 1890-1920* (W.W. Norton and Company, New York and London, 1981 (1st edn 1968)).

20. AHS to AJ, 16 July 1912, in AJ-IAV.

21. Carrie Chapman Catt (CCC) to AJ, 7 December 1912, in AJ-IAV.

22. Aletta H. Jacobs, *Herinneringen* (SUN, Nijmegen, 1978 (1st edn 1924)), pp. 307-8.

23. Eleanor Flexner, *Century of struggle: the Woman's Rights Movement in the United States,* revised edn (The Belknap Press of the Harvard University Press, Cambridge, Mass. and London, 1982), p. 283.

24. CCC to AJ, 16 July 1910, in AJ-IAV.

25. Adele Schreiber, Margaret Mathieson, *Journey towards freedom: written for the golden jubilee of the International Alliance of Women* (International Alliance of Women, Copenhagen, 1955): 'Much to the Board's regret, Martina Kramers who had founded the paper, *Jus Suffragii,* had to retire owing to ill-health' (p. 23). Other sources concur. I think that whenever 'ill-health' is used as an argument, it is wise to take a closer look.

26. CCC to Martina Kramers (MK), 21 May 1913, (copy) in SL-NYPL.

27. MK to CCC, 2 June 1913, (copy) in SL-NYPL.

28. Ibid.

29. AJ to Rosika Schwimmer (RS), 10 September 1906, in SL-NYPL.

30. Charlotte Perkins Gilman, *Women and economics: the economic factor between men and women as a factor in social revolution* (Small Maynard, Boston, 1899).

31. AJ to RS, 12 July 1904, in SL-NYPL.

32. Aletta Jacobs protests against Rosika's interpretation of her marriage in the same letter in which she writes that her husband has died. AJ to RS, July 1905, in SL-NYPL.

33. MK (Bobbie) to RS, 24 November 1906, in SL-NYPL.

34. Mary Gray Peck, *Carrie Chapman Catt: a biography* (The H.W.Wilson Company, New York, 1944), p. 157.

35. Ibid., pp. 160-1.

36. Schreiber, Mathieson, *Journey towards freedom.*

37. Jacobs, *Herinneringen*, p. 103.

38. AHS to AJ, 4 January 1915, in AJ-IAV.

39. CCC to AJ, 30 June 1915, in AJ-IAV.

Margot Badran

The origins of feminism in Egypt

Feminism emerged in Egypt while the modern state was in process of formation. It arose at a moment of growing urbanisation, with the expansion of capitalism bringing incorporation into the European-dominated world market system, and later British colonial occupation. Feminism appeared in Egypt, as in Western countries, amongst upper- and middle-class urban women. However, unlike in the West but as commonly in the Third World, feminism in Egypt became bound up with nationalism and found legitimisation in religion.[1]

In her book on the origins of modern feminism in Britain, France and the United States, Jane Rendall discusses the social conditions under which feminism emerges and draws attention to the increasing separation of women and men, with the growing division between the home and the place of work. She speaks of a new domestic world of women in which they created a culture of their own that gave them the opportunity for self-assertion.[2] In the case of Egypt, feminism emerged when the formerly strict seclusion of women imposed by patriarchal authority broke down increasingly in the last third of the nineteenth century. Women displayed new forms of self-assertion as they began to transcend the old world of imposed domestic confinement, broadening their horizon and paving the way towards a sexually integrated world. It was sometimes thought, because (middle- and upper-class) women in Egypt were separated within their own world, that there was a broad female community, but women were distanced from each other within individual households while female seclusion was at its strictest.[3]

Such historical differences demonstrate the diversity of social, economic and political conditions that have given rise to feminism. Feminism is a response and challenge to patriarchal domination and is at root a universal phenomenon. It is important to emphasise that feminism is a generic phenomenon with specific local or indigenous historical manifestations. It has been widely alleged in the Middle East and elsewhere in the Third World that feminism was (or is) a Western phenomenon, tainting and delegitimising it in countries in a colonial and post-colonial context. The aim of this paper is to contribute towards extending our knowledge of specific feminist historical experience, particularly in the Third World, and towards the expansion of theories on the origins of feminism.

Discovering these origins in Egypt is a far from simple task. It requires hypotheses, questions and methodologies generated by women's history. The emergence of the relatively recent discipline of women's history is a century younger than the appearance of feminism in Egypt as a nascent new consciousness. Why has the name of Qasim Amin, whose book *Tahrir al mar'a* (The liberation of the woman) was published in 1899, been more widely known in Egypt and elsewhere until quite recently than the name of Huda Sha'rawi, who was the pioneering leader of a feminist movement for a quarter of a century? Why have men, especially Qasim Amin (widely called 'the father of Egyptian feminism') been seen as the founders of feminism in Egypt?[4] Why has feminism in Egypt been frequently labelled 'Western'? Why has it so often been considered exclusive to the upper classes? The answers are related to the question: who has written history for whom, and why? The discipline of history, still mainly male-centred, has relied heavily on conventional questions, methods and sources. So far feminist history has been largely the history of men's feminism written within the framework of men's history.

Women's feminism and women's history

My quest, which began in the sixties, to find out about Huda Sha'rawi and other women who became feminists, and the nature of their feminism, is a story of other methods, sources and speculation.[5] It seemed logical to go to women to learn about an ideology and activism that concerned women's lives. I wanted to investigate women's accounts of feminism since feminism was concerned with changing women's lives. My first idea was to go directly to the women who were connected in various ways with Huda Sha'rawi. From them I learned the names of other early feminists. I found a mine of women's oral histories that exceeded expectations.[6] There was a richness of detail, interpretation and analysis, perspective and images I could not have found elsewhere, for they were only preserved through oral heritage. Through these women I gained access to written documents: the memoirs of Huda Sha'rawi - a unique testament - private memoranda and correspondence of early feminists, feminist journals and obscure books. Armed with these women's names, I proceeded to Dar Al Kutub, the national library in Cairo, where I was subsequently able to track down more material, including a substantial collection of women's journals, and I successfully scoured a number of smaller libraries and collections as well. My research continued to spread outwards, eventually leading me to the Public Records Office in London, where diplomatic and intelligence reports held important information about feminists in the early decades of the twentieth century, but because of their nationalist political activism rather than their feminism. The search led me on to sources I would not have known existed, had it not been for the particular way the material accumulated in a process that began with the Egyptian women who held the history within themselves.

I soon learned that when referring to feminism in Egypt, it was important to distinguish between women's feminism and men's feminism. Both arose in the late nineteenth century, although women's feminism preceded men's feminism. Women's starting point in the evolution of feminist awareness was a dissatisfaction with their own lives, which inspired them to change their way of living for their own sakes as women. The starting point for male feminists was linking the backwardness (to use the term of the day) of Egypt, a major contemporary concern, to the backward condition of women. Male feminists advocated the advancement of women in order to help the development of the nation, and for the good of society and the family as they saw it.

The historical literature on feminism in Egypt has produced two major lines of argument. One, illustrated by Juan Cole, explains the rise and appeal of feminism in class terms, seeing it essentially as a function of economic need and specifically identifying feminism in Egypt as an upper- and middle-class phenomenon. He argues that the Egyptian men, and the one woman, whom he discusses espoused the feminist cause because it served their evolving material interests in a changing economic order.[7] The other approach, articulated by Thomas Philipp, asserts that feminism is essentially Western, explaining its appearance in Egypt as a corollary of westernisation-cum-modernisation. He correlates the acceptance or rejection of feminism (which he discusses in conjunction with nationalism) by male thinkers with pro- and anti-Western political positions.[8]

This paper focuses on women's feminism in Egypt and draws primarily upon women's sources. My arguments derive from these sources. I argue that women's feminism in Egypt has been indigenous. This feminism, motivated and directed by women's own social, psychological, economic and political needs, was legitimised within religious - mainly Islamic - and nationalist frameworks. Historically, Egyptian women's feminism transcended class. Egyptian women's feminist ideology and agendas have not been a function of class interests, but one of gender concerns, cutting across class lines. This is not to say, however, that certain feminist goals have not been, in particular instances, more relevant to women of one class than another. Feminism originated in Egypt amongst women within the context of their everyday lives and preceded men's feminism.

The definition of feminism in this paper ranges from an emerging individual or collective awareness (feminist consciousness) that women have been systematically oppressed because of their sex, to a more complex analysis of oppression, the liberation of women and various forms of activism. The pivot of women's oppression is understood to be patriarchal hegemony which contains and restrains women. The term *feminism* was not publicly used by women until 1923, when they formed the Egyptian Feminist Union, and to my knowledge this term was not used by men when referring to themselves. The lack of documentation makes it difficult to know precisely when the term first circulated in the private domestic world from which feminism emerged. The term *women's liberation* was in existence at the end of the nineteenth century, as Qasim Amin's book testifies. The term *feminist consciousness* is far too recent a concept to have been used by early feminists in Egypt.

Because this paper focuses on the period from about the 1870s to the early 1920s, I use feminism and feminist consciousness purely as analytical terms relating to phenomena that antedated this terminology.

The nineteenth-century context

Early in the nineteenth century, Egypt won independence from the Ottoman Empire and a new ruling dynasty was established under the former Ottoman officer Muhammad 'Ali, who had been sent by Istanbul to end the recent French occupation of Egypt (1798-1801). To protect the autonomy of Egypt and his own power, the new ruler embarked on a process of massive social, economic and technological change. The state altered the agricultural system by introducing cotton as a cash crop for export, embarked on a programme of industrialisation, started modern health and education systems and promoted urbanisation. To assist in the agenda of change, Europeans were brought to Egypt, while study missions of Egyptian men were sent abroad to acquire new skills. During the last quarter of the century, in the midst of mounting economic and political pressures, Egypt came under British occupation.[9]

The city, the locus of emergent feminism, altered and expanded dramatically during the nineteenth century. By the end of the century, Cairo, the capital, had grown by two-thirds, and Alexandria, the commercial and trading centre, had become twenty times larger. With the physical expansion of the city, patterns of living in quarters segregated by sect and ethnicity gave way, especially among the elite, which moved into new residential areas and indeed into new or 'modern' houses which were less strictly responsive to the requirements of gender segregation. The urban sociology of Egypt changed dramatically. In addition to the expanding Turco-Circassian elite, which lived in the capital and which was connected with the new ruling dynasty (also of Turco-Circassian origin), Cairo, and to a lesser extent Alexandria, became home to a new class of absentee landowners, especially during the 1860s and 70s, when many men from the provinces were drawn into the central administration of the state.[10] The cities were also the home of the expanding new professional class of lawyers, doctors and engineers and the growing trade and commercial sector.[11] The impoverished peasants, displaced from their customary livelihood in the rural areas, swelled the urban population as well.[12] Amongst the Europeans arriving in Egypt in increasing numbers as new advisors and professionals were a number of women who entered the harems of the wealthy as governesses, nannies and seamstresses. All these different classes, living in closer daily proximity and gaining increased mobility throughout the country thanks to the recently completed networks of modern roads, railways and canals, were exposed to new experiences and different life-styles. The expanding Mediterranean steamship service also enabled women from wealthy families to travel to Europe, where they experienced at first hand life outside the harem system.

It was among the upper- and middle-class urban women living within the conventions of the harem system, which enforced their domestic seclusion and the segregation of the sexes, that a feminist consciousness arose during the last thirty-odd years of the nineteenth century. This institution for the control of women by the patriarchal family was linked to class. Seclusion in the home was not possible for lower-class urban women and peasant women because of their daily work, which necessitated a certain amount of interaction between the sexes. Veiling the face was required of all women in the city irrespective of class, but such was not the case in the countryside, where it was incompatible with the requirements of daily work. Observers could plainly see that the harem system and veiling were related to economic circumstances and not to Islam as had been alleged. The majority of Muslim women living in the rural areas of this predominantly agrarian country were not restricted by the harem system, whereas middle- and upper-class urban Christian and Jewish women obeyed harem conventions.[13]

However, in the context of nineteenth-century transformations, gender arrangements altered as well. Among the upper and middle classes, old patterns of female seclusion and sex segregation lessened in different ways, especially in the last third of the century, as daily life improved: new forms of transport facilitated movement, and new opportunities arose in education, recreation and social life. However, in the case of lower-class and peasant women, segregation and seclusion increased in proportion to the break-up of the home as a locus of craft manufacture and the decline of household-based subsistence and agriculture. It was at this moment of accelerating change that feminism arose among women in middle- and upper-class harems. From the altering daily experiences of women in nineteenth-century harems, the theoretical foundations of Egyptian (women's) feminism would take shape.[14]

In the second half of the century, with increasing contradiction and confusion in everyday life accompanying the transformations, the role of Islam in modern life was questioned. Shaikh Muhammad 'Abduh (1849-1905), of the Islamic university and religious centre Al Azhar, enunciated a doctrine for reconciling Islam with contemporary change, which became known as Islamic modernism. 'Abduh claimed that Muslims would find the necessary answers to the predicaments of modern life by an examination of the Quran and other sources of religion using *ijtiad* or independent inquiry (as opposed to relying exclusively upon the established religious authorities). He pointed out that Muslims had strayed from the correct practice of their religion, and that they should return to Islam in a freshly inspired way. Among the ills Muhammad 'Abduh drew attention to was the oppression of women by men in the name of Islam, especially abuses connected with wanton use of divorce and polygamy, thus paving the way for feminism within Islam.[15]

Egyptian women and men both articulated feminist ideologies within the context of Islamic modernism. Before proceeding to our central theme, I would like to mention men's emergent feminism by way of background information. The book that is said to have set the debate, and indeed sparked off *public* debate among *men*, was *The liberation of the woman*, published by the lawyer and judge Qasim Amin (1865-1908) in Cairo in 1899. He pointed out that the harem system of female seclusion and segregation, and the veiling of the face, were not required by Islam and that they prevented women from enjoying the rights Islam accorded them. In order for Egypt to progress women must progress. Five years previously Murqus Fahmi, also a lawyer, had set forth a similar argument in his book *Al mar'a fi al Sharq* (The woman in the East), which, however, did not generate broad debate. It was privately published and its author was not a Muslim, therefore his work would not pose the same threat as that of a Muslim. It is interesting to note that the year before *The woman in the East* came out, Amin published a book called *Les Egyptiens*, which was essentially an apologia to Western criticism and which argued that women in Egypt enjoyed their rights and were not oppressed.[16]

Sources of individual feminist awareness

The roots of feminism lay in women's own lives. The earliest evidence of emergent feminism appears in the generation of 'Aisha Taimuriyya (1840-1902), daughter of a Turkish government official and a Circassian slave who was born into a family of literary and intellectual men (there is no evidence that her mother was literate). She reached puberty about a decade or two before the migrations into Cairo of the new rural elite, in whose households the first publicly declared feminist activists were born. Through her writings and poetry she conveys a sense of being suffocated by seclusion, and an intense desire to acquire learning. She preferred the intellectual world, which she glimpsed in the literary coterie of her father when it met in the family house. Her father helped her further her education in the harem. Later she reached out through her writings to other women whom she would never see at a time when the harem system was still strict. She composed a long tale, *Nata'j al ahwal fi al aqwal wa al af'al* (The consequences of circumstances in words and deeds), to divert other women cocooned in isolation, while her deepest reflections of women's conditions were condensed in her poetry.[17] Warda Al Yaziji (1838-1924), a woman of Syrian origin and a contemporary of 'Aisha Taimuriyya, was also a poet who was sensitive to the plight of women. The words of both found resonance in Huda Sha'rawi (1879-1947) and other early feminist activists, who acknowledged 'Aisha Taimuriyya and Warda Al Yaziji as forerunners of feminism.

The first generation of the women who became public feminist activists in the 1920s were born in the last two decades of the nineteenth century. By that time, changes in the everyday lives of upper- and middle-class women were marked. Some constraints of the harem system had lessened, yet basic control over women remained firm. It was a time of accelerating contradiction, strain and confusion for women as well as for men. Huda Sha'rawi, the daughter of a Circassian mother and a wealthy landowner and politician from Upper Egypt, was born during this period and was brought up in an upper-class harem in Cairo. By this time tuition for girls in upper-class harems, mainly by European governesses, was usual. However, as she records in her memoirs, she encountered many obstacles when she tried to obtain instruction that exceeded the education allowed women of her class. She was, for example, thwarted in her desire to master Arabic - by the shaikh engaged to teach the Quran - which was not the everyday language of the upper classes and not deemed fitting for girls. By observing a famous poet, who made the rounds of upper-class Cairo harems, she discovered that eloquence and learning enabled women to communicate with men, gaining their respect, and to break through their own seclusion.[18]

In her memoirs, she recounts ways in which boys were given preferential treatment to girls merely because of their sex, and tells of the increasing restrictions females faced as they grew up, and the anger and psychological pain this caused her. She did not register her reaction to taking the veil at puberty, but noted the pain of separation from male childhood companions and being thrust without choice into a female world. However, when another first-generation feminist activist, Saiza Nabarawi (1897-1985), the adopted daughter of a friend of Huda Sha'rawi, who was brought up and educated in Paris, returned to Egypt at puberty and was forced to veil, she strongly rebelled at what to her was a strange practice before being made to acquiesce.[19]

There were a number of middle-class women, many of Syrian origin (whose educated middle-class families had emigrated to Egypt in order to escape Ottoman oppression at home), who were among the first women to be educated at school, and who wrote books and articles or founded women's journals in the 1880s and 90s. Their works have yet to be fully studied, but preliminary investigations indicate distinct forms of feminist consciousness. Zainab Fawwaz (1860-1914), who emigrated from Lebanon to Egypt when she was a girl, advocated education and work for women in her book *Al rasa'il al Zainabiyya* (Zainab's writings), and even supported political rights for women. Other women, too, promoted women's rights: Hind Nawfal, born in Lebanon, who founded the first women's journal *Al Fatah* (The young woman) in 1892, and Labiba Hashim, who founded *Fatah al Sharq* (The young woman of the East) in 1906, to mention only two.[20]

Middle-class women who were first-generation feminist activists included Malak Hifni Nasif (1886-1918) and Nabawiyya Musa

(1890-?). Women from the middle class were permitted by their families to take advantage of school education earlier than were upper-class women. Malak Hifni Nasif, a poet and writer known by the pen-name Bahithat Al Bad'iyya (Seeker in the Desert), and Nabawiyya Musa, also a writer, both attended the Saniyya School (created in 1899 to train women to become primary school teachers in the expanding state system, which was generating more facilities for females) and became teachers. Nabawiyya Musa was also the first woman to sit for the state secondary school certificate examination, which she passed in 1907. These women advocated broader education and work opportunities for women to enhance their own lives, as well as helping their families and society. Malak Hifni Nasif, who had unwittingly become part of a polygamous union and suffered from it, advocated women's rights in the family protected by Islam, which allowed polygamy only under stringent conditions. She favoured a gradual reduction in sex segregation, and during her short lifetime did not call for unveiling; she wanted women to be more fully self-fortified through education and wider experience first, to avoid sexual exploitation. Nabawiyya Musa makes it clear in her writings that she regarded appropriate work as being liberating for women. Of modest background herself, she was especially sensitive to the plight of poor women who were commonly forced to work in menial jobs, where they were exploited economically and sexually. Malak Hifni Nasif and Nabawiyya Musa, who experienced at first hand the advantages of education and work, made these advantages the cornerstones of their feminist goals for women.[21]

Collective feminist experience

The expanding social activities of women in the late nineteenth century, and the introduction of the salon, provided forums for debate and opportunities for women to broaden their networks. Huda Sha'rawi's memoirs recall the women's salon presided over by Eugénie Le Brun Rushdi (died in 1908) in the 1890s. A Frenchwoman who married Husain Rushdi, she only obeyed harem conventions as an adult. Having converted to Islam after diligent study, she realised that veiling and the seclusion of women were not required by the religion. The memoirs of Huda Sha'rawi and oral testimony indicate that women discussed issues such as veiling and seclusion, observing that these practices were not required by Islam but by social convention.[22] The nascent feminist awareness emerging in this salon was probably evident in other gatherings of women, of which there are no known recorded historical traces to date, but which further research might one day discover. We do know about two salons of well-known women where men also gathered. The salon of Princess Nazil Fazil, niece of the Khedive Isma'il, attracted prominent men of the day: intellectuals, statesmen and politicians, including Qasim Amin, whose feminist ideas are said to have been nurtured here.[23] Because of the Princess's status she could do what most other women could not. Early in the twentieth century, Mayy Ziyada (1886-1941), a Lebanese-born poet, writer and feminist, also held a salon where leading male literary figures met. Social practices had changed by then, and as a woman of non-Egyptian origin and a Christian it was easier for her to contravene the dying local norms.[24]

In 1908, coincidentally the same year in which the Egyptian University first opened, women began to hold women's lectures. These lectures were notable for being the first joint activity of middle- and upper-class women, and for being held outside the harem. Thus women broke down barriers of class and gender that the patriarchal system upheld, by meeting across class lines and in 'public' space customarily reserved for men. The lectures were held at the new Egyptian University on Fridays when there were no classes, or after working hours at the office of the Egyptian newspaper *Al Jarida*, founded not long before by liberal and pro-feminist men. The lectures were organised by upper-class women and given by educated middle-class women. Malak Hifni Nasif was a favourite speaker. When she died in 1918, Huda Sha'rawi took the floor for the first time to deliver a eulogy which became her first feminist speech. The lectures explored women's conditions in Egypt and made comparisons with women's lives in Europe.[25]

The significance of these women-initiated lectures is emphasised by the experiences of women at the new Egyptian University. Following the start of the lectures, and during the second academic year of this university (1909-10), a section for women was opened.[26] The pattern was repeated, with upper-class women attending as students and middle-class women lecturing. Among the latter were Nabawiyya Musa and Labiba Hashim. However, because of public opposition the women's section was closed down by 1912 (three men were sent to study in Europe on government grants with the money saved).[27] Women were not allowed into the university until 1929, when feminists quietly admitted a handful of women with the assistance of Ahmad Lutfi Al Sayyid, the pro-feminist rector, and Taha Husain, the pro-feminist dean.[28] Meanwhile, the women's lectures continued from time to time until the First World War, emphasising the importance of women relying upon themselves and building their own institutions until they could safely claim and retain their place in state institutions.

Not long after the women's lectures began, a group of upper-class women founded the Mabarrat Muhammad 'Ali (1909), which operated a dispensary for poor women and children. They were motivated by alarming statistics on infant mortality, published by the government the preceding year, and spurred on by the nationalist wish to conduct social service work within the framework of their own Egyptian society, and not through the British Lady Cromer Society. Although it was not in accordance with customary practice for women to congregate and acquire their own premises in public, the humanitarian and nationalist dimensions of the enterprise legitimised the innovation. Upper- and middle-class women joined forces, and women of the younger generation were also brought in to assist. The headquarters of the new society was located in a popular section of Cairo, bringing middle- and upper-class women into direct contact with less fortunate women in their own environment, and exposing them to social and economic needs as well as health problems. It gave women vital experience in organisation and management, as well as the opportunity to demonstrate their skills to others. Some women who participated in this work had a feminist understanding of the experience. It opened up their own lives and confirmed their conviction that there were basic health and economic requirements that women must meet as a pre-condition to feminism. It brought privileged women face to face with lower-class women from whom they had been distanced, and helped forge a lasting commitment to these women.[29]

Women in Egypt first attended feminist conferences and made feminist demands at political meetings while the harem system still prevailed. In 1899 - the year Qasim Amin's book *The liberation of the woman* appeared - Rahma Sarruf, of Syrian-Christian origin, attended the World Women's Conference in Europe and reported on its agenda of social, economic and political rights for women in the Cairo journal *Al Muqtataf*.[30] In 1911, Malak Hifni Nasif presented the first feminist demands at the Egyptian Congress in Heliopolis (at that time outside Cairo but now part of the city), a nationalist meeting, where she called for a wide range of women's rights, especially in the field of education and work, so that women might develop their potential for their own sakes as women, as well as bringing benefit to society. When she included the demand that women have access to the mosques for prayer as in early Islam, she underlined how even women's right to communal worship had been withheld by patriarchal hegemony.

Emergence of public feminist activism

While women's feminism arose with the decline of segregation and seclusion, women's first explicit public feminist act in Egypt was to unveil the face, proclaiming that women were putting an end at last to the harem system that patriarchal power had imposed upon them. This occurred in 1923, when Huda Sha'rawi and Saiza Nabarawi removed their veils at Cairo railway station on their return from their first feminist conference abroad. In the private, hidden phase of feminism, women had discreetly manoeuvred within the harem system, eroding it from within until they found the time was ripe to attack it directly.

This moment followed women's active participation in the Egyptian struggle for independence from 1919 to 1923. Their nationalist experience had further enhanced women's political and practical skills, and women feminists believed that the national independence for which they had fought should include independence from alien rule and freedom from internal gender and class oppression. The new Egyptian constitution guaranteed rights for all Egyptians, but an electoral law issued shortly afterwards rescinded political rights for women. This gave women two alternatives: to go back to the harem or to continue the fight for their own independence. They opted for the struggle.[31]

Egyptian women's agendas and timetables developed out of their own circumstances and their own goals for self-realisation. Despite men's articulation of a feminist ideology, and the promises made to women by men to assist their integration into society in the height of the nationalist struggle, during the aftermath of independence these male feminist claims were slow to find translation into practice. As history shows, they only came about later due to pressure by women's feminism.

Conclusion

I have discussed the context in which feminism arose and how it evolved from early consciousness, and have demonstrated that women's feminism preceded the feminism articulated by Qasim Amin, that it transcended class divisions and that it was specifically Egyptian. The answers to the question of why women's feminism arose and took the shape it did are illuminated by the lives and responses of the women discussed in this article. Middle- and upper-class women alike were able to create and take advantage of new opportunities within the climate of change. New forms of education and enlightenment through expanding contacts and experiences made them less willing to endure constraints imposed by patriarchal authority. While women were liberating themselves from strict seclusion, their own female world expanded (because, as I have pointed out, this strict seclusion also separated women from each other even within the same social class). Women from various parts of Egypt and of different religions and classes who had come to Cairo mingled with each other, as well as with women from the Caucasus, Turkey, Syria and Lebanon, providing each other with different examples of female life. In the mountains of the Caucasus, for example, society was considerably more liberal and sexually egalitarian. In Turkey, segregation and seclusion were far less strict, while women from Syria and Lebanon had been able to lessen the bond of confinement. We need to know more about the impact on each other of these Eastern women from such diverse backgrounds as a catalyst for feminism in Egypt. The contacts which Egyptian women had with European women (and Europe through travel), in different ways catalysts for change, have attracted more notice and have often been exaggerated.

When women in Egypt realised that their religion (Islam and Christianity) did not require the constraints of the harem system, their restiveness must have been exacerbated on the one hand,

and on the other hand they found legitimate cause within the framework of their religion to reach beyond these constraints. The rise of the state and the growth of a capitalist economy, which brought different forms of social and economic change, opened up - both by design and by accident - new opportunities for women, but also created new tensions. Out of the conflicts and setbacks, women forged an ideology and strategies to liberate themselves. A distinct understanding grew among women (however differently expressed) that the harem system was a patriarchal structure which deprived them of their rights, and which one day would have to be demolished.

This paper has set out a new framework for analysis. We are only just starting to create a historiography of Egyptian women's feminism. Much primary research is still required on most of the women discussed in this paper, as well as others not included here, whose stories need to be excavated by painstaking spadework. The Egyptian experience, I think, raises an overriding theoretical question: to what extent can men be called feminists? Those who have formal power and authority surely must help in changing structures imposed from within their own ranks, but in the end it is the oppressed themselves who must bring about their own liberation.[32] Britons (by their nationality affiliated with colonial oppression) who were sympathetic to the goals of Egyptian nationalism could, and did, assist to some extent the Egyptian cause, but finally independence had to be won and a new life constructed by Egyptians themselves. Ultimately only women can liberate themselves and perhaps only they can be called feminists.

Notes

1. See Kumari Jayawardena, *Feminism and nationalism in the Third World* (Zed Books, London, 1986).

2. Jane Rendall, *The origins of modern feminism: women in Britain, France and the United States, 1780-1860* (Shocken Books, New York, 1984).

3. Clearly there were positive aspects of the female cloistered world, and women were by no means only victims. However, seclusion had been imposed, and the world of women was ultimately controlled by patriarchal authority. Even within individual households there was a social (class and sexual) order that segmented women. See Mervat Hatem, 'The politics of sexuality and gender in segregated patriarchal systems: the case of eight-

eenth and ninetheenth century Egypt', *Feminist Studies*, 12, 2 (Summer 1986), pp. 260-1.

4. When I began my research on feminism in Egypt in the sixties, Saiza Nabarawi, who was then an elderly woman and veteran feminist, lamented that the younger generation did not know about Huda Sha'rawi and other early women feminists in Egypt. Jayawardena, *Feminism and nationalism*, Introduction, makes the same point about the ignorance of feminist movements in all the Asian countries she studied.

5. I began my research on Huda Sha'rawi and the feminist movement she led from 1923 to her death in 1947 for my PhD (1977) at Oxford. My thesis was entitled: 'Huda Sha'rawi and the liberation of the Egyptian woman'. My research began before women's studies had taken form as a discipline. I have continued research in this area and am currently completing a book on the subject.

6. In the sixties and early seventies, I interviewed more than sixty women in Egypt, most of whom have since died.

7. Juan Ricardo Cole, 'Feminism, class and Islam in turn-of-the-century Egypt', *International Journal of Middle East Studies*, 13 (1981), pp. 397-407.

8. Thomas Philipp, 'Feminism and nationalist politics in Egypt' in L. Beck and N. Keddie (eds), *Women in the Muslim world* (Harvard University Press, Cambridge, Mass., 1978), pp. 285-308.

9. For background see Roger Owen, *The Middle East in the world economy* (Methuen, London, 1981); Afaf Lutfi al-Sayyid Marsot, *Egypt in the reign of Muhammad Ali* (Cambridge University Press, Cambridge, 1984); Jacques Berque, trans. J. Stewart, *Egypt: imperialism and revolution* (Faber and Faber, London, 1972).

10. On this new class see F. Robert Hunter, *Egypt under the Khedives 1804-1879: from household government to modern bureaucracy* (University of Pittsburgh Press, Pittsburgh, 1984).

11. See David S. Landes, *Bankers and pashas: international finance and economic imperialism in Egypt* (William Heinemann, London, 1958).

12. Judith Tucker, *Women in nineteenth century Egypt* (Cambridge University Press, Cambridge, 1985), elaborates this in a study of lower-class urban and peasant women.

13. For more information concerning the harem see Margot Badran, 'Huda Sha'rawi and the liberation of the Egyptian woman', PhD thesis, Oxford, 1977, pp. 1-11.

14. Ibid., pp. 11-117.

15. See Albert Hourani, *Arabic thought in the liberal age* (Cambridge University Press, Cambridge, 1983), pp. 130-60.

16. On Qasim Amin see ibidem, pp. 164-70. According to Afaf Lutfi al-Sayyid Marsot, *Egypt and Cromer* (Murray, London, 1968), p. 187, Qasim Amin, Ahmad Lutfi Al-Sayyid and Sa'd Zaghlul (prominent intellectual

and nationalist figures) all worked on the book *The liberation of the woman* whilst on holiday together in Geneva in 1896. Murqus Fahmi presented his views through the medium of drama with an introduction. As a Copt he spoke more broadly about the ills of female seclusion and segregation, and did not present the threat that the Muslim Amin did. His book was privately printed and had a limited circulation, according to his daughter Andrée Fahmi. Men also expressed pro-feminist views in the press; for early examples see Byron D. Cannon in 'Nineteenth century writings on women and society: the interim role of the Masonic Press in Cairo - Al-Lata'if, 1885-1895', *International Journal of Middle East Studies*, 17 (1985), pp. 463-84. He notes that their ideas came from the West through international masonic connections.

17. 'Aisha Al Taimuriyya, *Nata'ij al ahwal fi al aqwal wa al af'al* (The consequences of circumstances in words and deeds) (Cairo, 1887). The foreword to this, translated into English by Marilyn Booth, will appear in a forthcoming book on Arab women's writings edited by Margot Badran and Miriam Cooke.

18. Huda Sha'rawi, *Harem years: the memoirs of an Egyptian feminist*, translated and introduced by Margot Badran (Virago Press, London, 1986), pp. 39-42.

19. Personal communication from Saiza Nabarawi in Cairo in 1967, who recounted that it was Huda Sha'rawi, her late mother's friend, who finally persuaded her to end her rebellion and put on the veil, saying that later they would take it off.

20. See Badran, 'Huda Sha'rawi', pp. 192-4 and Philipp, 'Feminism and nationalist politics'. Beth Baron has carried out research on women's early journal literature for her doctoral dissertation in progress for the University of California at Los Angeles. Her translation of the inaugural editorial in *Al Fatah* by Hind Nawfal will appear in the book edited by Badran and Cooke. Zainab Fawwaz also wrote poems, essays and novels, and published a biographical dictionary of Arab and European women entitled *Al durr al manthur fi tabaqat rabbat al khudur*. Marilyn Booth's translation of Zainab Fawwaz's 'Fair and equal treatment' in *Al Nil*, 15 (1891) will appear in the book of Badran and Cooke.

21. Bahithat Al Bad'iyya, *Al nisa'iyyat* (Feminist discourse) (Cairo, 1910) is a collection of her essays and speeches. Nabawiyya Musa, *Al ayat al aiyyinat fi tarbiyyat al banat* (A treatise on girls' education) (Cairo, 1920) and *Al mar'a wa al 'amal* (Woman and work) (Cairo, 1920).

22. Huda Sha'rawi, *Harem years*, pp. 76-82. Eugénie Rushdi wrote two books, *Harem et les Musulmanes* (Paris, 1902) and *Les repudiées* (Paris, 1908). At the turn of the century, Djavidan Hanim, an American-born woman of Austro-Hungarian descent and wife of Abbas Hilmi II (Khedive of Egypt), who also became a Muslim, learned through her study of Islam that veiling and the harem system were not required by religion, but in her position

she was isolated from Egyptian women and thus would not have been part of the contemporary debate. In the exile that followed the deposition of her husband, she wrote *Harem life* (New York, 1931).

23. Badran, 'Huda Sha'rawi', p. 85.

24. See *Al mu'allifat al kamila: Mayy Ziyada* (Complete works of Mayy Ziyada), compiled by Salama Al Haffar Al Kuzbari (2 vols., Beirut, 1982). Spanish translation: *Llama azul: cartas ineditas a Mayy Ziyadeh* (Instituto Hispano-Arabe de Cultura, Madrid, 1978). Marilyn Booth has done research on the life and works of Mayy Ziyada.

25. See Huda Sha'rawi, *Harem years*, pp. 92-143, and her 'Dhikra bahithat al bad'iyya' (Eulogy), *Al Miisriyya*, 1 November 1937.

26. The creation of the Egyptian University was generously supported by a woman, Princess Fatma, daughter of the late Khedive Isma'il: she donated the land for it and a collection of jewels to defray costs.

27. This information was communicated to me by Donald Reid, who obtained it from Cairo University Archives. His forthcoming book on the history of Cairo University deals with the Women's Section (1909-12).

28. Badran, 'Huda Sha'rawi', pp. 323-26.

29. Huda Sha'rawi, *Harem years*, pp. 94-7; Badran, 'Huda Sha'rawi', pp. 108-10; Afaf Lutfi al-Sayyid Marsot, 'The revolutionary gentlewomen in Egypt' in Beck and Keddie (eds), *Women in the Muslim world*.

30. For Rahma Sarruf's report on the conference see 'Mu'tamar nisa'i al 'amm' (The all-women's conference), *Al Muqtataf*, September 1899, pp. 675-7.

31. Margot Badran, 'Dubbele bevrijding: feminisme en nationalisme in Egypte, 1880-1925' in Selma Sevenhuijsen, Petra de Vries, Juliette Zipper and Joyce Outshoorn (eds), *Socialisties-Feministiese Teksten*, vol. 10 (Ambo, Baarn, 1987), pp. 204-26; also forthcoming in *Feminist Issues* under the title 'Dual liberation: feminism and nationalism in Egypt, 1880-1925'.

32. There were many Egyptian men who contributed to the cause of women's liberation, including Ahmad Lutfi Al Sayyid and Taha Husain (already mentioned), and other men whom members of the Egyptian Feminist Union asked to serve as advisors.

Jo Anne Preston

Female aspiration and male ideology: school-teaching in nineteenth-century New England

In 1863, Agnes Walker of Springfield, Vermont, wrote to her friend Kate Foster, who resided in Walpole, New Hampshire: 'I want to teach. Oh Kate, I am sold on teaching.' Why Agnes Walker and many other nineteenth-century New England women became 'sold on teaching' is the central question considered in this article. Here I compare the image of the female schoolteacher popularised by the school reformers with female schoolteachers' own descriptions of their motives and expectations. I found that nineteenth-century female schoolteachers' aspirations differed from those attributed to them by the reformers. The women wanted to achieve economic independence and to continue their scholarly pursuits; they expressed little interest in mothering the children or inculcating them with morals. My findings suggest that the sex-typing of teaching had a limited impact on a nineteenth-century woman's decision to become a schoolteacher.

This article considers the agency of women as a factor in their participation in the labour force; one which is frequently ignored in research on working women. All too often scholars have assumed that working women accepted the dominant gender ideology and behaved accordingly.[1] In this study, I inquire whether women's aspirations for themselves may have differed from those which were socially prescribed. This perspective questions the assumption that women chose an occupation because it confirmed their femininity. Recent scholarship on women in the labour force has suggested that several non-wage factors shape women's employment decisions: the limited number of occupations which are open to women, the need for jobs which are compatible with child-care arrangements, and the desire to affirm their womanhood in female-identified jobs.[2] I examine the third proposition: that women enter an occupation because they perceive it as being appropriate to their sex.

In the period concerned here, teaching was changing from a predominantly male to a predominantly female occupation, a phenomenon which caused both educational leaders and schoolteachers themselves to write about the nature of the occupation.[3] State school officials who actively promoted the feminisation of teaching wrote extensively about women's 'aptness' to teach. The opening up of the teaching profession to women also inspired many mid-nineteenth-century female teachers, the first generation of women to enter teaching in large numbers, to convey their expectations and experiences in their personal correspondence. I use the writings of both the school reformers and the female teachers to examine the relationship between gender ideology and the consciousness of working women.

Ironically, when for the first time the greater number of schoolteachers were women, a new set of beliefs which prescribed that women's place was in the home became culturally dominant. These beliefs, characterised by Barbara Welter as the cult of true womanhood, held that women were pious, pure, domestic and submissive.[4] The new social ideal, which emerged in response to the social and economic changes in the late-eighteenth and early-nineteenth century, relegated women to a separate sphere where they, because of their supposed biologically-determined qualities, were to uphold moral values.[5] Unlike eighteenth-century beliefs concerning femininity, which considered women to be similar to men but inferior in all respects, nineteenth-century gender ideology defined women as having special attributes which men did not possess. Although, prescriptively, women's educational duties were restricted to the moral instruction of their own children in the home, school committees drew on the nineteenth-century ideal of women to re-define teaching as a feminine vocation.

The new definition of teaching as women's work can be found in the writings of New England state school officials. Many mid-nineteenth-century state school committee members were leaders, or at the very least supporters, of the school reform movement. They believed that the employment of female teachers was critical to the implementation of the desired reforms. The school reformers perceived that female teachers would be more amenable to changes within the schools, such as a longer school year, graded classes and increased supervision. Furthermore, women's lower wages would allow local school committees to implement these changes without raising taxes.[6] Local school boards, however, were still reluctant to employ women. To convince the local employment committees of the advantages of taking on women, state school committee members argued in their essays and proclamations that women were not only equal but superior to men as teachers, because of certain 'natural' feminine qualities. The essays discussed here were found in the annual state school reports published between 1837 and 1880.

For data on female teachers' perceptions of their occupation, I have collected these teachers' unpublished writings. The correspondence and diaries examined were chosen from those written by women who taught in publicly-supported schools in New England between 1830 and 1880. Writings of women from prominent families and of those women who taught in exclusive private schools were eliminated from the sample. The unpublished letters of the remaining schoolteachers, although hard to find, are an important source of material for feminist historians. They reveal thoughts and experiences which are more representative of women in general than those of upper-class women.[7] The letters which I used to determine female schoolteachers' self-perceptions were written by New England women between 1830 and 1880, the period during which schoolteaching became statistically and ideologically women's work. The women were from families of moderate means, mostly farmers' daughters. All of the 43 women whose unpublished correspondence I found were unmarried and between the ages of 15 and 25 when they wrote their letters. By analysing their correspondence, I have attempted to construct their common view of teaching.

The state school committee members: the reformulation of teaching as women's work

School reformers, in their capacity as state school officials, wrote extensively on the virtues of female teachers in their efforts to persuade local school committees to employ more women. Horace Mann made a reference to this campaign in the 1841 Massachusetts State School Report: 'The expediency of employing a large portion of female teachers was first urged upon the consideration of the towns and districts in 1837.'[8] These men used the prevailing ideal of the 'true' woman to show that women had natural qualities which would enable them to be superior teachers. These arguments, which re-defined teaching as an appropriate female occupation, had appeared by the 1840s in the state school reports of four New England states: Massachusetts, Rhode Island, Connecticut and New Hampshire, and disappeared in the 1860s once female teachers began to be regularly employed. The state school committee members of Vermont and Maine (states where schoolteaching was not a predominantly female occupation until 1880) did not campaign for the employment of female teachers. The absence of a strong school reform movement in these states may account for this difference. In the following section, I examine the writings of the three state school officials who vigorously promoted the employment of female teachers - Horace Mann, Henry Bernard and Richard Rust - giving special attention to the way in which they used the major tenets of the cult of true womanhood (piety, purity, domesticity and submissiveness) to re-define teaching as women's work.

Horace Mann, during his tenure as Secretary of the Massachusetts Board of Education from 1837 to 1841, put forward numerous arguments for the employment of female teachers. In an essay dated 1841, he proclaimed that 'females were incomparably better teachers for young children than males'. Mann asserted that women were superior to men as teachers because of qualities they possessed 'by nature'. He claimed that women's 'manners' were 'more mild and gentle', attributes which were consistent with the 'true women's' docility. He also used the belief in women's domesticity to propose that 'women's stronger parental impulse makes [for them] the society of children delightful, and turns duty into pleasure'. Furthermore, according to Mann, because women are domestic by nature they are reluctant 'to break away from the domestic circle and go abroad in to the world, to build up a fortune for themselves'.[9] In this state school report essay, Mann tried to assure town school committees that women, unlike male teachers, would not leave teaching for more remunerative jobs in the West. In Mann's view, the female teacher was a submissive and reliable employee whose natural love of children would place 'their company' before a desire for high wages.

Although Horace Mann did on occasion mention women's purer morals, he placed more emphasis on their domesticity. In 1845 he wrote: 'All those differences of organization and temperament which individualize the sexes point to the female as guide and guardian of young children.' During the nineteenth century, women's relationship to children became primarily a nurturing one, which Mann claimed would continue in the classroom. According to him, women would develop a strong emotional bond with children in the school as well as in the home. Mann predicted that women would make ideal teachers because in the 'female character there is always the preponderance of affection over intellect'.[10] However, he never considered the obvious contradiction between the social prescription of women's place being in the home and his mandate for women's outside employment in schools.

Similarly, Henry Bernard, the first Secretary of Education in Connecticut and also an advocate of school reform, argued for more female teachers because of their 'peculiar talents'. He proclaimed in 1840: 'Heaven has plainly appointed females as the natural instructors of young children, and endowed them with those qualities of mind and disposition which pre-eminently fit them for such a task.' Like Mann, he stressed women's natural love of children: '[Women are] endued with a greater measure of the gentleness so winning and grateful to the feelings of a child.' Moreover, in Bernard's view, women have a special ability to control unruly students. He wrote: '[Women] have altogether superior success in managing...children, and I know of instances whereby the silken cord of affection, has led many a stubborn will, and wild, ungovernable impulse, into habits of obedience and study.'[11] According to Bernard, the female schoolteacher was to govern the classroom by affection, not by force.

After having been dismissed by the Governor for his attempts to reform the state school system, Bernard was appointed Secretary of Education for the state of Rhode Island in 1845. In his new position, he resumed his campaign for school reform and, as a part of that campaign, his arguments for employing female teachers. 'The peculiar talents of females', he reasoned, 'their more gentle and refined manners, purer morals...their power when properly developed, [are capable] of governing even the most wild and stubborn minds by moral influences.'[12] In this passage he claims that the female schoolteacher rules by moral suasion as well as by affection.

Richard Sutton Rust, the Secretary of Education for the State of New Hampshire from 1848 to 1851, wrote a special section in the 1849 school report entitled 'The employment of female teachers'. In this section he argued that most of the qualities of a good teacher are found in the female. The essential characteristics of such a teacher were kindness and affection, patience, purity of character, literary accomplishments, aptness to teach and ability to govern a school. Rust concluded that women possessed the first four characteristics - kindness, affection, patience and purity of character - 'in an eminent degree'. He did state, however, that women were deficient in natural brilliance and therefore in literary attainments, but he argued they could acquire enough education to teach in a district school.[13]

Through the efforts of these school reformers a new representation of the female schoolteacher emerged. Drawing on the Victorian ideal of femininity, they proposed that the female teacher was gentle, submissive and morally pure. Nineteenth-century gender ideology held that women's intellect was inferior to that of men; nevertheless, school reformers argued that a female teacher's capacity for reasoning, however limited, was sufficient to enable her to comprehend and therefore teach rudimentary skills. Since the nineteenth-century female teacher did not aspire after worldly goods, she could place the welfare of the students, and for that matter of society as a whole, before monetary gain. Finally, a female teacher's superior morals allowed her to control the class by moral suasion rather than brute force. Mann, Bernard and Rust, as well as other advocates of school reform, hoped that their depiction of the female teacher would persuade town employment committees to take women into consideration when recruiting new teachers.

Even though the prominent educationists Emma Willard and Catherine Beecher similarly described the female teacher in their campaign for more female academies, it was school reformers like Mann, with their greater political power, who re-defined teaching as an appropriate occupation for women.[14] Because they were frequently quoted in the popular press, and their school report essays were read by local school boards, the new image of the female teacher was widely disseminated throughout their respective states. The question still to be considered is, how did the school reformers' depiction of the female teacher affect the consciousness of New England women?

The female schoolteacher: aspirations and occupational choice

The vast majority of mid-nineteenth-century New England schoolteachers were native-born Protestant Americans of British or Northern Irish descent. They were primarily farmers' daughters who had received further education in a New England female academy or seminary after primary school. The women whose unpublished writings provide the evidence for this analysis share the above characteristics. The correspondence cited here was written either to their families or to close female friends. At the time they wrote the letters, most women were either attending a female academy, living at home after graduation or teaching.

The school reformers consistently portrayed female teachers as 'unaspiring', especially in their academic endeavours, which is not borne out by the New England women's writings under examination here. Women who were about to become teachers wrote from female academies or their familial homes of their desire to aggressively pursue their intellectual interests. Nellie Gay, a student at Glennwood Ladies' Seminary in Brattleboro, Vermont, wrote in 1860: 'When I get out of school I mean to read more than I ever have done. I mean to take a thorough course of History, and also cultivate a more intimate acquaintance with the poets.'[15] Other women who had begun teaching expressed their ambition to 'keep up with their German', 'practise composition' and 'read all the great masters'.[16] These New England women articulated the hope that schoolteaching would be a means of continuing an intellectual life, a motive not consistent with the attributes of the ideal female teacher as posited by the school reformers.

Another motive not mentioned by Mann, Bernard or Rust was the desire for good wages. Before applying for teaching positions, women carefully considered the wages offered. When Nellie Gay sought a teaching position in 1867, she wanted 'at least two dollars a week'. Aurelia Smith, a teacher in western Massachusetts in the

1840s, reported the wages earned for each of her teaching positions to show how she had bettered herself. When Mary Louisa Aldridge left teaching in 1871 to become a typesetter in Concord, New Hampshire, she wrote unabashedly of her greatly improved wages to her friends at home: 'I am getting rich fast - $11.26 last week and $11.68 this'. Her friends, who were soon to become teachers, approved of her ambition. From a female seminary in Providence, Rhode Island, Mary Rust wrote in 1873 to Kate Foster, who was then teaching in Walpole, New Hampshire: 'Do you ever hear from Mary Aldridge?...suppose she is in Concord earning money at a wonderful rate.'[17] Those teachers whose correspondence I have examined all considered good wages an important goal in seeking employment.

Good wages were important to nineteenth-century women because they enabled them to lead independent lives. Women who became teachers began to consider marriage an option, not a necessity. Mary Stackpole, a teacher in Waterborough, Maine, in the 1860s, wrote the following to her mother, who was trying to persuade her to marry someone she detested:

> 'I don't think he loves me so well... I wish I never met him or anyone else in Skowhegan...perhaps you think this is strange but Mother it is the truth. Oh Mother I had rather work hard and be happy than to have him and be unhappy.'[18]

Some female teachers yearned for even more independence. Mary Rust and many other New England women used their earnings from teaching to migrate west. Mary wrote in 1863: 'All I ask for is to get enough money to go West, you've no idea how terrible I have got the Western fever.'[19] Contrary to Mann's claim that women were reluctant 'to break away from the domestic circle', female teachers sought to lead autonomous lives through teaching.

As a further contradiction to the school reformers' claims, New England women did not become teachers because it suited their submissive nature. Female teachers were in frequent conflict with parents, students and local school boards. For example, they had many confrontations with school committee members over unsatisfactory boarding places. In 1839, Julia Pierce insisted that the Washington, Massachusetts school committee arrange for her 'to board at one place near the school house'.[20] Hannah Adams, a teacher in Sandown, New Hampshire, threatened to return home if she were not boarded within half a mile of the school. In 1832, she sent her sister the following account of her negotiations with the school committee:

> 'Mr. Teney...said I would board with Mrs. Hoyt, but the distance from the school house was more than half a mile and I should not walk any further. I would rather go home... Mon. morning he told me I might have my choice of boarding places.'[21]

Mary Aldridge, writing from Northhampton, Massachusetts in 1871, described her boarding-place as a 'wretched place generally' and demanded another.[22] In none of their letters did female teachers reveal a submissive attitude towards persons in authority.

I also found a great disparity between school reformers' and female teachers' descriptions of student-teacher relationships. State school officials portrayed female teachers as having a natural love and affection for all children. They claimed that women's positive feelings for children, as well as their superior morals, enabled female teachers to govern their students by 'the silken bond of affection' and 'moral suasion'. However, female teachers wrote only occasionally of positive feelings towards their students; their letters frequently described these students in more negative terms. In the 1840s, Julia Pierce described her students in Phoenix, Massachusetts, as 'backward'.[23] Agnes Walker wrote in 1865 that her cousin Amanda, who was teaching in the Connecticut River Lower District, 'had as disagreeable and rebellious a set of children as fell to the lot of any teacher', and described her own feelings towards students as follows: 'Some days I feel so cross I want to slap their ears. I have a class of Dunces in Arithmetic that try the life out of me.'[24] Mary Louisa Aldridge, when she began teaching in Hinsdale, New Hampshire in 1870, wrote home that her pupils were 'a pretty dirty set' whom she tried to 'govern by moral suasion', but she soon discovered that 'they are callous to soft soap or any of the milder forms of moral suasion'. She reported that: 'At the end of the fourth week I provided myself with a weapon in case I should need it - a leather strap one yard long by two inches wide.'[25] These female teachers, many of whom had recently graduated from female academies, were often horrified by their students' lack of personal hygiene and good manners. They wrote of their disapproval of the pupils despite their supposed 'natural affection'. Except for the one unsuccessful attempt by Mary Aldridge, these women did not try to 'govern by moral suasion'.

Ideology, women's self-perceptions and occupational choice

The promotion of a well-developed belief that women were by nature superior teachers demands that the impact of these ideas on women's employment decisions be considered. In the preceding section I presented nineteenth-century women's expectations and perceptions of teaching, which I determined by examining their correspondence and subsequently compared my findings to the new public image of the female schoolteacher. The evidence shows that the new representation of the female schoolteacher, although widely publicised, bore little resemblance to the female teachers' views of themselves or their aspirations. These nineteenth-century women had their own reasons for wanting to teach, and the propaganda campaign was possibly more effective in changing the attitudes of town school committees, which habitually discriminated against women, than in persuading women to seek teaching positions. And indeed that may have been its intent.

The results of my study also suggest that women had ambitions which were not shaped by the dominant ideology of their time. The female teachers whose correspondence I found wanted an independent life dedicated to their own self-improvement. The reasons for their rejection of the prevailing view of femininity are left to conjecture. Perhaps female academies and women's enduring friendships allowed women an opportunity to formulate their own identities. I do not make the claim that all female teachers shared the views expressed by those in this study; rather, I propose that many nineteenth-century women could and did formulate a perception of themselves which had not been prescribed by society. The disparity between these women's self-perceptions and the ideal of the female teacher demonstrates the importance of questioning the assumptions presented in prescriptive literature, and of examining the verbal and written evidence of the women themselves.

Notes

1. See Linda Gordon's discussion on the agency of women in 'What's new in women's history' in Teresa de Lauretis (ed.), *Feminist studies, critical studies* (Indiana University Press, Bloomington, 1986), pp. 20-30.

2. Barbara R. Bergman, *The economic emergence of women* (Basic Books, New York, 1986), pp. 36-8.

3. I discuss the causes of feminisation in my dissertation: Jo Anne Preston, 'Feminization of an occupation: teaching becomes women's work in nineteenth-century New England', Brandeis University, Waltham, M.A., 1982.

4. Barbara Welter, 'The cult of true womanhood 1820-1860', *American Quarterly*, 17 (1966), pp. 151-74.

5. Nancy Cott, *The bonds of womanhood: 'women's sphere' in New England 1780-1835* (Yale University Press, New Haven, 1977), pp. 197-204.

6. Preston, 'Feminization of an occupation'.

7. Caroll Smith-Rosenberg, 'Hearing women's words: a feminist reconstruction' in Caroll Smith-Rosenberg (ed.), *Disorderly conduct: visions of gender in America* (Oxford University Press, London, 1985), pp. 11-52.

8. Massachusetts State School Report 1846, pp. 25-6.

9. Massachusetts State School Report 1840, p. 45.

10. Massachusetts State School Report 1842, p. 24.

11. Connecticut State School Report 1840, pp. 6-7.

12. Rhode Island State School Report 1845, p. 11.

13. New Hampshire State School Report 1849, pp. 32-9.

14. Katherine Kish Sklar, *Catherine Beecher: a study in American domesticity* (W.W. Norton, New York, 1976), pp. 113-15; Thomas Woody, *A history of women's education in the United States* (Octagon Books, New York, 1966), vol. 1, p. 503.

15. Nellie Gay, Swansey, New Hampshire, to Kate Foster, Walpole, New Hampshire, 8 May 1860, Kate Foster Collection (private).

16. Lucy Britton, Walpole, New Hampshire, to Kate Foster, West Brattleboro, Vermont, 20 March 1859, Kate Foster Collection; P.A. Jennison, Worcester, Massachusetts, to Kate Foster, New Hampshire, 6 December 187-, Kate Foster Collection.

17. Nellie Gay, Swansey, New Hampshire, to Kate Foster, Walpole, New Hampshire, 12 April 1867; Aurelia Smith, West Otis, Massachusetts, to Smith family, Fulton, New York, July 1850, Hooker Family Collection, Schlessinger Library, Radcliffe College; Mary Louisa Aldridge, Concord, New Hampshire, to Kate Foster, Walpole, New Hampshire, 17 August 1871, Kate Foster Collection; Mary Rust, Providence, Rhode Island, to Kate Foster, Walpole, New Hampshire, 17 November 1873, Kate Foster Collection.

18. Mary Stackpole, Waterborough, Maine, to Elizabeth Stackpole, Topsham, Maine, 3 February 1863, Waterborough Historical Society.

19. Mary Rust, East Shelbourne, New Hampshire, to Kate Foster, Walpole, New Hampshire, 14 July 1871.

20. Julia Pierce, Windsor, Massachusetts, to Sally Smith and Fulton family, New York, 24 November 1839, Hooker Collection.

21. Hannah Adams, Sandown, New Hampshire, to Mary Adams, Derry, New Hampshire, 9 June 1831, Adams family Collection (private).

22. Mary Louisa Aldridge, Hinsdale, New Hampshire, to Kate Foster, Walpole, New Hampshire, 18 December 1870.

23. Julia Pierce, Phoenix, Massachusetts, to Sally Smith, Volney, New York, 1845.

24. Agnes Walker, Springfield, Vermont, to Kate Foster, Walpole, New Hampshire, 16 February 1865.

25. Mary Louisa Aldridge, Hinsdale, New Hampshire, to Kate Foster, Walpole, New Hampshire, 18 December 1870.

Alison Oram

'Embittered, sexless or homosexual': attacks on spinster teachers 1918-39

The image of the spinster teacher changed during the inter-war period and became increasingly negative; the idea of her as an embittered, thwarted woman with overtones of sexual frustration or deviance developed. This can be seen in the substance and tone of the many attacks which were made on single women teachers by the press, by anti-feminist men teachers and sometimes by the local authorities which employed them. I shall examine the terms of this increased hostility and suggest some reasons for it, and then go on to look at the response made by women teachers to it in the context of inter-war feminism.

My interest in spinster teachers and how they were portrayed stemmed in the first place from my wider research into the position of women teachers between the wars, and especially their response to the marriage bar.[1] The teachers I shall discuss worked in the state sector of education in England and Wales. They were mostly elementary (i.e. primary) school teachers, although some reference is made to state secondary school teachers. School-teaching was the only profession in which large numbers of women could earn a salary which was much above subsistence level, although they still received only four-fifths of men's pay. It was a public role; women teachers were visible and indeed important figures in their local communities. They also, of course, had authority and influence in relation to the children in their schools.

During the 1920s and 30s most women teachers were spinsters. This was due to the fact that in the early 1920s the majority of local education authorities introduced regulations requiring women teachers to resign on marriage. The censuses of 1921 and 1931 show that approximately 85 per cent of all women teachers (in all types of schools) were unmarried. Separate figures for elementary schools confirm this pattern, while for secondary schools the figure was probably higher. The actual number of spinster teachers working in state schools was about 150,000 throughout this period.

The large number of single women teachers at this time could also be explained by demographic factors. There had been more women than men in the population since the mid-nineteenth century, when it was first seen as a problem, and the high rate of mortality suffered by men during the First World War exacerbated the pattern. This situation obviously had an impact on a generation of women teachers, although during the inter-war period the balance between the sexes steadily became more equal and the marriage rate rose.[2] While the demographic facts showing women's reduced chances of marriage cannot be questioned, they do obscure the possibility that some women may have chosen not to marry, and that teaching may have been a route to secure this goal. Nevertheless, the predominance of spinster teachers could be explained by circumstances beyond their control: the loss of men in the war and the marriage bar. Why, then, should women teachers be abused as spinsters? My investigation into this contradiction was further prompted by my involvement in the Lesbian History Group in London, and by the general questions which were emerging as important ones to ask about lesbian history and how the definition and control of female sexuality had implications for all women.[3]

One major set of questions has concentrated on the effects of the newly developed science of sex, or sexology, at the turn of the century. While it identified women's capacity for sexual enjoyment, sexology privileged heterosexuality as the only acceptable type of sexual expression, and created a particular definition of 'lesbian'. The ideas of sexologists such as Havelock Ellis were popularised during and after the First World War in marriage manuals and psychology books. Several feminist historians in Britain have shown that this created a climate which emphasised active heterosexuality as normal and indeed essential for women's health and happiness, while increasingly stigmatising celibate women, spinsters and lesbians.[4] I wanted to examine how far this scenario applied to a particular group of unmarried women - teachers - in the period 1918-39. Did their treatment by colleagues and by the popular press reflect this wider change?

Other insights from lesbian history also helped me to evolve some explanation for these attacks on spinster teachers. Another important debate has been around the definition and use of the term *lesbian*.[5] Lesbian feminist historians today wish to reject an entirely sexual definition of themselves. That is how male sexologists have defined and controlled lesbians. While stressing love between women as the primary significance of lesbianism, a feminist approach has also emphasised the position of lesbians as women outside heterosexuality, who by their very existence challenge the myth of its inevitability. If heterosexuality is one of the ways in which men's power over women is maintained, then lesbianism is or can be a threat to that power. This aspect of resistance involves all women outside heterosexuality, including celibate or unmarried women.[6] Like lesbians, they are all women who are not subject to men's social and sexual power through a personal relationship. Thus, although attacks were made on unmarried women teachers primarily as spinsters rather than as lesbians, it will be argued that they were maligned for being outside heterosexuality. The use of lesbianism as a stigma is a way all women are controlled. While individual spinsters may well have felt that they had 'missed out' on marriage, they none the less could be seen as a threat because they were outside conventional womanhood. Some spinster teachers were undoubtably 'lesbians', whatever definition we take, but all were affected, and their status attacked, by accusations that they were warped, repressed and deviant.

However, I do not want to offer an explanation entirely dependent on changing ideas about women's sexuality. The particular kind of heterosexuality which was encouraged in this period assumed women's financial dependence on their husbands. Men feared economically independent married women, hence the marriage bar. Likewise, there were also economic reasons for these attacks on spinster teachers. It is important to look at women teachers' feminist politics and their position within the profession *vis-à-vis* men. Women teachers had a particularly high profile in this period because of their battles concerning equal opportunities in the profession. The most important issues were equal pay, equal promotion prospects and the marriage bar. A great deal of antagonism was created between women and men teachers as a result, and the National Union of Teachers (NUT) was split. Just after the First World War, some women teachers broke away to form the feminist National Union of Women Teachers (NUWT), and at much the same time a group of anti-feminist men teachers left to set up the National Association of Schoolmasters (NAS). Thus women teachers posed a feminist challenge to their male colleagues.[7]

One of my main sources for remarks about and attacks on spinster teachers in this period was the *Times Educational Supplement.* This weekly paper reflected informed opinion in the educational world, and also reported speeches made at teachers' conferences and in local government debates. By contrast, the popular press presented more sensationalised attacks on spinster teachers. To gauge the NUWT's response I used their reported speeches, together with articles in their journal *The Woman Teacher*, which reflected their united public face. However, since the union avoided discussing the issue of sexuality openly, more revealing material was found in personal correspondence in their archive.

Although I hope to show that unmarried women teachers were attacked as spinsters in a very negative way and with increasingly sexualised overtones, I have continued myself to use the loaded term *spinster* rather than the more neutral word 'single' in describing them. This is what they called themselves, and some of them were clearly trying to show that they were not ashamed of being spinsters.

Sexology and spinsters

Abuse of and contempt for spinsters was not, of course, a new development of the 1920s. In the Victorian era, popular prejudice had labelled spinsters redundant, superfluous women, and scorned them as old maids who had failed in the marriage market.

> 'For what else do women come into the world but to be good wives?... Poor profitless, forlorn creatures they are, when they live single and get to be old; unless indeed they are rich enough to keep up an establishment, with a parcel of dogs and cats and parrots.'[8]

Women's sexuality in the inter-war period, as in the nineteenth century, was still to a large extent conflated with maternal instinct.[9] For women teachers this had particular relevance. Maternal feeling sometimes seemed to be as much part of the job description for women teachers as intellectual capacity. As one educational writer put it: 'Indeed, this very mother-love is the most characteristic feature of the born teacher of "babies" - the hall-mark of her high calling.'[10] This commonplace observation was applied not only to infant teachers but right up to secondary school level. Teaching was seen as a substitute for actual motherhood, for those women who were unfortunate enough not to be able to find a husband and real children. 'Teaching was the greatest profession open to women, except motherhood itself.'[11]

It was rather a contradiction, then, that single women teachers were increasingly criticised for not being actual mothers themselves, despite the fact that they would have lost their jobs upon marriage in most areas. The pressure on women to marry and produce children had become more intense and overt by the 1930s, in the context of the alarm over the falling birthrate. There was a renewed emphasis on teaching mothercraft and domestic subjects in schools in the 1920s and 30s. Women who were childless were seen as unfulfilled and abnormal, and this prescription of women's role as mothers had a particular edge for teachers.

Single women teachers just could not win. On the one hand, they were necessarily using their maternal qualities in their work, but on the other hand they were wasting their eugenic qualities as 'the cream of British womanhood'. Spinster teachers' lack of participation in motherhood was not only inauspicious for the future of the state and of the race, but if they were not careful, it could also be psychologically harmful to themselves.

Abuse of spinster teachers as old maids who lacked the social and sexual qualities to find a husband was not new, but this acquired a new edge during the 1920s and 30s. This was a period when the notion of marriage as a psychological as well as a social necessity for women was introduced. Popular sexology texts proclaimed that sexual relations with men were the only way to psychological health and fulfilment for women. They characterised women without male sexual partners as frustrated, a prey to complexes and neuroses.

By the 1930s, women teachers who failed to marry were subjected to warnings with ominous psychological overtones. In an address to the 1933 conference, the President of the Association of Assistant Mistresses declared that most women desired marriage, but if it did not happen to them, then women teachers should use their energy in their work and avoid becoming abnormal and bitter. The answer to this newly discovered problem was 'great power of sublimation on the part of the unmarried teacher'.[12] Psychological theories would have carried particular weight in the world of education, where psychology was rather fashionable. Both education policy and teachers themselves were influenced by it during the inter-war years; for instance, there was a plethora of books on child development written for the teacher.

Attacks on women teachers' professional capability gained force if they were couched in sexual terms, and especially when they came from the medical world. This began to happen in the 1930s. 'A warning of the danger of rearing a generation of "spinsters' sons", by allowing boys in elementary schools to be taught only by women, was uttered by Dr H. Crichton-Miller... They were likely to be warped in their development.'[13] This accusation was part of a debate over whether boys should only be taught by men teachers.[14] However, neither were spinster teachers necessarily welcome in girls' schools, for different reasons.

The growing sexology literature suggested that single women and female friendships were potentially perverse. Therefore, as well as supposedly suffering heterosexual frustration and its consequences, spinster teachers were also at times depicted as more sinister. During the 1920s and 30s there was a widening public awareness of lesbianism, or rather lesbianism as defined by the sexologists, and by the 1930s spinster teachers were subject to much more aggressive attacks in sexual terms. In 1935 this report of an educational conference appeared in a national newspaper.

> 'Dr Williams had dealt with the effect on the temperament of the ductless glands, and said that games such as hockey and lacrosse develop that part of the suprarenal gland which presides over the combative element of a person's character. "You cannot confine the desire and aptitude for combat to cricket and football", he said. "They inevitably appear in the whole character, and what was originally a gentle, feminine girl becomes harsh and bellicose in all relations to life. The women who have

> the responsibility of teaching these girls are many of them themselves embittered, sexless or homosexual hoydens who try to mould the girls into their own pattern. And far too often they succeed." Dr Williams declared that girls who have no desire to play combative games are cajoled and coerced into taking part by "these thin-lipped, flat-chested, sadistic creatures".'[15]

This kind of accusation was fairly extreme; most did not go so far. What is interesting about this particularly outrageous example is that by the 1930s it was possible for attacks of this type to be made, backed up by supposedly serious medical evidence. This one echoes the sexologists' definition of real lesbians as being masculine creatures who were a danger to normal women, especially if, as teachers, they had influence over young girls.[16]

The date of this attack is significant. Media interest in lesbians began during and after the First World War. In a scandal which hit the headlines in 1918, the dancer Maude Allen failed in her libel action to counter the charge that she was a lesbian. Radclyffe Hall won an action for slander in 1920, which was also reported in the press. In 1921 lesbianism was discussed in Parliament, but the attempt to bring it within the scope of the criminal law in the same way as male homosexuality was defeated.[17] But it was the prosecution in 1928 of Radclyffe Hall's novel in defence of lesbianism, *The well of loneliness*, which really marks a watershed in public awareness of lesbianism. This obscenity trial aroused a huge amount of publicity that identified the existence of lesbianism and led to suspicion being cast on single women, a suspicion which could be extended to spinster teachers. The harsher condemnation of women's friendships as perverse after 1928 has been identified by other writers.[18]

These new ideas and awareness about sexuality were frequently used to attack feminism. It has been argued that the sex reform movement of the 1920s and 30s directly challenged militant feminism. The newly invented notion of the frigid woman became a problem of major concern, and a term applied to spinster feminists who had rejected marriage, allegedly on the grounds of 'man-hating'. One sex reformer suggested the harm which could be done by spinster teachers.

> 'As a teacher, the frigide wields considerable power over the unformed minds of her pupils. She rarely takes pains to examine the justice of her indictment of man, and her bias is obvious to those whom she instructs. Her prudery is often imitated by the girls she is able to influence.'[19]

The insinuation that spinster teachers were lesbians was also used when attacking them as feminists. Throughout the nineteenth and twentieth centuries, feminists have been attacked in terms of their sexual status: as spinsters who, it was implied, could not get a man and were therefore against men. They were unfemZinine, power-hungry, and wanted to be men themselves. At the 1924 conference of the NAS, it was said: 'The claim of the teacher feminist was no longer for equal rights, but for the canonisation of the spinster.'[20] By 1939 women teachers were accused by the NAS of wanting to be men. 'There is in the teaching profession a small politically-minded minority of advanced feminists who curse their Maker that He did not allow them to enter this world wearing trousers.'[21]

Anti-feminism and economics

The sexual threat that spinster teachers were seen to pose cannot be disentangled from the economic threat that they presented to men. They were attacked as sexually independent spinsters and as feminists, but also as economically powerful women who challenged men's authority by demanding equal opportunities in the profession. The stigmatisation of spinster teachers was not solely a result of sexology, but also part of a post-war climate which was hostile to women's economic and political power.

During and immediately after the First World War, women extended their sphere in 'male' areas of work and won the vote for women over 30.[22] Many groups of men feared and opposed the emancipation of women. In the slump just after the war, women workers were accused of stealing men's jobs and were told to 'go back to the home'. Women's work was considered to be marriage and housewifery, not outside employment, and domestic values were re-emphasised. Men's anxiety focused on the greater opportunities and higher wages for women which the war had opened up. Having experienced a greater degree of economic independence, women might have less incentive to provide domestic services for men and children in marriage, and might even be able to avoid wedlock altogether. This fear was at times quite explicitly expressed.

Women teachers were in the forefront of the economic challenge to patriarchal power relations. They had a high profile in feminist campaigns generally, and were very involved in various battles concerning their own profession throughout the period. During the First World War, women teachers obtained better representation within the NUT and achieved the acceptance of equal pay as union policy. Marriage bars were relaxed in most areas until the early 1920s, and more women became teachers in boys' schools. Women teachers obtained a higher proportion of men's pay than before, although they did not win equal pay. The cuts in education spending caused by the recession of the early 1920s (and again in the 1930s) destroyed some of the women teachers' gains, and also increased men teachers' anxiety to safeguard their jobs.

Equal pay was one focus of discontent. Antagonism towards women teachers' economic position was frequently expressed by the NAS, or by men teachers with similar views. The anti-feminist NAS had broken away from the NUT in 1919-22 after the main union had voted to adopt a policy of equal pay for men and women teachers. Women teachers had achieved this policy commitment after a referendum of all members, the majority of whom were female. However, male control of the union hierarchy ensured that the NUT quietly ignored their equal pay policy throughout the inter-war years. It is likely that many of the men teachers in the NUT privately agreed with NAS policies, but did not want to lose the benefits of belonging to the largest union.

In fact, national pay awards in the inter-war period fixed women teachers' pay at four-fifths of the male rate. The NAS argued that the differentiation should be even greater. For example, at the union's 1937 conference, a certain Mr Rice said: 'they had no desire to deprive women teachers of anything and they were not anti-women, but they were concerned about their own existence. What was an adequate wage for the spinster teacher was entirely inadequate for the family man.'[23] The battle over equal pay versus the family wage (i.e. an income sufficient to support a wife and children) continued intermittently throughout the period. Concern and hostility were expressed about women teachers' standard of living in relation to men's. It was frequently alleged by the NAS that even with unequal salaries single women teachers could afford to take holidays abroad and run cars, while men had to take on additional work such as evening classes in order to fulfil their family responsibilities.

Women teachers were seen as being too highly paid as female workers, irrespective of the type of work they were performing. It was quite a commonly held view that men teachers should get more money, not just for economic reasons - their assumed family responsibilities - but on the grounds of sex superiority alone. They were paying

> 'too much money to bachelor women... It must be obvious to anyone that in starting a young man at £172 10s, scale 2, and a girl of the same age and same scale with £160 was grossly unfair in the social system of the country. It was productive of late marriages, and was inclined to elevate the bachelor girl to a position in this country that she should not attain.'[24]

An article in the *Times Educational Supplement* in 1932 commented: 'they can usually earn a steady wage, higher than their fathers' or brothers'; and if the teacher happens to be a slip of a girl this is not pleasant'.[25] Clearly, women were not supposed to earn enough to be able to live comfortably and independently.

Nor were they supposed to be in positions of power and authority over male colleagues. Continuing concern of both women and men teachers that the other sex was gaining a disproportionate number of headships also led to acrimony. 'Nearly 4,000 women were teaching purely boys' classes. Only a nation heading for the madhouse would force on men, many married with families, such a position as service under spinster headmistresses.'[26] Thus increased hostility towards spinster teachers in the inter-war period was part of a post-war backlash against women, and against feminism in particular, a backlash which was strengthened by sexology and which reflected economic issues.

The feminist response

How did spinster teachers respond to this stigmatisation? This part of the paper will examine in particular their reaction to the hostility which was voiced in sexual terms. I shall look specifically at the response of the National Union of Women Teachers, the small feminist teachers' union which split from the National Union of Teachers in 1920. The majority of the most active feminists left the NUT to work within the NUWT at this point, and the women who remained in the NUT were not at all vocal about any women's issue which might be seen as divisive.

The evidence shows that feminist teachers in the NUWT themselves took on to some extent the negative attitudes towards spinsters, especially when arguing for a married woman's right to work. They ignored or deflected attacks which used sexological ideas about frustrated spinsters or lesbian teachers. Altogether they were on the defensive, having lost a feminist political analysis of sexuality which had existed before the First World War.

I shall start by describing the wider context of feminism in the period before going on to illustrate and explain feminist teachers' response in terms of this. Other historians have shown that many feminists, during the years before the First World War, argued that remaining unmarried was a personally and politically important decision for women to make.[27] For them, celibacy plus the freedom of a career, or work within the women's movement, was a more rewarding life than the subordination of marriage and slavery to men's sexual demands. If women remained unmarried, this would improve the position of the spinster, and indeed all women, give women a real choice between marriage and spinsterhood, and eventually improve the conditions of marriage for women. Among the prominent feminists who promoted celibacy in this period were Christabel Pankhurst and also Cicely Hamilton in her book *Marriage as a trade*, published in 1909.[28] Nowadays, the word celibacy is normally taken to mean abstinence from sexual activity, but then it meant simply unmarried. It may even have been used as a label by turn-of-the-century feminists to indicate that they gave priority to women in their lives.

Shortly before the First World War, however, a different attitude was developing among some other feminists, which was to become more influential between the wars. These feminists were influenced by sexology, especially the writings of Havelock Ellis. They supported 'free unions', divorce law reform and the use of birth control to separate sex from reproduction. These women, including Stella Browne, Dora Russell and Marie Stopes, demanded that women had a right to sexual pleasure in heterosexual sex. But at the same time - in accordance with the growing sex reform movement which stressed the necessity of heterosexual intercourse for women and the dangers of sexual repression - they also attacked lesbians and spinsters who remained outside heterosexuality.[29]

The changing politics of spinsterhood has some parallels with general changes within feminism. During the inter-war period a divergence developed within the women's movement between old-style equal rights feminism on the one hand, and the new feminism or welfare feminism on the other, with the latter predominating by the 1930s. The equal rights feminists, having won the franchise for women, were concerned with equality under the law and with obtaining 'a fair field and no favour' for women in employment. New feminism, associated with Eleanor Rathbone and the National Union of Societies for Equal Citizenship, stressed reforms which took into account the different nature and circumstances of women's lives compared to men's, such as demands for family allowances, birth control and other benefits for women as mothers.

While the equal rights feminists at any rate continued to concern themselves with spinsters' rights, this was mainly in the fields of employment and housing. They did not continue to assert the political value of celibacy, although lone voices like Winifred Holtby did challenge the increasingly prevalent view of the frustrated and neurotic spinster.[30] Inter-war feminists did criticise marriage, demanding more rights for wives and divorce law reform, etc., but they did not advocate avoiding it as earlier feminists had done. The increasingly influential new feminism only rarely questioned men's power in marriage and heterosexuality, and did not generally include any positive vision of the spinster's role in feminist action. By 1930 the feminist Labour MP Ellen Wilkinson - herself unmarried - could write (about spinster teachers):

> 'The Suffragettes were hungry for life and for freedom. They fought to open the great storehouses of learning to women,

> that they might make a big thing of life. Has that vision become blurred, till all it means is the right to a bed-sitting room and a pensioned old age? It is not good enough. There is something wrong when thousands of women spend the best years of life discontented, lonely and thwarted.'[31]

By arguing for a full life for women, including the right to personal relationships, she suggests that there is no longer a coherent and exciting politics of spinsterhood which includes a further option - that of women's communities.

So where did the NUWT fit into the world of inter-war feminism? Clearly its emphasis and campaigning was around the employment rights of women teachers, especially the fight for equal pay, and this put it firmly in the 'equal rights' camp. The union co-operated closely with other equal rights feminist groups, but it did also have links with some of the more welfare-orientated groups.

The women in the NUWT had formerly worked as a feminist pressure group within the NUT, but had broken away from the main union to form a separate organisation at the end of the First World War, believing that they would never be able to fight unhindered for feminist aims such as equal pay within a mixed organisation. They were a strongly feminist group of women teachers, a group which numbered between 5,000 and 10,000, with branches all over the country. Practically all its members were single women - as were the NUT's - because of the marriage bar. Many NUWT members had formerly been active in the campaign for women's suffrage. Two of its official organisers had been among the leaders of the Women's Social and Political Union, the Pankhursts' militant suffragette organisation, and several of its leading figures had been involved in the Women's Freedom League, another militant group before the First World War. As feminists of this generation it is likely that some of the older spinster teachers in the NUWT had remained single as a political decision. However, by the 1930s it was evident that a generation gap was emerging between these women and the younger post-suffrage women teachers, and in 1938 a youth conference was organised 'to give the younger members some knowledge of the significance of the women's movement'.[32]

This generation gap, and its associated political differences over spinster identity within the NUWT, was interestingly revealed in the response to the attacks on spinster teachers as sexually frustrated or deviant women. Generally the union seems to have tried to ignore or remain aloof from negative references to spinster teachers. In 1920 it attempted to brush off an attack on the NUWT as being composed of 'jaundiced spinsters'. Their accuser, a man teacher, quoted from a marriage manual to argue that the permanently unmarried were living abnormal lives.

> '"Those who can marry and do not are thus deliberately disregarding their biological duty to the race to which they belong. Those who would marry but cannot are supremely unfortunate. Both of them are a menace to the society in which they live." Now I submit that the N.F.W.T. [i.e. the NUWT] is dominated by such as are here described, and that the unrest exhibited by that organisation is not caused by inadequate salaries, but by the morbid condition of its militant members.'

The union's journal *The Woman Teacher* published this letter, but refused to comment on this accusation as it was in such 'bad taste'. 'It is so unspeakable that we refrain from commenting on [these] points.'[33]

But sometimes the attacks were so outrageous that the NUWT felt compelled to respond. To go back to the attack made by Dr Williams in 1935: 'The women who have the responsibility of teaching these girls are many of them themselves embittered, sexless or homosexual hoydens who try to mould the girls into their own pattern.' This accusation was angrily repudiated by the NUWT, but very interestingly in terms of women's sexual impulses being maternal ones. '... he should know that in the vast majority of cases a woman teacher's work is a complete outlet for her maternal instincts. Her womanly impulses are sublimated and diverted, but splendidly employed.'[34] The NUWT was resorting to an earlier idea of women's sexuality in order to deflect the attack on spinsters.

A tendency for the union to ignore spinsters' rights was first identified by some members in 1934:

> 'I ... suggest that the problem of the woman worker and also the status of woman as a whole will be easier solved if a little more decent attention is paid to the bachelor woman and her

welfare and dignity as a worker... This preoccupation with the rights and desires of the married woman has reached such proportions and the statements publicly made and circulated have become at times so disparaging both to the house-keeping family woman and to the wage-earning spinster...'[35]

The major clash within the union occurred in the context of the NUWT's campaign against the marriage bar. This was the regulation in many areas which required women teachers to resign on marriage. The NUWT was anxious to get the bar lifted, and part of their case involved arguing that the experience of marriage and motherhood enhanced women's teaching skills. The corollary of this, however, was that single women were inevitably less competent. Feminists might also fall into displaying negative attitudes towards spinsters if they were arguing that the marriage bar limited women's choices in life.

In May 1935 an NUWT official, Elsie Fisher, wrote an article for a popular newspaper on the marriage bar, with the headline 'Where are my children? Spinsterhood forced on the teacher'. This argued that the marriage bar forced young women teachers into clandestine marriages and illicit unions with men, and ended:

> 'Young teachers all over the country refuse to remain celibate, refuse to see their lives thwarted, refuse to deny themselves the love and companionship that means a fuller, deeper, richer life. Why indeed should they be sterilised by the order of town councillors?'[36]

Note how she portrays spinsterhood as so negative - as thwarted, denied and sterilised. One older NUWT member, Miss Morrison, took exception to the article, especially the suggestion that many young women teachers lived with men. She wrote to Ethel Froud, the General Secretary of the union, to complain that this was a serious libel on the habits and ethics of young women teachers. In the correspondence on this matter between Elsie Fisher and Ethel Froud, it emerged that Miss Fisher, rather than deploring free love as she did in the article, in fact privately endorsed it. 'As you probably know I personally believe profoundly in companionate marriage [meaning free love] and the freedom of the Russian system with regard to this relationship, but I carefully avoided committing the Union to this.' Elsie Fisher, then, presented herself as a good example of the post-war sex reform type of feminist thinking on sexuality. In her letter to Miss Froud she went on to say, 'I am really more concerned with your criticism than with that of the writer of the letter, because I hadn't realised how deep a division of opinion could exist *inside* the women's movement on this question.'[37] She underestimated the strength of Miss Morrison's convictions as 'an old campaigner in the fight for Votes for Women', and for that matter those of Miss Froud, who belonged to the same political generation.[38]

Two months later, in July 1935, came the debate in the London County Council over the abolition of the marriage bar in London. This was the fruition of the NUWT's long campaign over this issue. The report of the Council's Education Committee stated that 'the duties of both doctor and teacher call for certain personal qualities which may be thought to be enriched by marriage'. The *Times Educational Supplement* also commented that a staff composed of celibate women teachers tended to create an over-academic, cloistral atmosphere in schools, too much divorced from the normal home life to which the pupils were accustomed. In the debate itself, one London councillor 'agreed that they should not face with equanimity the prospect of the teaching service being entirely filled by spinsters'.[39]

Miss Agnes Dawson, a London councillor sponsored by the NUWT, also argued this line. The *Times Educational Supplement* reported her as saying:

> 'given a good teacher, marriage must bring fresh experience and more human understanding. To debar married teachers the opportunity to serve was to do a disservice to education. Men would not send their boys to schools where all the male teachers were celibates. They would consider it an unhealthy atmosphere. She claimed the same for the girls.'[40]

At this, Miss Morrison wrote again to the union to deplore the view that married women were better than single women teachers. She said that it was unfortunate that progressive women in 1935 should still consider a woman incomplete unless linked with a man:

> 'That "wives give best work" or are "enriched by marriage" (es-

pecially modern marriage) or are given "better understanding" or are in any way superior to a celibate woman I absolutely challenge; and a Union largely composed of devoted celibate teachers, giving their creative energy unstinted to their profession, that allows this attitude and these statements to go unchallenged is no good to me.'

In her reply, Miss Ethel Froud (the General Secretary) blamed the statement on the distortion of the male press and repeated the union line that married women should be as free as single women to follow their profession, but added, 'No, we can't have it said that we celibates are only some fraction of a human being.' Miss Morrison continued to press her point, saying that women are not improved or their intelligence augmented by intimate physical contact with a member of the male sex, and that it should not be implied that spinsters are unhappy, or less fortunate. Ethel Froud replied that to a large extent she shared her feelings.[41]

These fundamentally different attitudes towards spinsterhood among women in the NUWT reflect the changing position of mainstream feminism with regard to sexuality in the inter-war period. Miss Morrison is expressing her very positive political identity as a spinster in 1935, 20 years or so after it would have ceased to have a resonance for feminists generally. Views like Elsie Fisher's - of spinsterhood as a thwarted, negative state - were in the ascendancy in the women's movement, as well as in the wider world.

Conclusion

Hostility towards spinster teachers in the inter-war period focused on their failure to marry and produce children, on their unhealthy influence as celibates or lesbians in the schools, on their earning power and on their feminist politics. The popularisation of sexology explains some of these attacks. It emphasised heterosexuality as normal, and so any woman outside such a relationship was vulnerable to being labelled as frustrated, unfeminine or lesbian. The economic context is also important, however. Post-war unemployment and cuts in public spending led to increasing restrictions on women's work generally, as well as a backlash against feminism. Women teachers were strongly unionised, relatively highly paid, and spoke out as feminists for equal opportunities in their profession. Therefore spinster teachers could be seen as - and sometimes feared as - a group of economically independent women, not sexually subordinate to men, who were politically organised and had social power in their communities.

Sexology and the sex reform movement can also be blamed for the feeble response from spinster teachers. Without a firm critique of male-defined heterosexuality, they no longer had a feminist politics of sexuality to make sense of this stigmatising of spinsters. The women's movement itself in this period increasingly emphasised motherhood and incorporated sex reform ideas at the expense of spinsters.

Notes

1. See Alison Oram, 'Serving two masters? The introduction of a marriage bar in teaching in the 1920s', in London Feminist History Group (eds), *The sexual dynamics of history* (Pluto Press, London, 1983), pp. 134-48; Alison Oram, 'Inequalities in the teaching profession: the effects on teachers and pupils' in Felicity Hunt (ed.), *Lessons for life: the schooling of girls and women 1850-1950* (Basil Blackwell, Oxford, 1987), pp. 101-23.

2. N. Tranter, *Population since the Industrial Revolution* (Croom Helm, London, 1973), pp. 101-8; J.M. Winter, 'Some aspects of the demographic consequences of the First World War in Britain', *Population Studies*, vol. 30, no. 3 (1976), pp. 545-51.

3. The Lesbian History Group was set up in London in the autumn of 1984 by a group of lesbians who were interested in or doing research into lesbian history. It is a thriving, mainly non-academic group, which has fortnightly meetings to discuss lesbian history and its theory and politics.

4. See Lucy Bland, 'Purity, motherhood, pleasure or threat? Definitions of female sexuality 1900-1970s' in S. Cartledge and J. Ryan (eds), *Sex and love* (Women's Press, London, 1983), pp. 8-29; Sheila Jeffreys, *The spinster and her enemies* (Pandora Press, London, 1985), Chap. 5; Annabel Faraday, 'Social definitions of lesbians in Britain, 1914-1939', unpublished PhD thesis, University of Essex, 1985. It is important to point out that while each of these writers identifies these effects of sexology, they vary in their approach and emphasis. Lillian Faderman, in *Surpassing the love of men* (Junction Books, London, 1981), still the classic text of lesbian history, also discusses this change, while a British writer has argued the opposite case, that sexology stimulated the formation of a lesbian identity and

sub-culture: Sonia Ruehl, 'Inverts and experts: Radclyffe Hall and the lesbian identity' in R. Brunt and C. Rowan (eds), *Feminism, culture and politics* (Lawrence and Wishart, London, 1982), pp. 15-36.

5. For a useful discussion of this question see Sheila Jeffreys, 'Does it matter if they did it? Lillian Faderman and lesbian history', *Trouble and Strife*, no. 3 (1984).

6. Adrienne Rich's writing on the 'lesbian continuum' (A. Rich, *Compulsory heterosexuality and lesbian existence* (Onlywomen Press, London, 1981)) is relevant here. While there is a danger of including heterosexual women as lesbians under the banner of sisterhood, nevertheless for the purposes of doing research into lesbian history it is useful to have a fairly broad definition, since 'lesbians' in the past did not often readily identify themselves as such, even if the term was available.

7. Alison Oram, '"Sex antagonism" in the teaching profession: equal pay and the marriage bar, 1910-39' in G. Weiner and M. Arnot (eds), *Gender and the politics of schooling* (Hutchinson, London, 1987), pp. 276-89.

8. Geraldine Jewsbury, *The half sisters* (1848), pp. 66-9 (a novel) quoted in Rosemary Auchmuty, 'Victorian spinsters', unpublished PhD thesis, Australian National University, 1975, p. 63.

9. Bland, 'Definitions of female sexuality', p. 11.

10. P. Ballard, *The changing school* (Hodder and Stoughton, London, 1925), p. 314.

11. Professor Dover Wilson, quoted in the *Times Educational Supplement* (*TES*), 28 March 1931, p. 113.

12. Association of Assistant Mistresses, *Annual Report* (January 1933).

13. *News Chronicle*, 21 March 1934.

14. Oram, 'Inequalities in the teaching profession'.

15. *Daily Herald*, 5 September 1935.

16. Jeffreys, *The spinster and her enemies*, pp. 105-8.

17. J. Weeks, *Sex, politics and society* (Longman, London, 1981), pp. 116-17; Faraday, 'Social definitions of lesbians', pp. 210-25.

18. Jan Lambertz, in 'Single but not alone: interwar spinsters in England', unpublished paper, 1983, points out that older spinsters were likely to escape stigmatisation as lesbians, since they were not seen as sexual. For changes after 1928 in how female friendship was depicted in schoolgirl stories, see Rosemary Auchmuty, 'You're a dyke, Angela!', *Trouble and Strife*, no. 10 (1987).

19. W. Gallichan, *Sexual apathy and coldness in women* (T. Werner Laurie, London, 1927), p. 13, quoted in S. Jeffreys, 'Sex reform and anti-feminism in the 1920s' in London Feminist History Group (eds), *The sexual dynamics of history*, pp. 177-202.

20. *TES*, 26 April 1924, p. 180. NAS Conference.

21. *TES*, 15 April 1939, p. 142. Speeches at NAS Conference.

22. Other gains for women at the end of the First World War or shortly afterwards were the opening of the legal profession, divorce law reform and the greater availability of contraception.

23. *TES*, 3 April 1937, p. 112.

24. *Education*, 22 June 1923, pp. 401-2. Conference of Education Committees.

25. 'Why are teachers unpopular?', *TES*, 6 August 1932, p. 301.

26. *TES*, 15 April 1939, p. 142. Speeches at NAS Conference. For a detailed discussion of the debate over 'men teachers for boys' see Oram, 'Inequalities in the teaching profession', and Margaret Littlewood, 'Makers of men: the anti-feminist backlash of the National Association of Schoolmasters in the 1920s and 30s', *Trouble and Strife*, no. 5 (1985).

27. Lucy Bland, 'Marriage laid bare: middle-class women and marital sex *c.* 1880-1914' in Jane Lewis (ed.), *Labour and love: women's experience of home and family 1850-1940* (Basil Blackwell, Oxford, 1986), pp. 138-9; Jeffreys, *The spinster and her enemies*, pp. 91-3.

28. Cicely Hamilton, *Marriage as a trade* (1909, reprinted Women's Press, London, 1981).

29. Bland, 'Definitions of female sexuality', p. 17; Jeffreys, *The spinster and her enemies*, pp. 93-101, 115-21.

30. W. Holtby, *Women* (The Bodley Head, London, 1934), pp. 125-33.

31. *News Chronicle*, 20 February 1930.

32. NUWT, *A short history of the Union to 1956* (NUWT, London, n.d.).

33. *The Woman Teacher*, 2 Jan. 1920, p. 114; 30 Jan. 1920, p. 150. The National Federation of Women Teachers changed its title to National Union of Women Teachers in 1920.

34. *Daily Herald*, 5 September 1935.

35. *The Woman Teacher*, 12 October 1934, p. 5.

36. *The Star*, 24 May 1935.

37. NUWT Archive, Institute of Education Library, London. Box 176. This exchange of letters took place between 27 May 1935 and 31 May 1935.

38. *The Woman Teacher*, 12 October 1934, p. 5.

39. *TES*, 20 July 1935, pp. 257-8, for all the quotes in this paragraph.

40. Ibid.

41. NUWT Archive. Box 176. This exchange of letters took place between 7 and 20 July 1935.

Anne Laurence

Women's psychological disorders in seventeenth-century Britain

It is a commonplace that the description of psychological states or psychiatric symptoms is highly specific to different cultures, and differences between one society and another or one period and another are accentuated by differences in the language used to describe such conditions. Extremes of emotion in seventeenth-century England were very often described in religious terms. Thus sublime happiness was not necessarily distinguished from feeling at one with God, nor despair from the temptings of the Devil. Religious language is still widely used today when people describe their own emotions, but in seventeenth-century England the content of religious language had real meaning for most people.[1] To some extent, also, people were looking for religious experiences in order to test their faith, because of the emphasis placed by English Puritanism upon experiential religion.

There is, however, an important distinction to be made between the language which people use concerning their own feelings and that which is used to describe someone else's condition. Medical or legal language does not supply a suitable vocabulary for subjective experiences, but it does allow discussion of the state of mind of a third party, because it is concerned with behaviour rather than with feelings. The prevailing medical philosophy of the seventeenth century was humoral pathology, a system whereby the mind and body were believed to be governed by certain substances, or humours. As much emphasis was placed upon mood as upon physical symptoms. The vocabulary of humoral pathology had been assimilated into everyday language in much the same way as medical and psychological terms are used today. Words like choler and melancholy appear in writings of the seventeenth century in non-technical senses, much as we use terms like depression and schizophrenia. But while medical descriptions were bound up with notions of disease, they were not completely independent of religious language. The medical profession recognised the state of being possessed by the Devil, though it did not necessarily regard it as being within its domain; such cases were usually referred to a minister. The legal interest in psychological states lay in the issue of responsibility, since a person who was mad was not considered to be responsible for his or her own actions. Thus legal descriptions are less concerned with the details of someone's psychological condition than with the effect that that condition had upon their conduct.

The starting point of this paper is writings of women describing their own states of mind. Work on civil war churches led me to some collections of oral testimonies, which were given as a condition of entry to some nonconformist churches, and which were recorded by ministers and published. These contain testimonies by lower-class women, describing their spiritual trials and, incidentally, their domestic circumstances. They were, however, written down by men, and were required to fulfil certain preconceptions about spiritual advance towards godliness. Nevertheless, they are a unique type of record for seventeenth-century England, and work on them soon revealed that there were many autobiographical passages which were concerned with altered consciousness, described in terms of psychological disorder. This provoked the question: did men and women in the seventeenth century recognise psychological disorders, and if so, did they see any difference between those suffered by men and those suffered by women?

Previous historical work has tended to concentrate upon the kind of madness that led people into contact with the medical and legal professions, and has principally used the records of physicians, hospitals and courts. Both the medical profession and the law recognised states of altered consciousness in different ways and described psychologically disordered states. These were important in determining public attitudes to psychological disorder, but there has been little work on the idea of disorder from the point of view of the victim. My concern, then, is with the kinds of disorder which led women to comment in their own writing or speech upon their altered consciousnesses, and how these compared with public attitudes and with the supposedly objective views of medicine and the law.

Three main types of source have been used: women's own writings, the writings of the medical profession and legal records. Apart from the testimonies described above, there are many women's diaries from the seventeenth century. A high proportion of them were written as a form of Christian exercise, so periods of particular doubt and trial are mentioned. Many of the writers went through adolescent soul-searchings which they recount, and childbirth was necessarily a difficult and dangerous time, often a time for spiritual accounting in the face of the mother's possible death, or a time of trial at the loss of a child. These writings are predominantly by upper- and middle-class women. Sometimes funeral sermons and biographies can supplement this material. It could be argued that the overtly religious purpose of most of this literature necessarily suggests that all extreme emotions were seen in religious terms, and that censorship prevented the publication of any secular equivalent. It seems more likely that for those who wished to record their emotions, religion supplied both the motive and the medium. In these writings women examined their own behaviour and feelings in order to establish how far they had remained true to their faith. It is, therefore, important not to make too crude an equation between religious language and modern psychiatric disorders. On the other hand, religion did provide the vocabulary of abstract expression and provided explanations for extremes of mood, for doubt, ecstasy and despair.

Medical writings usually divided female diseases into the diseases common to all women, those found predominantly in widows and virgins, those found in 'barren and fruitfull' women, and those found in pregnant women and women who were breastfeeding.[2] The periods of adolescence and child-bearing were thought to be most significant for both physical and psychological maladies, whereas much less attention was devoted to the diseases of older women. John Pechey, in his work on the treatment of women's diseases, has chapters entitled 'Melancholy of virgins and widows' and 'Melancholy, madness, delirium and epilepsie of women in childbed'.[3] Sexual intercourse was considered to be beneficial, and many diseases of virgins and widows were attributed to abstinence. It was believed that 'if it be duly used, [it] conduces to Health', and that it was 'wholesome for melancholy persons, provided that it be acted seasonably, and with moderation'.[4] Indeed, many physicians shared Dr Pechey's belief that virgins, widows and barren women were more prone to melancholy than others.[5]

Two diseases featured largely in medical literature concerning women, both of which had a bewildering variety of symptoms, both physical and psychological, sometimes differing considerably from author to author. Neither can be classified solely as a psychological disorder, but in both cases this element was important. Green-sickness was a disease of adolescent girls, whereas suffocation of the womb, suffocation of the mother or mother-fits was seen most commonly amongst women of child-bearing age. Both diseases were believed to be caused by the retention of fluids that would otherwise be excreted, either by menstruation or in the discharge which follows childbirth. In both of these conditions some importance was given to the psychological state of the patient, since the womb was the seat of many emotions, especially melancholy.

It is almost impossible to know how patients felt about the diseases described in the medical texts. Neither green-sickness nor suffocation of the womb is mentioned in any of the women's own writings studied here, though green-sickness was recognised in plays and popular ballads (almost certainly because of the association of green-sickness with maidenly lustfulness, and the opportunities for comedy that this afforded). The reason for the inclusion of these two diseases in a discussion of women's psychological disorders is that, although the list of symptoms changed constantly, the psychological symptoms were always given prominence and were especially associated with the particular stage of life which the afflicted had reached. As humoral pathology did not distinguish between mind and body, this could be said of many diseases. However, as humoral pathology declined in fashion, both green-sickness and suffocation of the womb were classified as hysteric diseases.[6]

The third type of source is the records of coroners' inquests and assize courts, used here to look at two areas where women's responsibility under the law was particularly important: suicide and infanticide. It is important here because women were deemed to bear responsibility themselves; in other areas of the law, husbands or fathers bore it on behalf of their wives or daughters. Both suicide and infanticide are acts which, it can be argued, are rarely committed by anyone who is not psychologically disordered. These records are, like physicians' writings, accounts of behaviour symptomatic of psychological disturbance. Suicide and infanticide highlight public attitudes in that the courts were not concerned with particular diagnoses, but rather with whether a woman who had committed suicide or who had murdered her new-born child was guilty of a felony, a capital offence. There is, between the sixteenth and eighteenth centuries, a clear change of attitude towards responsibility in both these areas, which seems to be not merely the result of changes in the legal profession, but also in public attitudes. Attitudes to men's suicides changed as well, but few men ever appeared in court charged with infanticide, and the parallels in the courts' treatment of both offences are strikingly similar.

The use of these various kinds of material to examine women's psychological disorders presents a number of problems. There is the problem of vocabulary, there is the problem of the intention of the writer and there is the problem of twentieth-century prejudices and preconceptions. The intention of this paper is to look at women's psychological disorders through the eyes of the women themselves, and then through the eyes of the medical profession and, where appropriate, of the law. Because there is little common ground between the terms used in these different domains, there is an examination of the two stages of life at which women considered themselves to be most prone to psychological disorders, and at which the medical profession regarded them as being particularly susceptible, and then of the two acts which seemed most to embody disordered behaviour.

Adolescence

For many women, especially devout ones, adolescence was a time of particular spiritual doubt and temptation. It was the time when they became aware of sin and the dangers of this temptation. It was the time when they started to discover the extent of their religious faith. It is easy to translate these feelings as adolescent angst, but to do so completely is to diminish the importance of the religious motives in a culture which set a high value on such experiences. Mrs Elizabeth Walker, describing her own adolescence, wrote that she was dejected and melancholy:

> 'For half a Year I do not know that I slept, if I did it was very little; and yet I did not want either sleep or health... I did eat very sparingly, which, with much weeping, occasioned me some little inconvenience.'

Her father, noticing that all was not well, sent for a physician, but it soon became evident that hers was not a case susceptible to treatment by medicine.[7]

Self-starvation and *pica* (the consumption of inedible materials) were well-known phenomena. An account of Martha Taylor, 'The Famed Derbyshire Damosell', who fasted for twelve months, was given to the Royal Society in 1669.[8] Among the substances which sufferers from *pica* were supposed to eat were ashes, coal, chalk, unripe fruit and snow. One woman recounted how, as a girl, 'the devil did tempt me to rend the pillow, and pick out some of the feathers to swallow them downe, which I did, which had like to cost me my life, for I was very nigh dead by this means'.[9] These symptoms all appear amongst those most commonly mentioned in medical writings about green-sickness, or *chlorosis.* Other symptoms were palpitations and absence of menstruation. They were sometimes accompanied by 'great cares and disturbances of mind'.[10] Melancholy also frequently accompanied this malady. Sufferers were

> 'sad and full of thoughts, and Trouble at the Heart, and cannot express their grief; all things are tedious to them; they weep and laugh without a cause: they sleep little, and with trouble and fear: they have a Pain on the left side, and sometimes the left Breast: their Jaws are dry'.[11]

Women themselves seemed to recognise adolescence as a time of disturbance, but were less concerned than the medical profession to see their psychological symptoms as part of a larger medical problem. Unfortunately, all the women's own reports were made later in life, looking back on their teens, so there may have been some reconstruction of the past. The astrologer Simon Forman noted of one young woman that she 'hath the green sickness and hath taken thought and grief, very faint at the heart and her mind much troubled'.[12] Since the average age of marriage for women in seventeenth-century England was twentysix, it is probable that adolescence, for the purposes of diagnosing green-sickness, lasted until marriage, so there would have been many sufferers in their twenties.[13]

Child-bearing

Women themselves wrote about childbirth in a number of different ways. The three kinds of psychological state most commonly mentioned in women's writings in connection with child-bearing were suicidal feelings, melancholy and fears for the life of both mother and child. These are the kinds of state which would be mentioned in a spiritual autobiography; suicide and melancholy appear in the context of resisting temptation, and fears in the context of gratitude for a safe delivery. An anonymous woman reported that 'at the birth of a Childe I had very great temptations of destroying myself'.[14] Elizabeth Walker wrote of her own eighth delivery, 'In this Lying-in I fell into a Melancholy, which much disturbed me with Vapours, and was very ill', and of the illness of her daughter after the birth of her first child, 'The Disease took her Head which deprived her of her understanding.'[15] Mrs Veitch wrote how, eight days after the delivery of a child, 'I fell into a great exercise of mind, Misbelief and an ill heart got the Mastery of me too much.'[16]

For many women, the predominant emotion in childbirth was fear. An anonymous Scotswoman wrote in 1724:

> 'One time when I was with child and very distrest as to my bodily health... as my time drew near, I had reason to Conjecture that I was with Twins, which occasioned much fear to me, Thinking, That upon the bearing of one Child, if it should be told me that I had another to bear immediatly, it would be much more terrible to me than death.'[17]

Mary Carey wrote her spiritual meditations in anticipation of her death on the birth of her fourth child.[18] These fears were not just of death, but of the prospect of a difficult delivery - labour could last four or five days - and of continued ill-health afterwards. Mrs

Alice Thornton gave a detailed account of her nine deliveries and she was ill for several months after each of them with fevers and haemorrhages.[19] This is not to suggest that these women's feelings were in any way unbalanced; the whole process of childbirth was accompanied by intense anxiety and fears for the life of both mother and child which many mothers need not feel in the developed world today. Ralph Josselin's relief after one of his wife's deliveries, 'the easiest and speediest labour that ever shee had, and shee was under great fears', must have been shared by many people after a safe delivery.[20]

It is unusual to find seventeenth-century physicians identifying psychological problems with the precise time of childbirth. Richard Napier recorded a case of a woman who was recently delivered of a daughter, and noted that she 'useth to be light headed at this tyme of the yeare'.[21] The first account in an English medical text seems to be in a book written by John Pechey in the 1690s, where he described 'a very Beautiful Lady, that presently after delivery fell melancholy, and was mad for a Month, but by the use of a few Medicines recovered her Senses', and another woman, a Dutch merchant's wife, who was 'frequently distracted after delivery'.[22] These women were not, however, Pechey's own patients.

The disease known as suffocation of the womb, or suffocation of the mother, was identified by the medical profession as being one suffered by women of child-bearing age. No two medical writers could agree upon its symptoms, except to say that it often entailed difficulty in breathing, melancholy and loss of appetite. The classic early seventeenth-century description by Edward Jorden emphasised the psychological manifestations, but seemed undecided as to whether they were symptoms or causes. He wrote that 'there happeneth an alienation of the mind in this disease, whereby sometimes they will waxe furious and raging deprived of their right judgment of the rest', but he also claimed that 'perturbations of the mind are oftentimes to blame both for this and many other diseases'.[23] Nicholas Fontanus observed that sometimes 'they refuse wholesome meat and long after coales, chalke, a piece of an old wall, starch, earth, and the like trash which they devoure as ravenously, as a hungry Plowman will winde downe a good bag-pudding'.[24] The disease appears to have been seen as one which resulted from the fundamental state of being a woman, not just her physiology.[25] Edward Jorden put it down to her 'passive condition', and Sir Kenelm Digby believed that women were moist and passive, which made them subject to an 'unpleasing contagion of the imagination'. He cites as an example 'a very melancholy woman, which was subject to the disease called the Mother, and while she continued in that mood, she thought herself possessed'.[26]

Some physicians' notebooks refer to actual cases of suffocation of the mother. The Bedfordshire physician, John Symcotts, wrote of a woman who had 'been long troubled with fits of the mother, every day once at least'. He does not say what form these fits took, but in another case he says that a woman fell in these fits after having 'taken much grief for the death of her daughter', which suggests that the psychological component was important.[27] The astrologer Simon Forman was also consulted by women with a multiplicity of symptoms. Mrs Blague was afflicted with 'melancholy and wind. It makes her heavy, sad, faint, unlusty and solitary and will drive her into a melancholy passion.' Lady Monson was

> 'melancholy and full of fancies... She cannot sleep; she hath many ill thoughts and cogitations. She hath not her course and the menstrual blood runneth to her head... And she thinks the devil doth tempt her to do evil to herself.'[28]

Forman does not apparently call these collections of symptoms suffocation of the mother, but they are very similar in character to those listed in the medical textbooks.

It is tempting to believe that physicians simply used the idea of suffocation of the mother or mother-fits as a universal explanation for the multiplicity of gynaecological ailments from which women suffer, some of which, such as those resulting from large numbers of pregnancies, are very uncommon in the developed world today. Women themselves seem to have referred to individual symptoms without any apparent desire to systematise them. However, it is more likely that this diagnosis was an attempt by men to supply an explanation for differences in behaviour between men and women. Merely being a woman was often considered to be sufficient explanation of certain conditions.

Infanticide

In twentieth-century Britain it is usual to treat a woman who murders her new-born child as mentally unbalanced: as the victim of some kind of puerperal psychosis. The sentencing of a Glasgow woman to a two-year gaol sentence in 1986 after she had murdered her three children, the youngest of whom was ten weeks old, was described by one newspaper as 'chilling'.[29] However, nowadays the murder of new-born children is mercifully uncommon. The situation in early modern England was very different. Infanticide was not distinguished from murder and was a felony, a crime whose punishment was death and forfeiture of property; nevertheless it was not uncommon. It was a crime committed mainly by women, treatment of whom undoubtedly changed between the sixteenth and eighteenth centuries, and though the evidence is ambiguous, this change suggests public recognition that women might be subject to psychological disturbance after giving birth. No diaries written by women who committed infanticide are known to have survived; the reason for including the subject here is that it does seem to be suggestive of public attitudes to a predominantly female crime, and has some relation to the treatment of suicide, about which a number of women's writings have survived.

A survey of some of the court records shows that in sixteenth-century Kent 39 cases in which mothers murdered their new-born infants came to the assize court: 36 of these women were described as spinsters, one as a widow and one as a wife, and the marital status of the last one is not recorded.[30] The figures for Essex in the seventeenth century are not dissimilar. Of 84 indictments for infanticide, 73 were of spinsters, 7 of married women, 3 of widows and 1 of a woman who was either a wife or a widow.[31] Thus unmarried women were by far the greatest offenders, and many of them were domestic servants. This suggests that the commonest cause of infanticide resulted from female servants' need to dispose of unwanted children because they would otherwise have been unable to support themselves.

On the face of it, all but a very small proportion of the murders of new-born children were committed by women who were forced into it by economic circumstances and by the undoubted social censure that would follow the birth of a bastard child. In the sixteenth century the all-male juries which tried such cases usually found such women guilty of murder, though many of those tried at the Kent assize in the later sixteenth century were found guilty and then remanded because they were pregnant. This may have been a device to secure a stay of execution, though a high proportion of these women may have been pregnant when brought to trial. Juries seem to have become increasingly reluctant to find these women guilty of murder. By the late seventeenth century there was some recognition in the courts that women who had recently given birth might be in an altered psychological state. A servant girl who suffocated her child claimed to know nothing of it, saying 'that she had not her Senses, and was Light-headed', though her plea was not accepted and she was hanged, but a married woman from Buckinghamshire was acquitted, 'being delivered of a child and not having slept many nights fell into a temporary phrenzy, and kild her infant'.[32] Certainly by the eighteenth century it was unusual for women who had murdered their new-born children to be hanged.

It is difficult to establish whether this change came about because juries were acknowledging unalterable socio-economic circumstances, or whether they were becoming more aware of puerperal psychoses. Infanticide was a crime whose recorded figures bear no relation to its incidence in the community. It must have been extremely difficult to detect infanticide committed by a married woman with several children. Although few married women were brought to trial, a much smaller proportion of them was found guilty of murder than unmarried women. An act of 1624 made concealment of a still-birth a capital offence like infanticide. Women who had miscarried were sometimes interrogated and, in the eighteenth century, were often asked if they had had help at the delivery (not having help was sometimes considered to be evidence of an attempt to conceal the pregnancy). In 1755 a Wiltshire woman, Ann Mortimer, was acquitted of the murder of her bastard daughter, having been charged with being an accessory to her death by not having proper assistance at the delivery.[33]

Infanticide hovers in that uneasy area between crime and mental disorder. In our society one definition of insanity is murdering one's child; in the early sixteenth century this was murder, not insanity. Indeed, J.A. Sharpe has observed that the act of 1624 presumed a woman's guilt.[34] It does, however, seem that there was some change over the years. Whilst the law did not distinguish between the various possible reasons for infanticide, it apparently came to be treated less as an outright act of murder and more as a response to a particular socio-economic or psychological problem, though it is difficult to say whether this was the result of a greater awareness of women's altered psychological state after giving birth, or a recognition that the law demanded a penalty which did not fit the crime. The first seems the more probable, because there was apparently a similar kind of shift in attitudes to suicide.

Suicide

Suicidal feelings have an important place in the writings of the faithful, and are more often mentioned in women's diaries and testimonies than in men's. They were regarded as evidence of the Devil's temptings, to be wrestled against as a test of faith. A woman who was convinced that God had ceased to love her because of her transgressions reported that 'I had temptation by Satan to drown myself in a Pond', and another woman reported that it was only her unborn child which prevented her from destroying herself. Two other women mentioned suicide amongst the temptations offered by Satan, which they overcame thanks to God's intervention.[35] It is extremely difficult to know how far these are expressions of suicidal despair, or rhetorical devices to indicate the degree of temptation which the believer had overcome. Despair was considered to be a serious doubting of God's intentions. Suicidal feelings troubled Richard Napier's patients, and we have already encountered Lady Monson's fears that the Devil was tempting her to do evil to herself.[36] Attempted suicide was not uncommon either; Forman reported the case of a young woman who had tried to hang herself twice and had also been rescued from drowning.[37]

Although suicidal feelings and attempted suicide may often be distinct from the act of suicide, the act itself was not uncommon in early modern England. It was a felony, that is to say a crime whose punishment, paradoxically enough, was death and forfeiture of property. It had a religious significance too, for a person who had committed suicide could not be buried in consecrated ground. However, people who took their own lives whilst insane were not deemed to have committed a crime. John Sym, in the chief seventeenth-century theological work on suicide, stated that people

> 'destitute of understanding, or of the use of reason... as a child without discretion, a naturall foole, a madman in his mad fits, one in his sleepe; or in such fits of sicknesse as is accompanied with a delirium or phrensey, as, in a calenture [a fever]'

could not commit 'self-murder' because they could not be held wholly responsible for their actions or their moral consequences.[38]

There were about twice as many suicides as homicides, and about twice as many male suicides as female ones. Coroners' courts were required to consider all sudden deaths. The early sixteenth-century coroners' inquests for Nottinghamshire record 72 women's deaths, of which 21 were certainly suicides, and there are a number of other deaths by drowning which may or may not have been accidental. Most were declared to have committed felonies, with the exception of Alice Mee, who was 'lying in chylde bede' and suffering from 'an agew' and who, it was reported, in a frenzy from her illness, threw herself into a well at the instigation of the Devil. This would appear to have saved her from the charge of a felony. It is possible that fewer female than male suicides were concealed because fewer women had property which would be forfeit to the crown if a verdict of suicide were brought. No such consideration was shown Joan Wynspere, a spinster who, finding herself pregnant, took an abortifacient and died, and was judged to have committed a felony by slaying herself and murdering her unborn child.[39]

Rarely is a reason given for a woman's suicide. There are a few women who were pregnant. Martha Fishcock poisoned herself while pregnant, but this may have been another attempt to induce an abortion.[40] However, a similar process was at work in the verdicts found by coronors' juries as was at work in cases of infanticide. In the late sixteenth century, most suicides were found by juries to have committed a felony and were subject to the full penalties. By the eighteenth century, most of those who killed themselves were found to have done so while not *compos mentis*. Michael Macdonald has studied the figures for the seventeenth century and shows that *non compos mentis* accounted for about 6 per cent of the verdicts in 1660 to 1664 and about 40 per cent in 1710 to 1714.[41] In eighteenth-century Wiltshire, about eight times as many verdicts of lunacy were found as verdicts of felony.[42]

Suicide, unlike infanticide, is committed more often by men

than by women, but it gives us a particular insight into attitudes to mental disturbance, and shows that they changed considerably during the seventeenth century. The acts of infanticide and suicide were increasingiy viewed as symptomatic of psychological disorder. Thus those who committed them were treated not as felons, but as people not responsible for their own actions.

Conclusion

There is much that is familiar in the descriptions by seventeenth-century women of their mental and physical health, though the constructions which they put upon their afflictions are very different from the ones we might use. Neither green-sickness nor suffocation of the mother, both of which are widely described in the medical texts and which appear to have been used in diagnosis, is referred to by women themselves in their accounts of their own lives. They do, however, recognise the same periods of life as being times of trial as those identified by physicians as particularly problematic, and they describe many of the same symptoms, though in different terms.

It is difficult to chart a change in women's own perceptions of their psychological states; in England (though not in Scotland), spiritual diaries were less often kept in the later part of the seventeenth century. Nor was there much change in the attitude of the medical profession towards women's illnesses between the end of the sixteenth century and the end of the seventeenth century. Most physicians throughout this period would agree with Pechey, who asserted that 'there are many great and dangerous Diseases peculiar to Women arising from their Constitutions, monthly Purgations, Pregnancy, Labours and Lying-in. Their Constitution disposes them to Hysteric Diseases.'[43]

This seems to have been seen as sufficient explanation for the fact that women experienced certain kinds of psychological disorder which men did not have. It gave no recognition to the strength of the fears which many women felt as childbirth approached, although other men did appreciate them. Perhaps to have acknowledged them would have been to accept an implied criticism of their management of childbirth. On the other hand, physicians were prepared to accept that traumatic experiences like bereavement could affect both physical and mental health. It has been suggested that the first real change in the attitude of the medical profession came with the displacement in the eighteenth century of humoral pathology as the pre-eminent medical philosophy, and the recognition of psychological disorders as being distinct from physical ones.[44]

If the actions of the courts can be considered to be indicative of broad public attitudes, there does seem to have been a very considerable change between the end of the sixteenth century and the middle of the eighteenth century. There was apparently an increasing recognition that women's minds might, in certain circumstances, be sufficiently disturbed to render them no longer responsible for their actions. This is most noticeable in the treatment of both infanticide and suicide. However, it is difficult to know whether this was a change of heart on the part of the jurors themselves, or whether they were guided by the lawyers. Insanity was accepted as a possible reason for, though not an explanation of, infanticide and suicide.

Notes

1. Church attendance was enforced by law. This does not mean that everyone believed; it does mean that everyone was familiar with the language of religion. See G.E. Aylmer, 'Unbelief in seventeenth-century England', in Donald Pennington and Keith Thomas (eds), *Puritans and revolutionaries* (Oxford University Press, Oxford, 1978), pp. 22-46.
2. Nicholas Fontanus uses these divisions explicitly to organise his work *The womens doctour* (London, 1652), but other writers use them as well.
3. John Pechey, *A general treatise of the diseases of maids, bigbellied women, child-bed-women, and widows* (London, 1696).
4. John Pechey, *A plain introduction to the art of physick* (London, 1697), p. 92; Fontanus, *The womens doctour*, p. 73.
5. Pechey, *A general treatise*, p. 245.
6. Annabel Gregory is currently working on green-sickness and changing gender stereotypes.
7. *The holy life of Mrs. Elizabeth Walker* (London, 1690), p. 23.
8. John Reynolds, *A discourse upon prodigious abstinence* (London, 1669).
9. *Spirituall experiences of sundry beleevers* (London, 1651), p. 358.

10. Lazarus Riverius, *The practice of physick* (London, 1668), p. 401.

11. *Culpeper's directory for midwives* (London, 1676), p. 119.

12. A.L. Rowse, *Simon Forman: sex and society in Shakespeare's age* (Weidenfeld and Nicolson, London, 1974), p. 194.

13. Michael Macdonald, *Mystical bedlam: madness, anxiety, and healing in seventeenth-century England* (Cambridge University Press, Cambridge, 1981), paperback edn (1983), p. 41 shows how the physician Richard Napier treated many more young women in their twenties than in their teens.

14. *Spirituall experiences of sundry beleevers*, pp. 25-6.

15. *The holy life of Mrs. Elizabeth Walker*, pp. 63, 155.

16. National Library of Scotland, Adv. MS 34.6.22, p. 7.

17. National Library of Scotland, MS 1037, f.6v.

18. *Meditations from the notebook of Mary Carey* (Francis Meynell, Westminster, 1918).

19. *The autobiography of Mrs. Alice Thornton*, Surtees Society 62 (Durham, 1875).

20. Alan Macfarlane, *Diary of Ralph Josselin*, British Academy Records of Social and Economic History, new series III (1976), p. 111.

21. Bodleian Library, Ashmole MS 193, f.189v.

22. Pechey, *A general treatise*, p. 170.

23. Edward Jorden, *A briefe discourse of a disease called the suffocation of the mother* (London, 1603), pp. 13, 18.

24. Fontanus, *The womens doctour*, pp. 156-7.

25. This is discussed further in Hilda Smith, 'Gynaecology and ideology in seventeenth-century England', in Berenice A. Carroll (ed.), *Liberating women's history* (University of Illinois Press, Urbana, 1976), pp. 98-9.

26. Quoted in Richard Hunter and Ida Macalpine, *Three hundred years of psychiatry 1535-1860* (Oxford University Press, Oxford, 1963), pp. 71, 127.

27. 'A seventeenth century doctor and his patients: John Symcotts 1592-1662' in F.N.L. Poynter and W.L. Bishop (eds), *Bedfordshire Historical Record Society* 31 (1951), pp. 68-9.

28. Rowse, *Simon Forman*, pp. 136, 167.

29. *Sunday Telegraph*, 13 July 1986, p. 12.

30. J.S. Cockburn, *Calendar of assize records, Kent indictments Elizabeth I* (H.M.S.O., London, 1979).

31. J.A. Sharpe, *Crime in seventeenth century England* (Cambridge University Press, Cambridge, 1983), p. 136. These figures are borne out by Peter C. Hoffer and N.E.H. Hull in *Murdering mothers: infanticide in England and New England, 1558-1803* (New York University Press, New York, 1981), pp. 96-8.

32. Nigel Walker, *Crime and insanity in England* (Edinburgh University

Press, Edinburgh, 1968), vol. I, p. 126. See also Keith Wrightson, 'Infanticide in earlier seventeenth century England', *Local Population Studies*, 15 (1975), p. 11.

33. R.F. Hunnisett, *Wiltshire coroners' bills 1752-96*, Wiltshire Record Society 36 (Devizes, 1981), p. 5.

34. Sharpe, *Crime*, p. 136.

35. *Spirituall experiences of sundry beleevers*, pp. 35, 230, 235, 273.

36. Michael Macdonald, 'The secularization of suicide in England 1660-1800', *Past and Present*, 111 (1986), p. 55; Rowse, *Simon Forman*, p. 167.

37. Rowse, *Simon Forman*, p. 212.

38. John Sym, *Lifes preservative against self-killing: or an useful treatise concerning life and self-murder* (London, 1637), p. 172.

39. R.F. Hunnisett, *Calendar of Nottinghamshire coroners' inquests 1485-1558*, Thoroton Society 25 (Nottingham, 1969), pp. 140, 8.

40. Michael Zell, 'Suicide in pre-industrial England', *Social History*, 11 (1986), p. 315.

41. Macdonald, 'The secularization of suicide', p. 61.

42. Hunnisett, *Wiltshire coroners' bills 1752-96*, p. 1.

43. Pechey, *A general treatise*, Preface.

44. Ilza Veith, *Hysteria: the history of a disease* (University of Chicago Press, Chicago, 1965), p. 159.

Annelies van Gijsen

Pygmalion, or the image of women in medieval literature

In this paper, I intend to discuss some images of women in medieval literature that are generally considered to be more or less extremes. Medieval misogyny is thought to offer a very negative image of women, while the other extreme, the courtly image of women, is regarded as being positive. The question as to whether these judgements are justified will be central in this paper. I shall concentrate on courtly love, and use the stories of Narcissus and Pygmalion as illustrations.

Medieval society and literature

Medieval fiction may, of course, be considered a source of historical information. It is, however, a source of a special kind, offering a certain type of information. The study of medieval literature is very useful for reconstructing a history of ideas and ideals; it only incidentally provides a picture of actual medieval life. Medieval literature is generally normative and moralistic. It is a kind of mirror to show proper or improper behaviour, in which the good are rewarded and the bad are punished. Nowadays, this essentially optimistic view of life has lost its place in 'highbrow' literature; the sort of moralism that demands a happy ending - virtue rewarded, vices punished - is generally thought to be typical of mass market literature.[1] Therefore, medieval literature should not be read as descriptive of actual situations, but as a way of confirming the intended audience's moral standards: useful, edifying entertainment. This must be kept in mind when we turn to the concept of love in medieval literary texts.

Courtly love

The way courtly love is usually spoken of suggests it to be a certain specific, well-defined and authentic medieval concept of love. Unfortunately this is not the case. Even the term *courtly love* is not medieval. The first specialist who used it as a technical term for a specific kind of love was Gaston Paris. In 1883 he called the love between Lancelot and Guenièvre in Chrétien de Troyes' *Le chevalier de la charrette* (end of the twelfth century) the first example in French literature of *amour courtois.* This also happens to be the first text in which Lancelot appears as the Queen's lover, the part that is also played by him in later Arthurian literature. Gaston Paris' example is a very unreliable one. There are good reasons for assuming that Chrétien did not mean to show Lancelot and the Queen as exemplary lovers. The work has even been interpreted as a satire.[2] Another problem is the fact that the treatment of Lancelot's love for the Queen, a recurrent theme in Arthurian literature, shows a double standard. From a secular point of view, it is this love that makes Lancelot the perfect knight he is; on the other hand, it makes him unworthy to find the Holy Grail, and finally it causes the fall of Arthur's realm.

This shows a vital conflict between the passion of love and the social order, the cult of love and 'true' religion. Love sometimes assumes the role of an alternative religion, closely resembling the 'religious religion': the God of Love gives the lover his commandments, the lover serves him and his beloved, expecting his salvation from them; good lovers are rewarded, bad ones punished; Love teaches the lover all kinds of virtues, most of them secular, even social, some of them resembling the theological virtues - Hope, for instance - or the cardinal ones like Temperance, Fortitude, etc. Now there is one detail that requires attention. When we examine this description of love and test it on medieval courtly fiction, the word lover is not sex-neutral. The lover is a man; the beloved, or to put it more strongly, the object of his love, a woman.

I will now give a definition of courtly love that limits it to a certain concept of love. Of course, it covers only a small part of the love stories and ideas about love that actually appear in medieval fiction. This definition comes from Professor Gerritsen. He defines courtly love as: 'a concept of love in which love is considered to be a cult or worship of the beloved, demanding from the lover a voluntary submission that is sometimes experienced as sorrowful, but which, however, has an ennobling effect on him'.[3]

This leaves us in no doubt that courtly love is, indeed, essentially a matter of the feelings of a male lover towards a female beloved. He is the interesting partner, on whom all attention is focused: his feelings, his torments, his struggle to gain the love of his beloved, his development from boyhood to manhood, from youngster to perfect knight, all this he owes to love. But what about the lady? Well, she is merely a kind of catalytic agent for the development and change of her lover. She herself does not change. She does not need to change because she is perfect already, which means possessing all feminine virtues. It is her task to test and teach the lover until he has eventually proved to be worthy of her love, which should then be given to him as his due reward. The lady's feelings do not seem to matter.

It may be worth while to give an illustration from Andreas Capellanus' *De arte honeste amandi* (end of the twelfth century). A lady has two lovers. She loves the first one, but has promised the second one that, if she were to lose her first lover, she will accept him. She marries her first lover, and the second lover now demands her love because love and marriage are mutually exclusive. The lady disagrees. They decide to consult an expert: the Countess of Champagne. Her judgement is unequivocal: as love in marriage is impossible, the lady is obliged to give her love to the second lover. The 'voluntary submission' appears to be one-sided. Again, it is difficult to decide whether Andreas' treatise is really serious or a satire. It contains, for instance, a number of exemplary duologues between men and women of varying social classes. The subject is always the same: the man wants the woman to love him (or pretends to); she has her reservations (or pretends to). These duologues all demonstrate startling verbal aggression from the male partner. By strength of argument and reasoning, he tries to prove that it is the woman's duty to return his love. Most of the women are, however, not so easily trapped. The discussions are entertaining, but generally lack signs of any real emotional involvement of the partners. Eventually, in the Third Book of the treatise, the author advises his readers not to love women at all.[4]

Narcissus and Pygmalion

I shall now turn to two classic love stories, very well-known in the Middle Ages because they are told in Ovid's *Metamorphoses*:[5] the stories of Narcissus and Pygmalion. Both stories occur independently in the *Roman de la rose*: Narcissus in the part of Guillaume de Lorris (*c.* 1237) and Pygmalion in the part of Jean de Meun (*c.* 1277). In a medieval Dutch epic we find both stories incorporated in a discussion about love, where they are presented as opposites. The Narcissus story shows the punishment of a bad lover, the Pygmalion story the reward of a good lover. This is interesting because the stories have so much in common; both Narcissus and Pygmalion could be interpreted as models of the so-called courtly lover. I will first give a summary of the stories as they are narrated in the *Metamorphoses*.

Narcissus was a very beautiful youth. Many young men and girls fell in love with him, but he was so vain that he ignored them all. The nymph Echo tried to win his love, but he scorned her. She pined away from sorrow and was turned into bare rock; only her voice still survives. Then one of his other admirers prayed for revenge: 'May he himself fall in love, and be unable to gain his loved one!' Nemesis, goddess of revenge, granted this righteous prayer. One day, when Narcissus was hunting, he was thirsty and drank from a well. There he fell in love with his own reflection, believing it to be a beautiful boy. When he realised that his love would never be fulfilled, he was slowly consumed away with grief, died, and became a flower.

The story of Pygmalion is preceded by a story about the Propoetides, women who dared to deny the divinity of Venus and were punished by becoming the first prostitutes in history. This story then goes on: 'When Pygmalion saw these women living such wicked lives, he was revolted by the many faults which nature has implanted in the female sex, and long lived a bachelor existence without any wife to share his home.' Nevertheless, he carved an ivory statue of a lovely maiden and fell in love with his own creation. He vainly kissed and caressed it and adorned it with jewels and robes. At a festival of Venus, Pygmalion made offerings and prayed to the goddess of love. When he came home he found that the statue had come to life. Happy ending.[6]

I will now turn to the medieval Dutch tale *Roman van Heinric en*

Margriete van Limborch (after 1288, probably the first half of the fourteenth century).[7] In this 'medievalised' version Narcissus is a knight, Echo a noble lady. Narcissus' crime is that he is not only indifferent, but even enjoys making his - in this case exclusively female - admirers suffer. His indifference afflicts Echo; in her sorrow she complains to Venus that Narcissus will cause her death. She prays for revenge: may he also know hopeless love! The story continues in a similar manner to Ovid's story, except that Narcissus thinks his image in the well a fair maiden, and he drowns while vainly trying to kiss her. Conclusion: Venus will have her revenge on those who show no mercy to their lovers. In this case the lesson appears to be meant for men, or at least for both sexes; the text is not specific.

In the *Roman de la rose* version, however, there can be no doubt about the conclusion of the Narcissus saga. Here, the poem explicitly addresses the ladies in the audience. We might expect warnings such as: 'Ladies, do not love proud men', or: 'Ladies, never offer your love', but we find nothing of the kind; on the contrary, the text is as follows:

> 'You ladies, who refuse to satisfy
> Your lovers, this one's case should take to heart;
> For, if you let your loyal sweethearts die,
> God will know how to give you recompense.'[8]

The author may either have consciously reversed the sex-roles in the story, or automatically fallen back on a relationship between the sexes that possibly seemed the most 'natural' to him.[9]

I will now return to the Narcissus story and explain why I think Narcissus resembles the courtly lover. The parallels are: Narcissus refuses real love from a real woman (which, in fact, he has the right to do); he suffers in vain from a love that is essentially mere self-idolatry, a selfish feeling for a frigid image.

In the *Limborch* Pygmalion is presented as Narcissus' counterpart: his story is told to prove that true and constant love will be rewarded. As in the *Roman de la rose*, Pygmalion is portrayed as a professional artist, a sculptor, without a word about his original misogyny. Eventually Venus takes pity on him, because of his constancy and his promises to Venus to be her loyal servant. Then the goddess gives life and soul to the ivory maiden. As soon as Pygmalion returns home he is welcomed by the maiden, who tells him that she loves him sincerely and is his for ever. Conclusion: those who are constant in love, and have the patience to wait, will finally be rewarded.

To me it seems most instructive that in this story two elements are combined: Pygmalion is represented as the perfect lover, and he falls in love with the image of a woman that he himself created. In the end he is even granted his 'walking talking living doll'. There could hardly be a more significant example of the courtly lover. The statue he loves is as frigid and unattainable as the reflection in Narcissus' well; in a sense, it is also his own image he loves.[10] Both Narcissus and Pygmalion show an inability to love a real human being of flesh and blood that has a life and mind of its own.[11]

The image of women, dualism and inequality

The image of women in medieval literature has two faces: a so-called descriptive face and a prescriptive face, the one demonstrating what women are thought to be like, preferably 'by nature'; the other showing what women should be like, oddly enough also 'by nature'.[12] These could be called the realistic and the idealistic faces, bearing in mind that the image itself, by the very fact of being an image, is merely a product and tool of the human (read: the male) mind.

The idea that human beings consist of a material body and an immaterial mind, soul or spirit is more surprising than would appear at first sight. We are all familiar with it, and it is almost impossible not to experience this duality once one knows about it. Of course, distinctions and simplifications of this kind are essential to thought. We can only wonder why there has always been such a strong preference for bipolarity, for black and white instead of blue, red and yellow, for instance. The problem is not so much the mere distinction between two extremes, but rather the fact of their being linked to a hierarchy of values. In this system the soul or spirit is as infinitely superior to the body as light is to darkness, or good to evil.

The duality of body and soul and the duality of male and female are reflected in the lovers' attitudes towards women. Since they are incapable of experiencing themselves as a unity, they are unable to perceive this unity in their partners; because of the hierarchical nature of any duality involved, they cannot but regard them as essentially unequal. This means: either as beings of a higher order, all spirit, or as beings of a lower order, all body. In this hierarchy the 'purely spiritual' is always better than anything else. This explains why Andreas Capellanus regards 'pure love' as being superior to 'mixed love' (both kinds of love being erotic, but 'pure love' excluding 'the act of Venus').[13]

Now the image of men generally contains both poles; the dualism causes internal conflicts that are solved by establishing the proper inner hierarchy. Why, then, is the image of women reduced to either the 'all-evil' or the 'all-good'? This is possibly a result of the preconceived 'otherness' of women, which in its turn stems from the idea of dichotomy and hierarchy. If male and female are seen as opposites, like good and evil, light and darkness, soul and body, there is no room left to attribute complete humanity to both men and women. As men had already claimed this humanity and considered themselves as standard human beings, women must be either sub-human or superhuman. If the common humanity of male and female individuals is disregarded, either sex (but especially women) must be considered incomplete. This is incompatible with the one idea in the definition of courtly love I gave that appeals to me: the idea that love should be given voluntarily. If a woman wants the freedom of choosing to love or not to love, she must regard herself as a complete, autonomous and independent person, and her partner as her equal.

Notes

1. These ethics are often inconsistent; e.g. the virtue of being indifferent to material gain (often possessed by heroines in love stories) is usually rewarded by becoming rich and happy (through marrying a wealthy and apparently less scrupulous man), rather than staying poor and still being happy.

2. J. Frappier, 'Chrétien de Troyes' in R.S. Loomis (ed.), *Arthurian literature in the Middle Ages: a collaborative history*, 5th edn (Clarendon Press, Oxford, 1974), pp. 157-91.

3. 'Hoofse liefde' in 'Hoofdproblemen van de Middelnederlandse letterkunde', unpublished university reader, Instituut De Vooys, Utrecht,

1980, pp. 29-38.

4. Andreas Capellanus, *The art of courtly love.* With introd., transl. and notes by J.J. Parry (Norton, New York, 1969), pp. 122-35.

5. During the Middle Ages Ovid was widely read and commented upon. His stories often have an edifying moral interpretation. Cf. A.M.J. van Buuren, *Der minnen loop van Dirc Potter: studie over een Middelnederlands ars amandi* (Hes, Utrecht, 1979), pp. 192-239 *et passim*, and bibliography.

6. For these summaries I refer to Ovid, *Metamorphoses.* Transl. and with an introduction by M.M. Innes, 9th edn (Penguin, Harmondsworth, 1974), pp. 83-7; 230-1.

7. Editions: L.Ph.C. van den Bergh, Leiden, 1846-7, and R. Meesters, Amsterdam, etc., 1951 (Pygmalion: verses 1190-1259, Narcissus: verses 1298-1378, both in Book XI, ed. Meesters).

8. Guillaume de Lorris and Jean de Meun, *The romance of the rose.* Transl. by H.W. Robbins, ed. and introd. by Ch.W. Dunn (Dutton, New York, 1962). See also D. Poirion, 'Narcisse et Pygmalion dans le "Roman de la rose"' in R.J. Cormier and V.T. Holmes (eds), *Essays in honour of Louis Francis Solano* (Chapel Hill, 1970), pp. 153-65.

9. The 'true' Narcissus of medieval fiction should, of course, be female. I would like to suggest the heroine of *La belle dame sans mercy* (1424) for this role. See Alain Chartier, *La belle dame sans mercy et les poésies lyriques*, ed. P.A. Piaget (Droz, Lille, 1949). This poem inspired the writing of a play on the Narcissus theme; see A. Hilka, 'Das mittelfranzösische Narcissusspiel (L'istoire de Narcisus et de Echo)', *Zeitschrift für Romanische Philologie*, LVI, pp. 275-321.

10. I wonder if any woman would like to be addressed as 'Ruby, fair and noble statue by Pygmalion', even if this is apparently intended as a compliment (as is the case in a poem in *Die remedie der liefde* (Jan van Brecht, Brussels, 1583), f. 79v).

11. It only occurred to me later that this interpretation is really a modern continuation of a medieval tradition: the *Ovide moralisé*, in which Ovid's stories were given a contemporary and edifying explanation. This both amuses and worries me: it does little harm to put new wine in old bottles, as long as the bottles are kept in their proper places. My 'bottles', the stories of Narcissus and Pygmalion, are actually used in medieval texts to demonstrate ideas about love. My judgement, however, is twentieth-century and therefore a kind of projection or even a forgery. The best solution might be to consider the whole argument as a mere metaphor, serving only to show my point but essentially unfitted to prove anything.

12. A very clear account of the (mis)use of the 'nature argument' is given in Janet Radcliffe Richards, *The sceptical feminist: a philosophical enquiry* (Penguin, Harmondsworth, 1980), pp. 50-85.

13. See Andreas Capellanus, *The art of courtly love*, pp. 122-3. At the

International Conference on Women's History a striking parallel to this idea was discussed in Pirkko Heiskanen's paper 'Hierarchy as a structure in art history'; 'pure arts' are generally rated higher than 'applied arts'.

Anna Clark

Whores and gossips: sexual reputation in London 1770-1825

'You whore!'

What did this insult, shouted in streets or crowded pubs, mean to London women of the late-eighteenth and early-nineteenth centuries? 'Whore' literally means prostitute; it describes a woman's occupation as sexual commerce. But it is also a potent insult which could damage any woman's honour and sexual reputation.[1]

Anthropologists and historians have long stressed the way in which insults to female sexual reputation can control women's freedom in male-dominated societies. The classic studies have been of Mediterranean societies, where men's honour depended to such an extent on female relatives' sexual reputation that women were kept secluded, chaperoned and submissive.[2] J.A. Sharpe and Susan Dwyer Amussen have pointed out that the concept of honour worked somewhat differently in seventeenth-century England: unlike their Mediterranean sisters, English women engaged in commerce and public life. Instead of seclusion, gossip about their sexual reputations controlled women's behaviour.[3] By the eighteenth century, argues Polly Morris in her study of Somerset defamation, gossip about female sexual reputation expressed the contradictions between women's economic and social freedom, their low social status in a male-dominated society, and increasingly restricted notions of respectability.[4]

In London, these contradictions became even more acute between 1770 and 1820. This was a time of rapid change in women's economic opportunities, of concern over the prevalence of prostitution in the Metropolis, and clashes between libertinism and moral reform. This article concerns the impact of this turbulence on the everyday lives of plebeian women: small shopkeepers, milliners, mantua-makers, needlewomen, the wives of tradesmen and artisans, and ranging down to the level of the labouring poor. For them, sexual reputation was a volatile issue. Plebeian women defended their own definitions of honour against hostile men and middle-class authorities, but as sexual reputation became a marker of class status it sparked off resentment between women.

When the Regency Period ended in 1820, an era of conflicting moral standards ended as well. Up until that time, many aristocrats, especially the Prince Regent, were notorious for the number of their mistresses and the extent of their gambling debts. Radicals such as William Godwin and Mary Wollstonecraft undermined traditional notions of marriage from a more austere standpoint, arguing that love, not law, imparted virtue. However, the newly powerful middle class attempted to combat both these tendencies through the Evangelical moral reform movement. Identifying themselves as morally superior, these reformers portrayed the aristocracy as corrupt and the labouring poor as undisciplined. They also promulgated a distinctive ideology of separate spheres, which mandated that middle-class men should control the public world of economic and political life, while women remained secluded in the private domestic sphere of the home. By the early nineteenth century, the chastity of wives and daughters became a crucial marker of respectable middle-class status.[5]

These middle-class reformers were especially concerned with prostitution, which they perceived both as a danger to themselves and a sign of the degeneracy of the poor. Their definition of prostitution, however, was not universally accepted. In the opinion of the influential magistrate Patrick Colquehoun, any woman who indulged in extra-marital sex was a prostitute. He claimed there were 50,000 prostitutes in London, but this hugely inflated figure included 25,000 common-law wives.[6] As social historians have recently pointed out, many plebeian Londoners did not regard common-law wives as prostitutes, but considered them to be respectable women in recognised relationships.[7]

Plebeians were concerned with sexual morality, but they drew the line between moral and immoral behaviour at different points. Some accepted common-law wives but condemned women who sold sex on the streets; for others, friendship, sympathy and mutual aid were more important virtues than chastity. The open nature of plebeian morality derived from their social conditions. The number of out-of-wedlock births and common-law marriages rose sharply in the second half of the eighteenth century, caused by the passing of Lord Hardwicke's Marriage Act in 1753, which made it expensive and inconvenient for the poor to marry.[8] Furthermore, Londoners often migrated to the Metropolis from rural areas or left Britain to seek their fortunes abroad, a process which disrupted traditional courtship patterns and broke up many marriages. The American Wars at the beginning of this period, and the Napoleonic Wars at the end, also tore many men away from their sweethearts and wives. As a result, bigamy, common-law marriage and premarital sex were accepted as inevitable in plebeian culture.[9]

Definitions of sexual honour, then, differed according to class. But even within plebeian culture, there was a great deal of conflict and confusion about this issue. First, Methodists and other dissenters formed a small but influential minority among plebeian Londoners, and enforced strict standards of propriety on their followers. A tradesman's daughter might grow up in a neighbourhood where common-law marriage was unexceptional, but later in life find herself among religious people who considered her to be a whore. Second, many Londoners on the upper levels of plebeian culture - artisans, tradesmen and shopkeepers - existed in a nebulous class level between the labouring poor and the new middle class, uncertain as to which moral standards to adopt. 'Plebeian' means here the mass of people below the level of the middle class, ranging from the labouring poor up to these small shopkeepers and tradesmen. Until the 1820s, the cultural boundaries between those on the upper and lower levels of plebeian society remained very unclear. By the 1820s and 30s, some of these people would fall into the ranks of the working class as their skills became obsolete or bankruptcy robbed them of their shops. Others would profit from the new prosperity, and ruthlessly differentiate themselves from their poorer associates; in order to enter the middle class, they would adopt strict standards of propriety and move away from plebeian neighbourhoods.[10] Sexual reputation became a focal point of class tension during this transitional period.

Until the 1820s and 30s London artisans and shopkeepers of this ambiguous class level often retained the values of their poorer neighbours. Francis Place, a master tailor and influential radical, remembered that in the 1780s, when he was a young man, tradesmen did not care if their daughters became kept mistresses or the mothers of bastards; when he wrote in the 1820s, such behaviour was considered scandalous.[11] Sexual reputation, then, was a key element in a woman's social status; it affected whether her neighbours respected her, and whether she respected herself. But during the long transition from one morality to another, contradictory and fluid standards of sexual morality made it difficult for a woman to decide what behaviour was appropriate to her social status.

The insult 'whore' inhibited the ability of plebeian women to enjoy a public role.[12] This era witnessed a clash between the fact that plebeian women normally worked and socialised in streets and shops, and the new middle-class ideology of separate spheres, which impelled women to withdraw from the commercial and public world into domestic seclusion in order to be considered respectable. Descriptions of prostitutes as 'public women' or 'women of the town' brought into question the respectability of other Metropolitan women of business: shopkeepers, shoebinders, publicans, porters and costermongers, all of whom engaged in commercial public life.

Labouring and lower-middle-class women often went out to work or assisted their husbands, as they were expected to help support their families. In the largest London trades - tailoring, weaving and shoemaking - women helped their husbands, while other women kept their own small shops or businesses, especially in millinery and dressmaking, and a few engaged in such masculine trades as carting and printing.[13] Around the time of the Napoleonic Wars, however, the sexual division of labour was rapidly changing, creating anxiety among women who feared feminine trades would disappear or be taken over by men, and among men who attempted to exclude female labour as unfair competition for jobs. Women faced the dilemma of how to earn a living and still adhere to new middle-class standards of female chastity. In 1798, Priscilla Wakefield declared that women should follow their own useful occupations, but contradicted her own argument by warning them to avoid any situation which 'obliges them to mix in the public haunts of men'.[14] Mary Wollstonecraft echoed more conservative commentators when she lamented that the genteel trades of mantua-makers and milliners were synonymous with prostitution, for the wages were so low and the risks of seduction so great from the young rakes who frequented the shops.[15] London women were therefore extremely sensitive to the insult 'whore' because this was a fate often perilously possible. The drunken streetwalker clothed only in rags, grabbing and swearing at male passers-by on a freezing winter night, was a familiar and chilling sight to London women.

Even if labouring women did not accept middle-class definitions of sexual morality, they lived in a society where magistrates, charity officials, clerics and constables could punish them for deviations from bourgeois values. To be identified as a common prostitute could have serious material consequences for a woman. Any woman out on the street at night, soliciting men, drinking in a pub or merely walking home from work, faced the risk of being arrested as a common prostitute by corrupt constables, and then imprisoned by magistrates unless she was able to bribe them.[16] Such treatment of working women stemmed from the class-variable definitions of immoral behaviour; for the authorities, socialising on the street at night with men and/or streetwalkers would be taken as evidence of prostitution, but for working people this was ordinary courtship behaviour or association with friends.

Women united: friendship and compassion

Plebeian women had their own code of sexual honour. Many women would not shun a friend or neighbour simply because a constable or magistrate stigmatised her as a prostitute. In trials for theft, female witnesses defended their association with 'fallen' women or refused to accept middle-class definitions of female virtue.[17] Some women, especially among the labouring poor, associated with prostitutes because they did not care about sexual nonconformity. For more respectable women, the importance of neighbourliness, friendship, compassion, sociability or kinship outweighed the taint of unchastity in determining their relationships with 'fallen' women.

The rules of plebeian sociability allowed an easy intercourse between respectable and 'fallen' women. To the horror of moral reformers, 'profligates and prostitutes, mix[ed] with tradesmen's daughters and female servants' at pub dances and theatres.[18] Given the risk of damaging their own reputations in the eyes of the authorities, it is striking that some married women defended their association with prostitutes. For instance, during the course of Ann Tovey's trial in 1808 for stealing Mrs Elizabeth Hughes' purse, the prosecutrix revealed that she and her soldier husband had joined Ann, who was a prostitute, for a drink. This fact impelled the judge to ask incredulously, 'Are you really married...can you tell me how a decent woman should go with your husband, invited by a bad girl to drink?' Mrs Hughes replied simply, 'She asked me to drink'; for her, the polite response was to accept.[19]

One reason for this easy association of ordinary women with 'fallen' women was that the definition of prostitution remained very obscure. In fact, plebeian women were often determined to defend their sexual reputations, even though they had illegitimate children or engaged in sexual commerce. Clearly, they had their own definitions of virtue which were very distinct from those of the middle class. Although by middle-class standards an unmarried mother such as Mary Scully would have been considered a prostitute, she defended herself against this imputation in 1829. Trying to claim paternity before a magistrate, she declared, 'I am no bad woman. I tried all I could to support his child, and now he wants to make me a common streetwalker.'[20] Women whose low wages or unemployment forced them to resort to part-time sexual commerce did not consider themselves to be prostitutes. Explaining her quarrel with Ann Cottrell in 1796, Mary Parker admitted, 'I wash and iron, and go to gentlemen's houses sometimes, and she insulted me with that', but she claimed Cottrell 'had no right to charge me with being a common woman of the town'. Since she engaged in sexual commerce only occasionally, and then with 'gentlemen', she did not consider herself on the same level as a streetwalker.[21]

Furthermore, sexual reputation was only one factor by which working women judged whether they should associate with each other, for chastity was not the only important female virtue. Artisans' and tradesmen's wives and labouring women were described by their neighbours in depositions as 'industrious and sober' and as affectionate wives and mothers. Francis Place noted that among tradesmen's families in the 1780s, unchaste girls were not shunned if they 'were decent in their general conduct'.[22] One deposition in an adultery case in 1777 noted that Elizabeth Hicks of Shadwell had borne another man's child while her husband was away at sea and 'was much given to liquor', but 'she had no other faults'.[23] Mrs Hannah Vollar trusted Eliza Webb enough to make her a partner in her dressmaking business; as she told a magistrate in 1821, after Eliza had broken this trust and stolen some of the former's belongings, 'I knew she was an unfortunate woman, but thought her honest.'[24]

Even if a 'respectable' woman did not approve of sexual commerce, the ideal of rescuing lost souls might compel her to aid another woman. Unlike upper-class philanthropists who required the severe discipline of repentance, these women seemed to be motivated by humanity: the ruling principle among poor people was that they should have compassion for people in wretched circumstances, for they in turn might soon find themselves in need of help. In 1809, unemployed servant Elizabeth Tanner took lodgings with Harriet Collins, thinking she was in a similar situation; when Harriet confessed she was an 'unfortunate' girl Elizabeth merely asked, 'Cannot you reform and become a servant, it is better than going on the streets.' Harriet tearfully exclaimed, 'Thank God, I have found a friend at last', to which the rather gullible Elizabeth thankfully responded, 'There is more joy over one sinner that repenteth than over ninety-nine just persons.' Her joy was short-lived; the next morning Harriet had disappeared, taking Elizabeth's bundle with her.[25] When Mary Ann Sleeford, who kept a butcher's shop in Petticoat Lane, discovered in 1810 that her neighbour Bet Evens picked up men on the streets, she 'remonstrated with her on the impropriety of her conduct'. Despite her failure to reform Bet, she still allowed her own children to associate with her, and helped her to claim maintenance from her estranged husband, a Southwark cider merchant.[26]

Aid from female relatives saved many unmarried mothers from having to go on the streets. For such a relative, the fact that her niece or friend had lost her chastity did not release her from the claims of kinship or compassion. Even if they disapproved of premarital sex, mothers and aunts helped to conceal young girls' shame by providing shelter for them throughout the pregnancy and birth. Independent women who ran their own businesses or practised a craft had the most resources to aid girls in trouble. An aunt in the upholstery business took in Miranda Tusk, a dressmaker's apprentice, when she was starving and pregnant in 1815.[27] Such women could even defy male disapproval of 'fallen women', for fathers and other relatives tended to shun unmarried daughters who became pregnant. In 1817 Susan Badger's brother-in-law, an attorney, rejected her when he discovered her pregnancy, but his wife and sister, who kept a pub themselves, continued to support her.[28]

Women divided: gossip and insult

The pressures of respectability, however, increasingly limited the possibilities for economically independent women to defy convention, as did the declining opportunities for women to run their own businesses. Shopkeepers had to preserve a respectable reputation in order to retain their customers. For instance, Sally Blenheim's mother, a Greenwich laundress, feared 'all she has done will be in vain' if a charitable institution would not take in her unmarried daughter's baby after it was born in 1817, for if her workwomen or customers discovered this 'shame' they would no longer respect her.[29]

Women like Mrs Blenheim, who lived on the lowest ranks of the lower-middle class, were extremely vulnerable to the gossip of neighbours who resented their class pretensions and men who disapproved of women in business. The more a woman tried to attain a middle-class standard of respectability through her economic efforts, the more vulnerable she became to insinuations about her sexual reputation, for of course the ideology of separate spheres required women to stay in the home to be truly respectable.

The power of malicious gossip derived from its ability to erase the boundaries between public and private life, which made it especially dangerous for shopkeeping, artisan and labouring women whose sexual reputations could determine their credit at work. In part, when women gossiped they were succumbing to the reality of the importance of sexual reputation in women's lives, drawing upon the moral vocabulary of the dominant class to carry out their own vendettas. But they were also defying the linguistic constraints of ladyhood by being loud and aggressive and by refusing to respect the boundaries of the newly defined private domestic sphere. The disruptive force of gossip had long been legally recognised in the prosecutions of scolds, women who went to extremes in trying to monitor the *mores* of their neighbours or husbands.[30]

The danger of gossips who called women whores was also recognised in the provision through the church courts of prosecution for defamation. These church courts formerly exerted a powerful moral discipline over parishioners by imposing penance on adulterers, fornicators, unmarried mothers, blasphemers and other immoral types. By the late eighteenth century, the London Consistory Court seems to have heard only defamation and *mensa et thoro* (separation from bread and board) divorce cases. I have found 40 sets of such depositions for defamation cases from 1770-1810; these represent only 10 per cent of actual defamation charges, most of which never reached the deposition stage, probably because the complainant could not afford lawyers' fees, or had settled the case out of court.[31] The depositions are an extremely rich source for social history, containing detailed accounts of the original quarrels from the point of view of various witnesses. If the defendant was found guilty, the church courts meted out a largely symbolic but intensely humiliating punishment of penance: to stand in a white sheet in the church or church door and publicly apologise. However, very few of my cases were concluded by this penance; usually the dispute appears to have been resolved by a private apology.[32] Approximately one-quarter of the women plaintiffs in these defamation charges were solidly middle-class, the wives of attorneys, clerics or gentlemen, while the rest were artisans' and tradesmen's wives, or female shopkeepers themselves. They were particularly anxious to maintain not only their sexual, but also their social reputations, for defamation undermined their class status.

However, they also differed from conventional middle-class ladies in their desire to reclaim their reputation publicly, through church court proceedings (the civil courts were not generally available to them). A 'real lady' would never risk the exposure of the intimate details of her life which we find in these depositions. One-quarter of all the women plaintiffs had their own businesses or were involved in those of their husbands; they therefore needed to preserve their 'credit' as public figures. Half of them were married and half single, widowed or separated, unlike the married plaintiffs who formed the majority in the defamation cases Morris has studied in Somerset; a fact which reveals the vulnerability of single women's reputations in the turbulent Metropolis.[33] By the late eighteenth century, the church courts no longer heard defamation cases brought by men, due to the declining significance of sexual insults to men in an era of the double standard, although it must be noted that men remained extremely sensitive to imputations of homosexuality.[34]

Men, however, constituted more than half of those accused of defamation; despite the strong image of the female gossip, men gossiped too, spreading sexual innuendoes about their female neighbours and economic rivals.[35] As Polly Morris notes, 'Sexual language was used by men to discipline women who challenged their supremacy, and it referred, increasingly, to emerging definitions of femininity that denied the contemporary variety of female material roles.'[36] For instance, in 1796 Sarah Danton, a hotel-keeper, felt compelled to take proceedings against Mr E. Jervoise, Esquire, for calling her 'a damned bitch and whore' in a dispute over a hotel bill.[37] When Rebecca Cartwright asked William Kitchings in 1776 for the rent of his room, he scornfully replied, 'You are a whore and a dirty stinking whore and you are not the wife of John Cartwright but his whore.'[38] In 1793, after she refused to refer a customer to him, Alexander Ross shouted out to rival broker Mary Nowlan, 'You're a common whore and all your neighbours know it - there goes the Irish bitch with a feather stuck up her arse.'[39] Similarly, in 1796 Elizabeth Wilson worried that her credit among her neighbours would be damaged when the shopkeeper next door told her son, 'Go home to your Old Mother a Whore.'[40] Defamation proceedings were one way in which women could defend their contradictory position as respectable middle-class ladies and economic agents in public life against men who used insults to undercut them.

The fluidity of both class definitions and sexual morality during this period also increased social insecurity for the ambitious artisans, tradesmen and middle-class population of London. Keeping the family name unbesmirched seems to have been particularly difficult in the vast crowded parishes of the East End, source of half of the defamation cases in my study. In these newly-built but impoverished areas, prosperous families were few and far between, as most of the middle class and gentry had moved to more salubrious and prestigious neighbourhoods.[41] In Spitalfields, for instance, only a few master artisans and silk merchants lived among thousands of labouring and artisanal families.[42] The riverside districts of Wapping and Shadwell served as home both to the most violent, criminal and degraded population of thieves and prostitutes, and to respectable shipwrights and sea-captains.

While the poorer inhabitants of these neighbourhoods were not necessarily profligate, and indeed had their own moral codes, those with bourgeois aspirations could differentiate themselves from those below by ostentatiously upholding a middle-class standard of female virtue. Conversely, a woman's loss of reputation could drag her and her family down to the level of the labouring poor. As a result, socially ambitious families engaged in bitter disputes over respectability. For instance, one day Lewis Vanderpump and his wife Louisa went to see his sister Hannah Book in her chandler's shop in the East End, to ask why Louisa had been excluded from family gatherings. Much offended, Hannah replied, 'If he was so inquisitive to know what his wife has done he should go along with her to the place where she has transgressed.' Louisa retaliated by declaring to Hannah, 'You infernal Bawd you have reared all your children to be Whores from their Cradles...if I was to tell all that I know of your daughter Betty she would not wear such a high bonnet as she does', and then accused Betty, the wife of a man wealthy enough to own a counting house, of sleeping with Lewis Vanderpump before she married Mr Rudolph.

The real problem facing this family, however, was not solely rumours of adultery; tension over class status seems to have sparked off these insults. As a shopkeeper, Hannah Book aspired to middle-class respectability, but she was only a corner-shop keeper on a street inhabited by 'inferior' people in the poor parish of St George's in the East. She actually endangered her own reputation by loudly quarrelling with her own brother in the public arenas of shop and street. Conversely, Louisa Vanderpump resented the airs her niece assumed upon her marriage to a prosperous man, and insinuated that her respectability veiled loose morals.[43] Similar resentment towards class pretensions motivated other women who accused their neighbours of being whores. Lodgers could express their hostility towards more prosperous landladies in this way. When Mrs Butler, a dressmaker, quarrelled with her landlady, she spitefully declared, 'You Ma'am don't put yourself in such a style for you have been a whore to Mr Horton for these thirteen years.'[44]

Several of the women who defamed their socially ambitious neighbours turned out to be common-law wives themselves. The fact that women who did not conform to conventional marital morals called other women whores brings into question the connotations of the insult 'whore'. Its literal meaning of course is prostitute, but in the context of neighbourhood defamation it could also mean an unfaithful woman. Common-law wives did not necessarily regard themselves as whores, for they indulged in stable, monogamous relationships. The word 'whore' seemed to have a broader meaning as an insult, implying that a woman had no self-respect, that she did not control herself, that she was loud and sexually promiscuous, that she roamed the streets or that she did not conform to the control of husband or father. By calling other women whores, common-law wives asserted their own self-worth at the expense of female solidarity.

The power of sexual reputation divided women from each other. Even the association of a respectable woman with a prostitute could damage her reputation, and therefore have far-reaching consequences. A Mr Neale reduced his estranged wife's maintenance payments from 16 to 12 shillings a week because she was 'chum to a common streetwalker'.[45] While many women, as I have shown, ignored pressure to reject their 'fallen' friends, others felt compelled to disassociate themselves from them. Some female friendly societies (usually religious ones or those catering for tradesmen's wives) refused to accept common-law wives or prostitutes, and cut off annuities to widows who were thought to disregard sexual propriety.[46] When Elizabeth Harrison, the wife of a publican, found out in 1804 that her upstairs neighbour in the middle-class enclave of Goodman's Fields was not, as she had claimed, Mrs Rea, wife of a gunmaker, but Mr Rea's 'loose and abandoned' kept mistress, she broke off their formerly warm friendship.[47]

A clash in material, as well as moral interests, divided ordinary women and women who engaged in sexual commerce from each other. If a man associated with prostitutes or kept a mistress, he diverted money from the household exchequer and could expose his wife to venereal disease. When 'respectable' women shunned their 'fallen' sisters, therefore, they expressed their solidarity with injured wives, rather than with 'fallen' women. I have already told of how Elizabeth Harrison broke with her friend when she discovered her true position as a kept mistress, but the other side of the story is the plight of the real Mrs Rea, beaten, starved and infected by her profligate husband. Women of the labouring or artisan classes became very angry if prostitutes lured their sons or husbands away. In 1823, a 'respectable woman named Roberts' charged two teenage girls with 'seducing' her son 'from the paths of virtue and honor', causing him to lose his situation, and no doubt depriving her of his wages.[48]

From gossip to collective action

Plebeians tended to treat individual prostitutes and unmarried mothers as individuals who should be pitied for their misfortunes, but brothels could sometimes arouse community action. Neighbours of different classes, however, reacted from different motives and used different means to respond to the presence of bawdy-houses.

First, there was the traditional and collective means of popular justice. Women enthusiastically pelted brothel-keepers when they were set in the pillory, for exploitative bawds were unpopular even with prostitutes.[49] Rough music could also be used against brothels. In the 'warlike' district of Stepney, known for its 'pugnacious' women, one man and five women were indicted for a riot against Margaret Henley, who kept a brothel in Blue Anchor Alley. They gathered a mob around her house and raised rough music with 'cannisters, frying pans, saucepans, candlesticks, salt-boxes, tongs, pokers and other sonorous instruments'. Given that Stepney was a neighbourhood where artisans co-existed with thieves and prostitutes, these women may have been the wives of the 'mariners and shipbuilders' for whom the brothel catered, angry at the temptation it posed to their husbands.[50]

Middle-class people tended to use more genteel methods, such as private prosecutions, to rid their streets of brothels and prostitutes. As vast new stretches of middle-class housing were built in Islington, Pentonville and Marylebone, their inhabitants wished to ensure that these prestigious neighbourhoods remained free from the contamination of open immorality, which after all might damage property values.[51] Bourgeois women, anxious to uphold their own reputations, believed the presence of prostitutes exposed their daughters to unseemly influences - and their husbands to illicit temptation. In the 1808 trial of a brothel-keeper in Upper Titchfield Street, the wife of a cleric complained that 'she was constantly annoyed at the sight of women immodestly and indecently attired at the window of the defendant's house...nodding and beckoning at the gentlemen as they passed by'.[52]

A few years later, middle-class efforts to repress prostitution intensified, motivated by both Evangelical and commercial concerns. In 1812, committees were set up in every ward of the City of London to investigate and prosecute brothels. These reformers wished to assert their middle-class virtue by sharply differentiating themselves from the libertine life of the streets, but they also feared the ability of prostitutes to infiltrate themselves into their lives by seducing their sons and daughters into a life of crime. As some respectable inhabitants protested:

> 'No virtuous female, however protected, can pass through the streets in the evening without witnessing these disgusting scenes; and the utmost vigilance your Petitioners can use is insufficient to preserve their Sons and Servants from frequent Solicitations, even at their own Doors. Familiarity with the sight of these Women who practice various arts to entrap unwary Youth, gradually diminish their Disgust and Caution, and is too often followed with the most ruinous consequences.'[53]

As Place reminds us in his memoirs, their fears were based on reality, for he recounts that tradesmen's sons and daughters did associate with prostitutes and thieves.[54] When lower-middle-class Londoners took action against prostitutes, therefore, they were also setting themselves apart from their plebeian neighbours.

Immediately after the Napoleonic Wars, concern about prostitution increased as ex-soldiers and sailors competed with working women for jobs, driving many of the latter into prostitution. The Guardian Society was then founded to strengthen the fight against sexual commerce.[55] Although middle-class women apparently wished to join this struggle as part of a ladylike philanthropy, some moral reformers believed ladies should be completely removed from any concern with vice, let alone knowledge of its existence.

As an address to the Guardian Society stated in 1816, a 'virtuous woman ought not only to be pure in body, but in mind: she should be kept perfectly ignorant of all these things'. Ladies should not protest against brothels, nor try to rescue prostitutes. If a lady was seen conversing with a prostitute, 'she is immediately marked, as one who, if not already gone, is, at least, on the high road to destruction'.[56] This principle enabled middle-class men to assert their control over the task of reforming prostitutes, and precluded any possibility that ladies could find solidarity with their fallen sisters until the second half of the century.

Conclusion

After about 1820, women no longer brought defamation proceedings before the London Consistory Court. As Morris notes, this public way of defending sexual reputation, used so often by the independent businesswomen of plebeian London, offended the church court's sensibilities. Ladies were to retreat entirely into their homes, and should certainly not put themselves into situations where they could be insulted by belligerent, vulgar neighbours or saucy prostitutes on the street. Middle-class reformers also attempted to improve the loose sexual *mores* of the poor. Sexual reputation thus became a marker of class status, but one which limited the lives of women, not men.

Women's dependence on men divided them from each other. As women became more economically vulnerable, they competed for scarce male resources, pitting wives against prostitutes. However, the repression of prostitutes by the authorities and the use of the insult 'whore' served to restrict the freedom of all women, not just those engaged in sexual commerce. Yet some plebeian women did not always accept this morality; they valued the virtue of compassion above chastity.

Notes

1. I would like to thank Jan Lambertz, Alison Oram, Annemieke Keunen and Geerte Binnema for their help in revising this piece. Judith Walkowitz and John Gillis have also been most helpful in their comments

on the larger work on gender in London, of which this is a part. As the notes will reveal, I am also heavily indebted to the excellent scholarship and insight of Polly Morris's own work on defamation in Somerset.

2. Susan Harding, 'Women and words in a Spanish village' in Rayna R. Reiter (ed.), *Toward an anthropology of women* (Monthly Review Press, New York, 1975), p. 303; Julian Pitt-Rivers, 'Honor and social status in Andalusia' in J. Peristiany (ed.), *Honor and shame: the values of Mediterranean society* (University of Chicago Press, Chicago, 1966), p. 61; Yves Castan, *Honnêteté et relations sociales en Languedoc 1715-1780* (Plon, Paris, 1974), p. 40; also Bertram Wyatt-Brown, *Southern honour: ethics and behaviour in the Old South* (Oxford University Press, New York, 1982), p. 227.

3. J.A. Sharpe, 'Defamation and sexual slander in early modern England: the church courts at York', *Borthwick Papers*, 58 (1980), pp. 19-20; Susan Dwyer Amussen, 'Gender, family and the social order' in John Stevenson, Anthony Fletcher (eds), *Order and disorder in early modern England* (Cambridge University Press, Cambridge, 1985), p. 207.

4. Polly Morris, 'Defamation and sexual slander in Somerset, 1733-1850', unpublished PhD thesis, University of Warwick, 1985, p. 134.

5. Leonore Davidoff, Catherine Hall, *Family fortunes: men and women of the English middle class* (Hutchinson, London, 1987), pp. 103, 127, 153.

6. Patrick Colquehoun, *A treatise on the police of the Metropolis* (London, 1797), pp. vii-xi.

7. John R. Gillis, *For better, for worse: British marriages, 1600 to the present* (Oxford University Press, Oxford, 1985), p. 132.

8. Ibid. Weddings had to be announced three weeks in advance in case anyone objected to the marriage, and a fee was required.

9. Ibid., p. 111.

10. Ibid., p. 164.

11. *The autobiography of Francis Place 1771-1854*, ed. by Mary Thrale (Cambridge University Press, Cambridge, 1972), pp. 81-2.

12. For comparative studies, see Morris, 'Defamation and sexual slander', pp. 134ff; Susan Amussen, 'Féminin/masculin: le genre dans l'Angleterre de l'époque moderne', *Annales ESC*, vol. 40, no. 2 (1985).

13. Ivy Pinchbeck, *Women workers and the Industrial Revolution 1750-1850* (Virago, London, 1981 (1st edn 1930)), pp. 157, 282-303.

14. Priscilla Wakefield, *Reflections on the present condition of the female sex* (London, 1798), pp. 8-9.

15. Mary Wollstonecraft, *A vindication of the rights of women* (Penguin, Harmondsworth, 1978 (1st edn 1792)), p. 261; for comments on women's low wages, decline in employment and prostitution, see also *The Times*, 10 May 1785, 11 Jan. 1787, 10 Oct. 1803; Mary Ann Radcliffe, *Memoirs and the female advocate* (London, 1799), p. 409.

16. Hugh Phillips, *Mid-Georgian London* (Collins, London, 1964), p. 114; *Public Advertizer*, 21 Aug. 1790; *Universal Register*, 28 April, 17 Nov.

1785; 11 Sept, 14 Oct. 1788; *The Times*, 25 Oct. 1803; *Sun*, 14 Dec. 1816; *Weekly Dispatch*, 24 Nov. 1822, 25 April 1824.

17. Testimony found in trial transcripts in the printed 'Old Bailey Sessions Papers', abbreviated as OBSP.

18. *Address to the Society for the Suppression of Vice* (London, 1803), p. 59; for an earlier and similar complaint, see *Universal Register*, 23 Oct. 1789.

19. OBSP 1808-9, pp. 241-2.

20. *Weekly Free Press*, 28 March 1829.

21. OBSP 1796, p. 40.

22. *Autobiography of Francis Place*, p. 57.

23. Greater London Record Office, DL/C 280, 27 Feb. 1777, Hicks *v.* Hicks. Morris found a similar Somerset defamation case in which neighbours described an unmarried mother as 'a person of good life and sober conversation', 'Defamation and sexual slander', p. 458.

24. OBSP 1821-2, p. 147.

25. OBSP 1809-10, p. 18.

26. DL/C 293, 25 Oct. 1810, Evens *v.* Evens divorce.

27. Foundling Hospital petition, 1815, unnumbered. Names changed in accordance with archival regulations.

28. Foundling Hospital petition, 1817, rejected, unnumbered.

29. Foundling Hospital petition, 1817, accepted, unnumbered.

30. For the prosecution of scolds, see GLCRO, Middlesex Sessions Roll 3461, 1785, indictment 101 of Susannah Pardon of Whitechapel, and indictment 34 of Marmaduke Riley of St Andrew Holborn, both for being scolds; neither was punished. It was highly unusual for a man to be indicted as a scold, but Riley was apparently such a disruptive influence that his neighbours resorted to this tactic in desperation. In 1801 a female scold was ducked at Kingston (*The Times*, 6 April 1801), and in 1804 Ann Price was fined and imprisoned at the Surrey Sessions for being a common scold (*The Times*, 3 March 1804).

31. DL/C 179, 180, 181 for these other charges. For a further discussion of these courts, see Morris, 'Defamation and sexual slander', pp. 134ff.

32. Morris, 'Defamation and sexual slander', p. 239 for similar results in Somerset.

33. Ibid., p. 279.

34. Ibid., p. 239.

35. DL/C 179-181, defamation charges, 1770-1800.

36. Morris, 'Defamation and sexual slander', p. 391.

37. DL/C 287, 26 May 1796, Danton *v.* Jervoise.

38. DL/C 280, 3 June 1776, Cartwright *v.* Kitchings.

39. DL/C 285, 26 Feb. 1793, Nowlan *v.* Ross.

40. DL/C 641, 11 May 1796, Wilson *v.* Swears.

41. George Rudé, *Hanoverian London 1714-1808* (Secker and Warburg,

London, 1971), pp. 7-10.

42. William Hale, *Letter to Samuel Whitbread on the condition of the poor in Spitalfields* (London, 1813), p. 25.

43. DL/C 284, 23 Nov. 1789, Rudolph *v.* Vanderpump.

44. DL/C 283, 27 June 1789, Crompton *v.* Butler; see also DL/C 284, 12 May 1790, Myatt *v.* Allen.

45. *Weekly Dispatch,* 4 Sept. 1825.

46. Friendly societies were self-supporting and social organisations of women or men which met in pubs. Records exist in the Public Record Office, for example, the City of Refuge for the Benefit of Widows (PRO, FS/1/406A/111, 1795) and the United Sisters of Camomile St (PRO, FS/1/406B/115, 1795). Friendly society members sometimes took their disputes over morality to magistrates; see Guildhall Library, Collection of Newspaper Cuttings concerning the Guildhall Justice Rooms, 27 Sept. 1804, pp. 65, 68.

47. DL/C 290, 1804, Rea *v.* Rea divorce.

48. *Weekly Dispatch,* 17 Aug. 1823.

49. Edward Bristow, *Vice and vigilance: purity movements in Britain since 1700* (Rowman and Littlefield, Totowa, N.J., 1977), p. 25.

50. *Times,* 28 Oct. 1807.

51. Rudé, *Hanoverian London,* p. 14; for property values, Report of the Committee formed to prosecute brothels in the parish of St Sepulchre, 1 March 1826, Guildhall Ms. 3189.

52. *Sun,* 20 Oct. 1808.

53. *Report of the Committee...relative to common prostitutes* (London, 1814), p. 1.

54. *Autobiography of Francis Place,* p. 82.

55. Bristow, *Vice and vigilance,* p. 53.

56. *Address to the Guardian Society* (London, 1816), pp. 9, 11.

Maria Grever

On the origins of Dutch women's historiography: three portraits (1840-1970)

Some years ago Nathalie Z. Davis and Bonnie G. Smith were considering the historiographical roots of women's history.[1] They laid emphasis on the contributions of former women writers in several historical genres, such as biographies, historical novels and social history.[2] Most of these women devoted at least some of their studies to the history of women, or wrote about the prevailing customs and morals concerning their sex. In this way they contributed a great deal of information which is still relevant today. However, their work has been underestimated; few of the women scholars' names are known, and they deserve more recognition than has so far been forthcoming.[3] The obscurity of women historians seems to be one of the most dramatic features of women's history. To neglect these contributions would be to neglect an important part of women's history.

With regard to the situation in the Netherlands, I discovered a similar phenomenon. Many studies written by Dutch women historians in the nineteenth and twentieth centuries are relatively unknown. Others were criticised as non-feministic, and therefore unimportant. This article is about three Dutch women historians, and the niche they occupy within historiography. In order to demonstrate the significance of this subject, some theoretical notions will first be discussed.

Women's culture and 'herstoriography'

One of the central issues in women's history today is the concept of 'women's culture'. At first this concept was used to describe the nineteenth-century networks between women as studied by Carroll Smith-Rosenberg and Nancy Cott. Recently this concept has also proven to be fruitful when focusing on different types of female activities. In this way a new vision of female experience in the past can be formed.[4] For example, it is possible to examine how women dealt with oppressive ideologies, sometimes turning them to their own advantage. Women are no longer mere victims of a patriarchal system: they have become active participants in history. Instead of studying records about women which were composed by men, it is more useful to look at all kinds of documents written by the women themselves, in order to obtain a better understanding of their position in the private and the public spheres. Studying the writings of women is one way of gathering more information about their world and their consciousness.[5] The published work of women historians is therefore a very interesting source to consult when examining certain aspects of women's history. It should be possible to study the position of these women of letters, what strategies they developed to deal with the challenges they had to face, and how they analysed the history of the female sex in their work.

With regard to historiography, certain conditions are necessary to enable people to write history.[6] First of all, one needs access to material concerning the subject: written, printed or oral. Therefore one should be able to travel to find manuscripts or to visit monuments, ruins and inscriptions. Furthermore, an historian has to be familiar with the genres of historical writing and with the rules for classifying and expressing historical data. The historian needs to be in contact with a public sphere favourably disposed towards historical writing. Finally, there has to be an audience to appreciate the publications on these topics.

It is obvious that many women historians of bygone centuries were not in a position to travel alone in their search for documents. Due to their lack of professional education, women were mostly untrained as historians and knew little of the historical genres. Nor was it very easy to lead a public life, as many women were preoccupied with the private sphere. Some women historians were still able to write and publish historical studies, despite the difficulties which faced them. Although they were not allowed to study at universities, and it was very uncommon for women to publish their writings, they created their own ways of learning and gaining access to sources. In the salons and literary circles of the seventeenth and eighteenth centuries, upper-class women made many contacts of their own. At the end of the eighteenth century, translation was a major occupation for women scholars, and in this manner they acquainted themselves with different cultures and periods in history. Women historians were often helped by their fathers, husbands or friends to obtain access to specific records. As a result of this, several women were able to persevere and to produce many historical studies of various genres, an important part of which was devoted to women's history. Thus they were actors on the historiographical stage, and their works provide us with much information about the world as it affected women. Given this information, it is remarkable that many of these studies on women's history are little known.

There are, however, some plausible explanations for this phenomenon. Dale Spender analyses the production of knowledge within scientific communities as a cause of the neglect of preceding women writers. According to her, knowledge is socially constructed. By generating explanations of the world and devising schemata for the structuring of objects and events, not all of them become legitimate and acceptable: a selection process takes place, which has a power dimension.[7] Men took advantage of this selection process and in fact created 'men's studies', which they presented as human knowledge. They validated knowledge, as well as their authority to construct it. As for historiography, until the Second World War the history of politics and public events of men was validated. There was no room for women's history. The history of women cannot be captured through political occurrences in the public sphere, since there were few women who had an official career. Neither does it coincide completely with the private sphere. Women's lives were within both spheres, flowing smoothly from one to another. Biographies and historical novels are suitable genres to describe this process, as they provide a frame within which daily life and public events are integrated. Moreover, until the first half of the twentieth century, these genres were comparatively accessible for women historians.

Within the frame of social history, it is also possible to write women's history. Although they were not allowed to work in the archives, women were able to observe the daily customs and habits of people in their own country, and to write social history (family history, the history of manners and morals, or local history). They frequently wrote biographies of female relatives, or of some well-known lady. The fictitious background of the historical novel might be helpful to close gaps in historical discourse. The problem, however, was that these genres were hardly accepted in nineteenth- and twentieth-century historiography. The dominant aim was to construct 'real truth' based on 'real facts'. Literary forms of history were not taken very seriously. Biographies and historical novels about women were criticised because the framework of fiction made their historical facts 'unvaluable'.[8] What is more, if the genre was acceptable, women's history was excluded as a topic. It is remarkable that even the historians of the Annales School wrote incidentally and often very stereotypically of women's history.[9] Although they emphasised the intermingling of private and public spheres, daily life for the researchers of the Annales School was a male daily life. Women remained invisible; women's history was not validated as history, and often the genres that were used, were distrusted.

In order to overcome the obscurity of women's history, Bonnie Smith proposed the making of a genealogy of women's historiography running parallel to that of well-known men, by presenting lines of descent through names and titles that omitted any references to male contemporaries. To clarify the tradition of women's history gives a better understanding of recent developments in women's historiography.[10] For this very reason it would seem relevant to examine those Dutch women of former generations who wrote women's history. It would also be important to discover how particular historical studies written by these women were validated, and the way in which this process took place. However, this article is not intended to deal with the process of validation of knowledge; that would require a separate investigation. This case-study focuses on the strategies developed by former women historians which enabled them to study and write history, and the way they analysed the position of the female sex in their historical work. Special attention is given to Truitje Bosboom-Toussaint, Johanna Naber and Sini Greup-Roldanus. These three Dutch women historians represent the consecutive generations of the nineteenth and twentieth centuries, each with their different genres of historical writing.

A scholarly recluse

One of the greatest female writers in the nineteenth-century Netherlands was Anna Louisa Geertruida Bosboom-Toussaint (1812-86). Truitje, as she was called, wrote an impressive number of historical novels and stories. Her books were translated into several languages, such as English, French, German and Russian. She was the daughter of a pharmaceutical chemist in Alkmaar. Because of her liberal background she was not obliged, like most women in her situation, to do needlework. Instead she was allowed to read to her aunts while they were knitting.[11] Thus Bosboom-Toussaint became acquainted with all kinds of literature. The historical novels of Sir Walter Scott were her favourites. After being an unsuccesful governess in Hoorn, she returned in 1834 to her parents' home, were she studied history and literature all day in her own room. From 1847, until her marriage with Johannes Bosboom in 1851, she lived alone. After her work on some translations which were never accepted, a publisher suggested she write novels, and despite enormous prejudices she did so. People laughed at her and called her a savante: a woman writer was not a woman. Because people ridiculed her, she reacted by becoming a scholarly recluse;[12] her room was her fortress, and through her writing she took refuge in fantasy.

The publication of a short story in 1837 attracted the attention of the editors of a new literary journal called *De Gids* (The Guide). They took her under their wing, helped her to find documents and advised her on historical genres. Moreover, in 1841 she was engaged to one of the most important editors of *De Gids*: R.C. Bakhuizen van den Brink. His historical views influenced her greatly. In addition to this, she was involved with the Réveil, the Dutch religious revival. This new Protestant movement idealised the profundities of religion. Women had a special mission to protect the world from evil by means of self-sacrifice and humiliation. Most of Bosboom-Toussaint's historical novels were imbued by these values. Her first historical novels, like *Het huis Lauernesse*

(The house of Lauernesse, 1840), were successful; some of her later novels were not received so favourably. Such was the case with the *Leycestercyclus* (Leicester series, 1845-55), which was, in Bosboom-Toussaint's opinion, her most important work. Deceived by and let down by her fiancé Bakhuizen van den Brink in 1843, she recovered her strength by undertaking this huge project. In working on the *Leycestercyclus* she sought consolation, but Bosboom-Toussaint also considered this work as a special vocation. One of her aims was to expound how the Seven Dutch Provinces became more united inspired by the Protestant religion. It was based on historical studies and records which she usually studied at home. She borrowed the materials from the Royal Library, but she was not allowed to examine the records of the Public Record Office. The Master of the Rolls in The Hague, J.C. de Jonge, did not give her the chance to collect the archives necessary for her *Leycestercyclus*, because he did not take her literary work seriously. Yet the Keeper of the Public Records in Arnhem, I.A. Nijhoff, did hand her manuscripts. The historical research took her two years.[13] Bosboom-Toussaint wrote the *Leycestercyclus* without any advice from her literary friends of *De Gids*. The extended trilogy, whose second volume *Vrouwen van het Leycestersche tijdvak* (Women of the Leicesterian era, 1850) deals with the position of women in this period, had a total of 4,217 pages. The *Leycestercyclus* shed a completely new light on sixteenth-century Holland, and it is due to Bosboom-Toussaint that the Leicester Period attracted historical attention.

From 1585 till 1587, the Earl of Leicester governed the Seven Dutch Provinces which had declared themselves independent from their official sovereign, the Catholic King of Spain. However, an attempt was made by England through Leicester to incorporate the new Protestant Republic into the growing Empire. According to Bosboom-Toussaint, Leicester was more or less a victim of the conflicting interests of the Seven Dutch Provinces, Spain and England. To increase his country's influence, Leicester encouraged the war of independence against Spain and succeeded in diminishing the dominant role played by the Province of Holland over the other Provinces. Since he was a foreign governor, Leicester was automatically suspect. As a result, some Dutch ladies, such as the widow Van Hemert, tried to undermine Leicester's position, and a conspiracy was afoot to overthrow him. It was during this specific period that the Seven Dutch Provinces became more united.[14]

After the publication of the first volume an intensive debate between historians started about the significance of Leicester in the Netherlands. The historian H. Beijerman criticised Bosboom-Toussaint's historical opinion of Leicester, insinuating she had not carried out a thorough investigation of the records. She retorted in some annoyance that this opinion was the direct outcome of her profound study of the historical documents. She was regularly attacked by the critics for not telling 'the truth'; she was also accused of glorifying her heroines.[15] In the introduction of next editions, she defended herself several times and verified the story by means of the 'real records'. Several years later, in 1867, she poured out her fears and despondency about her position as a woman historian in a letter to the historian R. Fruin. She was ridiculed merely because she was a female writer; also, the fact that she used fiction to present facts, gave her historical reflections less value in the eyes of professional historians. Fruin subsequently responded that he respected her work very much; nobody should write about Leicester without carefully reading her *Leycestercyclus*.[16] The problem was, indeed, that the use of historical fiction was an excuse for some historians to sneer at Bosboom-Toussaint and her work. Nevertheless, she gradually achieved recognition as a writer of historical novels. This recognition reached its zenith when Bosboom-Toussaint was 57 years old; in 1869 she was the first woman to become an honorary member of the Society of Dutch Literature. Despite this honour, the feeling that she was neglected by male critics persisted. On later occasions she helped other women who wanted to write and publish. One of them was the moderate feminist Margaretha Maclaine Pont (1852-1928), who published several historical novels.[17]

Bosboom-Toussaint preserved a very detached attitude towards the women's movement. She hated being labelled a bluestocking, she emphasised her femininity and she disliked women fighters like the Dutch feminist Mina Krüseman. This is possibly the reason why another woman historian, the Marxist Annie Romein-Verschoor (1895-1978), neglected Bosboom-Toussaint in her thesis about nineteenth-century women novelists in the Netherlands, *Vrouwenspiegel* (Women's mirror, 1935). Romein-Verschoor claimed that ladies such as Bosboom-Toussaint and their novels were bourgeois. According to Romein-Verschoor, Bosboom-Toussaint's contribution to nineteenth-century Dutch literature was negligible.[18] It would seem that Romein-Verschoor did not really understand how nineteenth-century women like Bosboom-Toussaint coped with the strict moral codes, and she underestimated the significance of certain religious values. In this respect, Bosboom-Toussaint's historical novel *Mejonkvrouwe de Mauléon* (Milady de Mauléon, 1848) is very important. It is the story of an intellectual lady in the seventeenth century, whose independent life-style contravened the rules which governed her class, which was probably inspired by Bosboom-Toussaint's own experience. She was not accepted in her circle, and became the victim of gossip. However, her irreproachable behaviour, her religious devotion, and above all her self-sacrifice for the sake of her former fiancé, who became a prominent bishop, eventually restored her to grace. Henceforth Lady de Mauléon was able to live independently, without losing any respect. In this context the emphasis on 'female qualities', which originated with the Dutch Protestant revival, could traverse the boundaries of the nineteenth-century women's world.[19] Bosboom-Toussaint disliked the novel because it had been censored by her publisher. In the original version, a friend of Lady de Mauléon became an unmarried mother. The publisher demanded that she left out this part of the story. The content of the novel was therefore partly adulterated. Nevertheless, it is a typical example of an historical novel set in the seventeenth century, written with a vision of the world which had been inspired by the Réveil. In addition, an historiographical remark made by Bosboom-Toussaint about the neglected situation of women like Lady de Mauléon is of interest: apparently the Lady had become a victim of historical misjudgement. It was because of Lady de Mauléon that her former fiancé could further a brilliant career as a bishop, and enter French politics. Bosboom-Toussaint was of the opinion that in historical novels one could link dull data to people and events undeservedly forgotten. An example is the history of Lady de Mauléon that was restored in the novel mentioned above.[20]

Nowadays the public is only familiar with *Majoor Frans* (Major Frans, 1875), one of her contemporary novels. At that time it was considered to be a treatise on women's emancipation. Bosboom-Toussaint rejected this interpretation, as she had never wanted to be a feminist. Moreover, she found her historical work much more significant. Despite her antipathy against the women's movement, she herself was very emancipated. Although she had been married to Johannes Bosboom since 1851, she earned her own income by writing historical novels and lived a life of financial independence. At the age of 72, she became one of the first members of the Dutch Women's League for Public Morality. After her death in 1886, well-known feminists placed a monument on her tomb.

A writer of women's biographies

Born in the middle of the nineteenth century, Johanna Naber (1859-1941) belonged to the next generation of women historians: those who were allowed to attend secondary school. In 1876 she passed the entrance examination for the high school for girls. Naber became one of the most important feminists in the Netherlands, and wrote many historical studies on women and the feminist movement. Her publications numbered more than 250.[21]

She grew up in an intellectual and Protestant environment. Her father was a well-known professor of philology and classical languages. The Nabers entertained at home in the true intellectual and liberal tradition of their day. Whilst the daughters of the house busied themselves with needlework, animated debates took place. Johanna Naber was not allowed to study at university, despite the fact that at that time it was possible for girls to do so. As the daughter of a respectable family it was not considered to be decent; if she wanted to study at the library or attend lectures, she was to be chaperoned by her father or brother.[22] Naber never possessed a key to the house in which she lived. Her place was at home, where she was obliged to learn feminine tasks such as needlework, dressmaking, cooking, doing the laundry and cleaning oil lamps. Both her parents emphasised the importance of femininity. In the evenings, after she had completed her domestic duties, her father helped her with her studies. Since she never married, Naber kept house for her parents and later for her bachelor brothers. It was not until 1936, at the age of 77, that she had a home of her own. Sometimes she complained bitterly about the situation in which she found herself. Nevertheless, her double burden did not detract her from the significance of her work.[23]

The first book Naber wrote was directly linked to her position as a woman. The Dutch women's organisation Tesselschade had offered a prize for the best manual on art needlework. With her *Handleiding bij het kunstnaaldwerk* (Manual on art needlework, 1887), she won the first prize. She published the manual under the pseudonym Rechlindis, which was the name of a famous abbess living in the eighth century. Three years later, Naber published her first historical study written about the life of a French abbess in the sixteenth century: *Kracht in zwakheid: het beeld van Angélique Arnauld, abdis van Port Royal* (Strength in weakness, the image of Angélique Arnauld, abbess of Port Royal, 1890). This study was the beginning of a series of biographies, usually of women. Unlike herself, the historical figures Naber described were able to achieve an independent life. Because they were sequestered in a nunnery, Angélique Arnauld and her sister escaped the patriarchal authority of their father, who had placed his daughters in this Cistercian convent. In this way they were able to develop intellectually, and were involved in the Jansenist movement of the philosopher Blaise Pascal (1623-62). The Réveil had an important influence on Naber's work and helped her to show that women could attain a certain independence by emphasising moral virtues. There is a parallel with Bosboom-Toussaint's *Mejonkvrouwe de Mauléon.*

At first Naber was not very interested in the feminist movement, but she was encouraged to read about the subject by her mother. In 1896 she became a member of the committee which organised the large exhibition to show all the work that women did, the Nationale Tentoonstelling voor Vrouwenarbeid (National Exhibition on Women's Labour, 1898). The exhibition made such an impression on her that she became very enthusiastic for the feminist cause. Naber became a member of many women's organisations. She was the first Dutch feminist in the International Women Suffrage Alliance. As President of the Dutch National Council of Women from 1917 to 1922, she was also involved in the International Council of Women. In 1935 she set up the International Archives of the Women's Movement (IAV) in Amsterdam, together with Rosa Manus (President) and Willemijn Posthumus-van der Goot. Inspired by the feminist cause, Naber published many biographies of nineteenth-century feminists. She wrote biographies of Josephine Butler and Priscilla Bright-Maclaren in *Wegbereidsters* (Women pioneers, 1909), and *Van onze oudtantes en tantes* (Of our great-aunts and aunts, 1917) contained biographies of Dutch women. Her historical studies of the Dutch feminist movement, such as *Na XXV jaren* (After XXV years, 1923), are very important; she was in fact the first woman historiographer of the Dutch feminist movement.

Naber also wrote about other subjects; for instance a study of the French occupation in the Netherlands, and the publication of the Stadholder family's correspondence in five volumes (1931-6). Some of these studies were reviewed in professional journals, and the extended published documents were particularly respected. Her books on women's history were barely mentioned, and if they were, the remarks were somewhat negative. With regard to her study about the Port Royal abbey, she was accused of writing a history from the nun's point of view.[24] As a contrast to the attitude of the professional journals, her feminist studies and biographies of women attracted attention in many women's journals and daily papers. Her work was appreciated on a literary level as her style of writing was lucid. In 1898 she was awarded a gold medal by Dutch feminists for her journalistic work during the Nationale Tentoonstelling voor Vrouwenarbeid in 1898. She received awards from the literary society Het Teylergenootschap in 1901 and 1912. In 1918 she was the first female board member of the Society of Dutch Literature.

Naber did not consider herself to have an imaginative mind so she did not attempt to write historical novels. She regarded herself primarily as a biographer. According to her, history was a question of narrating, of sketching 'real' characters instead of writing about anonymous women in general. So Naber wrote about women with whom she could identify, and whom she regarded as predecessors of the feminist movement. An interesting example of these studies on women was a biography of Margaretha Wijnanda Maclaine Pont (1929), mentioned above as a friend of Bosboom-Toussaint. Naber wrote this book at the request of the Society of Dutch Literature. Her task was not to quote or to judge, but to relate the 'objective facts' of Pont's life, her career and her publications. However, having studied a large number of Pont's papers such as her correspondence with friends, writers and editors, her notes, her publications and many reviews, Naber decided to write a complete biography.[25] Pont was one of those deeply religious women of the Réveil who felt that their mission in life was to fight against the evils of the world. She succeeded in writing articles, essays and historical novels while she was manager of an institute for the protection of girls against prostitution. As the daughter of a prominent family, Pont had difficulties in convincing her parents of her aims in life. As in many of her other biographies, Naber was able to demonstrate the important role unmarried women like Pont had played in society. According to Naber, the celibate status of these women enabled them to work in all kinds of institutions so they could have a special contribution in civilising the world. In this way, she interpreted Pont as one of the predecessors of the Dutch feminist movement.[26] Moreover, Naber valued her historical novels for their feminism. Although Pont's historical interpretations were by no means new, Naber respected her work for the way it portrayed the women who played an active role in history.[27]

Naber is hardly ever mentioned in historical handbooks. She was never appreciated as a professional historian. In an interview in 1929, she regretted that some of her fellow historians did not take her studies very seriously.[28] Perhaps it was not the genres that she worked in that were considered inferior, but the topics she wrote about. Women's history, and certainly the history of the feminist movement, were not relevant in historiography. Naber died in 1941 at the age of 83, shocked and bewildered by the German occupation of the Netherlands. She left behind an impressive number of literary works.

A narrator of women's history

Sini Greup-Roldanus (1893-1984) lived at a time when women could study at universities relatively easily. As a member of the Dutch Women's Club, a cultural debating club of well-to-do ladies, and the first Committee of the IAV, she knew Johanna Naber well. She published several historical novels, all of them with female main characters.[29] As her full name, Dr S.C. Regtdoorzee Greup-Roldanus, was a little too long, she published under an abbreviated name: Sini Greup-Roldanus.

After finishing her secondary education, she studied literature at college. Although her parents were comfortably off, they were by no means rich.[30] This meant that Greup-Roldanus had to go to work immediately after she had qualified as a teacher. After several temporary posts she became a teacher of literature and history in

1916. A few years later she married Jan Regtdoorzee Greup, and in this way lost her job. It was common practice at that time to dismiss married women. However, since it soon became apparent that the couple was unable to have children, she was allowed to resume teaching. In 1924 she started to study history at the University of Amsterdam, and shortly afterwards she obtained a Master's degree. N. Posthumus, a well-known Professor of social and economic history, wanted her to write a thesis as she was an extraordinarily intelligent student. However, she refused because of her numerous occupations: teaching, meeting friends, attending concerts, making music and writing.

As a teacher she was able to hold her pupils spellbound by relating historical stories and anecdotes. She wanted to teach history within a narrative frame.[31] Her pupils encouraged Greup-Roldanus to write a novel, which she did: she published an autobiographical story of the only girl in a class of boys, called *De orchidee van 5a* (The orchid of 5a, 1924). It was very popular and was reprinted five times. Then her only brother, to whom she was greatly attached, suddenly died in 1930, and she mourned him bitterly. Her marriage was not a very happy one, so she was unable to rely on her husband for comfort and support. She decided to write a thesis after all.[32]

During one of his lectures Posthumus had suggested some historical subjects as matter for research. One of these was a study of linen-bleaching in eighteenth-century Haarlem. At that time linen-bleaching was a thriving industry. One of the male students remarked contemptuously that he would never write a thesis 'about a linen cupboard', but Greup-Roldanus was interested and accepted the subject. After nine years' research she obtained her PhD with honours. Her detailed thesis, *De Haarlemmer bleekerijen* (The bleaching industry of Haarlem, 1936), represents the social and economical views held by Posthumus on history in the inter-war period, and is sometimes quoted in Dutch handbooks.[33] In this book women are of little importance in comparison to the enormous number of historical facts that she discusses. It is a rather dull but profound thesis. Posthumus was enthusiastic about it and wanted her to take up a career at the University. In 1937 she published an article in the first annual of the IAV, about the role played by women in linen-bleaching, which was in fact her last professional article.[34] Greup-Roldanus did not accept her Professor's proposal, because her husband became incurably ill and she felt obliged to look after him. For nine years she helped him, sometimes under very difficult circumstances. There were no hospitals available as a consequence of the Second World War. Therefore she had to take care of him at home with the help of nurses. He died eventually in October 1945.

During his illness she tried to distract her mind by writing historical novels for girls as she sat by his bedside. She made use of the enormous number of historical documents she had collected for her thesis. Her first novels formed a trilogy about the lives of three girls in the seventeenth and eighteenth centuries. In the first two novels the action takes place in the linen industry of Haarlem; the last novel is set in Franeker. Despite her success with earlier novels, her publisher was rather reluctant to publish these books, as he thought they were written neither for girls nor for adults: they fell somewhere in between. Professor Posthumus was very angry when he heard about Greup-Roldanus' trilogy. Instead of occupying herself with professional research, his ex-student was writing novels. The reviews were divided. From an historical viewpoint, the critics formed a favourable opinion, but they were less enthusiastic about the literary form and style. One of the objections they made was that there were too many descriptions of kitchen equipment.[35] Romein-Verschoor, however, liked the trilogy very much. According to her, historical novels for girls were something new and different.

After the publication of this trilogy, Greup-Roldanus carried on writing historical novels for which she continued to do research in archives. She opted for fiction as a means of expression. The most likely explanation for this choice is that she preferred the narrative framework of historical novels to the strict accuracy of social and economic history. In the historical novel she could make the past come alive with characters created by herself. Her aim was to evoke women's history by creating an historical atmosphere, so that one imagined oneself to be living in a past era. In her novels bygone relics of daily life in eighteenth-century Holland, which she knew so well, were used by living girls and women.

After she had won a prize for a short historical novel in 1950, one of the members of the jury encouraged her to write novels for adults. She was then almost 60 years old. Greup-Roldanus wrote a total of seven historical novels for adults. The first novel, *De hu-*

meuren in de straat der weduwen (The moods in widows' lane, 1953), was awarded a prize by the town council of Middelburg. The novel tells the tale of five widows in seventeenth-century Middelburg. The reviews were very positive and the critics had great expectations. Only one critic objected to the archaic language that Greup-Roldanus used. Encouraged by this success, she published another historical novel a year later: *Een vrouw in rook en regen* (A woman in smoke and rain, 1954). This time the main character is an unmarried woman, Ronna, manageress of a linen factory. It seems that Ronna is in love with Jacob, the owner of another linen factory, who has been widowed three times. Ronna had always been a good friend of Jacob's former wives. At the end of the novel she saves his neglected business from ruin, and after all rejects Jacob's love because of his arrogance and irresponsibility.

This novel was also favourably reviewed, as was the one that followed. Her female characters in particular were given a great deal of praise. The dominant role that women and girls play in all her historical novels is striking. Often there is one woman in the background, whom Greup-Roldanus' acquaintances recognise as the author herself, who enacts the part of onlooker and gives support to many other characters. Superficially, men seem important, traditional sex relations are emphasised and women may never lose their femininity. However, in the heterosexual plots of her novels, men are merely an intermediary for the strong ties which exist between women. Women are usually responsible for bringing up the children, but also for several other social and economic aspects of life. This was indeed based on careful historical research. In the eighteenth-century Netherlands, men were the official owners of businesses like linen-bleacheries or printing-offices, although women often took care of the accountancy and management.

Greup-Roldanus' subsequent novels were received less enthusiastically. According to the literary critics, the novels were artificial and the language used was archaic. In a nutshell, they were considered to be light reading for ladies, not 'real literature' or 'real history'. Although Greup-Roldanus always based her novels on historical records, and most critics were of the opinion that she created a good historical atmosphere, the use of the fictional form made her work altogether of less value in the eyes of professional historians. This is probably one of the reasons why the books of

Greup-Roldanus rapidly sank into oblivion in the historiography. Finally, it is the literary level that determines whether an historical novel will be read by later generations. Most of the later novels of Greup Roldanus, however, are of little literary value. Yet it is my opinion that anyone who studies the eighteenth-century Netherlands should read the historical novels of Greup-Roldanus. Moreover, her work is very important with regard to contemporary women's history. In all her historical studies, novels and lectures she showes the important role that women played in society. Her work makes clear that widows and unmarried women took a decisive part in social and economic affairs. It was the daily lives of ordinary people which formed the foundation of her novels, rather than political history. According to Greup-Roldanus, trade and industry exercised a far greater influence on households than significant political events, and as a consequence, her novels were always set against a background of these two factors. Social and economic history was woven into a narrative tapestry in which women played an important role. The detailed descriptions of familiar everyday utensils, clothes, manners and expressions, based on research of very divergent eighteenth-century records such as notarial manuscripts, municipal bills, correspondence and lists of regulations of Dutch almshouses, represent an integral vision of history. This type of history is nowadays called the history of mentalities or cultures. In Greup-Roldanus' day it was not considered to be of much value. Neither the topics Greup-Roldanus wrote about nor the genre she worked in were generally taken seriously. Writing about women's history in a narrative style as a work of fiction did not fit into the then prevailing concept of serious historiography.

Besides writing historical novels, she gave lectures all over the country until she was almost 80 years of age. She was also kept very busy with her extensive correspondence; until late in life, she would often write as many as five letters a day. Due to a fractured hip she was obliged to be assisted with many tasks. As she hated to be dependent, Greup-Roldanus committed suicide at the age of 91 in 1984.

Women's heritage: invalid and insignificant?

Although they belonged to different generations, these three Dutch women historians had much in common. As women of letters, they experienced many difficulties. They were confronted with prejudices about femininity, the limitations of moral codes and the burden of household work. This did not prevent them from obtaining access to historical records or from acquainting themselves with rules governing the order and expression of historical material. Neither Bosboom-Toussaint nor Naber were able to study at university. Ridiculed as a woman writer, Bosboom-Toussaint was eventually helped by the male editors of *De Gids*. Despite being a scholarly recluse, she was involved with the religious revival in the Netherlands, so she did have some connection with the outside world which gave her inspiration for historical writing. While keeping house for her family, Naber received an intellectual education from her father at home and started writing about women's history. As she had been a passionate feminist since 1898, she was directly linked with the outside world, and wrote historical biographies and studies about the feminist movement. As a teacher in history and literature at secondary-school level, Greup-Roldanus was encouraged to obtain a doctorate by her Professor but was unable to fulfil her vocation as an historian at university. Instead of publishing articles in historical journals, her preference lay in the writing of historical novels. Initially supported by men, these women produced an impressive number of historical works in different genres.

It is hard to say to what extent the specific position of these lettered women influenced their historical achievements. Indeed, they wrote biographies and historical novels, the genres that fitted best with their possibilities. It is striking that all three of them more or less took refuge in their historical work. Bosboom-Toussaint and Greup-Roldanus regarded the writing of historical novels as a drug or therapy to survive. In her biographies, Naber wrote about women with whom she was able to identify. Nevertheless, writing women's history in these genres happened to be a positive choice as well. Narrating history was a way to create an historical atmosphere in which they could present women as central figures. It seems that the narrative framework of these genres, where the private and the public spheres are not separate entities, formed a setting for describing women's worlds. A careful examination of these studies can lead to the detection of hidden meanings.

In her historical novels Bosboom-Toussaint tried to expose the psychological motives of people in history. The emphasis on self-sacrifice or other 'female qualities' in these novels can be interpreted as a subversive strategy: in this way she intentionally recreated women who would otherwise have been forgotten. Naber wrote biographies of certain women whom she considered as predecessors of the feminist movement. In studying the life of an individual woman one can find a deeper understanding of the motives that are of influence on women's lives. After profound research in favour of using an historical framework, Greup-Roldanus created her own female characters. Despite the heterosexual plots in her novels the strong ties existing between women form the main theme.

These women historians were respected by a comparatively large public in their own time. However, the genres were often subject to distrust, and, which is perhaps more important, women's history was not a 'relevant' topic in historiography. Bosboom-Toussaint was criticised for glorifying her heroines, and Greup-Roldanus for her detailed descriptions of kitchen utensils, whereas Naber's biographies and feminist studies were barely mentioned in professional journals. As time went on, most of their historical studies were forgotten or misinterpreted. To write the history of an 'inferior' group (women), in genres which were not generally accepted, was to write non-history. The way women structured history within those historical genres was not validated. Therefore the dynamics in sex relationships are reflected in the validation of knowledge. Women writers and women's history were considered to be irrelevant in historiography. When women's history was accepted at universities in the 1970s, people were largely ignorant of the fact that the subject was not new. Although the same conclusions and genres were used, many of these women historians were relatively unknown.[36] One method of dispensing with this selection in historiography is to reconstruct women's hidden but strong intellectual past, to acknowledge former women historians as actors in historiography and to link this tradition with current women's historiography.

Notes

1. I want to thank my students for the discussions we had in a seminar about women historians in 1987, and especially Bas Holtzer and Monique Walboomers for their contributions about Truitje Bosboom-Toussaint and Sini Greup-Roldanus. I am also grateful to Karen Peters for the final corrections to this paper.

2. Nathalie Zemon Davis, 'Gender and genre: women as historical writers 1400-1820' in Patricia Labalme (ed.), *Beyond their sex: learned women of the European past* (New York University Press, New York and London, 1980), pp. 153-82; Bonnie G. Smith, 'The contribution of women to modern historiography in Great Britain, France and the United States, 1750-1940', *American Historical Review*, vol. 89 (June 1984), pp. 709-32.

3. Smith, 'The contribution', p. 710.

4. Nancy Cott, *The bonds of womanhood: 'women's sphere' in New England 1780-1835* (Yale University Press, New Haven, 1977); Caroll Smith-Rosenberg, 'The female world of love and ritual: relations between women in nineteenth-century America', *Signs*, 1 (1975), pp. 1-29; see also Mineke Bosch, 'Women's culture in women's history: historical notion or feminist vision?' in Maaike Meijer, Jetty Schaap (eds), *Historiography of women's cultural traditions* (Foris Publications, Dordrecht, 1987), pp. 35-52.

5. Elaine Showalter, *A literature of their own: British women novelists from Brontë to Lessing* (Virago, London, 1984); see also Fia Dieteren, 'De brief als bron voor vrouwengeschiedenis: beschouwingen naar aanleiding van Mina Krüseman', *Tijdschrift voor Vrouwenstudies*, vol. 8, no. 2 (1987), pp. 129-40; Mineke Bosch, 'Egodocumenten: bronnen van kennis en plezier', *Tijdschrift voor Vrouwenstudies*, vol. 8, no. 2 (1987), pp. 203-20.

6. Davis, 'Gender and genre', pp. 154-5.

7. Dale Spender (ed.), *Men's studies modified: the impact of feminism on the academic disciplines* (Pergamon Press, Oxford, 1981), pp. 1-3.

8. Joanna Russ, *How to suppress women's writing* (University of Texas Press, Austin, 1983). Quoted in Julie Abraham, 'De geschiedenis van de Player's Boy: het lesbische werk van Bryher', *Lust en Gratie*, 6 (1985), pp. 24-45, esp. 41.

9. Susan Mosher Stuard, 'The Annales School and feminist history: opening dialogue with the American stepchild', *Signs*, 7 (1981), pp. 135-49, esp. 139.

10. Smith, 'The contribution', p. 710.

11. Hans Reeser, *De jeugdjaren van Anna Louisa Geertruida Toussaint 1812-1851* (Tjeenk Willink, Haarlem, 1962), p. 10.

12. Johanna Naber, *Margaretha Maclaine Pont* (Tjeenk Willink, Haarlem, 1929), pp. 4-5; Reeser, *De jeugdjaren*, p. 46.

13. Gerben Colmjon, *R.C. Bakhuizen van den Brink: een markante persoon-*

lijkheid (Leidsche Uitgeversmaatschappij, Rijswijk, 1951), p. 185.

14. Reeser, *De jeugdjaren*, pp. 186-95; 281.

15. Reeser, *De jeugdjaren*, pp. 200-1. As in her historical novel *De Van Beeverens* (1854), about a young lady in a sixteenth-century Dutch town.

16. Hans Reeser, *De huwelijksjaren van A.L.G. Bosboom-Toussaint, 1851-1886* (Wolters Noordhof, Groningen, 1985), pp. 117-18.

17. Letters from Margaretha Maclaine Pont to Truitje Bosboom-Toussaint, 1878-1886. Coll. Letterkundig Museum, The Hague. Margaretha Maclaine Pont wrote *Elisabeth Blaeu, een Alkmaarsche burgemeestersdochter* (1899), for instance.

18. Annie Romein-Verschoor, *Vrouwenspiegel: een literair-sociologische studie over de Nederlandse romanschrijfster na 1880* (SUN, Nijmegen, 1977), p. 21.

19. See Bonnie G. Smith, 'Religion and the rise of domesticity: ladies of the North in the nineteenth century', *Marxist Perspectives*, Summer 1979, pp. 56-81.

20. A.L.G. Bosboom-Toussaint, *Mejonkvrouwe de Mauléon* (Ch. Ewings, Den Haag, undated), p. 129. The story was written in 1847, and first published in 1848.

21. List of official certificates including the membership card of the Bosboom-Toussaint committee of Johanna Naber, undated, Naber Society Archives, Bilthoven. See for the list of works Cora Vreede-de Stuers, *Johanna W.A. Naber: bibliografie* (IAV, Amsterdam, 1985). This bibliography consists of 250 titles. In the course of my research I discovered that Johanna published more articles and essays.

22. W. Itallie-van Embden, 'Johanna W.A. Naber' in J. Riemers-Reurslag, *et al.* (eds), *Het vrouwenjaarboek* (Becht, undated, probably 1930), pp. 190-8, esp. 191. In her short biography *Korte levensschets van Johanna W.A. Naber* (Utrecht, 1957), Angenita C. Klooster wondered whether Naber had been allowed to study at university. In the published interview by W. Itallie-van Embden, Johanna gave a clear answer to this question.

23. Klooster, *Korte levensschets*, p. 12.

24. Review Johanna W.A. Naber, *Correspondentie van de Stadhouderlijke familie 1795-1820*, vol. 4 in *Historische Zeitschrift*, Band 155, Hft. 2, 1937, by K. Menne; review of the same study in *Tijdschrift voor Geschiedenis*, vol. 53, no. 3 (1938), by M.G. de Boer; review Naber, *De nonnen van Port Royal* (Tjeenk Willink, Haarlem, 1924) in *Historisch Tijdschrift*, 5 (1926), pp. 214-19, by W. Nolet, p. 216; review Naber, *Vrouwenleven in prae-Reformatietijd, bezegeld door den marteldood van Wendelmoet Claesdochter* (Nijhoff, Den Haag, 1927) in *Tijdschrift voor Geschiedenis*, 43 (1928), by T.J. Geest, pp. 198-9. On p. 199 the reviewer accuses Naber of anachronistic interpretations in connection with the women's movement.

25. Naber, *Margaretha Pont*, pp. vii-x.

26. For instance, in the reprint of Angélique Arnauld in 1924, Naber

stated in a new preface that unmarried women often played a more important role than married women: *De nonnen van Port Royal*, p. 15. In her biography of Margaretha Pont, Naber praised Pont's pedagogic qualities as the latter prepared her girls not only for marriage. Naber, *Margaretha Pont*, p. 210.

27. In her biography of Margaretha Pont, Naber wrote a separate chapter about Pont's historical novels, Chapter III, 'Schrijfster van historische romans', pp. 94-136.

28. Itallie-van Embden, 'Johanna W.A. Naber', p. 196.

29. I was able to reconstruct the life of Dr Sini Regtdoorzee Greup-Roldanus from several sources: detailed information about Greup-Roldanus' life and work from her relatives in Goes, who looked after her estate; information in the shape of letters and reminiscences about her life as a teacher, vouchsafed to me by her former pupils; and finally the broadcast interview with Greup-Roldanus herself in 1983, when she was 90 years old.

30. Dr Regtdoorzee Greup-Roldanus in a letter to an ex-pupil, Paula van Duyl-de Groot, 24 April 1978. Correspondence of Mrs van Duyl-de Groot, Alkmaar.

31. Interview with Greup-Roldanus in the Dutch daily newspaper *Telegraaf* (7 Dec. 1959) by Wina Born, and an interview in another daily newspaper *Parool* (29 Sept. 1968) by Hanneke Meerum-Terwogt.

32. Broadcast interview with Greup-Roldanus in 1983.

33. For instance the encyclopedia of Dutch history, *Algemene Geschiedenis der Nederlanden*, part VII, 1959, p. 465, a contribution of J.G. van Dillen, and part VII, 1980, p. 394, a contribution of L. Noordergraaf.

34. S. Regtdoorzee Greup-Roldanus, 'De vrouw in een Oud-Hollands plattelandsbedrijf', *IAV-Jaarboek* (1937), pp. 38-72.

35. Review by Johan van Delden, *Boekennieuws*, vol. 8, no. 5 (June 1947).

36. For instance the work *Van moeder op dochter*, edited by W. Posthumus-van der Goot (Brill, Leiden, 1948), was one of the few books which was on the syllabus of feminist studies in the 1970s. It was a cumulation of female knowledge of former women historians such as Johanna Naber.

Helga Grubitzsch

A paradigm of androcentric historiography: Michelet's *Les femmes de la Révolution*

The history of women is usually related by men and the history of the women of the French Revolution is no exception.[1] Even their contemporaries presented a distorted picture of them: male journalists reported their activities in the newspapers or composed pamphlets about them; the National Assembly (of men!) gave their opinions and decided the outcome of their petitions; judges pronounced sentence upon them and doctors evaluated their state of mental health. Apart from very few personal accounts (the preservation of which is mostly the result of men's own interests), all of the available sources concerning the women of the Revolution show the filtration due to the perception of men. The historians then wrote their story, a history which reveals more about the ideas of men, their fears, desires and fantasies than it does about the women themselves.

In the context of my present research about the biography of Théroigne de Méricourt (1762-1817), I have continually encountered legends veiling her real life, images developed partly by contemporaries and partly by later historians, and handed down right up to the present day. For some biographers (e.g. A. Lamartine) she was a famous courtesan, *l'amante de la nation,* and for others (J.P. Beaulieu, J. Michelet) just the opposite: heroic maiden, Minerva in her armour. We see her described as a bloodthirsty murderess as well as a glorious heroine of the Revolution. Such contradictions inspired me to take a closer look at these images and to question the conditions which caused them to be formed, to expose their inaccuracy and to reveal the occluded reality.[2]

As feminist historians we cannot avoid the confrontation with such results of male imagination, as any approximation to a true account of the lives of women in history which is worthy of a claim to historical probability can only be attained through the decoding of these distortions. My preoccupation with the historical perception of the women of the French Revolution, for example, was an important step to help me distinguish between the biographical legends and the possible reality of these women's lives.

My work to date in the field of women's history has shown me that basically there can be no women's studies in a restricted sense. All research about and by women should examine the relationship between the sexes, where that which we consider to be female and male is actually mutually comparative, laid down with regard to social and cultural norms and further determined by class and ethnic origin. The behaviour of women in history is evaluated and handed down according to this relationship. Because of this, the discussion about androcentric historiography is not only of methodological significance, but is also an important prerequisite in the actual research work itself.

What is androcentric historiography?

'Aνηρ, the Greek word for man, also expressed the idea of man in the wider sense: that of mankind in general. This dual meaning allows the word *androcentric* to express far more than the more commonly used but more limiting expression 'male-centred'. Androcentric historiography relates history which has been filtered through a male interpretation of the world and presented as mankind's perception of events. The male sees himself as the centre of life. Historical events are reconstructed in a context which reflects a patriarchal perspective: male thoughts, concepts and values and sometimes secret desires, fears and fantasies, which, however, do not disclose themselves as being specifically male, but claim to be of neuter gender and valid for all mankind. Androcentric historiography then, purports to be able to record the activities and opinions not only of men but also of women. However, the patriarchal message hidden in the presentation is unmistakably revealed by a closer and more critical investigation.

An uncritical approach to androcentric history induces women to assimilate images of femininity created by men; they accept the male concept of mankind and fail to recognise the violence imposed upon their sex, or the distortions and mutilations of their history. Androcentric historiography is therefore a very effective instrument for maintaining patriarchal norms. It hinders the very awareness of suppression and obscures the struggle of the sexes.

Michelet

Jules Michelet was one of the first people to recognise the male character of historiography: 'History', he says, 'which we have rather stupidly allowed to remain feminine [grammatically] is a crude and wild male.'[3] His definition of history appears to him most appropriate for preparing the young male for the battle of life; the same history, however, would be unsuitable for a young woman, who ought rather to learn from nature, for nature is female like herself. In declaring history to be male and nature female, Michelet denies women their history on the one hand, and men their nature on the other. History for the young woman is the 'simple, true and bitter' life of a mother, an eternal cycle of childbearing and death, of pain and womanly self-sacrifice. The history of the mother will also be the history of the daughter, venerated by her as a 'dear legend', a 'religious memory' and 'first cult' in her life. Later will come the love for her country, for 'her second mother, the great mother, *la Patrie*'.[4]

The legends which Michelet created for the young woman correspond to his own ideal of femininity and that of many of his male contemporaries (e.g. P.J. Proudhon and A. Comte).[5] It is the portrayal of this perspective as generally valid and in accordance with natural laws that constitutes an androcentric construction of the history of women. This I intend to illustrate by taking a closer look at his book *Les femmes de la Révolution.*

There are several reasons for selecting Michelet in order to illuminate the problems caused by androcentric historiography. Firstly, Michelet's writings about women and love were extremely important in defining the image of women in the nineteenth century. His works *L'amour* (1858) and *La femme* (1859), which promised a renewal of morals and the importance of the family, were an enormous success.[6] They showed the historical need for more specific information about and agreement on the changing norms in the relations between the sexes.

A second reason for choosing Michelet is that, right up to the present day, his ideas remain topical and relevant. They have been incorporated as an unquestionable part of the current dominant gender-ideology. Th. Moreau, for example, demonstrates this in French school-books, and in the Federal Republic of Germany the Blüm theses reflect many of the thoughts and concepts which Michelet made generally popular in his *L'amour* and *La femme.*[7] Up to this very day, Michelet's book *Les femmes de la Révolution* is regarded as the standard work on the history of the women of the French Revolution. His influence on historical research to date should not be underestimated, in view of the fact that he is considered to be the founder of modern historiography - both in France and elsewhere.

A third reason for singling out Michelet is his republican sympathy. We should not assume that Michelet's thoughts were particularly regressive or conservative, for he had little in common with the royalist critics of the prevailing moral code, such as Nettement.[8] The concepts of man and woman which were gradually breaking through in the nineteenth century were formulated by men who sought change and democratisation of social relations (such as J.-J. Rousseau, B.P. Enfantin, Michelet, Proudhon).

Finally we must emphasise that Michelet's views give no indication that he is a misogynist. On several occasions he criticises the repression of women, quoting the difficult living conditions of servant-girls, female workers and women in the country.[9] His personal attitude repudiates right from the start any attempt merely to categorise him and his ideas as individually anti-women. The fact that women and love were the subject of so much interest in the sociological and historical literature of the nineteenth century, and the fact that the still-prevailing ideology of the sexes was further developed and firmly established by Michelet at that time, was basically effected by society itself, an aspect which will be considered in more detail after an analysis of *Les femmes de la Révolution.*

Les femmes de la Révolution

Les femmes de la Révolution appeared in 1854, a year after Michelet's last volume of the *Histoire de la Révolution française* (1847-53), from which he took large portions to use in his later book. In 1845 he had published *Du prêtre, de la femme, de la famille*, and in 1846 *Le peuple*, two works in which he had discoursed at length about women. We may then assume that his theories about womanhood, as popularised later in *L'amour* (1858) and *La femme* (1859), were already mature at this stage. They form the background against which he saw and evaluated the women of the Revolution.

In the first chapter Michelet refers to the historical origin of his image of women, this being the eighteenth century and Rousseau's *Emile*. In part five of *Emile*, Rousseau had already formulated the central themes which Michelet was later to take up and expound on: nature has appointed women to motherhood, which results in their physical weakness, their need for protection, their emotional nature and capacity for love, as well as their destiny of remaining at home, while men go about their business outside that home and advance the development of society. For Michelet, women in the eighteenth century, 'in the light of the dawning of a new belief', had opened their hearts to their intrinsic calling: humanity and motherhood.[10]

According to Michelet, there is always an affinity between motherhood and death: the woman who gives life risks her own life. This gives her the right and makes it her duty to take an interest in political affairs. Michelet's interest in the political involvement of women arises from his desire for 'a renewal of social conditions' in the Second Empire, a renewal in which 'the women should take the first step' (p. 266). They should champion the cause of the Republic and encourage republican virtues, just as the women of the Revolution did.

Michelet's evaluation of political action by women becomes clear in the opinions which he once more formulates in the summary at the end of his book. Firstly, women act in the way that they do because they follow the dictates of their hearts, and not because of a political will or rational awareness: 'the susceptibility, the heart, pity at the wretchedness of the people drove you in 1789 to revolution' (p. 267). 'Heroic courage in compassion' (p. 8) was displayed by Mme Legros when she rescued the prisoner Latude from the Bastille (ch. 2). 'Women of great heart' (p. 21) were those who could no longer bear the sufferings of the people, and marched on Versailles on the 5th and 6th October 1789 to bring the Royal Family to Paris. Pity impelled Olympe de Gouges to plead for the defendant King and 'brought her her death' (p. 87). It was also pity that caused Charlotte Corday to kill J.P. Marat; she hoped thereby to avoid further bloodshed (p. 163).

The atrocities of the Revolution made the women the 'most important agents of the Reaction' (p. 260), because they suffered along with the victims. Thus Michelet holds the women responsible for the uprising in the Vendée (1790-1), because, according to him, 'the deep-seated backlash of their pity, of their nature, moving the hearts of the women, was the real force of the counter-revolution' (p. 106). It was no wonder that terror finally forced the women to react: 'Mercy overflowed, blind and irresistible' (p. 261). When the heart speaks with such great force, the perception of the political context is obscured. Revolutionary acts spring from the 'burning of their hearts', which spurs women to action (p. 21). There is no rational control over this overpowering force of pity. Women are in its grip 'because of their passionate temperament dangerous in politics' (p. 236). This aspect of the heroic courage of women, their blind, emotion-inspired actions, is what Michelet blames in the last analysis for the failure not only of the Revolution of 1789, but of revolutions in general (p. 236).

When Michelet appeals to the women to 'concern themselves with the fortunes of their country' (p. 266), he certainly does not mean that they should become militantly involved in bringing about social change or even their own emancipation, even if he does express his admiration on several occasions for the initiative of the women revolutionaries (p. 17). Basically, Michelet claims that women are 'excluded from many important functions in political life' because of their nature, which destines them for motherhood, and because of their menstruation, which renders them indisposed for up to 14 days every month (!) (p. 236).

Women can best serve society with their love: by supporting and loving men who work for progress, and by making patriotism the guiding principle for their behaviour. This is the second message that Michelet wants to get across in his book. To allow the 'indolent' society of the Second Empire to renew itself and put an end to 'this pitiful half-century of reaction', the women should once more love 'the strong and vivacious', as their mothers did in the Revolution (p. 268, p. 15). The men of progress are those who promote science and technology and create new wonders every day, such as 'photography, railway and the electric telegraph' (p. 268):

> 'I call those alive, whose actions and works renew the world, who at least guarantee its movement, vivifying it with their activity, who move with its currents, breathing this great breeze which fills the billowing sail of the century, and whose motto is *Forwards!*' (Emphasis in the original (p. 268))

Those who swore 'to marry only righteous citizens, to love only the brave and to share their lives only with those who would give their lives for France' (p. 49) were held up as shining examples. Among these women who dedicated their lives to loving and supporting progressive men were Mme Roland, Mme de Condorcet and Lucile Desmoulins (see chapters 9, 10, 14, 15, 25).

A woman becomes significant through her relationship to a man. Mme de Staël achieved magnificence through her love for her father M. Necker, the banker and Minister of Finance whom she converted to support for the Revolution by her fiery enthusiasm. Her 'spiritual lovers', however, later 'reduced' her to comparative intellectual 'mediocrity' (pp. 61-2). It is not really surprising, then, that we often learn more about the men than about the women themselves, if we read chapters about the wives and daughters of famous men (see esp. ch. 9 and ch. 10 about Mme de Condorcet, and ch. 20 about G.J. Danton's wife, who is not even given a name). Michelet explains to us how important a loving wife is to a revolutionary:

> 'These men who spew out life in such a terrifying abundance, who nourish people with their words, with their burning breast, with their heart's blood, these men have great need of the homely hearth. The heart must be pacified, the blood calmed. And this is achieved only by a woman.' (p. 198)

If women are not completely engrossed in their love for their men, then there is only one other way for them to merit Michelet's esteem. They must dedicate themselves completely to the revolutionary cause and to their country; they should 'follow this noble impetus to the selfless beauty' and 'make the fatherland [French: *la patrie*] their dearest confidante and eternal right their lover' (p.

15). Sexuality appears to be incompatible with this image of women; the cause replaces the lover. For example, the virginal Charlotte Corday was 'pure and unstained', as were the maidens in white robes at the National Celebrations, who spoke such 'noble, enrapturing words' which would 'tomorrow bring forth heroes' (p. 49).

When Michelet speaks of womanly love, he means devotion, self-abnegation and willingness to sacrifice oneself. Sacrifice is 'the law of this world' (p. 271). After all, progress means struggle, competition and suppression; the utopian dream of a harmonious reconciliation of the classes and of equality of the sexes cannot exist under these circumstances. The oppressor, rather than admit his oppression, expects a sacrifice. Who is willing to make this sacrifice? One who loves. This brings Michelet to his next question: 'Who loves? Woman!' (p. 271). He believes this is the answer provided by nature, for nature has appointed woman to motherhood and thereby to 'an unlimited capacity for sacrifice'. By sacrificing herself woman becomes the 'initiation', 'the symbol and religion' (pp. 272, 53). She alone can give a sense of beauty and harmony to the sacrifice (p. 273). Here, too, lies the third message which Michelet imparts to women: they must always be willing to sacrifice themselves for their husbands, for their children, for the Cause; furthermore, to sacrifice their children for their country and their husbands for the progress of the world, and, which is the most important, they must forget 'transient love-affairs'. The sacrifice made by the woman is complete in the renunciation of her own need for love and tenderness. For how should the man achieve his great works for the advancement of civilisation, if wife or mother should bind him to the home with her 'indolent tendernesses' (p. 274)?

The positive female characters in Michelet's book all make a sacrifice of one kind or another. They consecrate their children with 'heroic abnegation' to their homeland (p. 51), they risk life and possessions to help others (as Mme Legros does in ch. 2), they place their own talents at the disposal of their husbands (like Mme Roland, p. 119), they even sacrifice their lives for the men they love and for the Revolution (Lucile Desmoulins, Mme Roland). These women dedicate their love for their husbands and children to the cause of the revolutionary ideal. Such self-abnegation in love inspires action, as opposed to the love which 'enfolds' the man and merely encourages 'his natural inertia', as in the case of the Girondist Vergniaud. Mlle Candeille's sacrifice was not great enough, although she 'left everything' to follow Vergniaud: 'The sweet, weak woman's heart held the lion-hearted Vergniaud fast' (p. 193). The man could not help but become weak. Michelet attributes the downfall of the Gironde to the 'dangerous influences' (p. 191) of women. They flatter, ensnare and pamper the men, who then 'become meek of heart and no longer have the cold severity in their blood to secure victory in battle' (p. 191).

The less women act according to the dictates of their womanly nature (as defined by Michelet) and the less they allow themselves to be guided by the precepts of love, the more dangerous they become. Their tenderness becomes a trap, a trap which proved to be the downfall of more than one revolutionary (see p. 255). Without the mantle of self-sacrificing love, their alluring physical attractiveness means destruction for the man. With regard to prostitutes, this means 'brutishness and the road to death' (p. 191). The woman who rejects the ideal of mother or virgin is a threat to decent female principles, and this rouses the animal instincts in men. Her power is destructive, 'an enervating force, a dreadful force which undermines and finally breaks the strength of the revolution' (p. 206). Untamed sensuality is the hidden power behind the terror: 'Under the apparent austerity of republican morals, amid the terror and the tragedies of the scaffold, women and physical love rule supreme in 1793' (p. 206). All this depravity was brought to light on the 9th Thermidor (27 July 1794), with the outburst of hate directed at Robespierre, whose moral strictness weakened the machinations of the streetwalkers, the gambling women and the ladies of the salons. As Robespierre was taken to the scaffold, the women presented 'an unbearable spectacle':

> 'Half-naked and shameless, under the pretext of the heat of July, their bosom decked with flowers, leaning on window-cushions and half-hanging out over the Rue Saint-Honoré, the menfolk behind them, they screamed with shrill voices: "Death! To the guillotine!"' (pp. 261-2)

As an indication that sexual licentiousness had now completely taken over, Michelet mentions drily: 'De Sade was released from prison on the 10th Thermidor.' When they saw Robespierre on his way to the guillotine, the women became 'furies', wild 'bacchantes' (p. 262). Robespierre was powerless to do anything but close his eyes to this spectacle. The Republic was drowning in blood and who was responsible?

> 'The Marchionesses, the Countesses and the royalist actresses returned impudently to France. They came out of the prisons and their hiding-places and worked untiringly to turn the tide of terror in favour of the royalists. They ensnared the Thermidorians, fascinated them, instigated them to murder, and sharpened the blade for them to drown the Republic in blood.' (pp. 262-3)

The political opponent becomes female, her power diabolical. Behind all this is fear - fear of that weak point which delivers men right into the hands of women: their own sexual desires. Sensuality for Michelet is animal, and the man who is dominated by it is nothing more than a 'wild hog' (p. 206, concerning Danton). To desire a woman who is not willing to make a sacrifice for the Republic is by definition a sign of uncontrolled sensuality. The women in the ranks of the political adversaries are adjudged to have the diabolical power to make the men slaves to their own sexual desires. It makes no difference whether a woman is reserved and 'of a respectable family', like Danton's second wife; she still has the magical power to transform Danton into 'a dismal, dejected creature of wild, insufferable sensuality' (p. 206). Unlike Danton's first wife, this lady did not sacrifice anything. According to Michelet, her family demanded that Danton go through a degrading wedding ceremony performed by a perjurious priest. In complying with their demands, Danton repudiated his revolutionary convictions and became a victim of 'the tyranny of his blind craving' (p. 205). For Michelet this is a model example of the destructive power of the female and physical love.

The loving, self-denying woman is strong only in sacrifice. This strength, however, requires her to be totally dependent on the man, since without him she is nothing. Appointed by nature to bear suffering such as menstruation and childbirth, her dependence increases her weakness.

> 'Greater miseries are absolutely wretched; they afflict the weak

> and maltreat the children and women much more than the men. The latter come and go, look here and there, bravely and resourcefully, and finally find something with which to survive the day. The women, however, the poor women, live for the most part shut away, huddled over sewing or knitting; they are hardly capable of finding sustenance when everything is gone. It is sad to contemplate that the woman, this dependant being that can only live in a couple, is more often alone than the man. He always finds company and makes new acquaintances, but she is nothing without her family.' (p. 20)

Single women are helpless, 'sorrowful creatures without a family'. 'When their housework can no longer sustain them, they know not how to supplement it; they retire to the attic and wait; sometimes they are found dead there when (by chance) a neighbour notices' (p. 21).

However, this picture drawn by Michelet in connection with his account of the women's march on Versailles on the 5th and 6th October 1789 contrasts sharply with the actual living conditions of these women. Most of them fought with great strength and courage to secure their daily bread, and handled their affairs cleverly and tenaciously. Those women who suffered the direst poverty did not merely stay at home knitting. They were forced to take up any kind of gainful employment, and those who did sewing or knitting at home were mostly paid to do this.[11] The isolation of the home is also pure fiction. Life, for the common people during the Revolution, was a public affair; much took place on the street, and the women participated in all these goings-on.[12] Nor were the participants of the march on Versailles weak, grief-stricken women as Michelet saw them but rather, as he elsewhere describes them, strong, brave and aggressive.

Michelet's concept of women includes strength only when it involves renunciation. Otherwise, it is for him a manly quality: positive in the case of those women whom he deems worthy of his respect (such as Mme Roland, 'earnest, strong, manly', p. 136), and negative with regard to those who reject the role of the self-sacrificing spouse and mother, thus becoming a threat to men. These manly qualities still cause him some unease, even those of 'honourable' women, as the paradox of 'honourable, *but* strong and brave' reveals (p. 22, my emphasis). There is a limit to female strength, which the loving woman must know and not transgress its boundary.

The truly feminine woman is weak, thereby giving men the opportunity to be considerate and chivalrous to her. She acts according to her nature, to which even 'the most intrepid' are subject. When in prison, Olympe de Gouges became 'again woman and weak, she trembled and was afraid of death' (p. 88). She did not fit into Michelet's picture of women, due to her earlier independence and commitment to women's rights. Nor could he very well categorise this woman who was 'full of noble ideas' as one of the 'wild bacchantes'. Instead, he now portrayed her as an 'unfortunate woman', a victim of her nervous sensitivity and not responsible for her actions (p. 87). Michelet simply glosses over Olympe's demands or criticisms. He does not even mention her 'Déclaration des Droits de la Femme et de la Citoyenne'.[13] This, indeed, would have been the relevant place to report on demands made by women during the Revolution for the improvement of their lot.[14] But Michelet remains reserved on this same point throughout his whole book. He tells us nothing about the Women's Societies because he had found mere 'traces here and there' in the sources (p. 86). According to him, the loss of the freedom of assembly for women in 1793 was merely a 'coincidence', which the historian deemed unworthy of further attention (p. 90).

In chapter seven, which also deals with the 'Emancipation of Women', two men are portrayed who worked earnestly to secure rights for women: Abbé Fauchet and M. de Condorcet. Michelet (again) does not bother to mention the content of the Abbé's speech, nor De Condorcet's essay on 'L'admission des femmes au droit de cité'.[15] Etta Palm d'Aelders, who played such an important role in the women's movement during the Revolution, who worked zealously to achieve better education for girls, and who brought many petitions before the National Assembly,[16] is merely spoken of as a friend of the Abbé Fauchet. Women first appear in this chapter as mothers of families, driven by want to the Jacobine Club, there to discuss with their husbands 'questions of means of subsistence' and the question 'of the public danger' (p. 60). With paternal indulgence, Michelet adjudges their activities to be the 'first, moving beginning of the women's societies' (p. 60). He forgets, however, to mention that the Jacobine Club did not give women the right to vote until 1791.[17] This was after other societies had been founded, due to the initiative of women, in which both sexes had equal rights, such as Les Amis de la Loi.[18]

By this determined avoidance of the question of women's rights, Michelet also solved the problem of coming to terms with the demands of the women revolutionaries. He makes no comment on the topic of women's right to vote, which was a demand made by many women of that time, including Olympe de Gouges; nor on the question of public education for girls, the subject of many women's petitions; nor on the question of the arming of women, a debate in which Théroigne de Méricourt and others were very active; nor even on the action taken by the Citoyennes Républicaines Révolutionnaires to control prices and eliminate profiteering.[19]

It is quite obvious, then, that Michelet selected and created images of the women of the Revolution according to his own personal concept of womanliness and completely in line with his Promethean male role.[20] These images bear little resemblance to the real people of the period. Michelet selected the historical material for his projections and related his story, a history which reveals more about him and his image of women than it does about the women themselves and their lives.

Social conditions for Michelet's image of women

Michelet's concept of women must be considered in the context of an historical development which had led to the well-documented modern form of gender differentiation as early as the eighteenth century.[21] This development was basically due to the partition of labour generated by the capitalist system of production, which divided this labour into employment outside the home and work which could be performed at home. With the industrialisation of the nineteenth century, the division into 'men's work' and 'women's work' became the norm. The task of ensuring social progress, through his untiring efforts on the production line or in science and technology, became the most important assignment for the man. He was the one who strove for advancement, who stormed the highest peaks, who bravely bore all burdens to assert himself in the struggle for existence.

The social theorists of the time, such as Michelet, Comte and

Proudhon, no longer sought mankind's happiness in an all-round development of abilities which a new division of labour would encourage. For example, C. Fourier, who was a propagator of such ideas,[22] was considered by Michelet to be a somewhat over-enthusiastic visionary. The search for happiness was now replaced by a belief in progress. Growth in material wealth and the development of production forces appeared to be the necessary conditions for this progress, which would be quite in harmony with the spread of large-scale industry, and which would automatically lead to better living conditions for the people.[23]

Progress, however, demanded sacrifice. The working world required discipline, rigour, performance-orientation, calculation and calculability, as well as ruthless competitiveness. These new virtues, imposed on the working population during the nineteenth century, necessitated the disavowal and control of many human needs, mostly in the emotional sphere. With the spread of paid work and exchange of goods - each salesperson approaches the buyer as an individual - society became more individual-oriented. In the wake of this individualisation, the social relations which obliged people in a hierarchical society to adopt a fixed standard of behaviour, gradually disappeared during the nineteenth century. Individual behaviour became a matter of psychic self-control. This implies a willingness on the part of each person to assume responsibility for her or his own life, a high level of self-regulation and the development of a moral conscience which controls behaviour through a sense of guilt.[24] Michelet describes these standards as he praises the virtues desirable in republicans and possessed by the revolutionaries of 1789:

> 'One must carry within oneself the inner republic, the moral republic, the only one which legitimises and forms the basis of the political republic; one must have command over oneself, a personal democracy; one must find one's liberty in subservience to one's duty.' (p. 117)

'Command over oneself' means in this context control over one's feelings, although Michelet allows and admits along with these virtues the contradiction in confirming the necessity of a certain 'moment of passion' which inspires revolutionary action (p. 117).

This social development - the striving for progress - requires men to adopt a psychic suit of armour to protect them from their own feelings.[25] The yardstick for individual male behaviour is capitalist rationality, which is by no means the same as reasonable behaviour; more often than not it implies submission to the principle of effectiveness - to achieve or produce a maximum in the shortest possible time.

The attribution of feelings and 'womanly qualities' to the female sex serves to construct a pseudo-world, the world of the home, as opposed to the world of outside employment and public life. Love is the magic cloak which enfolds this domestic world. The wife works at home for love and not for money, in contrast with those who are employed. The money which the man brings home is transformed by her work into loving care and attention for him and his children.

> '"For love" is in direct contrast with "for money". The construction of a domestic idyll in which love reigns, being complementary to the hard world of work in which money reigns, is the expression of the new order of life in the bourgeois society.'[26]

The human elements in man's nature which he learns to suppress can be projected into the reassuring intimacy of his own home. He ascribes as natural to woman all those qualities which have gradually disappeared during the 'process of civilisation' (N. Elias): sentiment, warmth, spontaneity, softness, patience, weakness and devotion. In contrast to the empire-building male Prometheus, the woman becomes quite simply a part of nature. Her life, feelings and thoughts are determined by the rhythm of her uterus. She embodies the cyclic form of life, the all-embracing liveliness which cannot be defined by linear rationality. The man re-creates his lost paradise in the woman and seeks the regeneration of his humanity in her harmoniously-run household.

However, nature is unpredictable; she has night and darkness on her side and a longing for another life. Prometheus recoils at his work. He may reveal his weakness to the woman, but who will guarantee that he will not thereby lose his strength? Now the woman also appears to be a seductive and menacing creature who threatens to rob him of his manliness. Sexuality lifts the individual physical barriers for a brief space of time. During the love-act the armour tends to melt away; the man experiences the power of his own nature through sensuality, repressed by the self-assumed process of civilisation. The fear of this power can only be overcome by subjugating the woman. Michelet warns the young man:

> 'Make haste to become her master. Because otherwise, I predict, she will speedily make herself your mistress... For the sake of your life and her life, both moral and physical, remain in command (she wishes it so, she wants it so), subdue her!'[27]

The battle of the sexes is rarely so openly described by Michelet. The woman of the capitalist society is not to be 'tamed' as she was in earlier times (this would, after all, presuppose her to possess some strength). The weapon of the bourgeois man is rather the domestication of the woman by inducing her to subjugate herself. Sacrifices are demanded of her, whereby she becomes the sacrificial victim offered to the cause of progress.

Michelet's women of the French Revolution reflect male expectations of the 'good' woman just as much as his own fear of the 'evil' and 'seductive' woman. This history is no 'wild male', but an account of events interpreted according to a concept of womanly nature, which very likely existed in this form only in the minds of men - a paradigm of androcentric historiography.

Notes

1. Feminist historians have pointed out the existence of this situation for many years: see, amongst others, R. Bridenthal, C. Koonz (eds), *Becoming visible: women in European history* (Houghton Mifflin, Boston, 1977); G. Lerner, *The majority finds its past* (Oxford University Press, Oxford, 1979); K. Hausen (ed.), *Frauen suchen ihre Geschichte* (Beck, München, 1983); H. Grubitzsch, 'Frauen machen Geschichte: Aspekte einer feministischen Geschichtsforschung' in H. Heer, V. Ullrich (eds), *Geschichte entdecken* (Reinbek, 1985), pp. 150-64.

2. H. Grubitzsch, 'Théroigne de Méricourt: Revolutionärin, Minerva oder Hure der Nation? Lebenswirklichkeit und biographische Legenden einer revolutionären Frau' in J. Dalhoff, U. Frey, I. Schöll (eds), *Frauenmacht in der Geschichte* (Düsseldorf, 1986), pp. 206-17.

3. 'L'histoire, que nous mettons très sottement au féminin, est un rude et sauvage mâle', J. Michelet, *La femme* (Flammarion, Paris, 1982), p. 148.

4. Ibid., p. 149.

5. D. Mey, '*Courtisane* oder *ménagère*? Zwei Pole des bürgerlichen Frauenbildes' in *Die ungeschriebene Geschichte: historische Frauenforschung* (Wien, 1984), pp. 187-98.

6. S.A. Kippur, *Jules Michelet: a study of mind and sensibility* (State University of New York Press, New York, 1981), p. 193; Th. Moreau, *Le sang de l'histoire: Michelet, l'histoire et l'idée de la femme au XIXe siècle,* Oeuvres complètes (Flammarion, Paris, 1982), p. 29.

7. Moreau, *Le sang de l'histoire*; N. Blüm, *Familie, Freiheit, Zukunft: Leitsätze und Entschließungen der 19. CDA-Bundestagung* (Mannheim, 1981).

8. H. Grubitzsch, *Materialien zur Kritik des Feuilleton-Romans: 'Die Geheimnisse von Paris' von Eugène Sue* (Athenaion, Wiesbaden, 1977).

9. A.R. Pugh, *Michelet and his ideas on social reform* (New York, 1966 (1st edn 1923)); H. Grubitzsch, L. Lagpacan, '*Freiheit für die Frauen, Freiheit für das Volk!' Sozialistische Frauen in Frankreich 1830-1848* (Syndikat, Frankfurt-am-Main, 1980), p. 208.

10. J. Michelet, *Les femmes de la Révolution,* Oeuvres complètes (Flammarion, Paris, 1982 (1st edn 1854)), p. 7. Quotations in the text have been translated by me from the Flammarion edition. All the page numbers in the following text refer to this edition.

11. O. Hufton, 'Women in revolution, 1789-1796', *Past and Present,* 53 (1971), pp. 90-108; A. Groppi, 'Le travail des femmes à l'époque de la Révolution Française', *Bulletin d'histoire économique et sociale de la Révolution Française,* 1979.

12. A. Farge, *Vivre dans la rue à Paris au XVIIIe siècle* (Gallimard/Julliard, Paris, 1979).

13. O. de Gouges, *Schriften* (Frankfurt, 1980); see O. Blanc, *Olympe de Gouges* (Paris, 1981).

14. P.M. Duhet, *Les femmes et la Révolution 1789-1794* (Paris, 1971); R. Graham, 'Loaves and liberty: women in the French Revolution' in Bridenthal, Koonz (eds), *Becoming visible,* pp. 238-54; L. Devance, 'Le féminisme pendant la Révolution française', *Annales historiques de la Révolution française,* 29 (1977), pp. 341-76; D.G. Levy, H.B. Applewhite (eds), *Women in revolutionary Paris: 1789-1795 selected documents* (University of Illinois Press, Urbana, 1979); *Cahiers de doléances des femmes 1789* (Paris, 1981); *Les femmes dans la Révolution française 1789-1794* (2 vols., Paris, 1982).

15. M.J.A. de Condorcet, 'Sur l'admission des femmes au droit de cité (1790)' in M.J.A. de Condorcet, *Oeuvres,* vol. 10 (Stuttgart-Bad Cannstatt, 1968 (repr. of 1847-9 edn)), pp. 119-30.

16. A. Dessens, *Les révendications des droits de la femme au point de vue politique, civil, économique pendant la Révolution* (Toulouse, 1905), p. 106.

17. Ibid., p. 151.

18. I. Bourdin, *Les sociétés populaires à Paris pendant la Révolution française jusqu'à la chute de la royauté* (Paris, 1937).

19. M. Cérati, *Le Club des Citoyennes Républicaines Révolutionnaires* (Paris, 1966).

20. 'Il faut que tu crées la femme, elle ne demande pas mieux... Nous sommes des ouvriers, créateurs et fabricateurs, et les vrais fils de Prométhée. Nous ne voulons pas une Pandore toute faite, mais une à faire.' J. Michelet, *L'amour,* Oeuvres complètes (Flammarion, Paris, 1982 (1st edn 1875)), pp. 85-6.

21. K. Hausen, 'Die Polarisierung der Geschlechtscharaktere - eine Spiegelung der Dissoziation von Erwerbs- und Familienleben' in W. Conze (ed.), *Sozialgeschichte der Familie in der Neuzeit Europas* (Klett, Stuttgart, 1976), pp. 367-93; B. Duden, 'Das schöne Eigentum - zur Herausbildung des bürgerlichen Frauenbildes an der Wende vom 18. zum 19. Jahrhundert', *Kursbuch,* 47 (1977), pp. 125-39; Grubitzsch, Lagpacan, *Freiheit für die Frauen,* pp. 19-56, 237-47.

22. Grubitzsch, Lagpacan, *Freiheit für die Frauen,* pp. 78-89.

23. Mey, '*Courtisane* oder *ménagère?*', pp. 187-98.

24. N. Elias, *Uber den Prozeß der Zivilisation* (2 vols., Frankfurt, 1981).

25. K. Theleweit, *Männerphantasien,* vol. 1 (Frankfurt, 1977).

26. Mey, '*Courtisane* oder *ménagère?*', p. 189, translated by me.

27. Michelet, *L'amour,* pp. 156-8, translated by me.

Willy Jansen

Ethnocentrism in the study of Algerian women

Historians and anthropologists have one thing in common: they both make a study of other cultures. Whereas the former focus on people in the past, the latter usually study people of other countries or of other ethnic groups. Both historians and anthropologists face similar problems of potential misrepresentation due to cultural distance. Historians should beware of *anachronism*, the tendency to account for past phenomena in terms of concepts and values of their own time, and anthropologists should avoid the pitfalls of *ethnocentrism*, the often subconscious tendency to form an interpretation of behaviour and phenomena in other cultures using the values and norms of one's own culture as a yardstick. These two disciplines could learn from each other by exchanging ideas on and experiences with anachronism and ethnocentrism.

However, the similarities between ethnocentrism and anachronism did not receive much attention at the International Conference on Women's History. Instead, the discussions at the Conference elaborated, amongst other problems, on the ethical acceptability of studying 'the other' if 'the other' was non-Western and black and the researcher Western and white. The cultural distance of space and ethnic diversity was seen as being much more difficult to bridge than the distance in time.

As with most ethical questions, there is no simple solution and this paper is not intended to provide one. However, it is necessary to mention my own opinions on the matter, as a background to the rest of this paper. I do not believe that it is unethical in principle to study other people. To deny categorically the right to study other people, as some critics of ethnocentrism seem to do, would be to deny the rationale not only of anthropology, but also of medicine, linguistics and history. Historians in particular would then be considered very unethical: unlike anthropologists, doctors or linguists, they cannot ask permission from the people they study. Nor do I believe in the idea that only women can study women, only blacks can study blacks, or only Dutch people can study Dutch people. The fact of being different, the ability to draw comparisons and to distance oneself from the norms, practices and constraints of the society studied, are all distinct advantages of cross-cultural research, despite their drawbacks. I do think, on the other hand, that it is unethical if one does not try to avoid ethnocentrism and if one ignores the problems of power.

The problem of ethnocentrism lies less in the difference between researcher and researched than in the power hierarchy this difference often creates, both on a personal and a social level. In order to redress this hierarchy, I would strongly advocate that more women study women (and men), more blacks study blacks (and whites), and more Algerians study Algerians (and French or Dutch people). Moreover, those of us with more power should actively support those of us with fewer opportunities to do such research. Social science or historical research by insiders both have the obvious advantages of intimate knowledge of language, thoughts and practices. If the foreign and the native researcher each have their specific advantages, the ideal situation would be to combine these advantages in a complementary working relationship. Of course this is difficult to put into practice, given the hierarchical structures within which human beings work, but by making the effort we can learn much from each other. Such coalition science presupposes a continuing critical reflection of both the cross-cultural and the intercultural researcher, and a willingness to discuss and change one's own culture-bound viewpoints. All research is influenced by the socio-cultural background of the researcher; no one can be absolutely free from ethnocentrism. This must be realised before one can attempt to reduce ethnocentrism to a minimum.

In this article I will present a model which reveals the various guises in which ethnocentrism presents itself, and illustrate how it works by applying it in a critical review of the anthropological literature on Algerian women. My aim is not to fit all forms of ethnocentrism into this model, but to offer a heuristical device which can detect the presence of ethnocentrism. Although this model was originally developed in a critique of the literature on the Middle East, it can also be used to criticise accounts of other cultures removed from the researcher by time and space. Another aim is to show which anthropological sources can be used to write Algerian women's history by giving a review of the literature on Algerian women. Very little has been written on the history of Algerian women. The bulk of the more substantial works dealing with this subject was written by travellers, one or two colonial administrators, a handful of Algerian sociologists and a number of French and American anthropologists. Few of these works treat women in an historical perspective, yet they can provide an interesting and important source for writing history if one makes allowances for their cultural bias.

Methods and sources

For the review I have used the literature in Western European languages which I read in preparation for my doctoral research on Algerian women. Much of it is included in the three main bibliographies on Algerian women.[1] Most works were obtained from various national and institutional libraries in Algeria, France and the Netherlands and from the French colonial archives in Aix-en-Provence. Short articles in newspapers, weeklies and monthlies have not been included, only those works with scholarly pretensions. The review is not a comprehensive one; some works were not accessible, and on others the notes I made were not extensive. The length of this article, too, does not permit me to go into as much detail as I would like. However, I think I have covered most of the scholarly literature on Algerian women written by Westerners between 1847 and 1987.

I will test our information about Algerian women against a model of ethnocentrism largely derived from the ideas of Edward Said in his book *Orientalism,* and from Philippe Lucas and Jean-Claude Vatin's *L'Algérie des anthropologues.*[2] Said is the best-known critic of ethnocentrism in Western views on the Middle East, and Lucas and Vatin apply their ethnocentrism critique specifically to anthropological studies of Algeria.

Guises of ethnocentrism: a model

Said argues that the Western literature about the Middle East tells us as much about the attitudes of Western writers towards the East as it does about the East itself. It reveals facts not only about the Arabs but also about Westerners; not only about how Arab society is, but also about how Westerners collectively think it is. He calls this way of thinking Orientalism. In his analysis the term *Orientalism*, originally indicating a philological discipline, is given a special meaning: that of one particular kind of ethnocentrism.

Independently from Said, Lucas and Vatin brought to light similar forms of ethnocentrism when showing how anthropologists writing about Algeria were influenced by the ideological, economical and political context in which they found themselves as French people in a period of French colonisation in Algeria. During the military expansion which began in 1830, the ethnographer was often a soldier, such as General E. Daumas for instance, and after 1900 often an administrator. In addition, other authors less directly part of the invading power were influenced by its ideology.

One characteristic of the Orientalist version of ethnocentrism is, according to Said, an underlying belief in the absolute and systematic difference between East and West, in which the East is considered irrational, inhumane, underdeveloped and inferior, and the West rational, humane, developed and superior. In the case of Algeria, the difference stressed was that between a barbarian and a civilised society in order to justify colonialism.

A second characteristic is a preference for abstractions, which is exemplified by the use of texts to help researchers understand social relations. The resulting 'philosophically idealist bias' leads, according to N.R. Keddie,[3] to a neglect of historical and contemporary realities, and of less normative sources which could tell us more about these realities, such as chronicles, geographies, travellers' accounts, autobiographies, actual legal cases, oral tradition, or contemporary anthropology, sociology and economics. This also leads to imagining the society to be more homogeneous than it is in reality.

A third characteristic is the concept of the Orient as static and unchanging. Lucas and Vatin defined this as *passéisme*: the predilection of ethnographers for exotic traditions and survivals from the past while refusing to look at the processes of economic deterioration and political upheaval in which the people they study are involved.[4] This glorification of old cultural forms reinforces the conception of 'the other' as different and inferior.

A fourth characteristic mentioned is the representation of Arabs and Muslims as dangerous. This danger is felt to be caused mainly by Islam. Ever since the Crusades, the word *jihad* (holy war) has sent chills down Western spines and created visions of bloodthirsty Arabs who force their religion on other people at the point of the sword. Islam is also feared because of its supposed brutality and repressiveness towards women and lax control of male sexuality.

These characteristics seldom reveal themselves openly and clearly. As time goes on they are presented in different forms and with changed justifications. It is easier to discover a cultural bias in retrospect; therefore the guiding presuppositions of a military ethnographer appear clearer than those of a modern trained anthropologist. However, this does not necessarily make the anthropologist less ethnocentric. The danger of ethnocentrism lies in the very act of conforming to the accepted, influential academic tradition of studying and writing about the Orient. It is in the conventional themes, methods and vocabulary that ethnocentrism is both expressed and hidden. Most authors reviewed here attempted to be objective and fair to the people they were describing, but not all were equally successful.

Said (as well as Lucas and Vatin) remarks that Western assumptions become apparent especially with regard to writings on Arab women.[5] I hope to demonstrate in the following pages how the topic of women is indeed a focal point of ethnocentrism, and what special problems this would pose for women's studies. The leading questions were: How pervasive is ethnocentrism in the main anthropological studies on Algerian women? Does it permeate these studies in the same way as has been noted in the general literature on the area in question? Do books on women have a special place in an ethnocentrism critique?

Symbols of inferiority

An ethnocentric view of Algeria as different and inferior comes to the fore in depicting its religion, Islam, as inhumane and backward by emphasising the way this religion subjugates women. From the literature they studied, Lucas and Vatin conclude that the world of Algerian women was the first aspect of Algerian life to be criticised, which led to the whole social system being accused and the barbaric nature of the society proven.[6] The misogyny of Islam and the degenerate position of Algerian women are easily used as symbols of the inferiority of Algerian culture.

B. Gastineau, who describes what he saw during his travels in 1852 and 1854, disregards all Algerian women when he writes: 'Algeria has all this boundlessness, all these riches, all these beauties, but she has no woman.' For him 'in Africa, as elsewhere, the real, unique woman is the French woman'. For him Algerian women prove the brutality of Islam:

> 'I was nauseated by this degrading spectacle that condemns Mohammedanism, which is declining today in Turkey as well as in Africa, for having committed the crime of equating woman with a slave, of not respecting in her a soul, dignity, modesty, moral liberty.'[7]

In the nineteenth century, the degenerate position of Arab-Algerian women was customarily illustrated by a comparison with Berber women. Gastineau thought that Kabyle women were freer because they went unveiled, and that the Kabyles only took what suited them from the Quran.[8] Kabyle society was seen as less Islamic and thus closer to French society. That he was not the only one to hold such views can be seen in a book by M. Daumas and M. Fabar, who compare nomadic Arab society with Kabyle society. For them, a Kabyle woman is more liberated, cleaner and more respected than an Arab woman.[9] Later authors continued to give an extraordinary amount of attention to the Berbers. This 'Berberism' served to justify colonialism as well as oppression of the Arab population and the attempts at civilisation bestowed on the Kabyles; it was part of a divide-and-rule policy. The treatment of women was used in this as a symbol of internal strife and different levels of inferiority. Up till the present day most monographs on Algerian women concern Berber women. The ethnic differences in Algeria are still stressed nowadays, but for other reasons.

Since the women's question served to depict Algerian society as different and inferior, most of the general works written during the nineteenth century and the first quarter of the twentieth century devote at least one chapter to it. In writings mainly concerned with women, a change takes place during this period from superficial, short and distanced judgements made by men on women's position,[10] to more elaborate descriptions and partisan stances by female authors who wanted to acquaint people with the Algerian woman's point of view. In the 1920s and 30s a wave of feminism swept through the Arab world. Feminist books appeared, women's organisations were founded and women's journals were started.[11] This international Arab feminism was concentrated in Lebanon, Egypt and Tunisia, largely by-passing Algeria. The Egyptian reformist Mohamad Abdou, who, like Qasim Amin, was an early male advocate of feminist beliefs and principles, greatly influenced the Algerian reformists, but his views on the status of women and the importance of their education were not emphasised.[12] Algerian feminist voices were absent in this period, but French women living in Algeria, such as Hubertine Auclert, Marie Bugéja and Henriette Célarié, stood up to speak for Algerian women.[13] Their works were more elaborate and more sympathetic to Algerian women, but they had in common with their male predecessors that they seldom went beyond appearances and that they overly victimised women. Algerian women were still depicted as dependent, inferior and in a state of semi-slavery to the men.

After the 1920s, the French outcry against the enslavement of Algerian women, which for a short time had swelled the chorus of international emancipatory voices, subsided somewhat, only to rise anew with the wave of feminism in the 1960s and 70s. Most recent feminist works continue the trend of describing Algerian women solely as victims, as oppressed objects instead of acting subjects in an hierarchical system. F. Corrèze's book, for instance, is one long lament about the deplorable situation of Algerian village women. Based on a superficial knowledge of their lives and rife with urban prejudices against country people, it forms a continuation of this image: the poor and illiterate but hospitable woman who passively accepts her lot.[14]

Fortunately, not all authors victimise women as blatantly as Corrèze, but sometimes this victimisation is the indirect result of condemnations of the way Algerian men treat women. F. M'rabet writes: 'The condition of the woman remains, entirely, the work of the man: it is the father, the brother, the [male] cousin, the uncle, the husband who make the laws, and the behaviour of the Algerian woman is only the consequence or the reflection of masculine behaviour towards her', and: 'Deprived of speech and of rights, reduced to the state of nature, the woman - and this is another glaring sign of her *cultural* non-existence - finds herself excluded from political action.'[15] Thus she accuses Algerian men of wielding extreme power over Algerian women, but in so doing she reconfirms the view of Algerian women as victims rather than as actors. M'rabet does refer to women who react, who resist, but her main focus is on how men see women, not on how women see themselves. Sweeping generalisations about women's oppression by men conceal the power of women and power differentials among women versus men. The same can be said of the articles on women in the special Algerian edition of *Autrement*, and in the special edition of *Tisuraf* on Berber women.[16] Again, the various articles written in an objective scientific jargon usually do no more than repeat the well-known list of weaknesses in the position of Algerian women which are due to misogynist family law, sexist cultural traditions and a lack of political representation.[17] These analyses are not untrue - the inequalities described do exist between Algerian women and men - and they are often inspired by a real concern for the plight of Algerian women. However, it is by this very conforming to the accepted feminist academic writing that an earlier form of ethnocentrism appears in another guise, namely the claim that Algerian social relations are inferior to those of the author's society, especially when it concerns the relationship between women and men. In order to avoid this form of ethnocentrism, the first step would be to make fewer generalisations about women's subjugation and to be more explicit about women's power potential or their actual ideas and worries, or how they resist or cope with this unfavourable social system. In the following pages I have suggested further steps that could be taken.

The method of research is important in realising this goal. To gain information, direct, intensive and sustained contact with Algerian women is essential. There are some studies available, based on this method, which provide a rich and detailed description of the everyday lives of illiterate peasant women. The first of these studies to appear was A.M. Goichon's work on women's lives in the Berber region of the Mzab in 1927, followed by a sequel in 1931. M. Gaudry wrote a book 1928 on the women of the Aurès, another

Berber region to the north-east of the Mzab. Her second study describes the lives of women in the Djebel Amour and the Ksel 1961.[18] Both Goichon and Gaudry carried out their research during the colonial period, and certainly must have been influenced by the context in which they worked, but they were unable to generalise as much as others about male power abuse or female victimisation because their generalisations were belied by their data. For instance, Goichon states: 'The religious and social context imprisons women',[19] but a large part of her text is devoted to how a group of women actually construct and manipulate this context to serve their own interests. The weakness of these studies and their lack of theory or interest in power relations, is to some extent an advantage in that it is less ethnocentric. Their strength lies in the minute descriptions of women's clothing, tools, work, food, ornaments, rituals and words. They should be considered as an important source for writing Algerian women's history, particularly because they tell us about people who are hardly ever represented in the written documents normally used by historians.

The method of participant observation over a long period was also applied in post-colonial Algeria. Studies on women or on gender relations were carried out by C. Lacoste-Dujardin, D.H. Parsons and myself.[20] Much attention was given to women in several anthropological monographs, such as the study of a village or region by M. Bennoune, D. Champault, Lacoste-Dujardin and J. Lizot, or of a theme by N. Zerdoumi and A. Ouitis, as well as in more theoretical works like those of G. Tillion or P. Bourdieu.[21] These monographs seem to follow the earlier trend of special focus on women. Whereas anthropological monographs often show a male bias in that they deal with men to a far greater extent than with women, in the case of Algeria there appears to be a female bias. It is also worth mentioning that most of the anthropologists writing about Algeria are women, and that the foreigners among them seem more attentive to the situation of women than the native anthropologists. This extraordinary interest in women may be appreciated from the aspect of women's studies, but it should also be evaluated for its ethnocentric implications. Does this mean that the position of women still serves as a focal point for the specialness of Algerian culture, as the main feature of Algerian culture which differs from that of the author?

All equal in the eyes of the law

The second characteristic of ethnocentrism is related to the conception of women's position as being symbolic of the backwardness of Islamic cultures. It displays a tendency to show a greater preoccupation with texts and abstractions than with actual social relations. One often finds references to Quranic verses, the Traditions of the Prophet or the writings of theologians, as if these were able to offer a sufficient explanation of social facts such as the percentage of polygamous marriages or the rate of divorce. Formal Islamic ideology is easily used to account for the socio-economic position of women in the Arab world, especially in popularised writings.

In anthropological studies this idealist bias is subdued, although not absent. It can be seen in the tradition of special interest in family law, which is not complemented by a similar interest in how real people deal with this law in everyday life.[22] Most authors who wrote about Algerian family law were interested in and critical of its discriminatory effects on women, but not all for the same reasons or to the same extent. Whereas L.M. Lefèvre was interested in how French decrees could overrule Kabyle customary law in favour of women, feminists such as M'rabet and M.V. Louis voiced the opposition of Algerian women's groups to various drafts of a new family law.[23] When the Family Code was finally approved in 1984, it again featured male privileges regarding polygamy, divorce, custody of children, inheritance and authority over women. The new Family Code will have a deleterious effect on many women, as Algerian feminists point out, and observers should of course take note of this. But they must also realise that this law is not the first preoccupation of many Algerian women, nor the sole factor which determines their position. In short survey articles on the position of Algerian women,[24] the overtly discriminatory laws still figure as an easy stick to beat the dog with, to the detriment of a more balanced description of discriminatory practices.

The philological and juristic bias does not pervade all literature to the same extent. Again the method of participant observation can help to reduce this bias. Grass-roots studies usually treat laws as only one element in a larger context. They also show how research can be done on an intermediate level between normative texts and real life by using oral traditions, poems, songs and actual legal cases. An example of the last is Gaudry's use of legal documents appertaining to court decisions on 'sleeping children'. (The notion of 'the sleeping child' refers to the belief that a child may be born more than nine months after its legal father's absence or death and yet be legitimate.) Many of these sources remain unexplored. A. Christelow, who used Algerian court cases for a research in which women are conspicuous by their absence, suggests nevertheless that marriage and divorce form a major category of the transactions and disputes brought before the judges of the Bureaux Arabes. The archival documents can be found in Aix-en-Provence and might prove interesting for women's history.[25] Another suggestion I would like to make to historians studying Algerian women is that they analyse legal documents on *habous* endowments. The *habous* system of making endowments to religious institutions was used to circumvent Islamic inheritance laws and actually disinherit women.[26] An examination of the friction between laws and actual practices is also theoretically interesting. Tillion demonstrates this when she relates differences in women's veiling and endogamy to differences in the acceptance of Islamic inheritance laws.[27]

Concerning the preoccupation with texts - especially Islamic texts - and laws, one more remark should be made about the relationship between women and Islam. Despite a readiness to connect the position of women with Islamic rules, very little research has been done on women's religious experiences and on women's influence on Islamic rules and practices. This relationship has generally been depicted as one-sided, with women as passive victims of a monolithic Islamic religion. What do anthropological sources reveal about women as active Muslims? Goichon portrays women in the Mzab as staunch defenders of the sectarian Islam practised by the Ibadites, especially the women who teach other women the Ibadi doctrine, the Quran and prayers. Religious education was seen as essential for both men and women, and because of strict segregation this education was left in the hands of the most learned women. Gaudry pays more attention to the adherence of women to *maraboutism*, the veneration of local saints, but says little about their practice of or attitude to a more formal Islam. H. Vandevelde-Dallière is more exact when she poses questions in her survey about the frequency of praying, the maintenance of the fast or the desirability of making a pilgrimage to Mecca.[28] In short, there are some references to women's religious practice, but most of this terrain lies open to further research.

A consequence of the idealist bias is that the female population is treated as being more homogeneous than it actually is, and that class, regional and age distinctions are overlooked. The generic term 'woman' (*la femme*) appears in many titles and is often an indication that the author has not bothered to take the differences between women into account. When the focus is on norms - *la coutume*, the Family Code or the Quran - instead of on the way people live with these norms, only women's common subjugation to them is noted, not their diverging interests and manipulation of these norms. Ethnographers who give a first-hand account of every-day life cannot easily overlook internal rifts, although some do. When J. Desparmet describes childhood, marriage and the family in Algeria, he consistently uses the term *les indigènes* when referring to Algerians, without specifying whether these are men or women, poor or rich.[29] Gaudry differentiates between women with regard to race, class and origins, but not to economic status, despite an elaborate description of women's economic functions. Nor does she question the application of inheritance laws.[30] Goichon does not treat women as one homogeneous group when she relates the coming to power of one small group of women through the religious monopoly of washing the dead.[31] Similarly, the encompassing term *la femme* fades into the background when particular cases of women's protests are revealed,[32] when Algerian women are extensively interviewed,[33] or when differentiating criteria such as age, civil status or even forms of veiling are analysed.[34]

From the above, it follows that the second step to be taken to avoid ethnocentrism would be to describe and explain gender inequality not only in terms of Islamic rules, but also by paying more attention to other factors, such as socio-economic developments which may affect gender relations in Algeria in similar ways as in other societies. Islam must be treated like other ideologies that reflect and influence gender inequalities: from the perspective of the people who create, use and obey its rules. Women must also be seen as active participants in this process, participants who are less influential on the whole than men, but not all to the same extent. Some Algerian sociologists have shown the merits of a relative disregard of Islam and a focus on other factors. Unfortunately their work is not easily accessible outside Algeria, and an international debate has yet to be started.[35]

Guardians of tradition

A third form in which ethnocentrism comes to the surface is the assumption that the other culture remains static and unchanging. To what extent is this assumption present in the anthropology of Algerian women? The only possible answer seems to be: to a great extent. The idea of women's position as an unchanging tradition and the central constant in Algerian culture over a long period of time is a recurrent theme in the literature.

In the early days of colonialism this image of women as guardians of tradition, exemplified in their lack of emancipation, served to reinforce the idea of absolute difference between colonisers and colonised. Later it came to be regarded as the last remains of a disappearing culture. French acceptance of women's unchanging role as the essence of Algerian culture, and their relative aloofness from indigenous family affairs, suddenly changed during the war of independence when the colonists tried to hurt the revolutionaries in their most sacred and vulnerable spot: their women. According to F. Fanon, the resistance movement reacted by making women's traditional position, represented by the veil, a symbol of Algerian identity.[36] Today the same image of women as guardians of valuable traditions and as representatives of essential values is still used, both by traditionalists who fear the encroachment of Western ideas and by modernists who complain about the backwardness of their society.[37] Today this image is duplicated, no longer by colonialists but by feminists, in many studies of Algerian society.

The view of women as unchanging is connected with the view of Islam as static and unchanging. The example of women is used to prove not only the inferiority and the ideological dominance of Islam, but also its immobility. In fact, Islam is not without history; many Islamic interpretations and precepts have changed over the centuries. It is true that the rules governing male-female relations have shown more resistance to change than other rules for proper behaviour. This is partly due to the fact that the former are more explicitly and repeatedly stated in the Quran and the Traditions.

However, this does not adequately explain why they are still obeyed to a greater degree than other rules. Many other historical factors, including East-West politics or forms of economic development, come here into play. However, as we saw above, such factors are considered less important than the impact of Islam.

Goichon, for instance, calls the Mozabite woman 'an element of stability', and considers her the rock to which the boat of the Ibadite doctrine is safely anchored. She writes that 'the Ibadite doctrine and the form of government which it inspired in the eleventh century have been consistently preserved up till the present day'. She implies that this doctrine, which she sees as dictating the position of women, has survived eight centuries, but at the same time she mentions that the family code which governs the Mozabite family was only drafted at the beginning of the nineteenth century.[38] J. Minces, like other modern authors, only reserves this static image for Algerian society before independence in 1962. She writes:

> 'Traditional society was a world ruled by Islam, at once law and religion, which regulated social and personal life in all its details... This traditional world had its own equilibrium, its coherence, its cohesion, and its security. In traditional society a woman had an inferior status from birth to death.'[39]

The disregard for religious processes was often accompanied by a disregard for social, economic or political processes. An historical perspective was only applied to specific aspects or periods. R. Descloitre acknowledges the changes in the Algerian family, but then proceeds to 'isolate that which endures'.[40] Gaudry, when describing women's economic functions, does not look at how they may be influenced by French economic policies. It is mostly from her expression of gratitude to colonial administrators for their help that we learn that her research was conducted under the protection of a colonial power.[41] Goichon gives an historical summary of the Ibadites' relation to other Muslims, but omits their relation to Frenchmen. She only tells us of the French occupation of the Mzab and the subjection of its inhabitants to military law in a footnote.[42] People who write about the post-colonial period tend more often to apply an historical contextual perspective, at least to the developments after 1962 as Minces does. A good example of this tendency is given by D.C. Gordon, who describes women's (political) position before, during and after the revolution.[43]

The concept of the other culture as being immobile, static and unchanging can be reflected and influenced by the theoretical orientations of the researcher. The anthropology of the Middle East, and North Africa in general, has been criticised for its lack of comparison and theory.[44] In the books on women reviewed here, it is partly this absence of a theoretical orientation which strengthens the image of women's roles and positions as static and immutable. It stands to reason that this form of ethnocentrism must be combated by an historical perspective of the 'people without history' *par excellence*: women. Even if they are indeed the guardians of tradition, of age-old Islamic rules, this must be explained. Historically!

Uncontrolled sexual beings

The last form in which ethnocentrism manifests itself is a fear of 'the other'. For Westerners, the danger of Islam lies especially in what they perceive as a failure to control sexuality. Fear explains why so much attention is paid to polygamy or to marriages between first cousins, although these occurrences are statistically rather insignificant, as well as bearing a remarkable resemblance to actual practices on the northern shores of the Mediterranean. According to Christian moral beliefs, to have a harem is adultery and to marry one's father's brother's daughter is incest, so their legalisation within Islam is perceived as a threat to the Western moral order.

Not only the topics chosen, but also the way these are treated, express the fear of promiscuous sexuality. Polygyny, for instance, is generally described in terms of its rules and sometimes its frequency, but seldom in terms of its effect on the lives of the people concerned. There are few accounts in the literature in question of what Algerian women actually think about living with a co-wife and how they manage in practice. Ignorance of other details, such as the extent to which it limits adultery or the reasons of women or their fathers for accepting such unions, makes it easier to generalise about the evils of polygyny. Why are Westerners far more negative about polygyny than about their own eternal triangles? An

Algerian co-wife has more rights than a Dutch mistress. What they should be criticising is that in both cases men have more rights over (more) women than women over men.

The attention foreigners lavished on Algerian women was not always positive. The image of them as lascivious harem women, painted by E. Delacroix in 1832, or as prostitutes, reproduced on thousands of colonial postcards,[45] can also be found in the literature. Gastineau called Algerian women 'strumpets' and accused them of impudence and voluptuousness; others used derogatory terms like intriguers, gossips or witches.[46] Most authors do not use such terms, but many do betray a fascination for female sexuality. They describe female sexual powers based on knowledge of abortifacient drugs, contraceptives or stimulants, on magical practices, or on adultery and prostitution more often or in more detail than they describe powers based on life-cycle status, fertility, age, female networks or income. Again the emphasis lies on uncontrolled sexuality, in this case not of men but of women.[47]

To overcome the ethnocentric fear for 'the other', one must first recognise it in one's own choice and treatment of certain topics. Secondly, one must examine the topics the women concerned think important, and establish new priorities and ways to discuss them by means of dialogue. This does not necessarily mean that polygyny, prostitution or magic can no longer be discussed, only that they must be put in the proper context, and in equal proportion to other important facets of gender relations.

Conclusion

Ethnocentrism is seldom straightforward; it appears in many different forms. In order to detect these forms a model was proposed, which warns us that ethnocentrism can manifest itself in viewing the other culture as different and inferior, as idealist and homogeneous, as static and traditional and as dangerous. When the literature on Algerian women was examined for the presence of these forms of ethnocentrism, it was found that the cultural values of the authors often affect their views and opinions. More significantly, it turned out that research on Algerian women was not neutral research at all, but a special case of ethnocentrism. Ethnocentrism concerning Algeria is concentrated in and expressed through the study of women.

Awareness of inherent ethnocentrism in the study of Algerian women poses problems for Western anthropologists or historians interested in these women. They have to overcome tangible barriers, such as government officials who do not want Algeria's image abroad to be dominated by the women's question. Moreover, they have to deal with some ethical problems. How can they avoid ethnocentrism if merely studying women is already seen as part of a colonial mentality and a depreciation of Algerian society? Is it cultural imperialism, or unethical, to unravel gender relations and gender hierarchy, and in so doing talk about taboo subjects like sorcery, abortion or faking virginity? Algerian feminists are faced with similar difficulties: how can they be critical of the gender inequality in their own country without being seen as Western spokeswomen or pawns in the hands of imperialist powers?

It cannot be denied that inequality between men and women in Algeria actually exists, as it does in other countries. How can it be ethically wrong to bring this inequality into the open? This is only the case if ethnocentrism is not reduced as far as possible. Some suggestions were made to bring about such a reduction: to focus not only on the differences but also on the similarities between cultures, which includes applying a similar variety of factors - not merely Islam - and a similar historical perspective to obtain an explanation of social inequalities; to discuss not only the disadvantages but also the advantages of a cultural system for women, in other words less generalisation and victimisation; to choose a method of research which does justice to the people most involved, and a topic of research which is based on what people actually say or do and not on the researcher's preoccupations based on fear, prejudice or general misinformation; and to confront external ideas with internal ideas. In addition, all this should be based on a constant awareness of personal and social values embedded in any science, and a willingness to discuss and change one's views.

Changing researcher and research, however, is not enough. Unravelling the threads of any social hierarchy is bound to raise objections, as it undermines the legitimacy of power. The dominant group in particular, but occasionally also the dominated group, has reasons for concealing inequalities. In cross-cultural studies these objections may be phrased as accusations of ethnocentrism or cultural imperialism. In Algeria it is mostly the male authorities who use this argument to object to research on women. As a result Algerian critics of the gender hierarchy may avoid contact with foreigners, and are afraid to speak out loud for fear of being accused of Western imperialist thinking. Western observers, if they are let into the country at all, may also swallow part of their critique so as not to forestall the chances of a dialogue. We saw that there are grounds for the accusation that studies of Algerian women are carriers of ethnocentrism, but the solution to this is not to forbid or stop writing about the lives and history of Algerian women, but to combat ethnocentrism in an open dialogue.

Notes

1. J. Déjeux, 'Connaissance du monde féminin et de la famille en Algérie: essai de synthèse documentaire 1947-1967', *Revue Algérienne des Sciences Juridiques, Economiques et Politiques*, vol. 5, no. 4 (1968), pp. 1247-1311; M. Raccagni, *The modern Arab woman: a bibliography* (Scarecrow Press, Metuchen, N.J. and London, 1978); A. Al-Qazzaz, *Women in the Middle East and North Africa* (University of Texas, Center for Middle Eastern Studies, Austin, 1977).

2. E. Said, *Orientalism* (Routledge & Kegan Paul, London, 1978); P. Lucas, J.-Cl. Vatin, *L'Algérie des anthropologues* (Maspero, Paris, 1979).

3. N.R. Keddie, 'Problems in the study of Middle Eastern women', *International Journal of Middle East Studies*, vol. 10 (1979), pp. 225-40, esp. p. 227.

4. Lucas, Vatin, *L'Algérie des anthropologues*, p. 51.

5. Said, *Orientalism*, pp. 188-90, 309, 311-16; Lucas, Vatin, *L'Algérie des anthropologues*, pp. 30-1. Other authors who discuss ethnocentrism in studies of Arab women, and who sometimes include studies of Algerian women, have influenced my thinking on this subject. They are: K. Adamson, 'Approaches to the study of women in North Africa as reflected in research of various scholars', *The Maghreb Review*, 5-8 (1978), pp. 22-31; L. Ahmed, 'Western ethnocentrism and perceptions of the harem', *Feminist Studies*, vol. 8, no. 3 (1982), pp. 521-34; A.A. Heggoy, 'Cultural disrespect: European and Algerian views on women in colonial and independent Algeria', *The Muslim World*, vol. 62, no. 4 (1972), pp. 323-34; S. Joseph, 'Study of Middle Eastern women: investments, passions and problems', *International Journal of Middle East Studies*, vol. 18, no. 4 (1986), pp. 501-9; A. Moors, 'Feministische wetenschap en de Oriënt', *LOVA-Nieuwsbrief*, vol. 8, no. 1 (1987), pp. 58-66; N. Tapper, 'Mysteries of the harem? An anthro-

pological perspective on recent studies of women in the Muslim Middle East', *Women's Studies International Quarterly*, vol. 2 (1979), pp. 481-7; J. Tucker, 'Problems in the historiography of women in the Middle East: the case of nineteenth-century Egypt', *International Journal of Middle East Studies*, vol. 15, no. 3 (1983), pp. 321-36.

6. Lucas, Vatin, *L'Algérie des anthropologues*, pp. 30-1.

7. B. Gastineau, *Les femmes et les moeurs de l'Algérie* (Librairie Michel Lévy, Paris, 1861), pp. 5, 16, 25.

8. Ibid., p. 16.

9. M. Daumas, M. Fabar, *La grande Kabylie: études historiques* (Hachette, Paris, 1847), cited by Lucas, Vatin, *L'Algérie des anthropologues*, pp. 104-14; see also Ch. Barbet, *La femme musulmane en Algérie* (Jourdan, Alger, 1903); and Gén. E. Daumas, *Moeurs et coutumes de l'Algérie* (Hachette, Paris, 1855), pp. 194-8, as well as his *La vie arabe et la société musulmane* (Slatkine Reprints, Genève/Paris, 1983 (1st edn 1869)).

10. Examples of early writings by Frenchmen on Algerian women are: J.-P. Bonnafont, *La femme arabe dans la province de Constantine* (Mateste, Paris, 1865); E. Mercier, *La condition de la femme musulmane dans l'Afrique septentrionale* (Jourdan, Alger, 1895); L. Milliot, *La femme musulmane du Maghreb (Maroc, Algérie, Tunisie)* (Rousset, Paris, 1909), and, in addition to his above-mentioned works, Gén. E. Daumas, *La femme arabe* (Jourdan, Alger, 1912).

11. L. Ahmad, 'Feminism and feminist movements in the Middle East, a preliminary exploration: Turkey, Egypt, Algeria, People's Democratic Republic of Yemen', *Women's Studies International Forum*, vol. 5, no. 2 (1982), pp. 153-69.

12. Ibid., p. 164.

13. H. Auclert, *Les femmes arabes en Algérie* (Société d'Editions Littéraires, Paris, 1900); M. Bugéja, *Nos soeurs musulmanes* (Revue des Etudes Littéraires, Paris, 1921); H. Célarié, *Nos soeurs musulmanes, scènes de la vie du désert* (Hachette, Paris, 1925). For a relevant review of these and other works on Algerian women see D. Brahimi, *Femmes arabes et soeurs musulmanes* (Editions Tierce, Paris, 1984).

14. F. Corrèze, *Femmes des mechtas: témoignage sur l'Est algérien* (Editeurs Français Réunis, Paris, 1976).

15. F. M'rabet, *La femme algérienne,* (suivi de) *Les Algériennes* (Maspero, Paris, 1979), pp. 14-15.

16. 'Algérie 20 ans', *Autrement*, 38 (1982) (special issue); 'Femmes berbères', *Tisuraf*, 4-5 (1979) (special issue).

17. K. Boals, 'The politics of cultural liberation: male-female relations in Algeria' in B.A. Carroll (ed.), *Liberating women's history: theoretical and critical essays* (University of Illinois Press, Urbana, 1976), pp. 194-213; K. Boals, 'The politics of cultural liberation' in J. Jaquette (ed.), *Women in politics* (Wiley, London, 1974), pp. 322-42; S. Khodja, 'Les femmes algéri-

ennes et la politique' in C. Souriau (ed.), *Femmes et politique autour de la Méditerranée* (Harmattan, Paris, 1980), pp. 251-61; J. Minces, 'Women in Algeria' in L. Beck, N. Keddie (eds), *Women in the Muslim world* (Harvard University Press, Cambridge, 1978), pp. 159-71; J. Stiehm, 'Algerian women: honor, survival, and Islamic socialism' in B. Iglitzin, R. Ross (eds), *Women in the world: a comparative study* (Clio Press, Santa Barbara, 1976), pp. 229-41. Those who generalise less are: M. Gadant, 'Les femmes, la famille et la nationalité algérienne', *Peuples Méditerranéens/Mediterranean Peoples,* 15 (1981), pp. 25-56; I. Rezig, 'Women's roles in contemporary Algeria: tradition and modernism' in B. Utas (ed.), *Women in Islamic societies* (Curzon Press, London/Malmö, 1983), pp. 192-210.

18. A.M. Goichon, *La vie féminine au Mzab* (2 vols., Geuthner, Paris, 1927/1931); M. Gaudry, *La femme Chaouia de l'Aurès* (Geuthner, Paris, 1928); M. Gaudry, *La société féminine au Djebel Amour et au Ksel* (Société Algérienne des Impressions Diverses, Alger, 1961).

19. Goichon, *La vie féminine,* p. 1.

20. W. Jansen, *Women without men: gender and marginality in an Algerian town* (Brill, Leiden, 1987); C. Lacoste-Dujardin, *Des mères contre les femmes: maternité et patriarchat au Maghreb* (La Découverte, Paris, 1985); D.H. Parsons, 'Change and ambiguity in male-female relations in an Algerian town', unpublished PhD thesis, University Microfilms International, Ann Arbor, 1979.

21. M. Bennoune, 'Impact of colonialism and migration on an Algerian peasant community: a study in socio-economic change', 2 vols., unpublished PhD thesis, University Microfilms International, Ann Arbor, 1976; D. Champault, *Une oasis du Sahara Nord-Occidental: Tabelbala* (CNRS, Paris, 1969); C. Lacoste-Dujardin, *Un village algérien: structures et évolution récente* (Société Nationale d'Edition et de Diffusion, Alger, 1976); J. Lizot, *Metidja: un village algérien de l'Ouarsenis* (Société Nationale d'Edition et de Diffusion, Alger, 1973); N. Zerdoumi, *Enfants d'hier: l'éducation de l'enfant en milieu traditionnel algérien* (Maspero, Paris, 1979); A. Ouitis, *Les contradictions sociales et leur expression symbolique dans le Sétifois* (Société Nationale d'Edition et de Diffusion, Alger, 1977); A. Ouitis, *Possession, magie et prophétie en Algérie* (Arcantère, Paris, 1984); G. Tillion, *Le harem et les cousins* (Seuil, Paris, 1966); P. Bourdieu, *Outline of a theory of practice* (Cambridge University Press, Cambridge, 1977).

22. M. Borrmans, *Statut personnel et famille au Maghreb de 1940 à nos jours* (Mouton, Paris/La Haye, 1977); L.M. Lefèvre, *Recherches sur la condition de la femme kabyle* (Carbonel, Alger, 1939), to name the more well-known examples.

23. Lefèvre, *Recherches sur la condition,* pp. 112-15; M'rabet, *La femme algérienne,* pp. 253-82; M.V. Louis, 'Les Algériennes, la lutte', *Les Temps Modernes,* vol. 39, no. 432-3 (1982) (special issue 'Algérie, espoirs, réalités'), pp. 152-93; 'Code de la famille: loi no. 84-11 du 9 juin 1984', *El*

Moudjahid, 20 and 21 June 1984.

24. See note 17.

25. Gaudry, *La société féminine*, pp. 485ff; A. Christelow, *Muslim law courts and the French colonial state in Algeria* (Princeton University Press, Princeton, 1985), p. 66.

26. Lefèvre, *Recherches sur la condition*, pp. 126-32; F. Peltier, G.H. Bousquet, *Les successions agnatiques mitigées* (Geuthner, Paris, 1935), pp. 147-9; Tillion, *Le harem*, pp. 176-8.

27. Tillion, *Le harem*, pp. 178-9.

28. Goichon, *La vie féminine au Mzab*, vol. 1, pp. 219-48; vol. 2, pp. 1-28; Gaudry, *La femme Chaouia*, pp. 230-79; H. Vandevelde-Daillière, *Femmes algériennes à travers la condition féminine dans le constantinois dépuis l'indépendance* (Office des Publications Universitaires, Alger, 1980), pp. 472-3; S. Andezian, 'Les conduites féminines à la domination masculine au sein d'une confrèrie populaire en Algérie' in A. Blok, H. Driessen (eds), *Cultural dominance in the Mediterranean area* (Department of Anthropology, Catholic University, Nijmegen, 1984), pp. 37-54; Jansen, *Women without men*, pp. 79-104.

29. J. Desparmet, *Coutumes, institutions, croyances des indigènes de l'Algérie* (Carbonel, Alger, 1939).

30. Gaudry, *La société féminine*, p. 210; *La femme Chaouia*, pp. 127ff. Here the *habous* system is said to apply, but this has not been analysed.

31. Goichon, *La vie féminine au Mzab*, vol. 1, pp. 219-48. Based on Goichon's study is: A. Farrag, 'Social control amongst the Mzabite women of Beni-Isguen', *Middle East Studies*, vol. 7, no. 3 (1971), pp. 317-27.

32. Louis, 'Les Algériennes, la lutte'; M'rabet, *La femme algérienne*, pp. 143-65; N. Aïnad-Tabet, 'Participation des Algériennes à la vie du pays' in C. Souriau (ed.), *Femmes et politique*, pp. 235-50.

33. F. Akeb, M. Abdelaziz, 'Algerian women discuss the need for change' in E.W. Fernea (ed.), *Women and the family in the Middle East* (University of Texas, Austin, 1985), pp. 8-26; M. Gadant, 'Fatima, Ouardia, and Malika: contemporary Algerian women' in M. Gadant (ed.), *Women of the Mediterranean* (Zed Press, London/Atlantic Highlands, 1986), pp. 15-46; C. Lacoste-Dujardin, *Dialogues de femmes en ethnologie* (Maspero, Paris, 1977). Most of the women interviewed by these authors live in France.

34. S. Rasmussen, 'Interpreting androgynous women: female ageing and personhood among the Kel Ewey Tuareg', *Ethnology*, vol. 26, no. 1 (1987), pp. 17-30; Jansen, *Women without men*; N. Chellig, 'L'espace sexualisé en Algérie et l'ambiguité du voile féminin', *Actes du colloque national: femmes, féminisme et recherches, Toulouse, Décembre 1982* (AFFER, Toulouse, 1984), pp. 457-62. The autobiography of T. Amrouche, *Histoire de ma vie* (Maspero, Paris, 1979) and M. Garanger's book of photographs, *Femmes algériennes 1960* (Contrejour, Paris, 1983), are also illustrative of the diversity among women.

35. For example F. Benatia, 'Some ideas about women's work in Algeria', *International Social Science Journal*, vol. 32, no. 3 (1980), pp. 464-78; F. Benatia, *Le travail féminin en Algérie* (Société Nationale d'Edition et de Diffusion, Alger, 1970); F. Talahite-Hakiki, 'Femmes et salariat urbain en Algérie: la salarisation bloquée et le nouveau procès de travail domestique', *Critique de l'économie politique*, 17 (1981), pp. 8-39; Vandevelde-Dallière, *Femmes algériennes*; or all the articles in *Actes des journées d'étude et de réflexion sur les femmes algériennes, 3-4-5 et 6 mai 1980* (Centre de Documentation des Sciences Humaines, Oran, 1980).

36. The Frantz Fanon thesis is discussed by D.C. Gordon, *Women of Algeria: an essay on change* (Harvard University Press, Cambridge, 1968), pp. 57-60.

37. Gadant, 'Les femmes, la famille', p. 27.

38. Goichon, *La vie féminine au Mzab*, pp. 1, 8.

39. Minces, 'Women in Algeria', pp. 165-6.

40. R. Descloitres, L. Debzi, 'Système de parenté et structures familiales en Algérie', *Annuaire de l'Afrique du Nord*, vol. 2 (1963), pp. 23-50, esp. 23.

41. Gaudry, *La société féminine*, pp. 223-313.

42. Goichon, *La vie féminine au Mzab*, vol. 1, pp. xiii, 12.

43. Gordon, *Women of Algeria*.

44. Moors, 'Feministische wetenschap', p. 59.

45. E. Delacroix, 'Femmes d'Alger', painting 1832.

46. M. Alloula, *Le harem colonial* (Slatkine, Genève/Paris, 1981).

47. For example E. Dermenghem, *Le pays d'Abel* (Gallimard, Paris, 1967); P. Potier, *Considérations sur la prostitution musulmane en Algérie* (Foulon, Paris, 1955); Alloula, *Le harem colonial*; A. Bouhdiba, *La sexualité en Islam* (Presses Universitaires de France, Paris, 1975).

Postscript

When the above contribution was already at press, a relevant article appeared by Marnia Lazreg entitled 'Feminism and difference: the perils of writing as a woman on women in Algeria', *Feminist Studies*, vol. 14, no. 1 (1988), pp. 81-107. Although our articles were conceived independently from each other and thus treat the topic from different perspectives, they share some remarkingly similar conclusions.

Notes on contributors with selected bibliographies

Margot Badran (1936) received her PhD from Oxford University. Her field is women's studies and history, specialising in the Middle East. She is a fellow of the Institute for Research in History in New York, and is at present a Fulbright Fellow in Egypt, engaged in research on Egyptian women feminists and fundamentalists 1930-60.

Publications:

Huda Sha'rawi, *Harem years: the memoirs of an Egyptian feminist,* intr. and transl. by Margot Badran (Virago Press, London, 1986).

Margot Badran, 'Islam, patriarchy and feminism in the Middle East', *Trends in History,* vol. 4, no. 1 (1985).

Margot Badran, 'Dual liberation: feminism and nationalism in Egypt 1880-1925', *Feminist Issues* (1987).

Lucia Bergamasco (1947) received an Italian doctorate from the University of Venice and a French one from the Ecole des Hautes Etudes en Sciences Sociales in Paris. She is doing research on a grant from the Italian government. Her work focuses on social history, especially the American colonial period, and lately cultural history and anthropology. She resides in France.

Publications:

Lucia Bergamasco, 'La naissance et la petite enfance en Nouvelle Angleterre à l'époque coloniale', *Revue d'Histoire Moderne et Contemporaine,* 31 (1984)

Lucia Bergamasco, 'Women's history e periodo coloniale: quattro studi recenti', *Memoria, Rivista di Storia delle Donne,* 7 (1983).

Lucia Bergamasco, 'Amitié, amour et spiritualité dans la Nouvelle Angleterre du XVIIIe siècle: l'expérience d'Esther Burr et Sarah Prince', *Annales ESC*, vol. 41, no. 2 (1986).

Mineke Bosch (1954) studied history at the University of Groningen. She works as a research assistant at the Erasmus University in Rotterdam to write a comparative history of academic women in the Netherlands. Her other research interests include lesbian history, collecting and preserving women's archives, personal documents of women and questions of philosophy of history in relation to women's history.

Publications:

Mineke Bosch, Annemarie Kloosterman, *Lieve Dr. Jacobs: brieven uit de Wereldbond voor Vrouwenkiesrecht 1902-1942* (Feministische Uitgeverij Sara, Amsterdam, 1985).

Mineke Bosch, 'Women's culture in women's history: historical notion or feminist vision?' in Maaike Meijer, Jetty Schaap (eds), *Historiography of women's cultural traditions* (Foris Publications, Dordrecht, the Netherlands and Providence, USA, 1987).

Mineke Bosch, 'A woman's life in a soapbox: the collection of egodocuments of women in the Internationaal Archief voor de Vrouwenbeweging in Amsterdam', *History Workshop Journal*, 24 (1987).

Anna Clark (1957) went to Radcliffe College and the University of Essex. For Rutgers University she wrote a PhD thesis on popular morality and the construction of gender in London 1770-1845. The article in this volume is part of a larger work called 'The struggle for the breeches: gender and the making of the London working class'. She is a lecturer in history at the University of North Carolina at Charlotte.

Publications:

Anna Clark, *Women's silence, men's violence: sexual assault in England 1770-1845* (Pandora, London, 1987).

Anna Clark, 'The politics of seduction in English popular culture 1748-1848' in Jean Radford (ed.), *The progress of romance* (Routledge & Kegan Paul, London, 1986).

Annelies van Gijsen (1953) studied Dutch language and literature at the Rijksuniversiteit Utrecht after she finished teachers' training college. Her thesis was on medieval astrology and its place in medieval Dutch fiction. She teaches Dutch to foreigners in Assen while preparing her PhD on Colijn van Rijsseles 'Spiegel der minnen'.
Publications:
Annelies van Gijsen, 'De "Spiegel der minnen": sterren en strekking', *Jaarboek de Fonteine*, XXXIV (1984).

Marijke Gijswijt-Hofstra (1940) graduated in sociology from the University of Amsterdam, where she is at present teaching historical sociology and early modern history in the Department of History.
Publications:
Marijke Gijswijt-Hofstra, *Wijkplaatsen voor vervolgden: asielverlening in Culemborg, Vianen, Buren, Leerdam en IJsselstein van de 16e tot eind 18e eeuw* (De Bataafsche Leeuw, Dieren, 1984).
Willem de Blécourt, Marijke Gijswijt-Hofstra (eds), 'Kwade mensen: toverij in Nederland', special issue of *Volkskundig Bulletin*, 12, 1 (1986).
Willem Frijhoff, Marijke Gijswijt-Hofstra (eds), *Nederland betoverd: toverij en hekserij van de 14e tot in de 20e eeuw* (De Bataafsche Leeuw, Amsterdam, 1987).

Maria Grever (1953) is a lecturer in women's history at the University of Nijmegen. She is conducting research on pioneers of Dutch historiography of women's history. She is also involved in developing final secondary-school exams on women's history for 1990.
Publications:
Maria Grever, 'Het verborgen continent: een historiografische verkenning van vrouwengeschiedenis in Nederland', *Tijdschrift voor Sociale Geschiedenis*, 3 (1986).
Maria Grever, 'Het vrouwelijk oculair: een historische beschouwing van vrouwengeschiedenis in de V.S. en West-Europa', *DIGO*, 4 (1987).

Helga Grubitzsch (1943) graduated in romance philology, Latin and psychology. After her doctorate, she was employed as a lecturer at the University of Bremen in different capacities, the most recent of them being lecturer in women's literature and social history.
Publications:
Helga Grubitzsch, Loretta Lagpacan, *'Freiheit für die Frauen - Freiheit für das Volk!': sozialistische Frauen in Frankreich 1830-1848* (Syndikat, Frankfurt-am-Main, 1980).
Hannelore Cyrus, Elke Haarbusch, Helga Grubitzsch (eds), *Grenzgängerinnen: revolutionäre Frauen im 18. und 19. Jahrhundert* (Schwann, Düsseldorf, 1985).

Willy Jansen (1950) received her PhD from the University of Nijmegen. As an anthropologist, she has done field work on the cultural and economic positions of widows and divorcees in Algeria. At present she teaches women's studies at the University of Nijmegen.
Publications:
Willy Jansen (ed.), *Lokale islam* (Coutinho, Muiderberg, 1986).
Willy Jansen, *Women without men: gender and marginality in an Algerian town* (Brill, Leiden, 1987).

Anne Laurence (1949) studied history and politics at the University of York, and she received her PhD from Oxford University. She is employed as a lecturer at the Open University and teaches various literary and historical subjects, including her speciality, early modern England.
Publications:
Anne Laurence, 'Parliamentary army chaplains: pay and preaching' in F. Heal, R. O'Day (eds), *Princes and paupers* (Leicester University Press, Leicester, 1981).
Anne Laurence, 'Daniel Defoe and imprisonment for debt', *Text and Context,* I (1986).
Anne Laurence, *Parliamentary army chaplains 1642-1651,* (Royal Historical Society, forthcoming).

Selma Leydesdorff (1949) works as an historian in the Department of Social Sciences at the University of Amsterdam. She has published on methodological issues regarding women's history and on

the position of women in the process of Dutch industrialisation. Her major research interests include oral history and the role of memory. Her latest study considers the effects of the Second World War on the memory of the Jewish proletarian community of Amsterdam.
Publications:
Selma Leydesdorff, *Verborgen arbeid, vergeten arbeid: een verkenning in de geschiedenis van de vrouwenarbeid rond 1900* (Van Gorcum, Assen/ Amsterdam, 1977)
Selma Leydesdorff, *Wij hebben als mens geleefd: het Joodse proletariaat van Amsterdam 1900-1940* (De Bezige Bij, Amsterdam, 1987).
Selma Leydesdorff, 'The screen of nostalgia: oral history and the ordeal of working-class Jews in Amsterdam', *International Journal of Oral History*, 7 (1986).

Alison Oram (1956) received a BA in Humanities from Bristol Polytechnic and an MSc degree from Bristol University. She works as a tutor-organiser for the London District Workers' Educational Association and teaches courses in feminist and lesbian history at London University in the Department of Extra-Mural Studies. She is currently preparing a book on women teachers and twentieth-century feminism.
Publications:
Alison Oram, 'Serving two masters? The introduction of a marriage bar in teaching in the 1920s', in London Feminist History Group (eds), *The sexual dynamics of history* (Pluto Press, London, 1983).
Alison Oram, 'Inequalities in the teaching profession: the effects on teachers and pupils' in Felicity Hunt (ed.), *Lessons for life: the schooling of girls and women 1850-1950* (Basil Blackwell, Oxford, 1987).
Alison Oram, '"Sex Antagonism" in the teaching profession: equal pay and the marriage bar 1910-1939' in G. Weiner, M. Arnot (eds), *Gender and the politics of schooling* (Hutchinson, London, 1987).

Jo Anne Preston (1943) lectures on sociology and women's studies at the University of Southern Maine. She is currently a visiting scholar at the Henry A. Murray Center: A Center for the Study of Lives, in Cambridge, Mass., where she is investigating the determinants of women's wages in the early New England textile industry.

The article in this volume is derived from her recently completed study on the feminisation of school-teaching in nineteenth-century New England.
Publications:
Jo Anne Preston, 'To learn me the whole of the trade: conflict between a female apprentice and merchant tailor', *Labor History* (1983).
Jo Anne Preston, 'Learning a trade in industrializing New England: Mary and Hannah Adams' expedition to Nashua, New Hampshire, 1833-1834', *Historical New Hampshire* (1984).
Jo Anne Preston, 'Millgirl narratives: representations of gender and class in nineteenth-century Lowell', *Life Stories/Récits de Vie*, 3 (1987).

Londa Schiebinger (1952) obtained her PhD in history at Harvard University. She teaches European history at the University of Georgia and is currently finishing a book on the position of women in the origins of modern science.
Publications:
Londa Schiebinger, 'The history and philosophy of women in science: a review essay' in Jean O'Barr, Sandra Harding (eds), *Sex and scientific inquiry* (University of Chicago Press, Chicago, 1987).
Londa Schiebinger, 'Skeletons in the closet: the first illustrations of the female skeleton in eighteenth-century anatomy' in Catherine Gallagher, Thomas Laqueur (eds), *The making of the modern body: sexuality and the society in the nineteenth century* (University of California Press, Berkeley, 1987).
Londa Schiebinger, 'Margaret Cavendish: natural philosopher' in Mary Ellen Waithe (ed.), *A history of women philosophers*, 3 (Nijhoff, Dordrecht, 1988).

Päivi Setälä (1943) wrote a dissertation on Roman brick stamps for the University of Helsinki, where she is currently employed as a lecturer in general history.
Publications:
Päivi Setälä, *Private domini in Roman brick stamps of the Empire: a historical and prosopographical study of landowners in the district of Rome*, Annales Academiae Scientiarum Fennicae, Diss. Hum. Litt. 10 (Helsinki, 1977).

Päivi Setälä, 'New aspects of the history of the family in Antiquity', *Scandinavian Journal of History*, 12 (1987).

Lydia Sklevicky (1952) graduated in sociology and ethnology from the University of Zagreb with a thesis on women and power. She is a research fellow at the Institute for the History of the Workers' Movement of Croatia, where she is preparing her PhD thesis on women in post-revolutionary Yugoslavia.
Publications:
Lydia Sklevicky (ed.), *Cultivating the dialogue: woman and society* (Biblioteka Revije za Sociologiju, Zagreb, 1987)

Amy Swerdlow (1923) obtained a BA at New York University, an MA in women's history at Sarah Lawrence College, and received her doctorate from Rutgers University. She is at present employed as director of the graduate programme in women's history and lecturer in US and women's history at Sarah Lawrence College. She has been a peace activist since the 1960s and was one of the founders of Women Strike for Peace.
Publications:
Hanna Lessinger, Amy Swerdlow (eds), *Class, race, sex: the dynamics of control* (G.K. Hall, Boston, 1983).
Amy Swerdlow (ed. and contributor), *Households and kin: families in flux* (Feminist Press/McGraw-Hill, New York, 1983).
Amy Swerdlow, *The politics of motherhood: Women Strike for Peace 1961-1973* (University of Chicago Press, Chicago, forthcoming).

Index

Abdou, Mohamad 295
'Abduh, Shaikh Muhammad 159
Abzug, Bella 123
academic status (women's history) 13-14
act of purgation 84
Acta Eruditorum 26
activism, public (Egypt) 165-6
Adams, Hannah 179
Addams, Jane 113
adolescence (psychological disorders) 205,206,207-9
adultery 303,304
Aelders, Etta Palm d' 282
Afer, Cn. Domitius 66
After XXV years (Naber) 259
agriculture (Egypt) 157
Aldridge, Mary Louisa 178,179-80
Algeria 12
    ethnocentrism study 289-306
Algérie des anthropologues, L' (Vatin) 291
'Ali, Muhammad 157
Allen, Maude 189
altered consciousness 204-5
America through women's eyes (Beard) 134
Amin, Qasim 154,156,159,163,164,166
amour, L' (Michelet) 273,274,275
Amussen, Susan Dwyer 231
anachronism 289
Andreas Capellanus 223,227
androcentric historiography:
    definition 272-3;
    Les femmes de la Révolution 273,274-83;
    Michelet 273-4;
    social conditions 283-6
Annales School 252
Anthony, Lucy E. 136-7,138
Anthony, Susan B. 135,136-7,138,146
anthropology 14;
    Algerian study 289-306

Anti-Fascist Women's Front 93,94-106
anti-feminism 186;
economics and 190-2
antiquity 61-2,64,67
anti-suffragists 147
Antonia, Iunia 68
Arabs 293-5,299
Arnauld, Angélique 258
Arnold, Christopher 23-4
arte honeste amandi, De (Andreas Capellanus) 223
aspirations, occupational choice and 177-80
Association of Assistant Mistresses 188
astronomy (women's role) 21;
craft tradition 22-5;
Winkelmann's achievements 25-7;
Winkelmann's attempts to enter Academy 27-33
Auclert, Hubertine 295
Augspurg, Anita 142,147
Augustine, Saint 79
Aurelius, Emperor Marcus 66
Avery, Rachel Foster 136-7,141

Babović, Cana 100
Badger, Susan 238
Baker, Russell 119
Bakhuizen van den Brink, R.C. 253,254
Balch, Emily 113
Baltimore Sun 114
bawdy-houses 243-5
Beard, Mary 134
Beauvoir, Simone de 61-2,71
Beecher, Catherine 176
Beijerman, H. 255
Bekker, Balthasar 83
Bennoune, M. 297
Bentley, Eric 119
Berber women 294,296-7
Berlin Academy 22,27-33
Bernard, Henry 174,175,176
Berus, Anka 98
bewitchment 76,79
bigamy 233
Birmingham Feminist History Group 123

birth control 193-4
Blague, Mrs 211
bleaching industry of Haarlem, The (Greup-Roldanus) 261
Blenheim, Sally 238
bonds of womanhood, The (Cott) 133
Book, Hannah 241
Bosboom-Toussaint, Johannes 253,257
Bosboom-Toussaint, Geertruida 252-8,265-6
Boston Evening Post 40,49
Boston Gazette 51
Bourdieu, P. 297
brick stamps 64-71 *passim*
Bright-Maclaren, Priscilla 258
Britain:
    psychological disorders 203-17;
    sexual reputation 231-45;
    spinster teachers 183-200
brothels 243-5
Browne, Stella 194
Bugéja, Marie 295
Buhle, MariJo 133-4
Burr, Aaron 53
Burr, Esther 39,40,48-52,53
Butler, Josephine 258

calendar-making 25,27-31 *passim*
Carey, Mary 209
Cartwright, John 240
Cartwright, Rebecca 240
catechism explanations 82-3
Catt, Carrie C. 131,135,144;
    letters to Aletta Jacobs 136,138-43;
    on suffragism 145-6;
    universal sisterhood 147-8
Célarié, Henriette 295
celibacy 184,193,194,198-9
Champault, D. 297
chastity 232,233,234
child-bearing 205,206,209-11,216
chlorosis 208
Chrétien de Troyes 222
Christelow, A. 299
Christianity 166

Chronological History of New England 40
church courts 239-40,245
cities (of Egypt) 157-8
class:
Egyptian society 154,156,158-9,160-3,166;
Roman society 67,70,71;
sexual reputation and 232-45
Cohn, N. 88
Cold War 112,116
Cole, Juan 155
collective action 243-5
collective feminist experience 162-5
Collins, Harriet 237
Colman, Benjamin 40,41-2,43,45-7
Colman, Jane 39-48,55
colonialism 292,294,301,302
Colquehoun, Patrick 232
comet (Winkelmann's discovery) 25-6
Committee for a Sane Nuclear Policy 112,114
Commodus, Emperor 68
common-law wives 232-3,242
communism (USA attitudes) 112,113,114,116,118
Communist Party:
United States 118;
Yugoslavia 93-4,95,100,102
compassion (women united) 235-8
Comte, Auguste 283
Condorcet, M.J.A. de 282
Condorcet, Mme de 277
Cook, Blanche W. 133
Corday, Charlotte 276
Cornificia, Anna 66
Corrèze, F. 295
Cott, Nancy 133-4,250
Cottrell, Ann 236
courtly love 222-3,224,225,227
craft traditions (astronomy) 22-5
Crichton-Miller, H. 188
Crispinilla, Calvia 63
cultural imperialism 305-6
culture:
ethnocentrism (Algeria) 289-306;
female (uses) 109-24 *passim*;

Jewish 16-17,19;
politics and 133-4;
suffrage and 145-7;
tradition and 292-3,301-3;
universal sisterhood 133,147-8;
women's historiography and (Dutch) 250-3
Cunitz, Maria 25

Danton, G.J. 277,280
Danton, Sarah 240
Daumas, M. 292,294
Davis, Nathalie Z. 249
Dawson, Agnes 198
Dean, Arthur 120
death, motherhood and 275
defamation cases 239-40,242
Delacroix, E. 304
Delrio, Martinus 80
Democratic Party (USA) 114
Denny, Deborah 48
des Vignoles, A. 31
Descloitre, R. 302
Desmoulins, Lucile 277,278
Desparmet, J. 300
Detroit Free Press 119
deuxième sexe, Le (Beauvoir) 61-2
Devil's pact 80-1,82,90
Devout Meditations 40
diaries 205,214
Digby, Sir Kenneth 211
Dinnerstein, Dorothy 113
discourse theory 96-7,106
divorce 63,159;
Algeria 298,299;
law reform (Britain) 193,194
dowry 62,63
dualism (in women's image) 226-7
Dutch women's historiography 249-66
Dutch Women's Suffrage Association 143

economic independence 19,20
economic opportunities (Imperial Rome):
antiquity studies 61-2;

brick stamps 64-5;
economic activity 67-9;
economic opportunities 69-70;
influence of women 70-2;
land owners 65-7;
law, status and 62-4
economics of teaching 186,190-2,199-200
Edes, Benjamin 51
education:
Egypt 161,162,163-4,166;
of Jane Colman 39,41-6;
of Sarah Prince 39,41-2,48-9;
Yugoslavia 98,100;
see also schools; teaching
Egypt (origins of feminism):
awareness sources 160-2;
collective experience 162-5;
nineteenth-century context 153,157-60;
public activism 165-6;
women's feminism/history 153-7,166-7
Egyptian Feminist Union 156
Egyptian University 163-4
Egyptiens, Les (Amin) 159
Eimmart, Georg 24,30
Elias, N. 285
Ellis, Havelock 184,193
emancipation process (Yugoslavia) 93-106
Emile (Rousseau) 275
employment aspirations 171-80
enchanted world, The (Bekker) 83
endogamy 299
endowment system 299
ethnocentrism 15
ethnocentrism (Algerian study):
characteristics 292-3;
conceptual problems 289-91;
idealist bias 292,298-301;
inferiority symbols 292,293-7;
inherent 304-6;
methods and sources 291;
sexuality (uncontrolled) 293,303-4;
tradition and 292-3,303
Eumachia 69

'Eurocentric' historiography 11-12
Europe:
suffragism 135,143,145-7;
suffragism (letters) 143-5;
see also Britain; France; French Revolution; Italy; Netherlands
Evens, Bet 237

Fabar, M. 294
Fahmi, Murqus 159
false consciousness 15,16
family:
privatisation 32;
Roman 63-4, 65-6,71;
wage 191
Family Code (Algeria) 298,300
Fanon, Frantz 12,301
fascism 11
Fatah, Al (journal) 161
Fatah al Sharq 161
Fauchet, Abbé 282
Faustina, Anna Fundania 66
Fawwaz, Zainab 161
Fazil, Princess Nazil 163
fear 209-10,216
'female' qualities 256,285
femininity 19-20;
appropriateness of teaching 171-7
feminism 4;
Algeria 295-6,298,301,305;
Arab 295;
Bosboom-Toussaint's 255-7;
Egypt 153-67;
international context 131-48;
Naber's 258-60,265,266;
United States 109-10,118-24;
Yugoslavia 93,94
feminist consciousness 156-7,158,161
feminist historians 10,11-13,133-5
feminist response to stigma 192-9
Feminist Studies (journal) 133
femme, La (Michelet) 273,274,275
femmes de la Révolution, Les (Michelet) 273,274-83

Figlinae Publilianae 68-9
Fishcock, Martha 215
Fisher, Elsie 197,199
Fontanus, Nicolas 210
Forman, Simon 208,211,214
Foster, Kate 171,178
Fourier, C. 284
France 11,271-86
freedom 15-16
French Revolution 11,271-86
friendship:
gossipy letters 131-48;
and lesbian relationships 184-5,188-90;
Prince-Burr 39,48;
women united 235-8,242-3
frigidity 189-90
Froud, Ethel 197-9
Fruin, R. 83,255

Gastineau, B. 294,304
Gaudry, M. 296-7,299-300,302
Gay, Nellie 177
gender hierarchy 305-6
gender ideology 171-80,274
Gerritsen, Professor 223
Gids, De (journal) 253,265
Gill, John 51
Gill, Moses 51,53
Gilman, Charlotte Perkins 144
Godwin, William 232
Goichon, A.M. 296-7,299,300,302
Gordon, D.C. 303
gossip (and sexual reputation) 231-4;
collective action 243-5;
friendship/compassion (women united) 235-8;
insult (women divided) 238-43
Gossip (Spacks) 132
gossipy letters:
from Aletta Jacobs 143-5;
to Aletta Jacobs 131,136-43;
suffragism 134,145-7;
universal sisterhood 133-5,147-8
Gratilla, Cusinia 66
Great Awakening 40

Greek women 61
green-sickness 206,208-9,216
Greup, Jan Regtdoorzee 261-2
Greup-Roldanus, Sini 252,260-6 *passim*
Guardian Society 244-5
Guide, The (journal) 253,265
guild traditions 22-5,29-30

Haarlemmer bleekerijen, De (Greup-Roldanus) 261
habous system 299
Hague peace conference, the 135,147,148
Hall, Radclyffe 189
Hamilton, Alice 113
Hamilton, Cicely 193
Hammer of witches (Institoris and Sprenger) 76,85
Handleiding bij het kunstnaaldwerk (Rechlindis) 258
harem system 158-61,163-6,303,304
Harrison, Elizabeth 242-3
Hashim, Labiba 161,163
Hay, Mary Garrett 138-9,140
Heidelberg catechism 82-3
Hellenistic women 61
Henley, Margaret 243
heterosexuality 184,185,188,194,199,200
Hevelius, Johannes 24,25,30
Heymann, Lida Gustava 147
Hicks, Elizabeth 237
historiography 11;
    absent/forgotten issues 19-20;
    androcentric *see* androcentric historiography;
    Dutch women's *see* women's historiography, Dutch (origins);
    feminist 10,11-13,133-5
history *see* women's history; women's history (writing of)
Hoffman, Johann Heinrich 29
Holtby, Winifred 194
home industries 18
homosexuality 184-5,188-90,193,199
Hopkins, M. 87
Horton, Mr 242
House Committee on Un-American Activities 118-19,123
house of Lauernesse, The (Bosboom-Toussaint) 253-4
Hughes, Elizabeth 236

huis Lauernesse, Het (Bosboom-Toussaint) 253-4
Huizinga, J. 83
humeuren in de straat der weduwen, De (Greup-Roldanus) 262-3
humoral pathology 203-4,206,217
Husain, Taha 164
hysteric diseases 206,216

Ibadites 299,302
idealist bias 292,298-301
identification 9-10;
    changes 14-16;
ideology 17,171-80
images of women 273,283-6
inequality 226-7;
    Algeria 292,298-301,305
infanticide 206-7,212-14,217
inferiority symbols 292,293-7
inheritance 62,63,65-6,70,71,298,299,300
Institoris 80
insult (women divided) 238-43
integrated emancipation 93-106
International Archives for the Women's Movement 131,260,261
International Conference on Women's History 1,9-10,39,289
International Council of Women 134,135,147
International Press Office 141
International Women's Suffrage Alliance 131,135
Isaurica, Flavia Seia 67
Islam 12;
    Algeria 293-4,299-303
    Egypt 156,158-9,165,166
Italy 11

Jablonski, J. 27-8
Jacobine Club 282
Jacobs, Aletta 135,146,148;
    letters from 143-5;
    letters to 131,136-43
Jacobs, Gerritsen 135
Jansenist movement 258
Jervoise, E. 240
Jewish culture 16-17,19
Jonge, J.C. de 254
Jorden, Edward 210-11

Josselin, Ralph 210
Journey towards freedom (Schreiber) 147
Jus Suffragii (journal) 141

Kabyle women 294,298
Karel, Duke of Egmond 78
Keddie, N.R. 292
Kennedy, John F. 111
Khruschev, Nikita 111
Kirch, Christfried 31
Kirch, Gottfried 22,24-6,27,28,30,32
Kitchings, William 240
Kloosterman, Annemarie 131
Kolb, Peter 27
Kramers, Martina 136,141-2,143,144-5
Krosigk, Baron von 30
Krüsemann, Mina 255

La Wisp 116-17,121
labour (female aspirations) 171-80
Lacoste-Dujardin, C. 297
Lady Cromer Society 164
land ownership 64,65-7,71
Larner, C. 84,88
Latin America 12
Laughing their way (Beard) 134
League of Women Voters 112,114,120
Lefèvre, L.M. 298
Leibniz, Gottfried 22,26-7,28-9
Leicester, Earl of 254-5
Les Amis de la Loi (society) 283
lesbianism 184-5,188-90,193,199
letters *see* gossipy letters
Leycestercyclus (Bosboom-Toussaint) 254-5
Lex Voconia 62
Liberation of the woman (Amin) 159,164
Lieve Dr. Jacobs (Bosch and Kloosterman) 131
literature (medieval) 221-7
Lizot, J. 297
London (sexual reputation) 231-45
London Consistory Court 239,245
Los Angeles Mirror 111
Louis, M.V. 298

love:
courtly 222-3,224,225,227;
in medieval literature 222-7;
womanly (Michelet's image) 275-80
Lucas, Philippe 291,292,294
Lucilla, Domitia 66

Macaulay, Catharine 51
Macdonald, Michael 215
machismo 12
magic 76,79,81,82-3
Majoor Frans (Bosboom-Toussaint) 256
maleficium 76,79,80-1,86,87
Malleus maleficarum (Institoris and Sprenger) 76,80,85,89-90
Mann, Horace 174-5,176,178
Manual on art needlework (Rechlindis) 258
Manus, Rosa 131,258
Mar'a fi al Sharq, Al (Fahmi) 159
maraboutism 299
Marat, J.P. 276
Marcia (court hearing) 70
marianismo 12
marriage (Roman law) 62,63,70,71
Marriage Act, Lord Hardwicke's (1753) 233
Marriage as a trade (Hamilton) 193
marriage bar 184,185,191,197-8
Massachusetts State School 174, 178-9
maternal instinct 187,196,197
maternalism 109,110-11,113-15,120-3
Mather, Cotton 41
media coverage (WSP) 115-16,119,120-1
medieval literature:
courtly love 222-3,224,225,227;
images of women 226-7;
medieval society and 221-2;
Narcissus and Pygmalion 224-6
Mee, Alice 215
Meitner, Lise 33
Mejonkvrouwe de Mauléon (Bosboom-Toussaint) 256,258
melancholy 204,205-6,208-11 *passim*
Memo 121
Memoirs of the life and death of the pious and ingenious Mrs. Jane Turell 39-40,43-8 *passim*

Memoria 11
men: androcentric historiography *see* androcentric historiography;
feminism of 154,155,159,163,167;
ideology, female aspirations and 171-80;
manly qualities 281-2;
men's studies 251;
sexuality (uncontrolled) 293,303-4;
witches 88,89-90
mentalities (study of) 16
Méricourt, Théroigne de 271,283
Metamorphoses (Ovid) 224,225
Michelet, Jules:
image of women 271,273-86;
Les femmes de la Révolution 273,274-83
Milady of Mauléon (Bosboom-Toussaint) 256
Minces, J. 302
misogyny 85,88-9,294,296
'mixed love' 227
moods in widow's lane, The (Greup-Roldanus) 262-3
morality, sexual reputation and 232-45
Moreau, Th. 274
Morris, P. 231
Morris, Polly 240
Morrison, Miss 197,198,199
Mortimer, Ann 213
mother-fits 206,210-11
motherhood, death and 275
Mozabites 302
M'rabet, F. 295-6,298
Muqtatf, Al (journal) 165
murder, infanticide as 212-14
Musa, Nabawiyya 161-2,163

Na XXV jaren (Naber) 259
Nabarawi, Saiza 161,165
Naber, Johanna 252,257-60,265-6
Napier, Richard 210,214
Napoleonic Wars 233,234,244
Narcissus 224-6
Nasif, Malak Hifni 161,162,163,165
National American Woman Suffrage Alliance 135-6,138,139,140-3
National Assembly (France) 271,282
National Association of Schoolmasters 186,190,191-2

National Liberation Movement 94
National Union of Societies for Equal Citizenship 194
National Union of Teachers 185,191,193,195
National Union of Women Teachers 186,193,195-9
nationalism 153,155-6,164-7 *passim*
Nawfal, Hind 161
Nazism 11
Neale, Mr 242
Necker, M. 277
neo-Malthusianism 143
Netherlands 11-12;
    witchcraft 75-90;
    women's historiography 249-66
Nettement 274
New York Times 119
Newsweek 115
Nijhoff, I.A. 254
nineteenth-century Egypt 153,157-60
Nowlan, Mary 240
nuclear arms 111,112,114-24 *passim*

occupational choice 177-80
Of our great-aunts and aunts (Naber) 258
oppression 11,15,16,17
oral histories 17,155
orchidee van 5a, De (Greup-Roldanus) 261
organisational model (AWF) 95,98-100,103-5
Orientalism (Said) 291,292
Ottoman Empire 157
Ouitis, A. 297
Ovid, *Metamorphoses* 224

pacifism 109-24
Palais de Nations 120
Pankhurst, Christabel 193,194
Papist superstition 82,83
Parallel lives (Rose) 132
Parent-Teacher Associations 114,121
Paris, Gaston 222
Parker, Mary 236
Parsons, D.H. 297
participatory democracy 118
Pascal, Blaise 258

passéisme 292
passivity 15,211
patriarchal authority 191;
androcentric historiography 272,273;
Egypt 153,154,156,158,163,165-7
patriotism 276-7
Pechey, John 205-6,210
Peck, Mary Gray 145
People's Government 94,97-100 *passim*
Peter the Great 31
peuple, Le (Michelet) 275
Philipp, Thomas 156
pica 208,210
Pierce, Julia 178,179
Pietism 40,50
pity 275-6
Pisan, Christine de 21,23
Place, Francis 234,236
Plebeian morality 232-45
politics:
culture and 133-4;
of historiography 12-13;
suffrage and 138;
women's history 9-20
polygamy 159,162,298,303
polygyny 303,304
'Pont' 30
Pont, Margaretha Maclaine 255,259-60
Popular Front 94,97,99-100,102-3
Posthumus, N. 261,262
Posthumus-van der Goot, Willemijn 258
premarital sex 233,237
prêtre, de la femme, de la famille, Du (Michelet) 275
Prince, Deborah 49
Prince, Mercy 49
Prince, Sarah 39,40-2,48-54,55-6
Prince, Thomas 40,41-2,48,53
Procula, Iulia 66
property rights 62,63,65-6,69-70
prosperity 62,63,68-72 *passim*
prostitution 144;
friendships within 235-8,242-3;
sexual reputation and 231-45

Protestants (Dutch) 253-4,256,257
Proudhon, Pierre Joseph 284
psychological disorders:
adolescence 205,206,207-9;
child-bearing 205,206,209-11;
descriptions 203-4;
infanticide 206-7,212-14;
source materials 205-7;
suicide 206-7,214-16
puerperal psychosis 212,213
'pure love' 227
purgation, act of 84
Pygmalion 224-6

Quadratilla, Asinia 66
Quartilla, Neratia 66
Quintilla, Pedania 66
Quran 294,298,299,300,301

Rathbone, Eleanor 194
Rea, Mr and Mrs 242-3
religion:
attitudes to witchcraft 81-4;
of Bosboom-Toussaint 253-4,256,265;
church courts 239-40,245;
of Colman 40-8 *passim*;
feminism and 153,156,159,165-7;
of Naber 257,258;
of Prince 40-1,49-54;
psychological disorders and 203-5,207,214;
see also Islam; Pietism; Protestants (Dutch); Réveil
Rendall, Jane 153
resistance-oppression dichotomy 15,16
Réveil 253,256,258
Richardson, Samuel 50
Robespierre, Maximilien Marie Isodore de 279-80
Roermond panic 77
Roland, Mme 277,278
Roman law 62-4
Roman de la rose 224,225
Roman van Heinrich en Margriete van Limborch 224-5
Rome *see* economic opportunities (Imperial Rome)
Romein-Verschoor, Annie 255-6

Rose, Phyllis 132
Ross, Alexander 240
Rossiter, Margaret 25
Rousseau, Jean-Jacques 275
Royal Academy (Berlin) 22,27-33
Rushdi, Eugénie Le Brun 162
Rushdi, Husain 162
Russell, Dora 194
Rust, Richard 174,176,178

Sabina, Iunia 68
sacrifice 278-9,280,281,286
Sade, Marquis de 279
Said, Edward 291-2
salons (in Egypt) 162-3
SANE Committee 112,114
Sarruf, Rahma 164-5
Sayyid, Ahmad Lufti Al 164
Scheltema, Jacobus 75
Schirmacher, Käthe 142
schools:
    spinster teachers 183-200;
    teaching in New England 171-80;
    see also education
Schreiber, Adele 147
Schuurman, Anna Maria van 41
Schwimmer Rosika 131,135-6,146;
    letters 143-5
science (women's role) 21-33
scolding 77
Scully, Mary 236
self-perception 173,180
self-starvation 208
sensuality 280,285-6
'serious gossip' 132,138
Severa, Aemilia 68
'sex cynicism' 146
sexology 184,185,186-90,192,193,199-200
sexual division of labour 110,114,234,283-4
sexual honour 231,233,235
sexual intercourse (as therapy) 205-6
sexual reforms 193-4

sexual reputation (in London) 231-4;
collective action 243-5;
women divided 238-43;
women united 235-8
sexuality:
uncontrolled 293,303-4;
see also heterosexuality; lesbianism
Sha'rawi, Huda 154-5,160-1,162-3,165
Sharpe, J.A. 213,231
Shaw, Anna Howard 131,133,135,144,146,148;
letters to Aletta Jacobs 136-9,140-1,143
slander 77,81,84,86
Sleeford, Mary Ann 237
'sleeping children' 299
Smith, Aurelia 177
Smith, Bonnie 134,249,252
Smith-Rosenberg,Carroll 133,250
social class *see* class
social conditions 275,283-6
social context (women's history) 16-19
socialism 145;
Yugoslavia 96,98,101,102,104,106
sorcery 76,79,80-1,86,87
Spacks, Patricia Meyer 132,135,145
Spender, Dale 251
spinster teachers (attacks on):
anti-feminism and economics 183,190-2;
feminist response 192-9;
negative image 183-6;
sexology and 184,186-90,199,200
spiritual life *see* religion
Spiritual Meditations 50,54
Sprenger, J. 80
Stackpole, Mary 178
Stadholder family 259
Staël, Madame de 277
Stalin, Joseph 101
Stanton, Elizabeth Cady 134,146
state school committees 173-7,180
status, Roman law and 62-4
Stearne, J. 87
still-birth 213
Stone, I.F. 121

Stopes, Marie 194
strength (women's role) 281-2
structural vulnerability 85-6,87
student-teacher relations 174-5,179-80
Students for a Democratic Society 118
Suetonius 71
suffocation of the womb 206,210-11,216
suffragism 134;
    Europe 135,143,145-7;
    teachers and 195;
    United States 135,136,138-48 *passim*
suicide 206-7,209,214-16,217
Sym, John 214
Symcotts, John 211

Tacitus 63,71
Tahrir al Mar'a (Amin) 154
Taimuriyya, 'Aisha 160
Tanner, Elizabeth 237
Taylor, Martha 208
teaching:
    female aspirations 171-80;
    spinster teachers 183-200;
    wages 173,177-8,183,185,190-2,195,199;
    see also education; schools
Terentia (Cicero's wife) 63,65-6,70
Third World 17,154
Thirty years of treason (Bentley) 119
Thornton, Alice 210
Tillion, G. 297,299
Times Educational Supplement 186,192,198
Tomšič, Vida 101-2
Toorop, Jan 18
toverij 76
Tovey, Ann 236
tradition, guardians of 292-3,301-3
transmission of directives 101-2
Trevor-Roper, H.R. 83
Turco-Circassian elite 157
Turell, Rev. Ebenezer 40,43,45,46
Tusk, Miranda 237-8

United Nations 122

United States:
school-teaching in New England 171-80;
suffragism 135,136,138-48 *passim*;
Women Strike for Peace 109-24
universal sisterhood 133,134-5,147-8
universities 13,22,24,32;
Egypt 163-4
unmarried mothers 237-8,243
urbanisation 153,157

Van Hemert 254
Van onze oudtantes en tantes (Naber) 258
Vancouver Sun 119
Vanderpump, Lewis and Louisa 241
Vandevelde-Dallière, H. 299
Vatin, Jean-Claude 291,292,293,294
veiling 12,158,159,161,299,300
Veitch, Mrs 209
Verus, M. Annius 66
victims, women as 14-15
Vietnam War 116,122
Voetius, G. 83
Vollar, Hannah 237
voting rights 282-3
Vrouwenspiegel 255

wages (teaching) 173,177-8,183,185,190-2,195,199
Wagner, J.W. 31
Wakefield, Priscilla 234
Walker, Agnes 171,179
Walker, Elizabeth 208,209
Watts, Isaac 50
wealth 62,63,68-72 *passim*
Webb, Eliza 237
Wegbereidsters (Naber) 258
Weiss, F.H. 25
well of loneliness, The (Hall) 189
Welter, Barbara 172
Wensky, Margret 23
'Western-oriented' historiography 12
white magic 76,79,81,82-3
whores (sexual reputation) 21-45
Wilkinson, Ellen 194-5

Willard, Emma 176
Williams, Dr 188-9,196
Wilson, Dagmar 112,114-15
Wilson, Elizabeth 240
Winkelmann, Maria 22;
  Academy ambitions 27-31,32;
  education and marriage 23-5;
  scientific achievement 25-7
witchcraft (Netherlands) 75-6;
  execution 77-81,86,87;
  religious attitudes 81-4,90;
  stereotypes 88-90;
  trials 77-8,83,84-90
Wollstonecraft, Mary 232,234
woman in the East, The (Fahmi) 159
Woman in Struggle 96,99,104
Woman Teacher, The (journal) 186,196
women:
  culture/historiography of 250-3;
  divided (gossip/insult) 238-43;
  images of 273,283-6;
  united (friendship/compassion) 235-8;
  'womanly qualities' 285
Women and economics (Gilman) 144
Women of the Revolution (Michelet) 273,274-83
Women pioneers (Naber) 258
Women Strike for Peace 109-24
Women's Christian Temperance Union 110,133,139
Women's Club 260
women's historiography, Dutch (origins):
  Bosboom-Toussaint 252-8,265-6;
  genres 249-53,265-6;
  Greup-Roldanus 252,260-4,265,266;
  Naber 252,257-60,265-6;
  women's culture and 250-3
women's history:
  concerning antiquity 61-2;
  Egypt 154-7,166-7;
  feminist 10,11-13,133-5;
  lesbian 184-5;
  petite histoire 131-2;
  study background and themes 1-5;
  study sources/methods 5-7

women's history (writing of):
absent and forgotten issues 19-20;
as academic subject 13-14;
contextual distance 16-19;
differences 11-13;
identification (changes) 14-16
Women's International League for Peace and Freedom 112,114
Women's League for Public Morality 257
Women's Peace Party 113
Women's Pentagon Action 110
Women's Social and Political Union 195
World Women's Conference in Europe 165

Yaziji, Warda Al 160
Young, Edward 50
Young Woman, The (journal) 161
Young Woman of the East, The 161
Yugoslavia (post-revolutionary) 93-106

Zerdoumi, N. 297
Zilsel, Edgar 22
Ziyada, Mayy 163
Zorin, Valerian 120